SMALL
STORIES
OF WAR

CARLETON LIBRARY SERIES

The Carleton Library Series publishes books about Canadian economics, geography, history, politics, public policy, society and culture, and related topics, in the form of leading new scholarship and reprints of classics in these fields. The series is funded by Carleton University, published by McGill-Queen's University Press, and is under the guidance of the Carleton Library Series Editorial Board, which consists of faculty members of Carleton University. Suggestions and proposals for manuscripts and new editions of classic works are welcome and may be directed to the Carleton Library Series Editorial Board c/o the Library, Carleton University, Ottawa K1S 5B6, at cls@carleton.ca, or on the web at www.carleton.ca/cls.

CLS board members: John Clarke, Ross Eaman, Jennifer Henderson, Paul Litt, Laura Macdonald, Jody Mason, Stanley Winer, Barry Wright

250 *The Art of Sharing*
The Richer versus the Poorer Provinces since Confederation
Mary Janigan

251 *Recognition and Revelation*
Short Nonfiction Writings
Margaret Laurence
Edited by Nora Foster Stovel

252 *Anxious Days and Tearful Nights*
Canadian War Wives during the Great War
Martha Hanna

253 *Take a Number*
How Citizens' Encounters with Government Shape Political Engagement
Elisabeth Gidengil

254 *Mrs Dalgairns's Kitchen*
Rediscovering "The Practice of Cookery"
Edited by Mary F. Williamson

255 *Blacks in Canada*
A History, Fiftieth Anniversary Edition
Robin W. Winks

256 *Hall-Dennis and the Road to Utopia*
Education and Modernity in Ontario
Josh Cole

257 *University Women*
A History of Women and Higher Education in Canada
Sara Z. MacDonald

258 *Canada to Ireland*
Poetry, Politics, and the Shaping of Canadian Nationalism, 1788-1900
Michele Holmgren

259 *Harriet's Legacies*
Race, Historical Memory, and Futures in Canada
Edited by Ronald Cummings and Natalee Caple

260 *Regulatory Failure and Renewal*
The Evolution of the Natural Monopoly Contract, Second Edition
John R. Baldwin

261 *Trade and Commerce*
Canada's Economic Constitution
Malcolm Lavoie

262 *Eye of the Master*
Figures of the Québécois Colonial Imaginary
Dalie Giroux
Translated by Jennifer Henderson

263 *Canadian Literary Fare*
Nathalie Cooke and Shelley Boyd, with Alexia Moyer

264 *Small Stories of War*
Children, Youth, and Conflict in Canada and Beyond
Edited by Barbara Lorenzkowski, Kristine Alexander, and Andrew Burtch

Edited by
Barbara Lorenzkowski, Kristine Alexander, and Andrew Burtch

SMALL STORIES OF WAR

Children, Youth,
and Conflict in Canada
and Beyond

Carleton Library Series 264

McGill-Queen's University Press
Montreal & Kingston • London • Chicago

© McGill-Queen's University Press 2023

ISBN 978-0-2280-1684-7 (cloth)
ISBN 978-0-2280-1685-4 (paper)
ISBN 978-0-2280-1836-0 (ePDF)

Legal deposit third quarter 2023
Bibliothèque nationale du Québec

Printed in Canada on acid-free paper that is 100% ancient forest free (100% post-consumer recycled), processed chlorine free

This book has been published with the help of a grant from the Canadian Federation for the Humanities and Social Sciences, through the Awards to Scholarly Publications Program, using funds provided by the Social Sciences and Humanities Research Council of Canada. Funding was also received from the Canadian War Museum.

We acknowledge the support of the Canada Council for the Arts.
Nous remercions le Conseil des arts du Canada de son soutien.

Library and Archives Canada Cataloguing in Publication

Title: Small stories of war : children, youth, and conflict in Canada and beyond / edited by Barbara Lorenzkowski, Kristine Alexander, and Andrew Burtch.
Names: Lorenzkowski, Barbara, 1969- editor. | Alexander, Kristine, 1979- editor. | Burtch, Andrew Paul, 1978- editor.
Series: Carleton library series ; 264.
Description: Series statement: Carleton Library series ; 264 | Includes bibliographical references and index.
Identifiers: Canadiana (print) 20230132707 | Canadiana (ebook) 20230132715 | ISBN 9780228016854 (paper) | ISBN 9780228016847 (cloth) | ISBN 9780228018360 (ePDF)
Subjects: LCSH: Children and war—History. | LCSH: Children and war—Canada—History. | LCSH: Children and violence—History. | LCSH: Social conflict—History.
Classification: LCC HQ784.W3 S63 2023 | DDC 303.6/6083—dc23

Contents

Acknowledgments | vii

Introduction | 3
Barbara Lorenzkowski, Kristine Alexander, and Andrew Burtch

Part One   Global Wars

1   Children's Images of War from the German Home Front, 1914–18 | 33
    Carolyn Kay

2   Sensing War: Childhood Memories of the Wartime Atlantic, 1939–45 | 63
    Barbara Lorenzkowski

3   "What Am I to Do to Save My Children?": Canadian Children
    in Civil Defence Planning | 93
    Andrew Burtch

Part Two   Family and Community

4   Children, Soldiers, and Correspondence in Canada's First World War | 121
    Kristine Alexander and Ashley Henrickson

5   Deconstructing a Canadian Military Family: The Taylor Mother and Son
    Remember the Cold War | 141
    Isabel Campbell

6   From Wartime Refuge to Peaceful Hippie Haven: Generations
    of Youth on Grindstone Island | 167
    Tarah Brookfield

Part Three   Telling Difficult Stories

7   Adolescents during Canada's Afghanistan Mission | 189
    Deborah Harrison and Patrizia Albanese

8   The Intergenerational Effects of Wartime Sexual Violence: Children Born
    of Wartime Rape in Northern Uganda | 206
    Myriam S. Denov

9   Politics and Emotion in Drawings by Children in Australian Immigration Detention | 224
    Mary Tomsic

Part Four   In the Spotlight
Editors' Introduction | 249

10 "Dear Daddy": Children, Writing, and the First World War | 258
    Kristine Alexander and Ashley Henrickson

11 Writing "Home": Letters from British Child Evacuees Sent to Canada during the Second World War | 266
    Claire L. Halstead

12 Charting the Social Spaces of Childhood in 1940s Halifax | 282
    Barbara Lorenzkowski

13 Surviving the Peace: Mine Awareness Education in the Former Yugoslavia | 294
    Andrew Burtch

14 "My Two Families": Experiences of Refugee Youth | 300
    Elizabeth Miller

15 "Donkeys Can't Fly on Planes": Intergenerational Storytelling and Artwork | 308
    Mary Tomsic

Figures | 315
Bibliography | 317
Contributors | 347
Index | 351

Acknowledgments

It seems trite to say that any manuscript is the work of many hands, but it is nonetheless true, and all the more so in an edited collection like the one you are holding, which was borne out of collaboration. The editors wish to first thank all of the organizers and participants in the 2016 symposium at the Canadian War Museum that inspired this collection: Sandra O'Quinn, Josh Boyter, Claire Corriveau, Ayanda Keith Dubé, Dominique Marshall, Marian Misdrahi, Susan Whitney, and Leontine Uwababyeyi all contributed their time and insight and it was in the post-symposium glow that we first discussed the possibility of a collection.

The book took shape over conference calls, Zoom meetings, and rewarding in-person editing sessions in Montreal and Ottawa. The editors offer profuse thanks to the contributors to this volume for their rich and valuable scholarship. We also appreciate their spirit of cooperation, collaboration, and above all their patience and understanding as busy schedules and COVID complications stretched this project's length.

The editors and contributors all owe a debt of gratitude to the excellent staff of McGill-Queen's University Press who shepherded the collection from manuscript to production, not least Kyla Madden whose expertise, generosity, and kindness made her the best possible editor we could have hoped for. It was Kyla who suggested the title that now graces the cover of this volume.

The images drawn from the collection were sourced from a variety of holdings, including the Canadian War Museum, and thanks go to Maggie Arbour, Meredith Maclean, Shannyn Johnson, and Susan Ross for their assistance in image scanning and reproduction. Many thanks to Vincent Lafond whose keen eye helped with ship identification. The editors and the press are grateful for the financial assistance offered by the museum to offset costs of including many colour images in this collection. Additional financial support was generously provided by the Canada Research Chairs program, the University of Lethbridge Faculty of Arts and Science. This book has been published with the help of a grant from the Federation for the Humanities and Social Sciences, through the Awards to Scholarly Publications Program, using funds provided by the Social Sciences and Humanities Research Council of Canada.

Finally, we would be remiss if we did not offer our thanks to all the young people whose insights, hopes, fears, experiences, and recollections have informed the production of each chapter in this collection.

SMALL STORIES OF WAR

Introduction

Barbara Lorenzkowski, Kristine Alexander, and Andrew Burtch

When visitors to the Canadian War Museum in Ottawa enter the Moriyama Regeneration Hall, they are greeted by the sound of wind, whistling through the sparsely adorned exhibition space. This subtle yet haunting sound is, like so much of the history of modern war, inextricably tied to childhood. Its origins lie in a memory recalled by Raymond Moriyama, the architect who designed the museum.[1] In 1942, during his boyhood in British Columbia, Moriyama and his family were displaced and dispossessed from their home as part of the Canadian nation-state's racist response to the Allied war against Japan. Labelled "enemy aliens," they were among the approximately 22,000 Japanese Canadians – three quarters of whom were Canadian-born or naturalized citizens – who were relocated to internment camps in remote ghost towns in interior British Columbia and sugar beet farms on the Canadian prairies.[2] When Moriyama's father refused to be separated from his pregnant wife, he was sent to a prisoner-of-war camp in Ontario, while twelve-year-old Raymond, his sisters, and their mother were interned in a camp in Slocan, British Columbia. "My mother then had a miscarriage and I lost the only brother I ever could have had," Moriyama would later write.[3]

A builder even at that young age, the boy secretly assembled a tree house from scrounged nails and scrap wood as an escape from camp life. Located on the banks of the Slocan River, the tree house exposed him to the natural elements: "the sound of wind at night, howling storms, the whisper of the river, serene moonlight in the mountains, crimson sunsets, the sweet fragrance of an autumn breeze, heavy and soft rain, sleet and icy snow."[4] "That tree house," Moriyama wrote with the hindsight of adult memory, "was my private school in the trees, a place of happy unstructured learning. It introduced me to solace, to solitude, to contemplation and to many inexplicable facets of life and human nature. In my sanctuary, I developed a new understanding of myself, of nature, of Canada and of the fragility of democracy."[5] Some sixty years later, when overseeing the construction of the Canadian War Museum, Moriyama heard the wind humming through the unfinished wall cladding. "Although it was a little more metallic, the sound was very similar to the one I remember hearing in the tree house, eerie yet comforting," he recalled. The museum recreated the sound – a soft and moving "song of the wind" – that envelops visitors as they enter the hall that now bears Moriyama's name.[6]

Moriyama's experiences, recollections, and vision highlight several threads that weave through *Small Stories of War*, a collection inspired by a symposium on young people and conflict hosted by the Canadian War Museum in 2016. The symposium, which featured research and reflections by scholars, survivors, and practitioners, was a powerful reminder of the fact that global processes of migration, displacement, and violence shape small people's lives in outsized ways. For Moriyama and many of the other youngsters discussed in this book, the invisible wounds caused by prejudice, family separation, trauma, and grief were made harder to bear by the realization that adults – in spite of high-flown rhetoric and good intentions – were often unwilling or unable to protect children and youth in times of crisis. As this book demonstrates, the intense feelings of hope, excitement, sadness, and betrayal engendered by armed conflict have shaped intergenerational relations and decisions made throughout the life course. Likewise, its chapters show how youthful imagination and critique could be mobilized to link past and present in the pursuit of a peaceful and more just world.

Like the history of war, the history of childhood and youth both exceeds and continues to be shaped by the borders of the modern nation-state. While acknowledging our debt to numerous foundational studies of young people and conflict in single national contexts, this volume takes a different approach, combining a sustained focus on Canada with case studies from Australia, Germany, Northern Uganda, Rwanda, and the former Yugoslavia. *Small Stories of War* thus builds on the methodological insights offered by the recent "transnational turn" in Canadian historiography.[7] It is also inspired by the musical practice of counterpoint: a compositional strategy that brings together individual melodies in order to create something more meaningful and complex. Thinking about different voices in place and time in relation to one another, we contend, opens up new possibilities for interpretation that only become possible when we listen to them together.

Modern Canada, the setting for the majority of the chapters in this volume, has been described as a modest middle power, "the linchpin of the English-speaking world" (to quote Winston Churchill), and a nation of peacekeepers.[8] Defined in many ways by its relationship to the British and American empires, Canada is also a settler colonial state whose leaders have continuously – in ways that were often violent and always contested – sought to erase and displace Indigenous populations in order to control land and resources.[9] During the late nineteenth and early twentieth centuries, the Canadian state's efforts to dispossess Indigenous peoples – pursued with the goal of creating what Australian historians Marilyn Lake and Henry Reynolds have called a "white men's country" – evolved in tandem with numerous other legal and social projects of racialized exclusion.[10] As Laura Madokoro reminds us, the internment of Japanese Canadians during the Second World War did not occur in a vacuum: the state had learned how to discriminate and dispossess "through the segregation of Black bodies, the 1876 Indian Act and the exclusion of Chinese migrants and settlers" long before developing the racist policies that changed the course of Raymond Moriyama's childhood.[11]

Canada's past and present, in other words, have been defined as much by racism and exclusion as by democracy, inclusion, and refuge.[12] While the tensions between these realities affected individual lives in different ways, it is also true that a majority of young people in twentieth and twenty-first-century Canada experienced war from a distance. The First and Second World Wars, the Cold War, and the early twenty-first century war in Afghanistan changed the rhythms and emotional-material realities of daily life for many Canadian youngsters: they created new patterns of mobility and family separation, encouraged young people to imagine and worry about violence and destruction in faraway places, and promoted new possibilities for political resistance and critique. It is important to note that, while disrupting lives and provoking intense emotions, these distant wars did not expose Canadian children and youth directly to the starvation, rape, terror, forcible confinement, and mass death that were witnessed and experienced by their counterparts in many other parts of the world. Putting the Canadian experience of childhood and modern war into conversation with stories from Germany, the former Yugoslavia, Rwanda, northern Uganda, and Australian migrant detention camps reveals a diversity of lived experience, while highlighting the often-unexamined privilege that shaped the wartime lives of the mostly white Canadian youngsters discussed in the pages of this volume.

By focusing on and interrogating the uneven effects of the "tyranny of distance" on young people's wartime lives, *Small Stories of War* expands on French historian Manon Pignot's important point that "the *place* where the war was experienced – not the *country* or the nationality – was essential."[13] Together, the chapters in this book demonstrate that it was young people's proximity or distance to violent conflict – in terms of geography *and* emotional intensity – that fundamentally influenced their experiences and memories. These questions of proximity, distance, and the intensity of wartime experience also offer valuable insights regarding the production of academic knowledge about young people.[14] The contributors to this volume cast a wide evidentiary net, and their arguments draw on a range of innovative sources including infantile scribbles, children's drawings, and post-traumatic nightmares. More conventional archival documents – correspondence, government records, and newspapers, for example – are also read creatively and against the grain in the chapters that follow, as are oral history interviews and qualitative social surveys.

Small Stories of War, in other words, supports ethnographer Dwight Conquergood's insistence that scholars should challenge the "hegemony of textualism" by attending to what he calls "another way of knowing": the local knowledge that "circulates on the ground within a community of memory and practice." Evoking Michel de Certeau's claim that "what the map cuts up, the story cuts across," Conquergood encourages researchers to engage with "two different domains of knowledge: one official, objective, and abstract – 'the map'; the other one practical, embodied, and popular – 'the story.'"[15] This storied knowledge is grounded in practice and place. It encompasses "the whole realm of complex, finely nuanced meaning that is embodied, tacit, intoned, gestured, improvised, coexperienced, covert – and all the more deeply meaningful because of its refusal to be spelled out."[16] The chapters contained in this volume foreground and prise open these complex meanings and experiences by drawing on a wide-ranging and interdisciplinary interpretive toolkit. They also – just as significantly – cut across the spatial and temporal practices of mapping and border work that remain at the heart of much historical research.

How did young people in different times and places make sense of war? How did they relate their experiences to powerful narratives of enemies and allies that were mobilized and consolidated in cultural imagery? How did young people and their communities construct and transmit stories about their experiences? How have social and intergenerational acts of remembering given form and shape to wartime memories? How can scholars uncover the perspectives and feelings of children and youth when so much of the archival and textual record remains adult-generated? What might listening to the memories of adult narrators tell us about the wartime and post-war subjectivities of young people?

In exploring these questions, *Small Stories of War* recalibrates historical analysis away from sweeping synthesis and toward the more granular level of young people's life-worlds. Playing with scale across the local, the national, and the global – between "big" and "small" – also brings to the fore structures and patterns that have been obscured by an earlier historiographical focus on master narratives and nation-based discourse.[17] The essays in this collection therefore revolve around five major analytical strands: experience, ways of knowing, time and temporalities, politics, and communities of memory. Separately and together, these strands situate young people's wartime lives and postwar memories in broader contexts while broadening the disciplinary frame of debates about children, youth, and armed conflict.

Experience

The historical study of children and modern war began in earnest in 1993, with the publication of French historian Stéphane Audoin-Rouzeau's monograph *La guerre des enfants, 1914–1918*. This groundbreaking work, which set the agenda for a generation of scholars, introduced the influential idea of a "culture de guerre," or war culture: the infusion of every aspect of daily life by the cultural mobilization of children as well as adults.[18] In this all-encompassing, total war, family, church, and school "set out to bring children to the heart of the conflict and keep them there."[19] Between 1914 and 1918, for example, French schoolchildren composed essays on "the five reasons why you love the little refugee children," practised spelling in dictations on a "mother's courage," and reflected, in the round and uneven script of beginning writers, on "what you will do in school this year, to show yourself worthy of your soldier father."[20] According to Audoin-Rouzeau and Annette Becker, "everything societies taught their youngest members during the Great War puts us in contact with what people thought was most important, and what each society believed it should communicate about the conflict." Such public stories about the war constituted "the inner core of the various war cultures."[21]

As historian of the American Civil War James Marten puts it (quoting Joseph M. Hawes), wartime – like childhood – is "where you catch a culture in high relief."[22] Given the volume and richness of wartime texts for young people produced by modern religious leaders, politicians, novelists, illustrators, and pedagogues, it is no surprise that so much historical scholarship about children, youth, and war has focused on the social construction of childhood by adults rather than on the experiences of young people. In the decades that followed the publication of *La guerre des enfants*, the concept of war culture and its associated analytical apparatus came to undergird much historical scholarship on children, youth, and conflict. Many of these studies, focusing on the two World Wars, represented these conflicts as moments of rupture: a "dividing line," as Rosie Kennedy writes, that "marked the moment when a part of … childhood and innocence was left behind."[23] In a series of important works, scholars from a range of national contexts including Kennedy, Andrew Donson, Susan Fisher, Manon Pignot, Julie deGraffenried, and Sabine Frühstück built on Audoin-Rouzeau's work by offering imaginative readings of the "war stories" that circulated in young people's print culture.[24] These novels and periodicals, George Mosse has argued, contributed to a "process of trivialization, cutting war down to size so that it would become commonplace instead of awesome and frightening."[25] Twentieth-century war culture also rested, as anthropologist Liisa Malkki suggests, on five closely related "registers" that displayed children "as embodiments of a basic human goodness (and symbols of world harmony); as sufferers; as seers of truth; as ambassadors of peace; and as embodiments of the future."[26]

The late twentieth-century interventions of Jacqueline Rose (who insisted that children's literature must be understood as a written response to adult anxieties and desires) and Joan W. Scott (who argued that all experience is mediated and constituted through discourse) clearly influenced the study of young people and conflict by the scholars named above.[27] They have also shaped the historiography of childhood more broadly: as Nell Musgrove, Carla Pascoe Leahy, and Kristine Moruzi remark, over the past three decades the field of history "enthusiastically developed its analyses around the notion that historical sources were 'discursive events' and abandoned its hope of recovering 'authentic experience.'"[28] *Small Stories of War*, by contrast, insists that it is possible – indeed imperative – for scholars to include lived experience in their analyses of children, youth, and conflict.

The authors of this volume readily acknowledge that historical experiences of young people – as captured in contemporary documents *and* adult testimony – are always subject to mediation, translation, and interpretation. But their work also demonstrates how we can wield the sophisticated research methodologies of the humanities and social sciences to unearth young people's experiences of war as they were entangled with cultural narratives. By foregoing the quest for authenticity as we piece together the fragments that remain, we can examine how young people's wartime lives were shaped both by the power of discursive practices and the subjectivities of a juvenile world.[29] Even in times of violent tensions and inflamed rhetoric, children and youth brought their own experiences to bear on their understanding of conflict, sought to make meaning of their changed social worlds, and developed a deep and often painful political understanding of the visible and invisible wounds that would shape their lives and communities for years to come. As part of what historian Rob Boddice has called a "re-turn to experience in history," *Small Stories of War* engages with a capacious and cross-disciplinary definition of lived experience that includes emotions and the senses.[30] Together, the chapters in this volume examine individual and collective experiences in ways that move the history of childhood beyond the boundaries imposed by poststructuralism, war culture, and the linguistic turn.[31]

The analytical tools offered by the history of emotions are particularly useful here. The concept of "emotional formations," proposed by Karen Vallgårda, Kristine Alexander, and Stephanie Olsen, describes patterns and processes of emotional education that articulate and often work to sustain relations of power.[32] Through emotional formations, they write, children have been "taught to express certain feelings in specific situations (such as grief at a funeral or gratitude when receiving a gift), and … expected to eliminate or at least curtail and refrain from expressing other feelings (such as envy at other people's luck or pleasure at their pain)."[33] In France, young Françoise Dolto, born in 1908, keenly felt the obligation to support her nation's soldiers during the Great War: "I spent my time knitting, I couldn't play anymore because that made me feel guilty, the soldiers were waiting, or so they said. There was a poor combatant in the trenches who was waiting for my scarf and who would freeze to death if I did not finish it."[34] Dolto's words illustrate the utility of Vallgårda, Alexander, and Olsen's concept of "emotional frontiers": the dynamic and often difficult boundaries between different emotional formations, as crossed for example in transitions between wartime and peacetime.[35]

We have also found the concept of "emotional echoes," as formulated by Vallgårda and Katrine Rønsig Larsen, to be helpful in the study of experience. "Emotional echoing," they suggest, "is the process through which individuals try on words, images, and practices borrowed from a cultural repertoire; emotive tools that they thereby help replicate and spread, often by bending their meanings, either subtly or markedly." If we conceive of the stories that young people told of wartime as a process of "emotional echoing," we become attuned to the "refractions, slippages, and adaptations" that echo the guidance of an adult world as well as the genuine acts of creativity by which children and youth reassembled and reshaped master narratives of war while simultaneously performing their own understanding of war, violence, and armed conflict. Such an approach directs attention to young people's struggles to make meaning of their wartime experiences, acknowledges the constitutive role that peer groups, families, and other communities played in the making of juvenile subjectivities, and "carries within it a potential for change," as Vallgårda and Larsen assert.[36]

Our authors examine the place of emotions in wartime family letters, the excitement with which children in Atlantic Canada explored a port city transformed by war, the anxiety expressed by North American young people during the Cold War arms race, the loneliness suffered by military children whose families were constantly on the move, the burdens shouldered by children born of wartime rape in northern Uganda who were ostracized by their families and communities, and the dread and despair experienced by refugee children in Australian detention centres, which they captured in drawings so violent and unsettling that newspapers and social media hesitated to circulate them, thereby limiting public debate to more conventional imagery.

Ways of Knowing

Reckoning with the complexities of lived experience raises important questions regarding the production of knowledge by, about, and with young people. Listening carefully to small stories that enrich and complicate official narratives of war has forced us to think carefully about young people as *targets* of knowledge (through propaganda, war culture, and pedagogy), as *subjects* of knowledge (studied by experts in the past as well as by scholars in the present), and as *producers* of knowledge – as knowers – in their own right.[37] Grappling with these multiple interrelated ways of knowing requires considerable self-reflexivity on the part of researchers.

The question of children's voices – a primary concern of scholars and activists since the passage of the 1989 United Nations Convention on the Rights of the Child – looms large throughout this work. While many scholars have striven to find and highlight the voices of young people in their research, this approach has also been subject to criticism. According to anthropologist Spyrous Spyrou, childhood studies scholars too often use "voice" as an uncritical shorthand for authenticity or truth in what he considers will ultimately be a futile academic quest for an independent, consistent, and knowable speaking subject. Instead of simply looking for and documenting the voices of young people, Spyrou suggests, scholars should "explore how children's voices happen."[38] Voices, as the sociologist Sirkka Komulainen reminds us, do not appear in a vacuum: they are products of social interaction.[39] Building on Komulainen's insights, Spyrou urges scholars to be reflexive and to think more carefully about how children's voices – like those of adults – are produced relationally and through performative practices. The chapters in this volume seek to do exactly this, by focusing "on the interactional contexts in which children's voices emerge, the institutional contexts in which they are embedded, and the discursive contexts which inform them."[40] Thinking about peer cultures and the "discourse that children shared with each other," as Aaron Willian Moore does in his work on children's life-writing in Second World War–era Japan, offers another powerful way to understand the multi-vocal nature of children's life-writings and the existence of juvenile worlds that were both entwined with, and separate from, the adult world.[41]

The centrality of place and space to young people's wartime and postwar worlds is another significant thread that weaves through this volume. Like other historians of wartime who have sought to emplace histories of the everyday, we seek to "demonstrate the embeddedness of particular lived realities in real places," as Lindsey Dodd and David Lees write.[42] The first two chapters of this collection explore space- and place-based ways of knowing by introducing readers to "spaces of childhood intimately known" and the "knowledge borne of habitual activities, emotional encounters, and sensory experiences," as Barbara Lorenzkowski notes.[43] In chapter 1, Carolyn Kay takes us to the working-class neighbourhood of Wilhelmsburg, Germany. Nestled in the meandering embrace of the Hamburg harbour, Wilhelmsburg was home to the children of workers, day labourers, and dock employees. Over the course of the First World War, these youngsters saw 4,500 of their neighbours and family members – fathers, brothers, uncles, cousins, family friends, and acquaintances – conscripted; 900 of these men would never return. When the neighbourhood's children captured the war in their school drawings, their artwork did "not appear to lament the deaths of the war," writes Kay, "but to revel in the victories and accomplishments," reflecting both the children's emotional investment in the war and the dictates of the school curriculum that was infused with "Prussian values of order, obedience, hard work, godliness, and loyalty to the Kaiser and the state."[44] German schoolteachers' innovative wartime pedagogy, which sought to nurture artistic expression, observational skills, and intuitive drawing, went hand in hand with a nationalist, militarist agenda. However, perhaps because these children were granted greater autonomy to express themselves in their artwork, Kay found tantalizing evidence of young artists seizing "the chance to express fears, reservations and doubts" about the war in their drawings.[45] These children did not create art in isolation, but found inspiration and a shared visual language in wartime postcards, children's books, illustrations in contemporary newspapers, colouring books, as well as the drawings of their classroom peers.[46]

Over two decades later, in the Canadian port city of Halifax, Nova Scotia (one of the Allies' most important naval bases in North America during the Second World War), children living close to the city's harbour and military bases were steeped in the sounds, sights, and smells of war. They could "read" the wartime Atlantic as youngsters elsewhere in the city could not, as Barbara Lorenzkowski posits in chapter 2. Childhood memories of the wartime Atlantic ring with sound and are bound up with place. Such "environmental autobiographies" underscore the central role of space in structuring childhood recollections.[47] To take seriously the spatial experiences of young people and examine the function of place-based stories in wartime testimony is not only to acknowledge the extent to which young people's lives are anchored in place, but also to contemplate the complex ways in which narrators frame their stories *through* place and space.[48]

Places could be tangible, physical sites that held meaning for children and youth, or figurative spaces created through the act of writing, as in the correspondence between youngsters and their parents. In the social space of wartime letters, parents tried to bridge the geographical distance that separated them from their children with words of affection and warmth as Kristine Alexander, Ashley Henrickson, and Claire Halstead observe in this volume. As scholars of wartime correspondence have argued, we should not be content to mine the voluminous letters exchanged between fathers on the frontlines and their families back home for their content and cultural conventions, but, rather, should listen to the ways "emotions carried through words."[49] In chapters 4 and 10, Alexander and Henrickson describe small hands holding and hoarding letters sent from the Western Front – a tangible connection to fathers who were physically absent yet emotionally and psychologically present. Correspondence was central to the emotional survival of Canadian soldiers as well as their families. In providing a "child-centred reading of adults' wartime letters," Alexander and Henrickson's chapters offer a compelling object lesson about the production and preservation of traces of young people's thoughts, actions, and feelings in the past.[50]

Oral testimony is another source rich in emotional resonance whose silences can be as telling as the words spoken.[51] In chapter 8, social work scholar Myriam

Denov examines the complex interior displacement of children born of wartime rape in late twentieth- and early twenty-first-century Uganda. These youngsters, Denov writes, were denied food, familial affection, and land rights upon returning to their families and communities after being forced to live and fight with the Lord's Resistance Army.[52] In recounting their experiences, they drew on culturally grounded understandings of coping and well-being. Theirs were embodied stories, their pain, injuries, and terrifying nightmares inscribed onto their bodies as either "spirit possession" or immobilizing sadness.[53] By heeding local understandings of suffering and healing – those cultural scripts within which young people make sense of their physical and spiritual experiences – Denov seeks to unlock the ways her narrators understood their life conditions. Her careful attention to "local ways of knowing, being, and doing" is a powerful reminder of the value of ethically pursuing participatory research with and about war-affected young people.[54]

Time and Temporalities

In addition to interrupting individual lives and taken-for-granted ideas about childhood, war also disrupts time.[55] The outbreak of war is often explained, by historians and survivors alike, as a temporal rupture: a moment of decisive change that creates an easily distinguishable "before" and "after." The idea that "wartime" is an exceptional and temporary state of crisis, preceded and inevitably followed by a more orderly "peacetime," has been used to justify the extension of state powers and the suspension of civil liberties in moments of crisis across the twentieth-century world. As historian Mary Dudziak explains, this way of thinking also makes it possible to ignore the persistence of conflict: to deny the fact, in other words, that war is "an enduring condition."[56] Stark distinctions between wartime and peacetime are easy to trace in many aspects of scholarship on the First and Second World Wars, but these lines become blurrier in later twentieth-century contexts like the Cold War (an ambiguous global conflict in which, Dudziak writes, "cataclysmic battles and great victories ... [were replaced by] small wars, surveillance, and stalemate"), asymmetrical and civil wars, and wars involving the deployment of relatively small numbers of troops (and, increasingly, drones) from the Global North in distant parts of the world.[57]

Small Stories of War investigates the multiple ways in which conflict disrupts and structures juvenile temporalities, while also resonating throughout the life course. For many of the young people discussed in these pages, the reverberations of conflict meant existing in a kind of limbo. The physical and affective experiences involved in this varied greatly, from youngsters on the Canadian home front waiting for news about deployed soldier-parents during the First World War and the war in Afghanistan, to the migrant children forcibly confined in offshore detention facilities by the Australian government. In addition to the emotions provoked by the experiences of waiting and forced confinement, this volume traces the complexities of returning to "peacetime" – a process that is neither instantaneous nor simple. As several historians of the First World War have written, demobilization was a complicated social, cultural, and psychological process as well as a military one.[58] Our authors therefore also address the experience of living in the aftermath, through the stories of soldiers' children dealing with grief and parental post-traumatic stress disorder (PTSD), as well as through the memories and future-oriented community-making of youngsters who survived war and genocide in Rwanda, Uganda, and the former Yugoslavia.

Chapter 7, by Deborah Harrison and Patrizia Albanese, provides a particularly compelling view of the complexity of "wartime" versus "peacetime" during the war in Afghanistan (2001–14), the longest military engagement in Canadian history. Writing about the adolescent children of Canadian servicemen and servicewomen, Harrison and Albanese discuss a conflict that was covered consistently by the Canadian media, but that had little broader impact on national culture, social discourse, and pedagogy. Like their counterparts during the First and Second World Wars, these teenagers waited, worried, and shouldered additional emotional and practical responsibilities at home. In taking on the emotional labour of supporting their parents, looking after younger siblings, and keeping their fears to themselves, they struggled with the dissonance of living with a war that most Canadians – including their schoolmates and teachers – only acknowledged in the occasional rallying cry of supporting the troops. In other words, while these teenagers' lives were upended by "wartime," most of their peers' lives were not. The invisible wounds caused by this disjuncture, exacerbated in many cases by returned parents with PTSD, set the adolescent children of Canadian military families apart from their classmates. These wounds were tended to in silence and voiced only in peer support groups where "you finally could breathe," as one teenager remarked in conversation with Harrison and Albanese.[59]

In addition to the often-difficult readjustments that characterize daily life in the immediate aftermath of conflict, *Small Stories of War* also highlights the ways in which long-past "wartimes" continue to resonate throughout the life course. A number of the oral history narrators discussed in this volume, for example, blurred established chronologies of war by insisting on "time maps" that encompassed both their pre-war and post-war worlds.⁶⁰ When granted the opportunity to situate their lives into broader temporal horizons, they movingly reflected on the ways that wartime tensions spilled over into the post-conflict period while also asserting their efforts to mend, fashion, and re-imagine social relations. As a marker of temporal distance between the present day and the past wars that shaped their lives, the chronological age of narrators is also worth considering closely. For the teenagers and young adult narrators interviewed by Deborah Harrison, Patrizia Albanese, Myriam Denov, and Elisabeth Miller, the act of translating experience into narrative offers insights into the making of youth subjectivities. For the elderly narrators discussed by Barbara Lorenzkowski, Andrew Burtch, Tarah Brookfield, and Isabel Campbell, remembered subjectivities of childhood and youth mingle with and complicate retrospective awareness of dominant narratives of war.

Broadening the temporal frame for telling stories of war, violence, and armed conflict can also yield life histories that sit uneasily with established historical narratives and chronologies. In chapter 5, for example, Isabel Campbell demonstrates that at the height of the Cold War, an era marked by widespread veneration of the traditional nuclear family and conventional gender roles, young Paul Taylor – whose father was an officer in the Canadian military – was never reprimanded by his mother Sheilagh for his sensitivity. A shy and gentle boy, Paul felt unmoored by his military family's frequent moves and was disheartened by the seeming impossibility of creating long-lasting friendships. His gregarious and sociable mother, by contrast, relished the adventure of family life on the move. She also created a home environment that allowed her son to express feelings that did not adhere to the masculine social norms promoted by political leaders, health experts, the military community, and her own husband. As an adult, writes Campbell, "Paul developed his own concept of fathering in direct counter-point to his father's model: a new age, post–Cold War father, insisting on staying in one place and sacrificing his career in order to spend family time with his wife and children."⁶¹ It is only in the wider temporal horizons of a life story, which invites the teller to shape and mould the narrative arc, that we can grasp the double burden of Cold War gender conventions and military mobility as well as the energy invested in breaking free of these constraints.

As oral historian Steven High reminds us, "the longue durée, with the requisite attention to the 'before' and 'after,' provides a different context in which to explore the meanings of mass violence: it becomes more deeply personal and more explicitly subjective."⁶² The value of taking a longer view is especially clear in chapters

8, 13, and 14. As our author Myriam Denov notes elsewhere, while "war embodied a terrain in extreme motion," the post-war context could be every bit as "dynamic, volatile and precarious."[63] "Conceived and raised in contexts of violence, brutality, and deprivation," the children born in captivity of the Lord's Resistance Army (LRA) were bearers of the "intergenerational legacies and memories of war," Denov writes. In navigating the transition from war to an uneasy peace, her sixty adolescent narrators were absorbed by the present moment: caring for younger siblings, countering the stigma associated with the circumstances of their birth, and trying to rewrite the communal narrative so that family members and community leaders would "guide them rather than fearing and punishing them." For them, the war had ended in name only as they continued to fight for food, respect, safety, education, and land rights.[64] A number of these Ugandan youths also explained that their uncertain access to education and land, like their unresolved positions within their families, prompted feelings of worry and hopelessness about the future. The fourth- and fifth-grade children from the former Yugoslavia, whose artwork is discussed in chapter 13, expressed similar emotions. As Andrew Burtch writes, many of these youngsters were "fearful of the risks from legacy munitions and landmines, and cautious about their future."[65] In chapter 14, documentary filmmaker Elizabeth Miller movingly centres the life story of Leontine Uwababyeyi. Having lost her family in the Rwandan genocide before the age of ten, Leontine eventually moved to Montreal – where, in her early twenties, she created what she calls "a new family" with other students and survivors.

The association of young people with futurity is a powerful one, perhaps especially so in times of conflict. As queer theorist Lee Edelman has argued, many modern political interventions have been justified in the name of an ideal imagined future child.[66] The understanding of children as the heart and future of the nation – innocent and vulnerable beings whose potential is worth fighting for – has been a central focus of the study of war culture for the past several decades. Taken together (and read with an eye to lived experience), the chapters in this volume reveal that the idea that children deserve protection in wartime because they "are" the future did not apply to everyone. As Robin Bernstein has written about the United States, the abstract idea of childhood innocence, "raced white" since at least the mid-nineteenth century, has been used simultaneously to protect some children while justifying the denial of rights to others.[67] Placing Claire Halstead's essay about British evacuee children in a slightly broader context makes this especially clear. The white middle-class British children Halstead discusses in chapter 11 spent most of the Second World War in Canada, because of familial and cultural

Introduction

ties and the belief that Britain's future was tied to its ability to protect its children from the physical and emotional toll of German bombs. While Owen and Richard Mackie, two of the evacuees featured in Halstead's essay, attended the private school run by their uncles in Vernon, British Columbia, Raymond Moriyama was interned with his mother and sisters a few hundred kilometres away on the banks of the Slocan River. At the same time and in the same province (and in numerous other parts of Canada), Indigenous children were living – and dying – away from their families and communities in government-funded and church-run Indian residential schools.[68] "A collective politics of aspiration" centred on white children, which Laura Ishiguro calls "settler futurity," has a long history in the territory currently known as Canada, and it is worth keeping this in mind while engaging with the contents of this volume.[69]

Politics

In addition to being the subjects of adult-led political interventions, children and youth were – and are – also political actors in their own right. Working from an expansive definition of politics that includes private and public emotions, actions, and words, our contributors insist that children and youth were, and are, engaged political actors who regularly articulate critiques and devise coping and community-building strategies in fraught and volatile circumstances. While dealing with the wounds of the past and worrying about what lay in store, many of the young people discussed in this book critiqued the political and material conditions that shaped their lives and sought to imagine and create better futures. In the Australian children's books examined by Mary Tomsic in chapter 15, for instance, young authors and their adult counterparts – all of whom had experienced violence and displacement in their journeys from South Sudan – narrated their lives in ways that "cast themselves and their families not as 'victims,' but, instead, as active subjects with life experiences to share."[70]

To represent children and youth as active political players is not to position them in opposition to the adult world or cast them as rebels against wartime society. As several of our contributors demonstrate, young people's political sensibilities were often nurtured in, and entwined with, the political cultures of their families and communities. Rather, this collection builds upon a burgeoning number of historical and anthropological studies that highlight young people's social and cognitive competencies in wartime as well as their moral capability.[71] As historian Olga Kucherenko argues in her study of Soviet children in the Second

World War: "Having grown up in a society where a young person's political activity was encoded in cultural norms, many Soviet child-soldiers acted as responsible and rational agents, exhibiting a mature understanding of not only their circumstances but also their place and role in the community."[72] In her work on children and youth in war-torn regions, anthropologist Jo Boyden similarly describes young people as "more aware and active politically, and more developed morally and socially, than adults generally assume." Accordingly, Boyden argues for "conceptualizing children as political actors with the capacity to make conscious decisions that are informed by analysis of personal and collective history and circumstances."[73]

Forged in moments of dissonance and disjuncture that pitted children, youth, and their families against prevailing codes and morals, the political consciousness of the young people featured in this collection manifested in political campaigns as well as subtle negotiations within familial and community networks. At the height of the Cold War civil defence campaigns of the 1950s and 1960s, Canadian youngsters lived uneasily at the crossroads of two contrasting sets of emotional precepts, as Andrew Burtch holds in chapter 3. As state authorities sought to regulate fears of nuclear war in the public consciousness, many children remained anxious and unsatisfied. In school newspapers, letters to politicians, and conversations with their parents, they critiqued the limited protections offered by bomb shelters and the directive to "duck and cover." In the 1980s, Burtch writes, Canadian teenagers concerned about nuclear war turned to collective political action. In 1986, a band of youth activists with Students against Global Extermination (SAGE) in Montreal embarked on a year-long Youth Nuclear Disarmament Tour, visiting schools across the country and encouraging communities to declare themselves a "nuclear weapons free zone."[74] In chapter 6, Tarah Brookfield takes readers to Grindstone Island, a twelve-acre private island located near Kingston, Ontario, which the children of Canadian and American peace activists remember both as an enchanted space of childhood and youth and – during the 1960s and 1970s – an intensely political place that offered workshops on non-violence, disarmament, and civil rights rather than more conventional summer camp activities. As one of the forty narrators interviewed for this project remarked, the youth who spent time on Grindstone felt "part of this revolution of change in the world." "Not only were their futures valued," concludes Brookfield, "they were considered valuable members of their families, communities, and nations."[75]

In chapter 9, Mary Tomsic turns to the interplay of politics and emotions expressed in drawings created by refugee and displaced children in the early twenty-first century. Having escaped war, violence, and political conflict in Iran, Myanmar, Sri Lanka, Vietnam, Iraq, Afghanistan, and Somalia only to endure the harsh conditions of remote detention centres run by the Australian state, the young subjects of this chapter used their artwork to create "map[s] of freedom and confinement" and to present themselves "as fully human and political subjects." Tomsic's close reading of the drawings and written statements these young asylum-seekers shared with the Australian Human Rights Commission in 2014 allows her to move beyond the more conventional reading suggested by contemporary media, which highlighted youngsters' sadness and despair. Instead, she argues that her subjects used pen and paper to make political claims. By reading the drawings of young asylum-seekers against the grain, Tomsic offers a probing examination of "how some children have represented and understood their experiences of forced displacement in the past and present."[76] Tightly intertwined, both cognition and affect – ways of knowing and feeling – have clearly shaped young people's political sensibilities and their political activism throughout the twentieth and early twenty-first centuries.

Communities of Memory

Finally, in exploring the relationship between narrators' "subjective truths" and "master narratives" of war, our contributors join a small but growing number of scholars who have brought the insights of memory studies to bear on the history of children, youth, and armed conflict.[77] No fewer than eight chapters in this collection are based on oral histories, featuring either teenagers or young adults looking back on their childhood and adolescence, or adult and elderly narrators, recalling their lives in the Second World War and Cold War.[78] In their embrace of oral testimony, many contributors to this collection engage in what Annette Kuhn has called "memory work": the art of historical detection that involves "working backward – searching for clues, deciphering signs and traces, making deductions, patching together reconstructions out of fragments of evidence."[79] "Telling stories about the past, our past," Kuhn writes, "is a key moment in the making of our selves."[80]

Much like the adults in their lives, young people belonged to multiple communities and were marked by their age, gender, social class, ethnicity, race, and geographical location. Yet they also belonged to "communities of memory," to quote anthropologists Loring M. Danforth and Riki Van Boeschoten, and recalled their wartime experiences "not as isolated individuals, but as members of social groups."[81] As recent scholarship has demonstrated, even in war-torn regions, many families and communities were able to mobilize resources that provided young people with layers of support, including "nurturing relationships with caretakers, supportive relationships with peers, meaningful interactions with adults, cognitive and emotional stimulation." By broadening the scope of inquiry to encompass the social ecologies of childhood, such works have emphasized the relational dimensions of young people's lives and noted that "a relationship with at least one emotionally available adult" afforded children in war zones with "one of the most important" layers of protection.[82]

Our contributors, as well, conceive of the relationships between children and adults as contextual and relational, thereby engaging with ongoing debates about the place of agency in childhood studies and the history of young people.[83] Rather than pitting children's experiences and perspectives against those of an adult world, historians should tend to what Mona Gleason calls "the messier 'in between'": the intergenerational exchanges between children and their parents, the complex dynamics of peer groups, and the varied relationships young people built beyond their nuclear families.[84] The chapters in this collection do just that by turning, for instance, to the "graphic community" of children whose drawings of war, displacement, and incarceration reflected their fluid engagement with the adult world – reworking, adapting, re-assembling, translating, embracing, and resisting the strictures of adult discourse.[85]

Small Stories of War also explores the dynamics of intergenerational storytelling, in stories of tragedy passed down through three generations of Halifax families and the memories of migration that circulated in Australian refugee communities and found expression in picture books, jointly authored by children and their parents. Perhaps most elusive are the juvenile worlds that children and youth shared with each other, and that constituted unique cultures with their own rules and rhythms.[86] Brookfield's elegant study of the youthful communities of peace activists on Grindstone Island offers an example of one such community of memory that was both emplaced and experiential, while Lorenzkowski's chapters in this volume reconstruct the fleeting sensory communities of children in Atlantic Canada who were bound together by the sounds of the wartime city. By adjusting the scale of our analysis to the fine-grained ways in which young people (and their adult selves) made sense of their wartime experiences, we may be able to leave behind the flattening effects of the war culture paradigm and explore new ways of telling the stories of young people and conflict.

In drawing upon oral testimony and young people's wartime accounts, this collection demonstrates how children and youth navigated master narratives of war – at times internalizing adult discourse, at times resisting it, but always trying to square their own experiences with the ways adult society was representing war, armed conflict, and political violence.[87] Several of the historical actors featured in this volume drew upon cultural scripts that gave shape and form to their memories, while others constructed their life-stories in counterpoint to dominant cultural narratives of war.[88] Some iconic moments of war burned themselves into the memory of children and youth in what historian William Tuttle has called a "flashbulb memory, the freeze-framing of an exceptionally emotional event down to the most incidental detail."[89] Other stories became part of family and friendship lore, recounted and shaped in dense social interactions and communal acts of remembrance, each adding a layer to the prisms of memory through which narrators glimpsed their childhood and youth. Some experiences were so perplexing or painful that they could be voiced only years later, while others yet were shrouded in silence so as to conceal difficult family histories. In the lovely turn of phrase of novelist David Ireland, "kids have plenty of thoughts, but not always the words to dress them up. They stay, the undressed ones, in you somewhere, then maybe you remember them later."[90]

"When we remember our childhood selves," writes Rebecca Clifford in her moving study of child survivors of the Holocaust, "we map our adult understanding of what is important and relevant onto our narratives." As a result, oral life stories "tell us as much about the journey to make sense of childhood as they do about childhood itself."[91] Whereas some historians remain profoundly ambivalent about memory's capacity to reconstruct the interior worlds of childhood, we agree with Graham Dawson that the value of post-war reminiscences lies precisely in their double vision that positions the remembering adult "both 'inside' and 'outside' childhood."[92] In her analysis of memoirs written by Holocaust survivors, Susan Rubin Suleiman similarly notes how, in these personal accounts, "we see both the child's helplessness and the adult's attempt to render that helplessness retrospectively, in language."[93] To embrace this double vision and acknowledge the multiple temporalities that are woven into the fabric of memory allows us to explore the processes by which youthful, middle-aged, and elderly narrators made meaning of war, violence, and armed conflict as they shared of their lived experience.

Conclusion

In February 2022, Russian forces invaded Ukraine. The war that ensued (which is ongoing at the time of writing) has affected young people in ways that are both devastating and unsurprising. Russian air strikes have targeted urban centres and civilian infrastructure, and hundreds of children in a range of locations have been killed. Thousands more shelter at night in subway stations and other makeshift bomb shelters, listening to the sound of explosions and fearing for their own lives and those of their loved ones. Children and youth also make up a significant portion of the over six-and-a-half million Ukrainians who have been displaced by the invasion and subsequent fighting, and photos abound on the internet of youngsters boarding evacuation trains, saying goodbye to fathers staying behind to fight, and adjusting to their new surroundings in makeshift shelters in Hungary, Poland, Slovakia, and Romania. Reports from areas of Ukraine under Russian occupation also suggest that Ukrainians civilians have been forcibly relocated into Russian territory.

The fighting in Ukraine, like other ongoing conflicts in the Middle East, North and Central Africa, and South Asia, provides further proof that war is indeed (in Dudziak's words) "an enduring condition."[94] The witnessing and testimony of young people in contexts of war and forced displacement, more widely available than ever before thanks to cell phone cameras and wireless internet, deserve to be taken seriously by politicians and citizens alike. As education scholar Aparna Mishra Tarc writes, looking closely at social media posts featuring war-affected youngsters reveals that "far from being helpless victims, children show themselves to be remarkably like adults or, more precisely, like adults ought to be in times of war. They console, uplift, despair, find beauty in devastation and join in armed combat."[95] Consolation, despair, beauty, and devastation also come together in Raymond Moriyama's "song of the wind," an earwitness memory of childhood and internment that – like this volume as a whole – reframes and complicates the study of young people and war culture.

Looking closely at the creation, collection, and circulation of voices and memories across time and space reveals much about the making and remaking of youthful subjectivities in conflict-ridden contexts. On one level, the emotional and sensory experiences discussed by our authors – from "skip[ping] over" human bones in the Ugandan bush to remembering the Second World War in Halifax as a "great time to be a kid" – can appear bewilderingly incommensurate. Yet the jarring nature of these juxtapositions, we contend, is precisely the point. What does it mean to consider pacifist experiments on Canada's Grindstone Island and tear-filled drawings produced by child refugees at Australian detention centres on Nauru and Manus Islands in the same frame? Does discussing adult concerns about white middle-class children's reactions to Canadian simulations of invasion and bombing alongside non-white youngsters' visceral memories of genocide and violence encourage us to see either of those events differently? These examples, which expose the often racist limits of protectionist discourse in particularly stark terms, are also reminders of the critical importance of place in young people's wartime lives. The "small stories of war" we offer here – from a parental embrace to the bars of a cage – therefore raise important questions about distance, proximity, confinement, and freedom. We hope they will inspire still more research about youthful imagination, critique, and the power of life stories in the midst and the aftermath of conflict.

NOTES

1 Moriyama, *In Search of a Soul*, 109 and 103.
2 Sugiman, "'Life Is Sweet,'" 187–8, and Sugiman, "Memories of Internment," 359–88. See also McAllister, *Terrain of Memory*; Oikawa, *Cartographies of Violence*; and Stanger-Ross and Sugiman, eds, *Witness to Loss*.
3 Moriyama, *In Search of a Soul*, 1.
4 Ibid., 39.
5 Ibid., 2.
6 Ibid., 109 and 39. Originally dubbed Regeneration Hall, this part of the museum was renamed in honour of Moriyama in 2021.
7 McKircher and Van Huizen, eds, *Undiplomatic History*; Madokoro, McKenzie, and Meren, eds, *Dominion of Race*; Dubinsky, Perry, and Yu, eds, *Within and Without the Nation*.
8 Quoted in Bentley, "Simile, Metaphor, and the Making and Perception of Canada," 67.
9 Lowman and Barker, *Settler*; Wolfe, "Settler Colonialism and the Elimination of the Native," 387–409.
10 Lake and Reynolds, *Drawing the Global Colour Line*.
11 Madokoro, "On Future Research Directions: Temporality and Permanency in the Study of Migration and Settler Colonialism in Canada," 3.
12 For more on exclusionary and genocidal aspects of twentieth-century Canadian history, see for example Abella and Troper, *None Is Too Many*; Truth and

Reconciliation Commission of Canada, *Honouring the Truth, Reconciling for the Future*; Woolford, *This Benevolent Experiment*; Backhouse, *Colour-Coded*; and Mathieu, *North of the Color Line*.

13 Pignot, "French Boys and Girls in the Great War," 173. See also Pignot, "Children," 29–45. Australian historians have led the way in the use of distance as a conceptual and analytical tool. See Blainey, *The Tyranny of Distance* and Bart Ziino, *A Distant Grief*.

14 Thanks to our second anonymous reviewer for encouraging us to expand on this point.

15 Conquergood, "Performance Studies: Interventions and Radical Research," 311–13, and de Certeau, *The Practice of Everyday Life*, 129.

16 Conquergood, "Performance Studies," 312.

17 Ghobrial, "Introduction: Seeing the World Like a Microhistorian," 16. See also Putnam, "Daily Life and Digital Reach: Place-Based Research and History's Transnational Turn," 167–81. Much in a similar vein, Lindsey Dodd and David Lees remark in their investigation of everyday life in Vichy France that "to examine the epistemology of the everyday" allows us to work productively on both the small-scale and the large-scale: "Understanding the multiple situated contexts of the everyday creates a history which is less satisfying in its wholeness, but more real, perhaps, in its messiness." See Dodd and Lees, "Introduction," 3 and 10.

18 Audoin-Rouzeau, *La guerre des enfants, 1914–1918*.

19 Audoin-Rouzeau and Becker, *14–18: Understanding the Great War*, 111.

20 Audoin-Rouzeau, "Children and the Primary Schools of France, 1914–1980," 43 and 47.

21 Audoin-Rouzeau and Becker, *14–18: Understanding the Great War*, 110. Studies of this phenomenon in various national contexts include Cave and Moore, eds, "Japanese Children Amid Disaster and War, 1920–1945: Special Issue"; Honeck and Marten, eds, *War and Childhood in the Era of the Two World Wars*; Carden-Coyne and Darian-Smith, eds, "Special Issue: Young People and the World Wars: Visuality, Materiality and Cultural Heritage"; and Cook and Wall, eds, *Children and Armed Conflict*. See also Maksudyan, *Ottoman Children & Youth during World War*; Plum, "Lost Childhoods in a New China: Child-Citizen-Workers at War, 1937–1945," 237–58; Peacock, *Innocent Weapons*; and Embacher et al., eds, *Children and War: Past and Present*.

22 Marten, "Childhood Studies and History: Catching a Culture in High Relief," 52.

23 Kennedy, *The Children's War: Britain, 1914–1918*, 1.

Introduction

24 Donson, *Youth in the Fatherless Land*; Fisher, *Boys and Girls in No Man's Land*; Pignot, *Allons enfants de la patrie*; Kennedy, *The Children's War: Britain, 1914–1918*; deGraffenried, *Sacrificing Childhood*; Frühstück, *Playing War*; and Chatani, *Nation-Empire*.

25 Mosse, *Fallen Soldiers: Reshaping the Memory of the World Wars*, 126.

26 Malkki, "Children, Humanity, and the Infantilization of Peace," 60. For this reference, we are indebted to Frühstück, "'And my heart screams,'" 183.

27 Rose, *The Case of Peter Pan, or The Impossibility of Children's Fiction* and Scott, "The Evidence of Experience," 777–8.

28 Musgrove, Leahy, and Moruzi, "Hearing Children's Voices: Conceptual and Methodological Challenges," 10 and 6–7.

29 Vallgårda and Larsen, "Emotional Echoes: Young People, Divorce, and the Public Media, 1960–2000," 230.

30 Rob Boddice, "The Re-turn to Experience in History," public lecture at the University of Lethbridge (15 October 2021). See also Boddice and Smith, *Emotion, Sense, Experience*, 18–22.

31 As Josephine Hoegaerts and Stephanie Olsen suggest, writing histories of experience through "thick layering[s] of accounts and meanings of the past" – based on textual and non-textual evidence – opens up the possibility of "includ[ing] historical actors whose 'voice' may have been lost, but whose 'experiences we can at least partly come to know." See Hoegaerts and Olsen, "The History of Experience: Afterword," 382 and 378.

32 Vallgårda, Alexander and Olsen, "Emotions and the Global Politics of Childhood," 20–2.

33 Ibid., 21.

34 Dolto, *Enfances*, 28. As quoted in Pignot, "French Boys and Girls in the Great War," 169.

35 Vallgårda, Alexander and Olsen, "Emotions and the Global Politics of Childhood," 22–6.

36 Vallgårda and Larsen, "Emotional Echoes: Young People, Divorce, and the Public Media, 1960–2000," 226–53. Historians Sarah Glassford and Amy Shaw similarly emphasize "the importance of listening to individual women as they voice their experiences and of giving their assessments as much analytical weight as the hopes or expectations that governments, or Canadian society more broadly, held for them." Glassford and Shaw, "Conclusion: Making the Best of It," 261.

37 This formulation is inspired by Bowen and Hinchy, "Introduction: Children and Knowledge in India," 317–29.

38 Spyrou, "Troubling Children's Voices in Research," 106. On the use of "voice" and "agency" by historians of childhood, see Gleason, "Avoiding the Agency Trap," 446–59.
39 Komulainen, "The Ambiguity of the Child's 'Voice' in Social Research," 13. See also James, "Giving Voice to Children's Voices," 261–72.
40 Spyrou, "The Production of Children's Voices," from his *Disclosing Childhoods*, 86.
41 Moore, "From Individual Child to War Youth," 357. See also Moore, "Reversing the Gaze," 181–201.
42 Dood and Lees, "Introduction," 10.
43 Barbara Lorenzkowski, "Sensing War: Childhood Memories of the Wartime Atlantic, 1939–1945" in this volume.
44 Carolyn Kay, "Children's Images of War from the German Home Front, 1914–1918" in this volume.
45 Ibid.
46 Ibid.
47 The term "environmental autobiographies" is Moore's, *Childhood's Domain*, 19.
48 Cole, "(Re)Placing the Past," 30–49; Lorenzkowski, "The Children's War," 116; and Lorenzkowski, "The Small Spaces of Childhood."
49 Roper, *The Secret Battle*, 266. See also Hanna, "A Republic of Letters," 1338–61.
50 Kristine Alexander and Ashley Henrickson, "Children, Soldiers, and Correspondence in Canada's First World War" in this volume.
51 See also Layman, "Reticence in Oral History Interviews," and Greenspan, "The Unsaid, the Incommunicable, the Unbearable, and the Irretrievable," 229–43.
52 For studies on the interior displacement of children born to occupation forces, see also Fehrenbach, *Race after Hitler*; Ericcson and Simonsen, eds, *Children of World War II*; Hamilton, *Children of the Occupation*; and Lee, *Children Born of War in the Twentieth Century*.
53 See also Boyden, "Anthropology under Fire," 252–3 and Boyden, "Children under Fire," 1–29.
54 Denov, "Co-Creating Space for Voice," 425. In a trenchant criticism of Western concepts of trauma and associated Western health practices, some scholars have suggested that "it is not emotional expression or talking through past traumatic events but culturally prescribed rituals that are required for healing and social reintegration." See Kostelny, "A Culture-Based Integrative Approach: Helping War-Affected children," 25; Mieth, "'What Is the Use of Talking-Talking?,'" 38–59; and Bragin, "Editorial: Special Issue on Children Affected by Armed Conflict," 179–86.

Introduction

55 For more on childhood and temporality, see Millei, "Temporalizing Childhood," 59–73.
56 Dudziak, *War-Time*, 5.
57 Ibid., 68.
58 Alexander, "Domestic Demobilization," 177–89; Cabanes, "Negotiating Intimacy in the Shadow of War," 1–23.
59 Deborah Harrison and Patrizia Albanese, "Adolescents during Canada's Afghanistan Mission" in this volume.
60 Zerubavel, *Time Maps*. See also Sheftel and Zembrzycki, "'We Started Over Again, We Were Young': Postwar Social Worlds of Child Holocaust Survivors in Montreal," 20–30.
61 Isabel Campbell, "Deconstructing a Canadian Military Family: The Taylor Mother and Son Remember the Cold War" in this volume.
62 High, *Oral History at the Crossroads*, 40.
63 Denov, "Social Navigation and Power in Post-Conflict Sierra Leone," 192.
64 Myriam Denov, "The Intergenerational Effects of Wartime Sexual Violence: Children Born of Wartime Rape in Northern Uganda" in this volume.
65 Andrew Burtch, "'What Am I to Do to Save My Children?': Children in Canadian Civil Defence Planning" in this volume.
66 Edelman, *No Future: Queer Theory and the Death Drive*.
67 Bernstein, *Racial Innocence*, 4.
68 There is now a large body of scholarship about the history and legacy of Indian residential schools in Canada. Relevant examples include: Giancarlo, "Indigenous Student Labour and Settler Colonialism at Brandon Residential School," 461–74; Fraser, "T'aih k'iighe' tth'aih zhit diidich'uh (By Strength, We Are Still Here)"; Woolford, *This Benevolent Experiment: Indigenous Boarding Schools, Genocide, and Redress in Canada and the United States*; Leeuw, "Intimate Colonialisms: The Material and Experienced Places of British Columbia's Residential Schools," 339–59; Milloy, *A National Crime*; Kelm, *Colonizing Bodies*; Miller, *Shingwauk's Vision*.
69 Ishiguro, "'Growing Up and Grown Up … in Our Future City,'" 15.
70 Hage, "Migration, Food, Memory, and Home-Building," 419.
71 See, for instance, Zahra, *The Lost Children: Reconstructing Europe's Families after World War II*; Shalhoub-Kevorkian, "Negotiating the Present, Historicizing the Future"; Barber, "Making Sense and No Sense of War," 281–312; and Baron, ed., *Displaced Children in Russia and Eastern Europe, 1915–1953*.
72 Kucherenko, *Little Soldiers*, 7.
73 Boyden, "Anthropology Under Fire," 250.

74 Andrew Burtch, "'What Am I to Do to Save My Children?': Children in Canadian Civil Defence Planning" in this volume.

75 Tarah Brookfield, "From Wartime Refuge to Peaceful Hippie Haven: Generations of Youth on Grindstone Island" in this volume.

76 Mary Tomsic, "Politics and Emotion in Drawings by Children in Australian Immigration Detention" in this volume.

77 For a sustained examination of wartime memories of childhood and youth, see Danforth and Van Boeschoten's *Children of the Greek Civil War*, in particular chapter 9 on "Communities of Memory, Narratives of Experience" (quotation on page 222). A more literary rendition of children's experiences during wartime is provided by the Belarusian writer Svetlana Alexievich, who is among the rare Nobel Prize laureates to have been honoured for her oeuvre of non-fiction, including *Last Witness: An Oral History of the Children of World War II*. William M. Tuttle's *Daddy's Gone to War: The Second World War in the Lives of America's Children* provides an empathetic reading of 2,500 wartime childhood memoirs that his respondents offered up in the form of letters, while Lindsey Dodd's *French Children Under the Allied Bombs, 1940–45: An Oral History* is attuned to the sensory and emotional experiences of childhood in wartime. In her important work *Children Born of War in the Twentieth Century*, Sabine Lee offers a sharp and sensitive reading of oral histories to uncover the impact of official policies on children born of sexual violence. Rebecca Clifford's *Survivors: Children's Lives After the Holocaust*, finally, traces the decade-long attempts of child survivors of the Holocaust to piece together their childhood histories and origin stories in an elegant, often moving account that draws upon both archived oral history collections and her own oral history research.

78 For an expansive view of oral history research practices, see Janesick, "Oral History Interviewing: Issues and Possibilities," 300–14.

79 Kuhn, *Family Secrets*, 4 and 165.

80 Ibid., 2. Feminist scholars, who have fruitfully explored the intersection of gender, culture, and memory – and, as such, much to offer to historians of children and youth – include Hirsch and Smith, "Feminism and Cultural Memory" and Srigley, Zembrzycki, and Iacovetta, eds., *Beyond Women's Words: Feminisms and the Practices of Oral History in the Twenty-First Century*.

81 Danforth and Boeschoten, *Children of the Greek Civil War*, 222.

82 Kostelny, "A Culture-Based Integrative Approach: Helping War-Affected Children," 26 and 28.

83 Alexander, "Agency and Emotion Work," 120–8; Gleason, "Avoiding the Agency Trap," 446–59; Miller, "Assent as Agency in the Early Years of the American Revolution," 48–51; Karen Vallgårda, Kristine Alexander, and Stephanie Olsen, "Against Agency," Commentaries section of the Society for the History of Children & Youth (SHCY) website. October 2018. http://www.shcy.org/features/commentaries/against-agency/.

84 Gleason, "Avoiding the Agency Trap," 448.

85 Pignot, "Drawing the Great War," 174.

86 For pioneering studies of the worlds that children created beyond the purview of the adult gaze see Opie and Opie, *Children's Games in Street and Playground*; Opie and Opie, *The Lore and Language of Schoolchildren*; Nasaw, *Children of the City: At Work and At Play*; and Sutherland, "Children in the Culture of Childhood" from his *Growing Up*, 220–53.

87 For studies that have traced the interaction between personal testimony and dominant cultural narratives of war, see Thomson, *Anzac Memories*; Summerfield, *Reconstructing Women's Wartime Lives*; and Down, "Au Revoir les Enfants: Wartime Evacuation and the Politics of Childhood in France and Britain, 1939–45," 121–50. Works that are intent on exploring what historian Michael Roper calls the "'underlay' of memory," namely the ways speakers construct a sense of self in both present and past, include Roper, "Re-membering the Soldier Hero," 181–204 (quotation on 184); Sugiman, "'These Feelings That Fill My Heart': Japanese Canadian Women's Memories of Internment," 69–84; and James, *Dona Maria's Story*.

88 For a point of comparison, see Portelli, "Oral History as Genre," from his *The Battle of Valle Giulia*, 7–8, and Summerfield, "Culture and Composure," 65–93.

89 Tuttle, *Daddy's Gone to War*, 3.

90 As quoted in Sutherland, *Growing Up*, 14.

91 Clifford, *Survivors*, 13. As Alessandro Portelli argued in 1979 in a brief and brilliant essay that left behind the defensive posture of early oral history, we should be mindful that "memory is not a passive depository of facts, but an active process of creation of meanings. Thus, the specific utility of oral sources for the historian lies, not so much in their ability to preserve the past, as in the very changes wrought by memory." See Portelli, "What Makes Oral History Different," from his *The Death of Luigi Trastulli and Other Stories*, 52.

92 Dawson, *Soldier Heroes*, 241.

93 Suleiman, "The 1.5 Generation: Thinking about Child Survivors and the Holocaust," 292.

94 Dudziak, *War-Time*, 5.
95 Aparna Mishra Tarc, "We Need to Pay Attention to the Experiences of Children during the Ukraine Invasion," *Conversation* (9 March 2022), https://theconversation.com/we-need-to-pay-attention-to-the-experiences-of-children-in-ukraine-during-the-russian-invasion-178772.

PART ONE
GLOBAL WARS

1
Children's Images of War from the German Home Front, 1914–18

Carolyn Kay

> In my classes every youth must depict war. This is a beloved subject for boys. You can see with what sort of joy and passion they make these images and how much care and imagination they expend on this art.[1]
> Franz Cižek, 4th International Congress for Art Education, Dresden, 1912

The historical memory of the First World War is marked in terms of its losses rather than its triumphs: what prevails are images of mud and muck, mass slaughter and exploding shells, and the senseless deaths of millions of young soldiers. Yet for the young German child who experienced the war on the home front, the images of war were something very different. Most children had fathers, brothers, uncles, and grandfathers who went off to war triumphantly in 1914; within the schools and certainly within the family such soldiers were held up as national heroes and the children became subjects of intense wartime pedagogy and propaganda. Male and female teachers presented the war as a glorious struggle for Germany's civilization and as a testing ground for personal honour and service. The children internalized these ideas, giving voice to strong nationalistic sentiments. We can see their fervour for war in some of the surviving examples of school drawings addressing the theme of the European conflict. That is the subject of this chapter.

Today the historiography of the First World War includes many excellent studies of the home front (such as Andrew Donson's *Youth in the Fatherless Land*), and thus addresses the transformation of society experienced by ordinary citizens during this tumultuous period.² Still, the lives of children and their education in schools during wartime merits more attention by historians of modern Europe. As Gert Geissler has noted about the German case: "From 1914 onward war defined the education of youth and of schools, from the ordinary school to the university. The parental home, the school, the church, youth groups, and the military came together and created in various efforts a unified and nationalistic form of education that was very powerful. The military and the school marched in close formation as they embraced war as the continuation of politics through other means."³ Christa Hämmerle, in her recent book on Austrian children during the war, also makes the point that students in Austrian schools, already influenced by military ideas before 1914, were encouraged to positively support the war and to defend the war aims: "For this purpose the entire scope of learning was placed in service to the nationalistic war."⁴ Likewise, the path-breaking scholarship of French historians Stéphane Audoin-Rouzeau and Manon Pignot (who has analyzed wartime children's art in Paris) has shown that French children were saturated with war propaganda in the home, in the street, and especially at school. Here they encountered what Audoin-Rouzeau calls "war culture." "Presented to children as a war to protect their safety, the conflict was also portrayed as a war to build ... their future. In such circumstances, the pressure exerted on children from the outset was extremely heavy. It was a matter of making use of the war to transform the children of the war period into a generation of outstanding adults."⁵

In wartime Germany, young children faced a barrage of incessant propaganda from July 1914 onwards. There were approximately ten million school-age children in 1914 out of a general population of 67.8 million Germans and thus the number of young Germans was substantial.⁶ In the Volksschule – primary public schools – students from age six to fourteen were immersed in war propaganda, especially in the first two years of the conflict.⁷ Notably, these schools had been instrumental in the socialization of workers' children before 1914, teaching boys and girls to respect God, Kaiser, and the Fatherland.⁸ Songs, classroom decorations, school assemblies, and daily lessons – all were affected by the fervour of war. At the same time, nationalistic authors like Adolf Matthias (the author of a popular advice book for parents entitled *How Do We Raise Our Son Benjamin?*) wrote books, pamphlets, and essays on wartime pedagogy, praising the war as a great teacher of individual virtues, including duty and service to the community and the nation.⁹

In all of these ways, German children became the objects of intense war culture. Within the classroom a war frenzy arose in the first two years of the war. By 1916 the Social Democratic writer Clara Bohm-Schuch was arguing in *Children in the World War* that in the Volksschule a disturbing "Kriegsrausch" or war cry had exhibited itself in children, accompanied by expressions of intense hatred of the enemy and the playing of very rough war games.[10] She called on schools to change this environment of intolerance. In the same year Spartacist Karl Liebknecht – a prominent opponent of the war – complained that "war, war and always war is the only solution proposed by schools."[11] We know now that the intense period of wartime nationalism in the schools was in fact limited; as Kathrin Berdelmann and Joachim Scholz have argued, the effects of war pedagogy diminished after 1916 for many reasons, including the loss of teachers, disease and hunger affecting students, absenteeism from the schools for work or because of illness, and classroom fatigue about the war.[12] To be sure, the wartime suffering of children because of the child's separation from parents and the economic hardships faced by families on the home front affected all combatant nations, as Kristine Alexander and Ashley Henrickson make clear in their chapter on Canadian soldiers' letters to their families during the "Great War." In Germany such conditions affected the education of children and thus their indoctrination, meaning that the pedagogy at school was often inconsistent after 1916. Furthermore, we need to consider other factors when assessing wartime pedagogy at any point in the war, including the ages of children in the schools, their class background, whether they lived in the city or country, whether they experienced reform pedagogy or not, and what gender these children were. Were younger children more susceptible to school propaganda than teenagers? Did it make a difference to learning about the war if you were a boy or a girl?

In addition, one of the greatest challenges for the scholar is uncovering the attitudes of children during this time. The voice of the child is not found within the prescriptive literature of the age (i.e., advice literature for parents or books on wartime pedagogy), or in the accounts of school directives and activities during the war. What did children actually think? How much did they understand about the war? My research has convinced me that children's perspectives – and thus their "voice" – can be found in the school artwork of the war years, encouraged by teachers of the reform movement in arts pedagogy (the "Kunsterziehungsbewegung" or art education movement) which promoted free drawing and the creativity of children.[13] During the war years, such classes inspired children to draw and paint on the subject of the great conflict. Admittedly, these school exercises by their very nature could shape the ideas of children's work, since boys and girls were told by teachers to revel in the war and thus to draw or write on the war as

Figure 1.1
Austrian forces attack. R. Übleis, age fourteen, Doppel-Bürgerschule Graz, 1914.
Österreichische Nationalbibliothek.

an essential task of the nation. Nonetheless, as we will see, children brought individual perspectives to bear on their essays and artwork in terms of what they chose to draw or how they imagined the war. With caution, the historian can analyze such works to discern the voice of the child.

Research on children's wartime drawings is very exciting and yet is limited by the number of available sources. Not many examples of children's art survived the two wars or were collected by schools. However, there is an extraordinary collection of children's drawings – in pristine condition – in the Elbinsel-Wilhelmsburg Museum, drawings originally done for the Volksschule III Wilhelmsburg.[14] As well, at the Library for Research on International Education (Bibliothek für Bildungsgeschichtliche Forschung) in Berlin, children's school drawings from 1914–45 reveal distinct political, national, and military influences.[15] Likewise, in the Austrian National Library examples of boys' artwork from schools in Graz during the First World War are a rich resource on the war.[16]

My other sources are photographs of children's artwork in books and journals from the First World War. For example, in 1915 educational authorities in Berlin held an eight-month exhibition of children's work, called *Schule und Krieg* (School and War), for which a book and catalogue were produced.[17] In the *School and War* publication one sees many examples of children's artwork on the war. As well, in wartime Vienna, an art teacher named Richard Rothe arranged for an exhibition in November 1915 of wartime drawings by his young students, and a book from that exhibition, called *Die Kinder und der Krieg* (Children and the War), shows the artwork created.[18]

Analyzing the children's art leads to the conclusion that war pedagogy was intensive in the period from 1914-16, and that in the reform pedagogy of art classes in the Volksschule children experienced a deep connection to the war: certainly, they were directed by teachers to celebrate the war and support the national army. As Eberhard Demm notes, the wartime propaganda had a specific goal: "to teach children to have unshakable trust in the heroism of the army and the principled wisdom of the High Command" while stressing to children "that we are not in this world in order to be happy, but to do our duty."[19] What strikes me as very significant, in all of this art, is evidence that the youth of Germany and Austria-Hungary were immersed in a culture of war and violence after 1914, akin to the French experience described by Pignot and Audoin-Rouzeau.[20] They were encouraged by teachers to be celebratory about the war – and to accept its legitimacy, including the violence and killing – because the conflict was being waged on behalf of the beloved nation.

Art Classes in School

To understand the children's drawings in the war years, one must also understand the *Kunsterziehungsbewegung*: the arts education movement. This pedagogical approach to art was part of the new wave, or reform movement, of German education, dedicated to nurturing the child.[21] German art education had changed dramatically, to be sure, since the early nineteenth century. At the start of this century, educators considered drawing a luxury for children and thus not an essential part of instruction. A much different approach emerged with the pioneering work of Johann Heinrich Pestalozzi and Friedrich Fröbel, who encouraged children's drawing of geometric shapes and daily play with balls and blocks as a means of developing skill, intellect, and personality.[22] In the aftermath of the 1848 revolutions, Fröbel's ideas were rejected by Prussian educational authorities as socialist, and once again the Volksschule became an institution of rote learning – what one scholar has described as "a dark age for the teaching of drawing."[23] Finally, towards the end of the century efforts by a variety of educational reformers, including Alfred Lichtwark, the director of the Hamburg Kunsthalle, helped return educators' attention to the arts in instruction.[24] Allied with the teachers' reform movement in Hamburg and a passionate advocate of arts education named Carl Götze, Lichtwark wrote "Die Kunst in der Schule" (Art in the School) in 1887, urging art instruction, and he helped organize an exhibition in the Kunsthalle of children's art in 1898, entitled *Das Kind as Künstler* (The Child as Artist).[25]

Lichtwark urged teachers to expose children to art and to art instruction, so that they would become enlightened citizens of thought and culture – able to lead Germany into the future. In the Hanseatic capital, the Hamburg reform movement introduced an innovative and modern approach to teaching art in the classroom, with teachers inviting children to explore their creative ideas and to study nature, utilizing ideas taught to them by artists in special courses and conferences.[26]

The art reform movement in Hamburg promoted a modern approach to teaching art and was backed by modernist artists in the Hanseatic capital. Indeed, throughout Germany during the fin-de-siècle, art teachers and educational reformers described children's art as the result of their instinctive, deeply perceptive, and essential creativity (what Rothe described as the "*Urinstinkte*" or "primal instincts" of children).[27] Modernist artists such as Wassily Kandinsky, Gabriele Münter, and Paul Klee believed in such ideas, showing an often intense interest in children's "primitive art" and seeing the child as the "pre-history" of adulthood, and thus as "a kind of domestic noble savage."[28] In such an approach, the nature of the child was supreme – and psychologists of the era interested in child development defended the idea of allowing the child to express herself without adult influence.[29] As Clive Ashwin has argued: "the theorists of the reform movement centered their attention, especially in relation to the very young child, on the child's developing personality and intellect, accepting from the start that its perception of the world was not the same as that of the adult and that its drawing should not be measured according to the adult criterion of objectively verifiable truth, but in relation to its own private and often highly idiosyncratic view of reality."[30] Thus the art reform movement was inextricably linked to emerging ideas on child development and psychology.

On 15 October 1872, the Prussian cultural minister Adalbert Falk called for the introduction of drawing classes in the Volksschule;[31] by the time of the First World War, educational reformers in German cities like Hamburg, Breslau, Munich, and Berlin dominated the classroom and they focused upon the cultivation of the child through imaginative exercises and arts instruction. They were also supporters of the war and of wartime pedagogy. As such, their art instruction invited the children's participation in the war. Indeed, most Volksschule teachers accepted the

Children's Images from the German Home Front

Figure 1.2
Flags of Prussia, Germany, Austria, and the Ottoman Empire. Elfriede Taube, age eleven, Lyzeum Berlin Pankow, 1915. Bibliothek für Bildungsgeschichtliche Forschung, DIPF/BBF/Archiv: BDK SZ 704.

idea of Germany being under siege from aggressive and jealous nations: their support for the war was very strong.[32]

Today in Berlin's Library for the History of Education (BBF) one finds a small collection of drawings from the early war years by children – featuring German and Allied flags (Prussian, German, Habsburg, Ottoman), and anthems and weapons of war, especially Zeppelins.[33] The progressive lessons of the arts reformers ultimately became linked with an oppressive war.

Indeed, once the war broke out, teachers viewed the creation of war art as a crucial, positive, and indeed progressive experience for young students. Rothe said of his students: "The war lives in all of their activities, in all their play and dreams. It has awoken in the innermost souls of these children – boys and girls – something holy that they had never learned to recognize before. The war has awoken the slumbering primal instincts in these children and has made the boys more active and the girls gentler and more compassionate."[34]

Rothe also begins his book with a stirring proclamation of support for the German struggle, depicting the conflict as a result of the aggressive actions of the "enemy" who seeks to make Germany and Austria-Hungary their "Knechte" or slaves.[35] His nationalism and his traditional view of gender roles are evident throughout the book and he would have certainly communicated such ideas to his students, influencing their perspectives.

The Breslau artist and arts teacher Colestin Kik was another leading proponent of the reform method of teaching drawing; in 1915 he wrote an article about his students' artwork in the 1915 *School and War* exhibition in Berlin.[36] Praising the elemental quality – the artistic value – of the drawings and arguing that these drawings were the very best means of hearing the children's voices during the war, he described the process of creation. Kik pointed out that teachers did not tell the children what to draw, specifically. All the children's works were original, he proclaimed: the teachers told the children to draw a "*Kriegsbild*" (a war picture) or to set down on paper their impression of the war.[37] The children then used their imaginations to create the art. Kik argued that to express the enormity of the war – its tragedy and heroic greatness – required of an artist neither natural talent or a trained ability. Children could create drawings of spontaneous expression and power, and in their efforts they expressed truthful recreations of their sense of reality. Thus he argued that the war drawings offered tremendous insight into their thoughts and feelings – perhaps more than any medium.[38] Rothe's and Kik's bias and preconceptions were plainly evident in their writings: both stressed that the war encouraged children's bravery, loyalty and passion for the nation, and that few expressed any sense of suffering or opposition. Furthermore, they made the case for boys being better artists than girls, as boys were supposedly more talented at drawing forms and utilizing detail, while girls – who had a good colour sense – tended to cram too many objects into the picture or get lost in the decorative details.[39] They also made the false assertion that girls did not draw many battles scenes. Conservative and nationalistic viewpoints emerged clearly in the writings of these two bourgeois men – projected onto the children and inherent in the idea that all German boys and girls loved the war.

The specific pedagogy that was used by art teachers in the wartime classroom is also revealed in accounts by teachers published between 1914 and 1918, in wartime journals for art instruction. One such teacher, Ignatz Göth, described his pedagogy in great detail, explaining how he first showed his class of working-class Austrian boys (twelve years old) a model of a submarine, alongside images of subs and warships from a wartime book for children. Then he described a battle scene to the class, whereby an unmarked ship appeared at night on the sea, only to be sunk by a German submarine with a periscope. The students did drawings based on this story, and also made a model of a periscope, which apparently aroused enormous interest among them.[40] Another teacher, Gustav Kolb, wrote in 1915 that his class in Göppingen (in a secondary school for middle-class boys) read about the German troops fighting the French in the Argonne forest and the class took on the project of depicting this conflict in their art. To prepare, students went to a nearby forest and studied individual trees, foliage, boughs, and limbs. They later drew such images from their memory. To create the French and German figures they spent a second week studying their own bodies crouching, kneeling, jumping, falling, and lying on the ground. As well, one student dressed in a French uniform for the class to observe. In the final week of preparation the students were given the freedom to create the drawings on their own, using their imagination – although clearly they would have been influenced by the preceding exercises. Kolb's belief in the elevating powers of the war, to draw forth the students' finest qualities and their connection to the German struggle, is evident in his description of the popularity of his classes and in his conviction that the war art of these boys was exceptional.[41] Yet another teacher, in Vienna (Otto Kunzfeld), emphasized how obsessed his students were with the war; their hearts and minds were filled with images of war events. Some of his female students were the daughters of officers and when they drew scenes of struggle they felt their hearts soar, he claimed. In impassioned exchanges between teachers and students the subjects of the art were set down: mobilization, departure of soldiers, attacks by infantry, battle scenes, and care of the wounded. Kunzfeld also described the progression in girls' drawings of the war – from stick figures he defines as symbolist to more mature images that are naturalistic. War art, he concluded, enriched the students' creativity.[42]

The Drawings of War by Children

Kunzfeld's observations about the different styles and skills of student art on the war ring true in the actual examples of children's wartime art available to historians. The drawings vary from rudimentary sketches of figures – by young children up to the age of twelve, done in a free style – to polished studies of soldier engagements, with careful delineation of the human figure in movement – usually by children aged thirteen to fifteen.

Many examples of this art originated in the Volksschule. As noted by Colestin Kik and other teachers, the children chose the subjects themselves, although it is not always clear how children knew *what* to draw. Where did the images they chose originate from? Were children influenced by illustrations in popular newspapers or in children's books on the war,[43] or was it toy soldiers, images hung in classrooms (the *Schulwandbilder*), and wartime postcards that influenced the children's ideas? Several reviewers of children's wartime art, in newspaper articles of 1914 and 1915, suggested that the children saw illustrated newspapers and that these images likely influenced their work.[44] Colouring books from the war years were another possible influence, and a popular one by the prolific illustrator Willy Planck features dramatic scenes of battle that likely influenced children's perspectives.[45] The drawing of the human figure in the children's war art covers the range from what proponents of the art education movement described as primitive and symbolic expressions of war (akin to ancient Egyptian friezes), to very detailed and skillfully rendered images of troops at war. There are similarities, nonetheless, for all of the child artists in terms of what is depicted in this war art. Very few of the drawings show the trenches, or the war of stalemate. According to Kik, "a boy does not appreciate boring, static battles and dreary trenches. Close battles and charges with bayonets and rifles are what he loves so much more, attacks by riders on horses and the pursuit of a fleeing enemy … The blood flows in streams and the red from the box of watercolours is heavily used."[46] In such student artwork there would be no depiction of gas or gas attacks, and few indications of machine guns. Most of the soldiers would be in movement in a field or on a hill or they would be storming a town and capturing a flag.

Kik's view that students loved portraying dramatic scenes of battle is borne out in the surviving examples of wartime children's art. To date, the collection of wartime children's drawings from the Hamburg area is the most extensive and remarkable collection of German children's drawings from the war years; the collection originated in Schule 3 in Wilhelmsburg (today a Waldorf school) and the students were boys and girls in classes "II" and "IV" between the ages of ten and fourteen. The area of the school lay in a section of expansion for the Hamburg docks; thus the children were likely of working-class background (the children of workers and dock employees). In this school Prussian values of order, obedience, hard work, godliness, and loyalty to the Kaiser and the state prevailed. A school flag contained the motto "Religion, Virtue, Devotion to Work, Diligence – with God for Emperor and the Empire."[47]

In the classroom drawings of 1915 the children explored four main subjects: the battles on land, on water, and in the air, and the care provided by nurses in war hospitals. Weapons such as cannons, bombs, machine guns, airplane bombers, submarines, and Zeppelins are featured, but one also sees a lot of bayonets and swords. There are no scenes of gassings or tanks; such aspects of the war would have been unknown to the children in the first few years of the war. Also missing are graves or cemeteries. The drawings do not appear to lament the deaths of the war, but to revel in the victories and accomplishments. Notably, Wilhelmsburg was the place of 4,500 conscripted soldiers in the First World War; of this number, 900 died.[48]

In the Wilhelmsburg drawings, most of the battle scenes by children show German soldiers against French soldiers. The only references to British or Russian forces are in the marine drawings. In the drawings by younger children, German soldiers are distinguished by their helmets (with the Pickelhelm, or spiked helmet) and by flags of the German nation. French soldiers wear red pants and blue jackets, or they are distinguished by their round caps, the kepi.

Analyzing Children's Art

The art historian Olga Ivashkevich has described children's art as a dialogue; she argues that children "reinvent" ideas, personal experiences, cultural values, and social conditions in their art.[49] They are also influenced by other children's art, especially if they are creating drawings in a group setting. This does not necessarily imply that they imitate others' work, but that seeing a friend's drawing can be a starting point for a child's personal impression of war, nature, and home life. And whether a drawing is made at home or at school, created alone or with friends, the child's unique impressions are set down – so that the artwork becomes "an artefact of lived experience."[50] Ivashkevich points out, too, that other researchers of children's art have noted the impact of gender differences, and thus of the socialization that can reinforce gender stereotypes as seen in the children's art.⁵¹ Historian Nicholas Stargardt has uniquely addressed children's art within the context of the Holocaust; he argues that surviving drawings and paintings such as those at Terezin (produced in peer groups under the direction of art teacher Friedl Dicker-Brandeis) should be seen "as the frozen moments of a social history lived in a very particular time and location."⁵² They are like photographs, and we don't know if the child wanted to say more or offer different stories. As Stargardt points out: "there is no established historical method for looking at the visual material produced by children themselves. Should we interpret their drawings as depicting real life or expressing their fantasies? ... Do children paint the world around them or do they go on painting the same picture, taking it with them like an expressionist autobiography? And what roles do age and sexual and cognitive development play?"⁵³ These are crucial issues for the historian; whether or not one can accurately interpret a child's drawing is up for question. However, in the case of the wartime art of German children, the sheer number of works depicting battlefield killing and showcasing the power and superiority of the German/Austrian forces is notable, and this is my starting point for utilizing the artwork as documents of the children's attitudes.

Analysis of the Wartime Art by German Children

When we turn to the examples of German children's wartime art it becomes clear that most drawings from 1914–16 show an unequivocal support of the war, which is certainly not surprising considering the extensive propaganda children were exposed to in the opening years of the war. What is intriguing, nonetheless, is the ways in which children imagine the German soldier or German nurse, and how they depict the German body. In the artwork of the children patriotic support of the German nation and its "just" cause is a constant theme, and the German soldier is depicted as brave, heroic, and triumphant. An extension of his power is the explosive cannon and the firing gun. The war is imagined as a battle of movement, with hand-to-hand combat, running troops, exciting weapons, and enormous Zeppelins. The bodies of these German heroes are drawn as monumental figures of strength and heroism: vigorous, purposeful, youthful, victorious, on the move, determined, skilful, carefully armed. Nurses are set on the page as goddesses of care and comfort, often drawn like mothers (with the wounded soldiers depicted as children). In the scenes of battle the enemy doesn't stand a chance of victory. He is shown as inept and clumsy, with legs and head akimbo, falling backwards, clownish, out of battalion order, overwhelmed, with inferior weapons. Sometimes the body of the enemy is bleeding profusely or blown apart. Civilians flee bombarded cities in disarray, their tiny bodies no match for the mighty Zeppelin. Essentially, in the children's artwork the body becomes a symbol of the nation. Notably, some children revel in showing violence to the body – imagining violence as something positive, exciting, and fun.

Specialists on children's art – including the psychologist Rhonda Kellogg and art historian Claire Golomb – have argued that children's drawings express several intense desires, including their demand to be in control and to be seen as grown up.[54] The war drawings encapsulate such desires and also show an attempt to make order out of the dramatic world of 1914–16. Indeed, as Claire Golomb points out: "The themes children portray reflect their experiences, joys, interests, and sorrows, hopes, fears, struggles, victories, and defeats. However, children do not live and create in isolation. They are part of a larger community and events that affect all of its members are depicted."[55] She also stresses that children draw their own symbols of the world, their own images; they know that what they are drawing and what they are representing are two separate things.[56] With such ideas in mind, let us consider several of the original drawings by young children of the Wilhelmsburg Volksschule.

In this first drawing by Martha Dieckmann, aged twelve, we see two groups of soldiers engaging each other in conflict; on the right are the Germans, on the left the French. Dieckmann used coloured pencils to depict four German soldiers in blue, with Pickelhelm, advancing on four French soldiers. One falls from a plane. The German soldiers are in a straight horizontal line, close together, carrying firepower (shown by bursts of yellow and red lines) and with a huge cannon. One soldier, closest to the cannon, carries a sword. They have managed to shoot down the French flier. The girl draws the bodies here with one arm, each extended by a weapon (the body and the weapon becoming one), a common method of depicting the body by younger children. The cannon is the centrepiece of the work, celebrating the enormous firepower of the Germans. In contrast, the French soldiers, delineated with red trousers and hat, and with blue jackets, stick out awkwardly. Their bodies express ineptitude; their uniforms give away their position. The first French soldier falls back – having been struck by gunfire from the second German soldier (and this French soldier also holds a sword). The last three are spaced far apart and fire towards the Germans, without luck. They will soon be victims. We also see two red objects, perhaps bombs, descending upon the French soldiers

Figure 1.3
German and French soldiers in combat. Martha Dieckmann, age twelve, Wilhelmsburg III, 1915. Museum Elbinsel-Wilhelmsburg, Hamburg, Germany.

from their own force's plane. Note that the girl draws the heads of the Germans as larger. Even though the Germans are outnumbered here, they are the victors. Their power, strength, unity, and weaponry are superior.

Similar images are captured in drawings by Frieda Bischoff and Emma Burmeister, girls who were in Dieckmann's class, and presumably of the same age; here we see evidence of possible copying or collaborative work by the girls. It could also be the case that the teacher showed an illustrated image to the class, or described a particular scene from battle, which they copied. In Frieda Bischoff's work the French outnumber the Germans, but to little avail. Although she did not draw a cannon, she repeated the story of German success: three German soldiers defeat four French soldiers and a flier. The Germans have shot down the plane and the pilot, having also killed the first French soldier at close range. They move forward purposefully and in close ranks; meanwhile she shows the French as

Figure 1.4
French and German soldiers fire at each other. Frieda Bischoff, age twelve, Wilhelmsburg III, 1915. Museum Elbinsel-Wilhelmsburg, Hamburg, Germany.

Figure 1.5
Battle scene of the First World War, as rendered by the twelve-year-old artist. Emma Burmeister, Wilhelmsburg III, 1915. Museum Elbinsel-Wilhelmsburg, Hamburg, Germany.

clumsy and too far apart, sticking out awkwardly with their garish French uniforms. The first soldier's body is blown backwards with enormous force. Emma Burmeister's work shows a tighter concentration of five German soldiers with heavy firepower, including a mighty cannon, clearly overwhelming a doomed group of four French soldiers (the Germans outnumbering the French in this unique example), with one again falling from a plane. The German bodies here are taller and the French are out of order, firing up rather than forward.

In a related drawing by Elsa Tilch, five German soldiers with three cannons decimate the French. Here the Germans are on the left and the French lie on the ground, near death or dead. One smiles at us. The soldiers are distinguished by their headgear. The theme again is of German superiority, strength, power, leadership, and success. Death is depicted with a grin, not with a face of terror.

The subject of German superiority is echoed in boys' art too, as in this work by Wilhelm Bade, where French soldiers fall back, are out of position, and certainly appear weak and inept. In contrast the German soldiers' bodies press forward,

Figure 1.6
German troops use cannons to kill French soldiers. Elsa Tilch, age twelve, Wilhelmsburg III, 1915. Museum Elbinsel-Wilhelmsburg, Hamburg, Germany.

Figure 1.7
Inept French troops face superior German soldiers. W. Bade, age twelve, Wilhelmsburg III, 1915. Museum Elbinsel-Wilhelmsburg, Hamburg, Germany.

Figure 1.8
German soldiers, behind barbed wire, fire on French soldiers. W. Regutzki, age twelve, Wilhelmsburg III, 1915. Museum Elbinsel-Wilhelmsburg, Hamburg, Germany.

Figure 1.9
German troops on the move against French soldiers. Erich Raschke, age ten, Wilhelmsburg III, 1915. Museum Elbinsel-Wilhelmsburg, Hamburg, Germany.

moving with precision and determination. The Germans are outnumbered, but in control. Notably, the French troops are shooting the wrong way and in one case the gun is turned upside down.

Wilhelm Regutzki, in his drawing, offers another scene of German precision versus French disorder, in this case indicating trenches and barbed wire, and setting the French forces as easy targets in their blue and red uniforms. Erich Raschke's work shows the precision and order of the German troops, vis-à-vis their French enemies – and adds in a Zeppelin for emphasis. The German forces operate as a coordinated machine, the French as a sputtering failure.

For the children drawing such scenes of combat, wartime propaganda provided plenty of examples of German superiority. Perhaps the most intriguing instance of this idea appeared in Willy Planck's 1915 colouring book, *Kriegsbilder*.

Children's Images from the German Home Front 51

Figure 1.10
German soldiers fire cannons against the French. Cover of a popular wartime colouring book for children. Willy Planck, *Kriegsbilder: Ein Malbuch für die Jugend* (Ravensburg: Maier, 1915).

The cover page, for example, shows German soldiers firing on the enemy, carefully camouflaged, gathered into a cohesive unit, and with a huge cannon. The French are fatally confronted by German strength; they wade forward into death, wearing ridiculous uniforms that betray their position immediately, carrying heavy packs, and without adequate firepower. One is already on the ground; several are struck and falling backwards. Other scenes in this colouring book celebrate and romanticize German troops in the war, giving the children the opportunity to copy, colour, and internalize such images.

Another possible influence as to the children's idea of German greatness was Arpad Schmidhammer's work – the prolific children's author and illustrator. Among the many popular books he created during the war, *Hans and Pierre* stands out for its satirizing of the French.[57] Schmidhammer celebrates the clever German

Figure 1.11
Caricature of the French soldier, in a children's picture book on the war. Arpad Schmidhammer, *Hans und Pierre: Eine lustige Schützengrabengeschichte* (Mainz: Jos. Schulz Verlag, 1916).

soldier in the trench who outwits, outlasts, and outdoes his hapless foe, Pierre. (Of course the book reveals nothing of substance about the actual conditions in the trenches.) On the cover, the contrast between the sturdy German fighter and the effeminate French fop is evident.

Alongside the theme of the monumental German body in war, artwork by children from the Wilhelmsburg school shows fixation with weaponry – cannons, guns, Zeppelins, submarines, and aircraft. In some works, such weaponry dominates with great effect. We see scenes of gigantic yellow Zeppelins, red cannons, and explosive bombs and rifles, all dwarfing the troops; dramatic air battles that decimate a town without human agency (Wilhelm Regutzki); and submarines (the famous U9) dispatching deadly missiles against British battleships (C. Möller). Such weapons are celebrated by the children – depicted in awe.

Figure 1.12
German airplanes attack. W. Regutzki, age twelve, Wilhelmsburg III, 1915. Museum Elbinsel-Wilhelmsburg, Hamburg, Germany.

Figure 1.13
The German U9 submarine hits a British warship. C. Möller, age twelve, Wilhelmsburg III, 1915. Museum Elbinsel-Wilhelmsburg, Hamburg, Germany.

Figure 1.14
The caring nurse. Ella Bostelmann, age twelve, Wilhelmsburg III, 1915. Museum Elbinsel-Wilhelmsburg, Hamburg, Germany.

Figure 1.15
Nurses and the soldiers' hospital, the "Lazarett." Erna O., age ten, Wilhelmsburg III, 1915. Museum Elbinsel-Wilhelmsburg, Hamburg, Germany.

Children's Images from the German Home Front

In contrast, when the children draw the wounded and the nurses who care for them, the predominant tone is one of nurturing and gentleness. In the images of the nurses, done here by three girls (Bostelmann, Erna O, Bernhardt), one sees that the children occasionally draw the nurses as quite large – to show their importance? – and design the hospitals as domestic places of refuge. Oftentimes the wounded appear like children and look out directly at the viewer, a suggestion of their identification with the war and their personal sense of refuge and safety in the arms of the loving mother. The wounded are not doomed or destroyed in these images; they are watched over by smiling goddesses of care.

Yet in a few drawings of nurses, executed in a more sophisticated style by older female students (Scharweit and Müller, fourteen years old), the story of war becomes one of death and suffering, with the wounded in precarious condition and the nurses unsmiling and serious. Here we do not see the laurel wreath of the national hero or the romantic idea of dying for one's country.

Figure 1.16
Soldier, nurse, and horse-drawn ambulance at the Red Cross hospital tent.
Minna Bernhardt, age ten, Wilhelmsburg III, 1915. Museum Elbinsel-Wilhelmsburg, Hamburg, Germany.

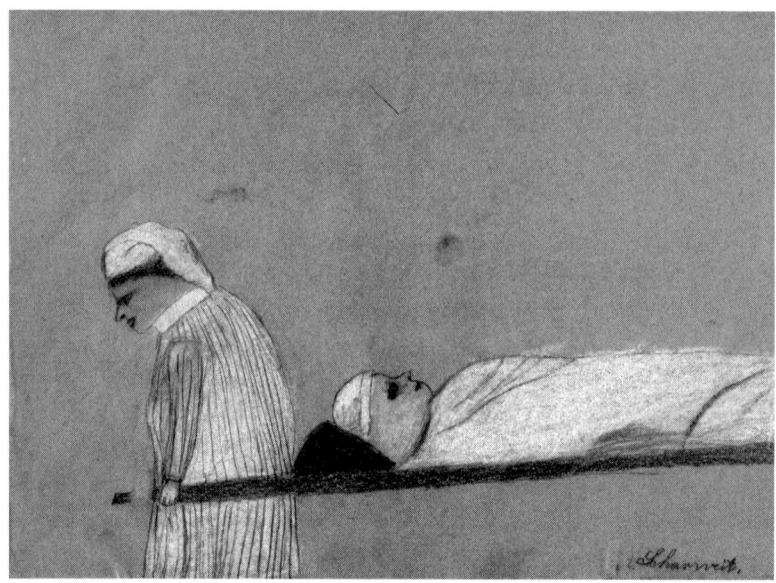

Figure 1.17
A nurse carrying a soldier with a head wound. A. Scharweit, age fourteen, Wilhelmsburg III, 1915. Museum Elbinsel-Wilhelmsburg, Hamburg, Germany.

Figure 1.18
A nurse cares for a severely wounded soldier. J. Müller, fourteen, Wilhelmsburg III, 1915. Museum Elbinsel-Wilhelmsburg, Hamburg, Germany.

Children's Images from the German Home Front

Figure 1.19
German Zeppelins and aircraft attack and kill civilians in a French village. G. Gerns, age ten, Wilhelmsburg III, 1915. Museum Elbinsel-Wilhelmsburg, Hamburg, Germany.

Likewise, there is one drawing in the Wilhelmsburg collection that could be described as anti-war, or at least as ambiguous in its meaning. The drawing is from 1915 and was done by a ten-year-old boy named Georg Gerns. The scene shows a French town being attacked by two Zeppelins and a bomber, with flames erupting from the main buildings. The French defenders have already lost several soldiers, even as the remaining troops fire a cannon towards the foe. In the forefront of the work, however, stand a mother and child; the mother wears a feathered hat – a child's indication of French style? – holding the hand of her daughter, who wears a similar smaller chapeau. Both look out at the viewer, as do the remaining French troops. Thus in this drawing we have a child drawing another child with her mother, doomed to destruction, looking directly at us in the last moments. Is the artist suggesting empathy with these imagined victims? Admittedly, this drawing is an anomaly; the majority of the drawings celebrate the war. But it is intriguing to think that school art classes could allow the individual student the chance to express fears, reservations, and doubts as much as it gave children the opportunity to support the war.

Conclusion

In the First World War, German and Austrian children connected their personal ideas and feelings with idealized notions of war and were yet unaware of the enormous losses soon to change their nations. Teachers in schools urged children to support the nation's cause and taught them that violence, death, and sacrifice were joyous and beautiful. We see such ideas in the artwork of German children, instructed by teachers of the art-reform movement who celebrated children's originality and creativity. These same children collected foodstuffs and metals for the war effort, packed Christmas gift-boxes for the troops, sang patriotic songs during school assemblies, visited wounded troops in military hospitals, and longed for the victorious conclusion of the war. However, by 1916–18 some were becoming war weary, as schools shut down for lack of teachers and paper, and as food and fuel provisions became scarcer. Schools also faced increasing instances of truancy as children stayed home to help their mothers, or roamed the streets causing trouble. Throughout Germany teachers and state officials expressed alarm about juvenile delinquency, as instances of crime (stealing) and "immoral" behaviour (smoking, going in couples to the cinema) were on the rise, especially among working-class youth.[58] Notably, schools also began reporting on children who were traumatized by the war; in Freiburg it was claimed that children who had lost parents and siblings to the war openly expressed emotional distress in class.[59] Thus, how deeply patriotic ideas of war penetrated into the minds of these children and remained stubbornly resistant to trauma or to defeatism in the last few years of the war (or in the Weimar era) is an important and yet difficult question to answer. Andrew Donson argues that even in the midst of war weariness children's attitudes to the war remained patriotic in 1918: "School directors observed a growing 'indifference' about the war among schoolchildren. They also claimed, however, that most pupils, even in working-class neighbourhoods, still believed that Germany's army was superior and would therefore win the war."[60]

What, then, did these children think when the war was lost and they were asked to support the Weimar Republic's peaceful liberalism? How did they feel about the nation as they grew into adulthood? The children of Wilhelmsburg III would have been thirty-one to thirty-three years of age in 1933 and thus of voting age in the Weimar years. By the start of the Second World War they would

Children's Images from the German Home Front

have reached the ages of thirty-seven to thirty-nine. And thus in the Third Reich adults who had once been children in the "Great War" would be asked to support another war, to sacrifice themselves for the defence of Nazi Germany, and to exult again in weaponry, war, and service to the Fatherland. This time many of them would be sent to the battlefields to witness first-hand the actual conditions of a brutal war.

NOTES

The author gratefully acknowledges that the research for this article was funded by the Social Sciences and Humanities Council of Canada and the German Academic Exchange Service.

1 Quoted in Hagedorn and Winkler, "Der Wandel des Kunstunterrichts zur Zeit des Ersten Weltkrieges (1914–1918)," 88. Cižek was a path-breaking arts educator for children, working in Vienna.
2 For the German home front see Donson, *Youth in the Fatherless Land*; Chickering, *The Great War and Urban Life in Germany*; Davis, *Home Fires Burning*; and Daniel, *The War from Within*.
3 Geißler, *Schulgeschichte in Deutschland*, 362. See also Günter, *Geschichte der Erziehung*, 488–9. The chapter entitled "Schule und Lehrerschaft im ersten Weltkrieg" emphasizes the chauvinism of many schoolteachers and schools.
4 Stekl, Hämmerle, and Bruckmüller, eds, *Kindheit und Schule im Ersten Weltkrieg*, 28.
5 Audoin-Rouzeau, *La Guerre des enfants, 1914–1918*, 39–40; Pignot, *La guerre des crayons*. See also Audoin-Rouzeau, "Children and the Primary Schools of France, 1914–1918," 39–52.
6 Geißler, *Schulgeschichte in Deutschland*, 313.
7 Ibid., 233–4.
8 Ibid., 243–4.
9 Adolf Matthias, *Wie erziehen wir unseren Sohn Benjamin* (Munich: Beck, 1911. First edition published 1896). The wartime tract is Adolf Matthias, *Krieg und Schule* (Leipzig: Hirzel, 1915).
10 Clara Bohm-Schuch, *Die Kinder im Weltkriege* (Berlin: Internationale Korrespondenz, 1916), 10.
11 Demm, "Deutschlands Kinder im Ersten Weltkrieg," 92. Demm also notes that the writer Friedrich Wilhelm Foerster warned about a generation of youth taught to hate the enemy and to seek revenge.

12 Scholz and Berdelmann, "The Quotidianisation of the War in Everyday Life at German Schools during the First World War," 92–103.
13 Kay, "German Children's Art during World War I," 195–212.
14 The drawings (over 270 examples) are in the archive of the Museum Elbinsel Wilhelmsburg. See http://www.museum-wilhelmsburg.de/index.php/bibliothek.html.
15 The examples of school assignments of children's art have been collected by the archive and placed on CD-Rom and are accessible at the Archiv der Bibliothek für Bildungsgeschichtliche Forschung des Deutschen Institutes für Internationale Pädagogische Forschung, Berlin.
16 Österreichische Nationalbibliothek (The Austrian National Library), "Erster Weltkrieg, Europeana Collections 1914–1918, Kriegssammlung." There are 235 works available online and in the archive.
17 Zentralinstitut für Erziehung und Unterricht, *Schule und Krieg: Sonderausstellung* (Berlin, 1915). The exhibition began on 21 March 1915.
18 Richard Rothe, *Die Kinder und der Krieg* (Wien: Schalk, 1915).
19 Demm, "Deutschlands Kinder im Ersten Weltkrieg," 63.
20 Pignot, *La Guerre des crayons*, 34–51.
21 See Kerbs, "Kunsterziehungsbewegung und Kulturreform," 378–97; Siepmann, ed., *Kind und Kunst*. See also Wittmann, *Bedeutungsvolle Kritzeleien*, 141–86.
22 Ashwin, *Drawing and Education in German-Speaking Europe 1800–1900*, 2–3.
23 Ibid., 99, 138.
24 On Lichtwark and the arts in Hamburg see Jenkins, *Provincial Modernity* and Kay, *Art and the German Bourgeoisie*.
25 Alfred Lichtwark, "Die Kunst in der Schule," in *Alfred Lichtwark: Eine Auswahl Seiner Schriften*, Vol. 1, ed. Wolf Mannhardt (Berlin: B. Cassirer, 1917), 31–48; *Das Kind als Künstler: Ausstellung von freien Kinderzeichnungen in der Kunsthalle zu Hamburg*, ed. Carl Götze (Hamburg: Boysen & Maasch, 1898).
26 Ashwin, *Drawing and Education in German-Speaking Europe*, 174.
27 Rothe, *Die Kinder und der Krieg*, 9.
28 Fineberg, *The Innocent Eye*, 6, 11.
29 Ashwin, *Drawing and Education in German-Speaking Europe*, 174–5.
30 Ibid., 175.
31 Kerbs, "Kunsterziehungsbewegung und Kulturreform," 379.
32 Geißler, *Schulgeschichte in Deutschland*, 359. A huge number of teachers were conscripted: 40,000–60,000 in the first year alone. See ibid., 361.
33 See, for example, the drawings by Elfriede Taube (0704), Hermann Frihsing

(0774), and Elizabeth Johanniswerth (8493). Bibliothek für Bildungsgeschichtliche Forschung, Berlin, archival collection of children's drawings from schools.
34 Rothe, *Die Kinder und der Krieg*, 9. "In allen ihren Beschäftigungen, in allen ihren Spielen und Träumen lebt der Krieg. Er hat sowohl Knaben und Mädchen in innerster Seele erfasst, ein hohes heiliges Etwas in ihnen wachgerufen, das sie in Friedenszeiten nie und nimmermehr kennen gelernt hätten. Der Krieg hat in den Kindern die schlummernden Urinstinkte geweckt und hat die Knaben aktiver, die Mädchen milder und sanfter gemacht."
35 Ibid., 7.
36 Colestin Kik, "Kriegszeichnungen der Knaben und Mädchen," in *Jugendliches Seelenleben und Krieg, 12: Beiheft zur Zeitschrift für angewandte Psychologie und psychologische Sammelforschung*, ed. William Stern and Otto Lipmann (Leipzig: J.A. Barth, 1915): 1–21.
37 Ibid., 3.
38 Ibid., 2–3.
39 Ibid., 3–4.
40 Ignatz Göth, "Das Unterseeboot. Eine Unterrichtsskizze im 5. Schuljahr," *Schaffende Arbeit und Kunst in der Schule* 4 (1915): 237. For an example of a female teacher's experience of teaching war art see Bertha Marten, "Krieg und Zeichenunterricht," *Deutsche Blätter für Zeichen- und Kunstunterricht* 20 (1915): 66–9. Marten also claims that her students were enraptured by the war. The educational theorist Georg Kerschensteiner who had written a very influential book on children's art entitled *Die Entwickelung der Zeichnerischen Begabung* (München: Carl Gerber, 1905) also supported war art. See his *Deutsche Schulerziehung in Krieg und Frieden* (Berlin: B.G. Teubner, 1916).
41 Gustav Kolb, "Der Zeichenunterricht und der Krieg," *Kunst und Jugend* 4 (April 1916): 49–54.
42 Alois Kunzfeld, "Krieg und Jugendkunst," 153–8.
43 A superb new book on this topic is Zunino, *Die Mobilmachung der Kinder im Ersten Weltkrieg*.
44 Paul Busson of Vienna argued in a review in 1914, for the *Neues Wiener Tagblatt*, that the illustrated newspapers were the source of the children's art. See Rothe, *Die Kinder und der Krieg*, 40.
45 Willy Planck, *Kriegsbilder: Ein Malbuch für die Jugend* (Ravensburg: Maier, 1915). Another fascinating example of illustrations for marine battles is John Gleich, *Der Seekrieg: Ein Malbuch für die deutsche Jugend* (Ravensburg: Maier, 1915).

46 Kik, "Kriegszeichnungen der Knaben und Mädchen," 8.
47 The children's drawings are in the archives of the Museum Elbinsel Wilhelmsburg and were featured in an exhibition in 2014 commemorating the war and the children's art. For more information see the museum's catalogue from 2015: Jürgen Drygas, "Erster Weltkrieg 1914–1918 … und so weiter," *Die Insel: Museum Elbinsel Wilhelmsburg* (2015): 9–21. For details about the school see ibid., 10–12.
48 Drygas, "Erster Weltkrieg 1914–1918," 12.
49 Ivashkevich, "Drawing in Children's Lives," 57.
50 Ibid., 56–7.
51 Ibid., 51.
52 Stargardt, "Children's Art of the Holocaust," 234. See also Stargardt, *Witnesses of War*.
53 Stargardt, "Children's Art of the Holocaust," 234.
54 See Kellogg, *Analyzing Children's Art*, and Golomb, *Child Art in Context*. The quote is from Thomas and Silk, *An Introduction to the Psychology of Children's Drawings*, 64–5.
55 Golomb, *Child Art*, 44–5.
56 Ibid., 4.
57 Arpad Schmidhammer, *Hans und Pierre: Eine lustige Schützengrabengeschichte* (Mainz: Jos. Schulz Verlag, 1916). Schmidhammer was also the author of several popular picture books on the war including *Die Geschichte vom General Hindenburg* (Mainz: Jos. Schulz Verlag, 1915) and *Lieb Vaterland magst ruhig sein! Ein Kriegsbilderbuch mit Knüttelversen* (Mainz: Jos. Schulz Verlag, 1914).
58 Donson, *Youth in the Fatherless Land*, 154.
59 Chickering, *The Great War and Urban Life in Germany*, 508–9.
60 Donson, *Youth in the Fatherless Land*, 177.

2

Sensing War:
Childhood Memories of the Wartime Atlantic, 1939–45

Barbara Lorenzkowski

Between 1939 and 1945, H. Bruce Jefferson, the wartime censor for Atlantic Canada, had a front-row seat in witnessing the changes that transformed Halifax, Nova Scotia, into the most important naval base of the Allied forces in North America.[1] In his office on the seventh floor of an art deco building overlooking the harbour, Jefferson monitored the press coverage as closely as he did the movement of naval vessels in the harbour. Merchant ships crowded into the Bedford Basin, the city's natural harbour that extended deep inland. About every eight days, convoys sailed from Halifax in carefully orchestrated departures to carry goods and supplies across the North Atlantic.[2] At the peak of shipping congestion on 6 April 1941, 182 ships jostled for space in the Basin and the stream, not counting minor war crafts, ferries, and harbour crafts. It was, Jefferson wrote, "the biggest day in the whole history of the harbor."[3]

As a port city, Halifax had always been a nodal point of trade and migration, embedded in the networks of the Atlantic world. In wartime, it would become a nodal point of conflict. Halifax was home to six military headquarters, including North West Atlantic (Navy), District No. 6 (Army), and Eastern Air Command (RCAF).[4] The city also served as a way station for massive troop movements. Close to half a million Canadian service people passed through Halifax to embark on one of the 150 troop convoys headed overseas during the war.[5] Skilled dockyard workers flocked to the city, as did family dependents of service men and merchant mariners, young Maritime women in search for clerical and domestic work, and the refugees and sailors who "poured in from Poland, Norway, Belgium, France, Denmark, the Netherlands and other nations."[6] The city's population surged from around 66,000 in 1939 to 95,459 in early 1944, putting immense pressure on the local infrastructure. "The Halifax area is a war zone, and should be treated as such," wrote an exasperated David B. Carwell, controller of ship repairs and salvage, to the minister of munitions and supply, Clarence Decatur Howe, in May 1943. "Good food is difficult to procure, sleeping space is not available for workers to rest, transportation facilities are inadequate."[7]

With the ease of a seasoned journalist, Jefferson captured the city's wartime transformation. His was the gaze of the professional observer. In his typewritten journal, he revelled in the panoramic perspective from his censor's office that afforded stunning views of convoy movements. Jefferson looked at the city as if through the lens of a camera, his eye schooled in his close friendship with a local photographer. Akin to the frames of a film, his journal entries have a keen visual quality and are infused with light, colour, and perspective. "Last evening's convoy was the most spectacular in months," he wrote appreciatively on 25 June 1943. "There was brilliant sunshine, and exceptionally clear atmosphere extending to the horizon where there appeared to be a bank of fog."[8] To Jefferson, the sense of sight was all-important; it complemented the knowledge he gleaned from exchanges with government and military officials, port administrators and service personnel. The observations he recorded in his near daily journal entries speak to an urban experience that prized knowledge and information.

Whereas Jefferson was dazzled by the dramatic visual appeal of wartime Halifax, children experienced the city at a different scale; they encountered the war at street level. If the censor was the archetypical "voyeur," who – in Michel de Certeau's influential formulation – looked down upon the city as if it was "a text that lies before one's eyes," to be made legible and rationalized in a single sweeping glance, children were walkers in the city. "Their story begins on ground level, with footsteps," de Certeau writes.[9] It was in the act of walking that children made sense of their surroundings and claimed play-spaces in back-alleys, city streets, fields, parks, and on the shores of the harbour. Children possessed an intimate knowledge of the physical spaces, the micro-topographies, and the texture of their local neighbourhoods. As the philosopher Henri Lefebvre holds, such lived space, which is inhabited and made intelligible through daily acts of use, "is alive; it speaks. It has an affective kernel or centre."[10]

This chapter turns to Halifax, Nova Scotia, to examine how children experienced the sounds, sights, touches, tastes, and smells of war. Drawing on close to thirty oral history interviews I conducted in Halifax in the summer of 2009 as well as archival sources, this study explores how children made sense of the urban environment and how their sensory experiences, in turn, shaped and mediated their understanding of the war. In their play, their work, and their urban explorations, children learned about the Second World War through their senses. In the long hours spent outdoors, children – and especially boys who were less likely to be confined to the home to tend to younger siblings and household chores – acquired an intimate understanding of their neighbourhoods and began to decipher the social world of the wartime city with the help of sensory clues. The narrative stance of my interview partners was not the detached, ironic gaze of the urban flâneur, but that of the walker in the city who experienced wartime Halifax as a vibrant and exciting place.

This chapter makes three interrelated claims. First, just as the industrial revolution had transformed cityscapes in the nineteenth century and wrought corresponding changes into the urban "sensorium," so, too, did the war years reshape the urban environment of Halifax.[11] Between 1939 and 1945, the port city became louder, dirtier, and more congested. As the war amplified the sounds of the city, the soundtrack of ordinary life became interlaced with the steady beat of war. The heightened sensory and emotional intensity of the war years echoes through the memories of my respondents and helps account for the vividness of their childhood recollections. Second, childhood memories of the wartime Atlantic do not accord primacy to the visual. Rather, they ring with sound, a sense that is rooted in place, dynamic and action oriented, immediate, and resonant with emotions. As a sense, sound has a special affinity with the life-worlds of children. Whereas sight implies distance, the sense of sound is grounded in proximity. As the geographer Yi-Fu Tuan holds, "we are usually more touched by what we hear than by what we see … because we cannot close our ears as we can our eyes."[12] There is an intimacy to sound, a resonance more likely to evoke an emotional response. Although all the senses were at play as children walked the streets of wartime Halifax, the power of aural memories is striking. Third, children inhabited sensory worlds markedly different from that of adults.[13] What registered as urban pollution, overcrowding, and incessant noise for adults, childhood memories describe as exciting. Even when a naval magazine at Bedford Basin exploded on 18 July 1945, hurtling debris across the Halifax peninsula, children experienced the explosion as a moment of excitement, in which the social rules and emotional protocols of ordinary life were temporarily suspended. Their sense of danger not yet honed by life experience, children's bemused fascination stood in stark contrast to the terror expressed by their parents and grandparents, whose lives had been shaped by the devastating Halifax Harbour Explosion of 1917.

Children in Sensory History

The central premise underpinning the field of sensory studies is the importance of historicizing the senses. As Mark Smith, one of the pioneers of sensory history, holds, the senses are neither "universal nor transhistorical," but have to be understood in their historical and social contexts.[14] Hearing, seeing, smelling, tasting, and touching all constitute physical as well as a cultural acts.[15] The senses are "historically and culturally generated ways of knowing and understanding," Smith posits.[16] Accordingly, any investigation of the sensory past must go beyond a mere description of historic sensations to examine the meanings people attached to those senses.[17]

In studying the Allied aerial bombing of cities in Nazi Germany and Vichy France, historians Nicholas Stargardt and Lindsey Dodd have examined how children and youth made sense of the novelty and intensity of wartime sensory experiences. Children possess "a different sense of danger and threats from adults," Stargardt observes in his seminal study *Witnesses of War*. During the sustained bombing of German cities, children "often marvelled at the sight of fires burning across cities." They described the fire brought by Allied planes as spectacular, the colours captivating and magical. "Again and again," Stargardt writes, "children compared such sights with being at the theatre, watching a show greater than any they had ever seen." Whereas childhood memories emphasize the commanding visual spectacle of buildings engulfed in flames, it was sound that communicated vital knowledge about the proximity of danger. German children, their ears schooled in the relentless repetition of bombs falling onto cities, learned to distinguish between the "Crash bang!!!" of high-explosive bombs and the "'muffled crack' of the incendiaries," their earliest memories of the war entangled in the sound of sirens and explosions.[18] In France as well, sound was the single most prominent sense recalled in childhood recollections of Allied bombing. As the historian Lindsey Dodd notes, "the sound of bombs and their destructive explosions and blasts nearby imprinted on memory, leaving strong emotional reverberations into adult lives."[19]

In the port city of Halifax, children and youth grew up at a remove from the horrors of the Western Front and the sounds of Allied bombing whose destructive force shook children in Vichy France and Nazi Germany.[20] Yet for Halifax youngsters, too, city sounds were insistent, demanding of attention, and inescapable.[21] In wartime Halifax, sound told of motion – of foghorns blowing; practice shells exploding; dockyards working; locomotives whistling; children yelling; brass bands marching; soldiers parading; bells ringing; and army trucks roaring through city streets.[22] Unlike the eye, which directs its gaze into one direction, the "world of the ear" is "multidirectional."[23] Playing on their local street, children might hear the rumbling of the milk-cart, the noise of an approaching army truck, the laughter of friends at the end of the block, the angry shouts of a drunken father, and the hush that fell on the street when bike messengers arrived, carrying a black-rimmed telegram that announced the death of a local boy. Familiar and knowable sounds were heard as comforting; they anchored children in the aural texture of their neighbourhoods. By contrast, a sudden silence or unfamiliar noise spoke of potential danger and commanded attention.

It is the body that acts as a repository for such sensory experiences. As the historian Joy Parr reminds us, "this visceral knowledge, which we carry corporeally, often wordlessly, marks us as of our time, as much as do the values and chronicles we carry in language."[24] Yet such embodied knowledge, acquired in daily habits and routines that are carried out without any conscious thought, is difficult to put into words.[25] Not surprisingly, perhaps, my early attempts to uncover childhood memories of sensory experiences fell flat. Whereas my interview partners readily shared stories about their explorations in the wartime city, my questions about the sights, sounds, smells, touches, and tastes of 1940s Halifax met with puzzlement and one-word answers. "Horse-shit," Owen Hamlin said laconically.[26] As I would come to learn, the "tacit knowledge" of the sensory past that was garnered in daily routines was more likely to reach me in place-based stories.[27] "We are not only in places but of them," the American philosopher Edward Casey has remarked. "More even than earthlings, we are placelings, and our very perceptual apparatus, our sending body, reflects the kind of places we inhabit."[28] The senses anchored children in place, all the more so because the young were walkers in the city. Children were attuned to the sounds of their neighbourhoods, familiar with its sights, accustomed to its smells, and attentive to its feel – the uneven surface of cobblestone streets, the touch of the tall grasses on Dalhousie grounds, or the soft rumbling of street cars running through Halifax neighbourhoods. It is in these small spaces of childhood that memories of the war reside.

Sensory Postcards

Children marvelled at the maze of movement in the harbour where the war was at its most tangible. Born in 1930, Marjorie Ferguson grew up in the North End of Halifax, right next to the naval base HMCS *Stadacona*. As we sat on the patio of her Halifax home in July 2009, she took out a handwritten account she had penned the evening before and began reading: "As I sit here, I remember so much about the war years. I don't know where to start or how to put it in some sort of order. The harbour, Bedford Basin started to fill with ships. The streets with the military and sailors of many nations, and bases on every vacant piece of land. The lights were dimmed and the neon lights were put out."[29] To Halifax residents, the sight of convoys assembling in Bedford Basin became the visual shorthand of the war. "Hundreds of ships would gather in the Basin," James MacFadzean recalls, "and then they'd all move out during the night or during an afternoon, and that was an *incredible* sight to see, all these ships moving out of the harbour."[30] Many of my narrators commented on the dramatic contrast of the Bedford Basin, filled to the rim with ships one day, and then empty the next morning. Hildegard Jangaard's father liked to take his children for an evening drive around the Basin.

Figure 2.1
Convoy in Bedford Basin, Halifax, Nova Scotia. Canadian War Museum, accession no. 199100001-028.

"And the whole Basin would be full of ships," Jangaard remembers, "maybe as many as sixty, seventy, eighty ships. And the next, you'd go down there and there'd be none. They would all have slipped out of the port quietly at night."[31]

Under wartime censorship regulations, Halifax residents were asked to refrain from any discussion of convoy departures and troop movements, while newspapers and radio broadcasts were instructed to refer to the city obliquely as "An East Coast Port."[32] The Maritime Telephone and Telegraph Company issued a card that subscribers were to post next to their telephones at home: "WARNING. It is Forbidden to Mention Ships or Ship Movements, Aircraft, Troops, War Industries, or the Weather during Long Distance Telephone Conversations."[33] It was an admonition that Jeannie Hill and her sister took to heart. Several times each week, the young girls travelled back and forth on the ferry between Dartmouth to Halifax to attend gym classes at the local YMCA or visit their cousins in the Halifax South End. "And the convoys would be going out *right* in front of us," Jeannie Hill says, "but we *never said a word*. You didn't discuss it. You didn't talk about it ... But sometimes, the poor ferry would be jogging around these ships going out."[34] Enveloped by the waters of the Bedford Basin, the harbour, and the Northwest Arm, the Halifax peninsula bore "daily witness to vital information" which, as historian William Naftel notes, "was impossible to conceal but illegal to discuss."[35] Throughout the city, "great big billboards" carried stern reminders that "loose lips sink ships," a wartime slogan that echoes through childhood memories.[36] It was in the harbour that the city's children could see the scars of the Battle of the Atlantic, observing in disbelief vessels with their "rear end literally *blown off.*"[37]

In the evening of 9 April 1942, the American freighter *Trongate*, in harbour for repairs, urgently signalled for help. A fire had broken out below decks, threatening to set off the ammunition and light bombs in the cargo hold. "The timing and location could not have been worse," as historian William Naftel writes. "The port was jammed with 200 vessels, the second highest tonnage of the war, including four American army transports loaded with troops and anchored in the stream and two British transports loading Canadian troops at the seawall." After the crew abandoned ship, HMCS *Chedabucto* carefully scuttled the burning freighter by firing a series of non-explosive practice shells.[38] In his office, censor Jefferson and his colleagues "sat down for tea and sandwiches" at the midnight hour to watch the unfolding drama: "The bright lights, the dim shapes of ships, the flashing of the signal lamps, the movement of rugs and harbor craft, the banging of the four inch gun, the leaping flames, must have been a close replica of a rather one-sided naval engagement, and formed a sight not soon to be forgotten. Every few second

Figure 2.2
Norwegian MV *Kronprinsen* awaiting repairs at Halifax dry dock. The merchant vessel had been torpedoed by a German submarine on 9 June 1942 and went on from Halifax for further repairs in Boston before being put out back to sea. Canadian War Museum, accession no. 19810715-084.

red and gold signal rockets, which seemed to form part of the cargo, roared aloft, singly and in groups, while at one stage of the fire incessant rattling like the distant explosion of firecrackers told of small arm ammunition (probably .303) exploding by the thousand."[39] Curious onlookers gathered on Citadel Hill and along the waterfront, but there was no panic. As the wind carried the sounds of the explosion seaward, most people in the city slept through the night, oblivious to the drama playing out in the harbour.

Jefferson recorded the incident as a visual spectacle, slightly unsettling, but fascinating nonetheless. But to young Thomas Wheatley, it was an auditory attack. As the freighter drifted across the harbour towards Dartmouth, HMCS *Chedabucto* fired upon the burning vessel for several hours until it finally settled to the harbour floor. "And we didn't know what it was," Thomas Wheatley says. "And all the windows in the house would *rattle* and *bang*. Everybody was afraid. We didn't know if we were being *attacked*. And the air raid went off, and everyone took their places, waiting. And then the word came around that it was a ship caught fire in Halifax. They thought it might be another Halifax explosion." Instead of evoking the visual effects of a potentially devastating accident, as censor Jefferson did in fluid prose, Thomas Wheatley's recollections are rendered home in brief, pointed remarks. He is recounting how war sat at the very doorstep of his family home, threatening young and old alike. His account is laced with uncertainty and emotion.[40] The youngster's knowledge of the accident was partial; news reached his family and neighbours in bits and pieces only. Waiting anxiously, the residents of Eastern Passage heard each "rattle" and "bang" as potential harbinger of yet another Halifax Harbour explosion. Meanwhile, censor Jefferson occupied "the space of detached seeing" that Michel de Certeau has associated with the urban flâneur.[41] Ensconced on the upper floors of his office building, Jefferson listened serenely as a colleague, schooled in reading the quick play of light signals flickering back and forth between various ships and the dockyard, offered a "blow by blow" description of the unfolding events in the booming, authoritative voice of "a veteran witness in court."[42]

The congested waters of the wartime harbour would remain a dangerous place. Two of my interview partners lost their fathers when the harbour tug *Erg* was run down by a Norwegian freighter on 6 June 1943. Obscured by fog and rain, the *Erg* had carried workers and repair equipment to vessels anchored in the stream. It sank almost immediately; nineteen men on board the tug drowned.[43] Yet so omnipresent was the movement of corvettes, destroyers, harbour crafts, ferries, troop carriers and merchant ships, and so frequent accidents and near misses that Halifax residents became inured to danger. When the USS *Wakefield* was towed into the harbour in early September 1942 – flames still spurting from the deck after the troop ship had caught fire off the coast of Nova Scotia on 3 September 1942 – it was greeted with nonchalance. "People at last are becoming indifferent to war conditions," censor Jefferson observed. "A year ago or even 6 months ago arrival of a burning ship like the 'Wakefield' would have been the signal for hundres [*sic*] of phone calls and Citadel Hill would have been covered with spectators. Actually we had only half a dozen calls, and hardly anyone bothered to go up to look at the ship."[44]

Having been bombarded with the sights and sounds of war, the city's children increasingly took them for granted. Their eyes became habituated to wartime sights, while the noise of the wartime city faded into the background: the fog horns blowing in the harbour; the ringing of ship bells; the constant din of shore fog whistles; the racket of squadrons of planes flying low over the harbour; the roar of local traffic; and the shunting of locomotives.[45] As Catherine Cable, born in 1933, mused, "You became very used to all of the people, all of the ships that were in the Bedford Basin. The Basin was filled with these ships. And it was awesome at first, but then very ordinary. It was nothing for me to see ships *galore*, and to hear their horns."[46] "You didn't even think about it," Laurence Griffin concurred.[47]

Much to the consternation of a CBC crew that arrived in town to record the shrill voice of sirens during an air-raid drill, the microphone kept picking up sounds ordinary and mundane: to the north, "the steam whistle of the NSL&P power house (which always sounds for raids)," to the west "a bunch of children playing tag in Cornwallis Park," and to the east "the engineer of a CNR shunter which kept chuffing unconcernedly up and down behind the hotel all through the 'raid.'"[48] Disappointed, the crew returned home empty-handed. The journalists did not realize that their "failed" recording had captured the sounds of 1940s Halifax, if not in the way they had hoped. They had come in search of an auditory landscape, dominated by a single keynote of war that would ring above the urban din. Instead, they found a patchwork of sounds that braided together sounds of wartime and the everyday.

Like the patches of a quilt, each Halifax neighbourhood had an aural texture all its own, composed of distinctive aural practices and traditions, local rhythms and volume, and a subtle modulation of city sounds.[49] In the South End, Bernard Miller heard the melodies of Strauss waltzes wafting over from the skating rink at the foot of his street. Each winter, the naval officers at nearby King's College,

Childhood Memories of the Wartime Atlantic 73

which served as a naval base during the war, built a rink that civilians were welcome to use in the evenings. "So I remember that," Bernard Miller said. "On a crisp winter night there was the Skater's Waltz playing and the people kind of twirling around the rink. It's quite a memory that I have of it."[50] Living on the Northwest Arm, Shirley Hill heard dance music and laughter drifting over from the Jubilee Boat Club, a short block away: "We would hear the sailors coming down the Jubilee Road with their girlfriends and they'd rent the canoe and go out. And because we lived on the Arm, we'd hear them singing and talking, the voices, just generally having a grand time."[51] In Eastern Passage across the harbour, Thomas Wheatley grew up next to the base of Eastern Air Command. As he remembers: "The airplanes would fly right over your house; you could hear the house actually *vibrate* when the planes would go over. Lights would shine in the bedroom window. And I could tell what airplane was going by the sound of the airplane … You knew all the airplanes. The DC-3s, the Hurricanes, the Harvards, or the Lancasters. Whatever airplane was going over top, we pretty well knew it. And we knew if they were too high or too low from listening to them coming."[52] "Such sounds are kept as souvenirs," the geographer Fran Tonkiss has observed. "Such sound memories make us what Elias Canetti has called an 'earwitness' to the scene."[53]

Sound offered not only sensation, but also information.[54] "Sound was a vital element within an urban information system," as David Garrioch has held. "Those who belonged to a particular neighbourhood recognized its sounds and responded in ways that outsiders did not. Any interruption to the normal local sounds immediately put them on the alert."[55] In the North End of Halifax, children possessed a familiarity with the sounds of the wartime Atlantic that children elsewhere in the city did not. In Marjorie Ferguson's evocative phrase, "you quickly learned to read the harbour. From the sounds you knew the weather and how busy it was."[56] During the war years, the dockyards worked around the clock, repairing and outfitting over 7,000 ships.[57] Growing up in the North End, children fell asleep to the sounds of riveting guns from the nearby dockyards. "It never stopped," Frederick Allen recalls. "At 3 o'clock in the morning, I can still hear the riveting guns going."[58] Children's ears were attuned to the boom of firing from the harbour batteries, the distinctive "whoop, whoop, whoop" of corvettes, and even the settled signal that would announce a convoy's arrival in the Narrows. Owen Hamlin, a self-described "little, slight sprite" of a boy living next to the naval base Stadacona, liked to cross North Street with his older brothers whenever he heard ships blowing for Bedford Basin. "We knew that signal. We also knew the signal coming the other way," he remembers, "and as soon as you heard them, you'd cross the street and wait till you saw the ships."[59]

As the historian Joy Parr has observed in her work with the residents of Iroquois, Ontario, a town located on the banks of the St Lawrence prior to its relocation in 1954, "People didn't so much walk to the river, or walk by the river, as they lived with the river, their walking bodies attuned, even when not attentive, to its presence."[60] In a similar vein, children in the North End lived with the harbour. They were embedded in the web of sound, spun by the wartime Atlantic, familiar with its auditory threads, and attentive to its rhythms, even when they were not listening consciously. Children in the South End, too, heard the foghorns blowing, but could not read their subtle meanings. "There was a *constant* noise," Robert Dickie recalls. "They'd be horns blowing. You'd hear the ships making these funny, different noises." The young South End boy heard as noise what children in the North End understood to be the back and forth of auditory signals.[61]

When sharing their memories, my interview partners represented the city not unlike the poets of urban life such as Walter Benjamin have done. They portrayed Halifax as an enchanted place, a source of pleasure and sensory stimulation.[62] "The air was almost as thick as water, the grey, the smoke, the soot. And the city was dingy and grey. But we didn't care. We enjoyed it," Robert Dickie laughs. "It was a great time to be a kid. We just saw things and experienced things that were so much fun." "You knew full well that war was a dreadful thing, but yet, you're really excited with all that was going on around you," Frederick Allen recalls.[63] If there is a *leitmotif* in their childhood recollections, it is this: that the war years were a time of sensory and emotional intensity. This sentiment should not be dismissed as a mere expression of nostalgia. In this regard, it is instructive to note that the concept of the adventure playground was born in post-1945 Britain when social scientists observed children playing in the bombsites and ruined buildings of British cities. Deemed dangerous by adults, these sites offered children a means of urban exploration, freedom from adult supervision, and a space to create their own games and play-structures.[64]

If children engaged with the city at street level, Jefferson represented another urban type, that of the urban flâneur. An insatiable collector of wartime stories, Jefferson found the war years both exhilarating and exhausting. From his office on the seventh floor of the post office, he fielded phone calls, handed out censorship judgments, observed convoy movements, and, in direct contravention of the rules he was to enforce, took hundreds of photographs of the Halifax harbour.[65] He was fascinated by the spectacle of the wartime city and relished the stream of

Figure 2.3
View of the Halifax Dockyard during wartime. Courtesy of the family album of Ronald Gilkie.

information that flowed through his office, but began to tire of the auditory overload. As he complained in July 1944, the wartime city was growing ever noisier: "Halifax has grown extremely noisy ashore as well as afloat. Nearly all the public services have become defective through heavy traffic and few repairs. Motor cycles, army and commercial trucks roar through the streets, dozen of locomotives shunt day and night with the usual bell ringing and whistling, and last but not least the street cars, now about 80 or 90 in number, pound over the dilapidated rails with a clatter that makes conversation almost impossible."[66]

The strain of the war was beginning to show. In the evenings, when walking back from his office to the Nova Scotian Hotel, Jefferson observed the "growing toughness of the city."[67] "There were singing drunks, crying drunks, fighting drunks, arguing drunks, and drunks talking to themselves as they ambled along," he wrote in his journal in January 1943.[68] Working in the post office building at the Ocean Terminals, there was no escape from the noise. "This morning," an exasperated Jefferson noted on 13 September 1943, "a brass brand, probably the visiting CWAC's invaded the Terminal and marched up and down playing for an hour or so. At the same time a squadron of planes flew low overhead, adding to the racket of ship whistles, a concrete mixer at the Power house and the yells of officers and NCOs trying to direct troops." The never-ending round of military parades only added to the urban cacophony.[69] "All this is rather hard on the nerves," Jefferson sighed.[70] Dazzled by the drama of the visual, the censor found the bombardment of the aural difficult to contend with.[71] Whereas sound anchored children in the local life-worlds of their neighbourhoods, the censor heard the sounds of the city as auditory assault.

Spatial Stories

To my interview partners, wartime Halifax represented a space of memory. Reminiscent of Walter Benjamin's chronicle *Berlin Childhood around 1900*, "there is little sense of a flow of time" in their childhood stories.[72] Instead, their memories are intricately interwoven with the sites of their childhood. Space is the narrative device that structures their recollections. As walkers in the city, children traversed neighbourhood streets, the wide-open spaces of Citadel Hill, the hayfields on the ground of Dalhousie University, the expanses of Point Pleasant Park, and the shorelines of Eastern Passage. Six decades later, they would take great care to teach me about the geographies of their childhood in the stories they told, the maps they drew, and the driving interviews they gave.

Several of my interview partners took me on extended driving interviews to acquaint me with the geography of wartime Halifax and the neighbourhoods of their childhood. We drove out to York Redoubt, driving up the steep hill that young Gerald Dempsey had biked up every day to deliver *The Halifax Mail* to the soldiers stationed at the fort. We circled Bedford Basin to head to Port Wallace where Gerry Lethbridge had grown up, visiting the site of the old family business, his father's gas station, next to the Dartmouth ferry terminal. We drove through Point Pleasant Park and to Pier 21, where the father of Ernie Nickerson had worked as Port Secretary during the war. It was "right at those piers, just near Pier 20, 21, and 22" that young Ernie Nickerson liked to look at the troopships, painted in camouflage patterns and towering over the boy. Across the harbour, at Eastern Passage, Thomas Wheatley brought me out to the old family home, sitting on a steep hill next to the fields of Eastern Air Command. Once or twice a week, the boy and his friends coasted downhill to the army camp at the bottom of the road to join soldiers watching the latest movie, while feasting on crackers, jam, and butter.[73]

These emplaced stories served a dual purpose. They were meant to teach me about the geography of wartime Halifax. Only by knowing about the location of bases, coastal batteries, the submarine net held up by the gate vessels in the harbour's entrance, the vantage points from which to look out to the waterfront and dockyards, the airfields at Eastern Passage, and the magnificent natural harbour that was the Bedford Basin could I hope to make sense of the stories I heard. As the anthropologist Julie Cruikshank has observed in her work with women elders in the Yukon Territory, such place-based storytelling provides "a kind of cultural scaffolding, the broad framework I needed to learn before I could begin to ask intelligent questions."[74] In turn, the locations we visited prompted memories of the micro-geographies of childhood. Gerry Lethbridge gestured to a hill in downtown Dartmouth where drunken servicemen had poured cornflakes into the gutter after raiding Forsythe's grocery store during the Victory in Europe (VE) riots on 7–8 May 1945. After years of wartime rationing, the sight of the flakes floating downhill struck the young boy as delightfully absurd. In Herring Cove, Gerald Dempsey pointed to Black Rock Point where the *Clare Lilley*, a British ammunition ship, had run aground on 22 March 1942, loaded with lard, sugar, fruit cocktail, chocolate, and American cigarettes. The boy went out to the ship with some fishermen to help salvage the cargo and marvelled at the stacks of Lucky Strike and Chesterfield "that started Herring Cove smoking pretty good!"[75] Soon, Herring Cove and Halifax pantries were stocked with good-quality lard, which started "an epidemic of doughnut making all over the Halifax area," alongside large quantities of flour, egg powder, concentrated orange juice, and bacon.[76] These spatial stories reflected not the bird's eye-view of the port city that censor Jefferson enjoyed, but a street-level encounter with the war.

The Halifax harbour was a social space that anchored memories of both home and play. At Eastern Passage, Thomas Wheatley and his friends witnessed the wartime pollution of the harbour up close: carcasses of animals and orange crates floating in the water and a thick film of oil glistening in the sunlight. The boys went for a swim anyway, but came to the beach prepared. Each brought a can of kerosene to wash the oil off their bodies after their swim. "We'd float and stay in the water … You were so buoyant floating around that you found it hard to walk for the first few feet when got back on land," Thomas Wheatley recalls. "And then we'd wash ourselves off with kerosene, and then home we'd go."[77] Avid walkers in the city, boys embraced the opportunities the wartime city offered for play and exploration, at times with devastating results. Looking out of his office window, censor Jefferson noted heavy smoke at Eastern Passage on 5 December 1942. Large quantities of oil, some twenty feet wide and five feet deep, had floated to a little inlet and washed up on shore. Curious as to the effect, some neighbourhood boys threw burning matches onto the beach, causing a fierce blaze that roared through the centre of Eastern Passage village, emitting "the most spectacular belching flames and billowing black smoke seen in these parts" since the *Nueva Andalucia* had burned on Mars Rock in March 1942. "The fire burned a small wooden highway bridge, seven houses, a store, part of a church, 10 fish houses, 10 motor boats, and considerable quantities of fishing gear," Jefferson recorded.[78]

Touching Danger

These localized worlds of childhood intersected on 18 July 1945 when a naval magazine exploded nearby the entrance to Bedford Basin, scattering flaming debris all over the ammunition grounds.[79] The explosion shook the city's residents more dramatically than even the VE Day Riots of early May 1945. All my interview partners remember this "hot, hot day" when the earth trembled, windows broke, and families evacuated their homes to hurry to the wide-open spaces of the city.[80]

In his room at the Nova Scotian Hotel, Jefferson watched the explosion unfolding "right in front of my eyes" – from the initial "heavy gun fire" at 6:40 pm, when "fireworks began to shoot into the air," to the dramatic moment when the lights "suddenly mush-roomed into a ball of reddish flame, and a huge ball of black smoke soared into the air above it."[81] As the fire spread across Magazine Hill, setting alight caches of stacked ammunition, it produced an ominous soundtrack. The steady staccato of the popping of smaller shells reached a violent crescendo, whenever the fire devoured a new store of gun charges and shells. Explosions did "roll and roar and burst for about an hour" in a fevered pitch, then "died away to a mutter" before increasing in violence once more. The constant sonic barrage culminated in three violent explosions at 19:40, 22:00, and 4:00, each, in turn, producing a blast so intense it lifted amateur photographers off the ground, made solid steel and concrete buildings in downtown Halifax sway back and forth on their foundations, and broke nearly all the shop windows on Barrington Street, leaving the heavy plate glass scattered across the sidewalks.[82] It was, Jefferson wrote of the 4:00 a.m. explosion, "a hell of a bang."[83]

In the childhood memories of my interview partners, the Bedford Magazine Explosion acted as a sharp temporal marker, precisely because it was felt so viscerally. The blast of the first explosion shook the foundation of family homes, lifted adults and children off the floor, and made ships in the harbour rock dangerously. Across the Halifax peninsula and along the shores of the Bedford Basin, families had just sat down for supper when they heard the "boom, boom, boom" of the first explosion. "And what did we do?" laughed Carolyn Crowell, whose father O.R. Crowell served as the city's director of civil defence. "We all ran outside to see what it was. The very thing you are told not to do."[84] "I remember being alone in the bathroom. It was around supper time," Catherine Cable recalled, "and all I remember was the house shaking and this terrible noise. And, of course, I ran downstairs."[85] In the Lord Nelson Hotel next to the Halifax Public Gardens, Charles Grantham was working in the kitchen when the first explosion made the building tremble. "And all the dust and dirt and chandeliers came down off the ceiling in the dining room. And I got my little bicycle and pedaled my butt right for home as fast as I could," he remembered.[86] In Melville Cove on the shore of the Northwest Arm, some fifteen kilometres from the site of the explosion, young Ronald Gilkie was walking home from the neighbourhood store when he heard "this Ka-boom." At the sound of the first detonations, his father had run to the front door of the modest family home, camera in hand, to take a picture of the mushroom cloud hovering over the Bedford Basin. The force of the blast knocked him off his feet: "Dad, apparently, just hit the front door, about to take the picture, just took the picture and then was *blown* right through the living room back into the kitchen! And thankfully, all the doors and windows were open because it was a hot, hot day. Otherwise it probably would have taken the windows out and everything, the force of the explosion. But he has the picture of the big mushroom cloud."[87] Arrested in the moment of the explosion, these recollections amount to what historian William Tuttle has called a "flashbulb memory, the freeze-framing of an exceptionally emotional event down to the most incidental detail" that interrupted the rhythms of family life and encroached upon the small spaces of childhood.[88]

When the explosion made the earth shake, Halifax residents were catapulted back to the morning of 6 December 1917, when the French steamship *Mont Blanc*, carrying a large quantity of munitions, had collided with another ship in the Narrows, causing the largest man-made explosion prior to the bombings of Hiroshima and Nagasaki. About 2,000 people had died in the blast – hit by debris, buried in collapsed buildings, killed by fires – while another 9,000 were injured.[89] In the

Figure 2.4
The Bedford Magazine Explosion, 18 July 1945. Courtesy of the family album of Ronald Gilkie.

areas bordering the Halifax harbour, memories of the 1917 Halifax Harbour Explosion had settled so deeply into collective memory as to trigger intense emotions. The parents of my interview partners had witnessed the violence wrought by the Halifax Harbour Explosion as children, youth, or young adults. To their children, they bequeathed stories of loss and pain alongside more gentle tales of lives miraculously spared.[90]

As the early rumblings of the Bedford Magazine Explosion reached Halifax and Dartmouth households, the families of my interview partners acted out a collective script: they evacuated their homes, took the children, and headed to safe ground. Sitting at an open window on this balmy summer evening, the blast of the first explosion thrust six-year-old Russell McManus across his sister's bedroom. His father rushed home to shepherd the family to the Halifax Common, a city park located on high ground: "We bundled everybody up, they opened the windows of the house, and we put my sister in the carriage and we went down that street with Dad and Mum, Nanny and Gramps and myself ... And as we are walking down the street, there'd be this great big bang! And windows, glass would come flying down. Gramps would lean over my baby sister and protect her."[91] Living nearby the Northwest Arm, Shirley Hill and her cousins were eating supper in the garden when they heard the crescendo of exploding shells. Bearing the emotional scars of the 1917 Halifax Harbour Explosion, Shirley Hill's aunt decided to usher the children to safety: "My mother and my aunt had both been children during the big Halifax Explosion. My aunt had a very bad cut on her face ... And as soon when that explosion happened ... it was determined ... She said, 'We are getting out of here; we're taking the children.' So they had a car and she and my four cousins and my mother and my brother and I, two dogs, got in this big old Dodge and headed out the road and drove down to where my summer place is now, twenty-two miles away ... My aunt was so nervous, knowing what she went through."[92] Many families had already left their homes or the city of their own volition when naval headquarters broadcast the order to evacuate the Halifax North End at 9:00 pm. All citizens living between the Bedford Basin and Quinpool Road – more than half the city's population – were asked to leave their homes. Across the harbour, more than 10,000 Dartmouth citizens were relocated to the A-23 artillery camp beyond the Eastern Passage airport, a safe eight miles distance from the Bedford Magazine.[93]

It was a city on the move. People from the North End crowded into city parks to find shelter from flying glass and debris. Thousands headed to Point Pleasant Park on the southern tip of the peninsula where they camped out overnight. "I don't know how many people were sleeping out on our little front yard there, on the grass that night," Charles Grantham recalled, "but there must have been twenty-five or thirty people."[94] "Citadel Hill was black with people afraid to stay within glass range of buildings," the censor Jefferson remarked. As army trucks patrolled the streets of the North End to prevent the looting of stores and private homes, the city provided free sandwiches and coffee for the multitude sleeping outdoors.[95] Other families headed out of the city altogether, venturing as far as Herring Cove, as Beatrice Risser remembered: "This ammunition dump is blowing up. And it wasn't very far from us, as the crow flies, because Chester Avenue is across the Basin; it wasn't very far. So this was supper time and my father had an old car, and everybody that was in the house – there was a man and a woman that boarded at our place, and all of us children; I think there was nine of us in the car. And we had to leave, we had to leave the city ... You just didn't *stick around* ... So [laughs], we went down to Herring Cove and we slept on the side of the road all night with everybody else. You know, you had your blankets and everything. And you could hear 'pop, pop, pop' all night long."[96] Hundreds of families defied the evacuation order, sitting on gardens, backyards, and sidewalks in the North End while looking out to the Bedford Basin. "We got out of our home," Catherine

Cable recounted, "but we stayed in our backyard and spent the whole night just camping out."[97] In a collective choreography, the onlookers would duck after each detonation so as to avoid the blast in the explosion's wake.[98]

Set against a "brilliant red sunset behind the magazine," the Bedford Magazine Explosion offered a commanding sensory spectacle that H.B. Jefferson likened to "the color motion pix of a volcano crater," replete with the "periodical 'eruption' and boiling up of the 'lava' as the fire reached new stores of shells and gun charges." In the fading daylight, clouds of dust hovered over the basin. As darkness fell, the main fire at the magazine glowed with a "sinister dull red glare," framed by the black silhouette of the surrounding hills. Alongside the waterfront and in the North End, "dense clouds of yellow smoke" wafted over from the magazine, while "occasionally the acrid smell of burning cordite could be whiffed."[99] The blast of successive explosions could be felt as far away as the Northwest Arm.[100]

But for children and youth, it was sound that signalled the moment of rupture. In painting with sound, my interview partners recreated the auditory moment when the force of the explosions intruded on their neighbourhoods and family homes – a loud, insistent, and violent shouting that ebbed away only to build up again in a dramatic crescendo. Sound resonated with children more deeply than even the trembling ground or the powerful blasts of successive explosions. Spontaneously, my interview partners re-enacted and performed the aural theatre of the Bedford Magazine Explosion, infusing their memories with the "ka-boom," the "bang," the "pop, pop, pop," and the "boom, boom, boom" of subsequent explosions.[101] These auditory memories are so vividly remembered precisely because they stood in sharp contrast to the day-to-day. As such, these memories – recounted with a chuckle and light-hearted laughter – carry a meaning very different from memories of the "screaming wail" of sirens that heralded sustained aerial bombings in wartime Germany and France.[102]

If the Bedford Magazine Explosion spelled danger for adults, its meanings for children were more ambiguous. While young children looked to their parents and older siblings for reassurance, children in middle childhood noted, with curiosity rather than fear, how the Bedford Magazine Explosion upended social protocols. Gerry Lethbridge and his family were strawberry picking in the outskirts of Dartmouth just "two, three or four miles as the crow flies, direct from the Magazine" when the explosions began. Rushing back home, the family could hear the small shells detonating: "Pop-pop. Bang, bang, bang. Pop-pop. And *boom!*" Gerry's parents transformed the dining room into a makeshift communal bedroom, clearing out the dining table and bringing down mattresses from the second floor. "And

Figure 2.5
Cloud hovering over Halifax in the wake of the explosion at Bedford Magazine. Canadian War Museum, accession no. 20080094-528.

we went to sleep, although there wasn't too much sleeping going on. There was too much excitement," Gerry Lethbridge recalls. When a "tremendous explosion" shook the house at midnight, "my dad said that was enough. He gathered us up, and my mother's home was in the little community down the eastern shore, called East Chester Cove, and it was about twenty-five miles from Dartmouth. So he drove us down there." His father returned to Dartmouth to help service the gas station, while his mother stayed with the children. Lying awake worrying all night – at four o'clock, another explosion lit up the sky as far away as East Chester Cove – she, too, decided to head back to Dartmouth: "So the next morning, and Mom was a *very* conservative person, but the next morning, she went to get out on the road, and she hitchhiked her way back to city. And I mean that's just something that Mom would *never* ever do! But she hitchhiked back in."[103]

In this moment of heightened danger, adults abandoned social protocols of touch. Owen Hamlin's mother typically resisted any attempts at physical affection: "To hug my mother, she would recoil, all the time. Her affection was: You are fed. You are clean. You are disciplined." But when the Bedford Magazine Explosion pushed in the window of the family home, hurtling sharp glass splinters across the room, Owen's mother gathered her son protectively into her arms: "I can remember my mother screaming, and pushing me down, and shielding me from the window. She was afraid that there was more to come."[104] The Bedford magazine explosion was a time out of time when the usual rules of propriety no longer applied.

In Halifax, children and youth did not share in their parents' fear. To them, the 1917 Halifax Harbour Explosion was a story, vividly known, but not viscerally felt. Children revelled in the topsy-turvy excitement of the moment: running to Gottingen Street to snap a picture of the mushroom cloud over the magazine with a "little $2 baby brownie camera"; camping on the roadside with strangers; being treated to a picnic-style dinner of herring and potatoes in Herring Cove; and watching the dazzling fireworks display that lit the skies throughout the night.[105]

Even the youngest of my narrators had vivid memories to share of the Bedford Magazine Explosion. Whereas war remained an abstract concept for the very young, the explosion was an event both tangible and dramatic. It reached into the small spaces of childhood where it excited the senses: it could be heard, felt, smelled, and seen. "And I do remember a series of explosions," Catherine Cable recalls whose family refused to leave the North End. "The sky would light up like huge lightning bolts … And then this *huge*, huge explosion that would just make the earth vibrate. You know, I hate to say it, but it was somewhat exciting."[106] On the Halifax Common, Russell McManus marvelled at the "spectacular fireworks display." His father taught the young boy how to shield himself against the blasts: "Dad said that when you see that big flash over there, you're going to feel the ground tremor, so you stood on your tiptoes and had your head up like that against your arm."[107] Parents provided not only emotional security and reassurance, but also taught their children the meaning of sensations. Drawing upon their knowledge of the 1917 Harbour Explosion, they explained the sequence of violent explosions and instructed their children how to protect themselves.[108]

As they were camping out in the late hours of 18 July 1945, my narrators remained embedded in dense social networks. In Herring Cove, Ronald Gilkie saw the night turn into day when the explosion at four o'clock in the morning lit the skies. "As a kid it was great," he smiles. "We got to stay up all night."[109] As the historian Lindsey Dodd has observed in her oral history of French children under the Allied bombs, "Ignorance protected children from frightening knowledge."[110] Yet, so, too, did the social context in which Halifax children and youth experienced the Bedford Magazine Explosion. Surrounded by their parents, grandparents, siblings, cousins, family friends, and neighbours, children experienced the emergency as an intensely social time. The intimate webs of family and community were carried outdoors, as children, parents, family members, neighbours, and strangers slept side by side in city parks, backyards, parking lots, and military camps, the blasts of successive explosions puncturing their sleep. The 1945 explosion was an intense sensory experience and a communal event in which parents and grandparents mediated – through their actions and words – the meaning of a potentially devastating explosion. If my narrators' memories speak of fear, it was not their own; it was the adults in their lives who struggled to maintain their composure.

Having lived through the 1917 Halifax Harbour Explosion, adults could fathom the cost of a second. Their concern broke through their reserve in protective gestures and hurried actions: a mother holding her son in tight embrace; an elderly man shielding his baby granddaughter from flying glass splinters; an aunt bearing the emotional and literal scars of the 1917 explosion; a father piling up his family and boarders into the old car to leave the peninsula; a mother hitchhiking across the countryside. It was a sense of danger forged in a local trauma, still painfully recalled after twenty-eight years.

Conclusion

Just as searchlights were piercing the Halifax sky during blackout exercises, the war years shone a bright spotlight on wartime memories. War transformed the city's urban environment. Its auditory landscape became infused with the sounds of war, while its busy waters, crowded with vessels and convoys, offered an engaging visual spectacle. Much like children of earlier decades, who had mastered the grammar of their urban neighbourhoods in the act of walking, Halifax children and youth relished the sensory richness of their neighbourhoods.[111] Whereas time was frozen in a series of memory pictures, the social spaces of childhood that children inhabited day in, day out had a solidity and texture that were vividly recalled. Children who lived in proximity to the harbour or military bases were exposed to particularly rich sensory experiences that, in adulthood, often translated into memorable wartime accounts. As children's ears and eyes became habituated to the wartime landscape, the novelty of these sounds and sights wore off, but its dramatic impact lingered, demarcating the war years clearly in memory.

In wartime Halifax, there was no single sound that came to represent the war. Instead, the memories of my narrators evoke an aural quilt that blended neighbourhood keynotes of war and the rhythms of everyday life. By 1943, the cacophony of the wartime city was beginning to weigh on the censor Jefferson who prided himself in the objective gaze of the professional observer. Yet to children, the wartime pollution of the Halifax harbour, the streetcars groaning under the weight of a burgeoning population, the escalating housing crisis, and the increasing pitch of city sounds registered not as a sensory burden, but a source of excitement. Their sensory preferences still unburdened by cultural expectations, youngsters marvelled at the "stink" of soldiers marching through Point Pleasant Park, the young men sweating in their "old, heavy, khaki uniforms," a "musty smell" hanging in the air.[112] In the South End, boys roared on their bikes through piles of manure.[113] At Eastern Passage, they dove into the harbour's waters, cutting through a thick film of oil, oblivious to the animal carcasses and orange crates floating nearby.[114] Not even the ominous echoes of the 1917 Halifax Harbour Explosion could unsettle the city's children and youth.

When the Bedford Magazine went up in flames on 18 July 1945 in what was the local bookend of the Second World War, the explosion catapulted the parents and grandparents of my interview partners back in time. Their voices, gestures, and hurried actions bespoke their fear. Recalling the devastation of the 1917 Halifax Harbour explosion, their response was visceral and immediate; they gathered their children and sought safe shelter. By contrast, the city's youngsters heard not danger, but a counterpoint – and a fascinating one at that – to ordinary life. The sounds of the Bedford Magazine Explosion constituted a shared aural thread in the tapestry of their recollections. The auditory sensations of the explosion were imprinted on the memories of my narrators, who performed the sounds experienced and remembered in our conversations some sixty years later. The amused tone of their recollections reflects the benefit of hindsight; only one life was lost on 18 July 1945.[115] But it also speaks to children's capacity for wonder that was not yet circumscribed by the knowledge of danger.

To attend to the child's sensorium carries us into spaces of childhood intimately known. It was a knowledge borne of habitual activities, emotional encounters, and sensory experiences. To Halifax children living within earshot and sightlines of the harbour, this nodal point of global conflict was a life-world, made familiar in daily exploits. Though children and adults lived side by side in over-crowded wartime quarters, they did not necessarily inhabit the same sensory worlds. Children, whose memory did not reach back into a time before the war, embraced the wartime city on its own terms. In reading the urban landscape, they picked up sensory clues that spoke not of death, violence, and destruction, but of novelty and excitement. Growing up in 1940s Halifax, children and youth were immersed in a theatre of war that was safe, yet dramatic – a stage upon which the local and the global entwined.

NOTES

1 White, "Conscripted City: Halifax and the Second World War," provides the most comprehensive treatment of the city's transformation during the war years. Other studies with a more popular bent include Kimber, *Sailor, Slacker, and Blind Pigs* and Naftel, *Halifax at War*.

2 Library and Archives Canada (LAC), RG 24, Vol. 11696, File D.H. 1003-7-3, Vol. 1, "Convoy Schedules – Monthly Schedules of Arrivals and Sailings to CAN. For RCMP From 26/3/32."

3 Nova Scotia Archives, H.B. Jefferson Journal, Accession No. 1992-304 489 A [hereafter H.B. Jefferson Journal], 6 April 1941.

4 White, "Conscripted City," 15, 4, and 13–20.

5 Ibid., 13–14.

6 Ibid, 15. For detailed results of the 1944 population survey see LAC, RG 19, Vol. 9, File H-13, 1942–1944, "Letter by E.L. Cousins to the Honourable C.D. Howe, Minister of Munitions and Supply, Ottawa, Ontario, 17 July 1944, Census Returns – Halifax, Dartmouth," 1.

7 LAC, RG 19, Vol. 9, File H-13, 1942–1944, "Letter by D.B. Carwell, Controller of Ship Repairs and Salvage to the Honourable C.D. Howe, Minister of Munitions & Supply, Ottawa, Canada, 8 May 1943."

8 H.B. Jefferson Journal, 25 June 1943.

9 de Certeau, *The Practice of Everyday Life*, 97.
10 As quoted in Tonkiss, *Space, the City and Social Theory*, 115.
11 Ong, "The Shifting Sensorium," 47–60.
12 Tuan, *Topophilia*, 8.
13 As scholars of sensory history have contended, sensory perception might be sharpest in childhood and early youth. "Unburdened by worldly cares, unfettered by learning, free of ingrained habit, negligent of time, the child is open to the world," writes the human geographer Yi-Fu Tuan with characteristic abandon. This contention, as Wendy Parkins holds, is the "romantic myth of the child's acuity of perception, the capacity of children to feel deeply and experience a sense of wonder as they encounter phenomena – both natural and social – for the first time." Anthropologists Constance Classen and David Howes further observe that children are socialized into "culturally-modulated ways" of sensing the world around them. Most sensory preferences, in other words, are learned rather than innate. Tuan, *Topophilia*, 56; Parkins, "Feeling for Beauty," 2–638; Howes and Classen, *Ways of Sensing*, 4.
14 Smith, *Sensing the Past*, 3.
15 Classen, "Foundations for an Anthropology of the Senses," 401.
16 Smith, *Sensing the Past*, 3.
17 Hamilton, "The Proust Effect: Oral History and the Senses," 220, and Smith, "Producing Sense, Consuming Sense, Making Sense," 841.
18 Stargardt, *Witnesses of War*, 16, 241, 234–6.
19 Dodd, *French Children under the Allied Bombs, 1940–45*, 99.
20 As Mark Smith holds in his sensory history of the American Civil War, the violence of war pushes the senses "to their limits": "War is hell on them; the violence of it engraves sensory memory in ways other experiences cannot approach, memory so powerful it can be relived, over and over again." See Smith, *The Smell of Battle, the Taste of Siege*, 7. See also Jug, "Sensing Danger: The Red Army during the Second World War," 219–40.
21 For a point of comparison see Pascoe, "City as Space, City as Place," 1–30, and Faire and McHugh, "The Everyday Uses of City-Centre Streets," 18–28.
22 Fran Tonkiss, "Aural Postcards: Sound, Memory and the City," 306. "Sound is dynamic," as anthropologists Constance Classen and David Howes note. "We can see things that are completely still, but when we hear something we know that an activity is taking place." See Howes and Classen, *Ways of Sensing*, 8. One of the best studies on soundscapes remains Corbin's *Village Bells*.

23 Sui, "Visuality, Aurality, and Shifting Metaphors of Geographical Thought in the Late Twentieth Century," 335.
24 Parr, "Notes for a More Sensuous History of Twentieth-Century Canada," 720.
25 As Alain Corbin notes: "The historian needs to know that the banal is frequently silent ... The noise of traffic is today tending to disappear from the evocation or description of big cities, although it is not clear whether it is no longer noticed because of its omnipresence and the fact that no one heeds it, or whether its extreme banality leads insidiously to it being passed over." See Corbin, "Charting the Cultural History of the Senses," 135.
26 Owen Hamlin, interview by author, 12 August 2009, Halifax.
27 Parr, "Notes for a More Sensuous History," 731.
28 Casey, "How to Get from Space to Place in a Fairly Short Stretch of Time: Phenomenological Prolegomena," 19.
29 Marjorie Ferguson, interview by author, 28 July 2009, Halifax.
30 James MacFadzean, interview by author, 13 August 2009, Halifax.
31 Hildegard Jangaard, interview by author, 25 July 2009, Halifax. See also e-mail correspondence with Colin Craig, 19 July 2009, and author interviews with Marjorie Ferguson, 28 July 2009, Robert Dickie, 31 July 2009, and Jeannie Hill, 12 August 2009, in Halifax, and Barbara Whyte, 3 August 2009, and Susan McNeill (pseud.), 27 July 2009, in Dartmouth.
32 Naftel, *Halifax at* War, 29–31.
33 Quoted in ibid., 30.
34 Jeannie Hill, interview by author, 12 August 2009, Halifax. In a similar vein, Robert Dickie regularly crossed over to Dartmouth on the ferry to visit his cousins. Dickie, interview by author, 31 July 2009, Halifax.
35 Naftel, *Halifax at War*, 30.
36 Author interviews with Barbara Whyte, 3 August 2009, and Susan McNeill (pseud.), 27 July 2009, in Dartmouth.
37 Gordon Perks, interview by author, 5 August 2009, Halifax.
38 Naftel, *Halifax at War*, 236–7.
39 H.B. Jefferson Journal, 9 April 1942.
40 Thomas Wheatley, interview by author, 7 August 2009, Dartmouth.
41 DeFazio, *The City of the Senses*, 65.
42 H.B. Jefferson Journal, 9 April 1942.
43 Author interviews with Gerald Dempsey, 30 July 2009, Herring Cove, and Doris Pope, 4 August 2009, Halifax. See also Naftel, *Halifax at War*, 124.

44 H.B. Jefferson Journal, 12 September 1942.
45 Ibid., 25 May 1942, 20 July 1943, and 13 September 1943.
46 Catherine Cable, interview by author, 6 August 2009, Halifax.
47 Laurence Griffin, interview by author, 22 July 2009, Halifax.
48 H.B. Jefferson Journal, 29 September 1942.
49 Steward and Cohen, "Introduction," 13–14.
50 Bernard Miller, interview by author, 4 August 2009, Halifax.
51 Shirley Hill, interview by author, 17 August 2009, Halifax.
52 Thomas Wheatley, interview by author, 7 August 2009, Dartmouth.
53 Tonkiss, "Aural Postcards," 304, 307.
54 Rodaway, *Sensuous Geographies*, 95.
55 Garrioch, "Sounds of the City," 6, 14.
56 Marjorie Ferguson, interview by author, 28 July 2009, Dartmouth.
57 White, "Conscripted City," 20.
58 Frederick Allen, interview by author, 29 July 2009, Dartmouth.
59 Owen Hamlin, interview by author, 12 August 2009, Halifax.
60 Parr, "Notes for a More Sensuous History," 724.
61 Robert Dickie, interview by author, 31 July 2009, Halifax.
62 See also Sleight, *Young People and the Shaping of Public Spaces in Melbourne*, 10, and Thrift, "With Child to See Any Strange Thing," 398–409.
63 Author interviews with Robert Dickie, 31 July 2009, Lawrence Griffin, 22 July 2009, and Frederick Allen, 29 July 2009, in Halifax.
64 Ward, *The Child in the City*, 73; Bell, "Heroes or Hooligans?," 89–95; Kozlovsky, "Architecture, Emotions and the History of Childhood," 95–118.
65 William Naftel, "H.B. Jefferson: Newspaperman and Wartime Press Censor," in "An East Coast Port: Halifax in Wartime, 1939–1945," Virtual Exhibition of the Nova Scotia Archives at: https://novascotia.ca/archives/eastcoastport/.
66 H.B. Jefferson Journal, 29 July 1943.
67 Ibid., 13 September 1943.
68 Ibid., 15 January 1943.
69 Ibid., 13 September 1943.
70 Ibid., 29 July 1943.
71 Urry, "City Life and the Senses," 389–90.
72 Tonkiss, *Space, the City and Social Theory*, 121.
73 Author interviews with Gerald Dempsey, 30 July 2009, Herring Cove; Gerry Lethbridge, 21 July 2009; and Thomas Wheatley, 7 August 2009 in Dartmouth.
74 Cruikshank, *The Social Life of Stories*, 27.

75 Author interviews with Gerald Dempsey, 30 July 2009, Herring Cove and Gerry Lethbridge, 21 July 2009, Dartmouth.
76 H.B. Jefferson Journal, 7 April 1942.
77 Thomas Wheatley, interview by author, 7 August 2009, Dartmouth.
78 H.B. Jefferson Fonds, Nova Scotia Archives, MG 1, Vol. 486, File: XXXV, Ruling Halifax, November 1942, # 1778 – # 1822, HBJ 1832, 5 December 1942.
79 For brief accounts of the Bedford Magazine Explosion see Raddall, *Halifax – Warden of the North*, 302–5, and Naftel, *Halifax at War*, 238–41.
80 Author interviews with Ronald Gilkie, 19 August 2009, Halifax; Beatrice Risser, 8 August 2009, Lunenburg; Shirley Hill, 17 August 2009, Halifax; Frederick Allen, 29 July 2009, Halifax; and Owen Hamlin, 12 August 2009, Halifax.
81 Nova Scotia Archives, H.B. Jefferson Fonds, MG 1, Vol. 487, File: XLIX, Ruling HFX, 2421–39, July–August 1945, 1–2.
82 Ronald Gilkie, interview by author, 19 August 2009, Halifax.
83 Nova Scotia Archives, H.B. Jefferson Fonds, MG 1, Vol. 487, File: XLIX, Ruling HFX, 2421–39, July-August 1945, 6.
84 Carolyn Crowell, interview by author, 11 August 2009, Halifax.
85 Catherine Cable, interview by author, 6 August 2009, Halifax.
86 Charles Grantham, interview by author, 9 August 2009, Bridgewater.
87 Ronald Gilkie, interview by author, 19 August 2009, Halifax.
88 Tuttle, *Daddy's Gone to War*, 3.
89 Raddall, *Halifax: Warden of the North*, 244–50.
90 Author interviews with Barbara Whyte, 3 August 2009, Dartmouth and Catherine Cable, 6 August 2009, Halifax.
91 Russell McManus, interview by author, 30 July 2009, Halifax.
92 Shirley Hill, interview by author, 17 August 2009, Halifax.
93 Raddall, *Halifax: Warden of the North*, 302 and Nova Scotia Archives, H.B. Jefferson Fonds, MG 1, Vol. 487, File: XLIX, Ruling HFX, 2421–39, July–August 1945, 3.
94 Charles Grantham, interview by author, 9 August 2009, Bridgewater.
95 Nova Scotia Archives, H.B. Jefferson Fonds, MG 1, Vol. 487, File: XLIX, Ruling HFX, 2421–39, July–August 1945, 3.
96 Beatrice Risser, interview by author, 8 August 2009, Lunenburg.
97 Catherine Cable, interview by author, 6 August 2009, Halifax.
98 As the historian Thomas Raddall writes, "From time to time, a major explosion sent a huge yellow flame towards the zenith and all threw themselves flat, counting the seconds along and waiting for the blast" that would reach them ten to fifteen seconds later. See Raddall, *Halifax: Warden of the North*, 303.

99 Ibid., 3–4. See also Raddall, *Halifax: Warden of the North*, 203.
100 Ronald Gilkie, interview by author, 19 August 2009, Halifax.
101 Author interviews with Ronald Gilkie, 19 August 2009, Halifax; Robert Dickie, 31 July 2009, Halifax; Beatrice Risser, 8 August 2009, Lunenburg; and Carolyn Crowell, 11 August 2009, Halifax.
102 See Stargardt, *Witnesses of War*, 234–6, and Dodd, *French Children under the Allied Bombs, 1940–45*, 87–100.
103 Gerry Lethbridge, interview by author, 21 July 2009, Dartmouth.
104 Owen Hamlin, interview by author, 12 August 2009, Halifax.
105 Author interviews with Frederick Allen, 29 July 2009, Halifax; Ronald Gilkie, 19 August 2009, Halifax; Beatrice Risser, 8 August 2009, Lunenburg; Russell McManus, 30 July 2009, Halifax; and Carolyn Crowell, 11 August 2009, Halifax.
106 Catherine Cable, interview by author, 6 August 2009, Halifax.
107 Russell McManus, interview by author, 30 July 2009, Halifax.
108 For a point of comparison, see Dodd, *French Children under the Allied Bombs, 1940–45*, 92–5.
109 Ronald Gilkie, interview by author, 19 August 2009, Halifax.
110 Dodd, *French Children under the Allied Bombs, 1940–45*, 90.
111 For pioneering accounts of children in the public spaces of the city that are rich in sensory accounts see Nasaw, *Children of the City at Work and at Play*, and Davin, *Growing Up Poor*.
112 Gordon Perks, interview by author, 5 August 2009, Halifax.
113 Robert Dickie, interview by author, 31 July 2009, Halifax.
114 Thomas Wheatley, interview by author, 7 August 2009, Dartmouth.
115 Raddall, *Halifax: Warden of the North*, 304.

3
"What Am I to Do to Save My Children?": Canadian Children in Civil Defence Planning

Andrew Burtch

Five bodies lay strewn across Ava Street on a sunny afternoon in Ottawa's Manor Park neighbourhood on a sunny day in May 1953. Their features were partially obscured by sheets of blood, embedded glass granules, wood splinters, and burns. Exposed bone poked out of clothing from compound fractures. A young boy stood silently over one of the bodies as first responders arrived on the scene, taking in the carnage. As his mother ran out to bring him into the house, a "magnificently unsympathetic grin" spread over the boy's face, and he turned to another child and remarked, pointing at the corpse, "Don't he look funny?"

The "bodies" in this case were volunteers from Ottawa's Civil Service Civil Defence corps, an Ottawa-based group briefly set up during the 1950s to train and provide emergency workers to respond to a possible nuclear attack against the nation's capital. Their wounds were applied as part of casualty simulation training, and other volunteers raced about during a daytime exercise to practise first aid, as well as how to safely load and transport casualties in stretchers.

Unlike a military exercise, however, this drill did not play out between uniformed men on a mock battlefield, but by men and women in civilian dress in a residential neighbourhood. The exercise's objective was to inform local residents through the day's work and subsequent press coverage that nuclear war was a possible outcome of the Cold War, and that there were measures they could take to prepare. The exercise instead elicited parental outrage; a neighbourhood mother had previously begged the organizers not to upset children on their return home from school.[1] For the residents of this quiet street, the Cold War had come home.

The stated objective of civil defence was to protect lives and infrastructure at home so that Canadians could survive the initial wave of a nuclear attack and continue fighting the third world war. Of course, the advice offered to Canadian citizens was somewhat different – the strategic goal of civil defence was laid aside to instead emphasize the survival of the family, the city block, and the community. It would be the job of every citizen to survive, offer assistance to the afflicted, and to rebuild after the initial danger had passed. Much of this advice was directed, sensibly, to adults. Children had an implicit and explicit role to play in most of Canada's survival plans, but officials rarely addressed children directly – assuming them to be mostly passive recipients of governmental or familial direction, or used in civil defence imagery as symbolic props to persuade parents to take measures to protect their children. In Canada as elsewhere, civil defence planners made free use of the image of children at risk to argue in favour of civil defence preparations and to mobilize their followers. These plans were as much about shielding children from negative emotions as they were about actual measures that would improve their safety. The Cold War child knew the risks of nuclear war, and they participated in community preparations, usually along rigidly prescribed gender lines for boys and girls.

Children and their families in Cold War Canada learned about the risks of nuclear war in the public school of emotions that were the civil defence campaigns of the 1950s and 1960s. As the rich historiography on civil defence in the atomic age demonstrates, fear, uncertainty, and anxiety underpinned both strategic government planning and contemporaneous popular contemplation of nuclear war.[2] To grow up amid the existential threat of nuclear warfare shaped the Cold War subjectivities of children and youth, though not necessarily in the way civil defence planners envisioned.

Like other Western governments, civil defence experts in Canada sought to manage emotions through the illusion of control and the rhetoric of patriotism. As Elaine Tyler May has argued persuasively, the Cold War orthodoxy infiltrated the home even on the level of family relationships, prompting "domestic containment" and, for a time, the diminution of dissent.[3] But emotions were not so easily contained. The very campaigns that hoped to inculcate emotional composure and patriotic sentiment among the young could, instead, inspire fear and anxiety. Such an emotional disposition was not, as the Canadian prime minister John Diefenbaker held with some exasperation, an irrational and purely affective response to rising Cold War tensions.[4] Fear and anxiety, too, as the historian Frank Biess has argued, are "emotions with significant cognitive elements."[5] In the burgeoning disarmament movement of the 1980s, youth activists would draw upon the strength of these emotions to formulate their sharp criticism of civil defence programs, denounce the dangers of radiation from atomic testing, and loudly reject the binary Cold War logic of deterrence or annihilation.

This chapter turns to the history of emotions to examine the experiences of Canadian children and youth in the atomic age. In a pioneering work that spans the disciplines of psychology, history, and anthropology, William Reddy has developed the term "emotional regimes" to describe collective efforts to construe certain emotional codes as desirable.[6] The emotional scripts that informed civil defence efforts aimed at replacing "negative" emotional reactions, such as fear, panic, or anxiety, with "positive" or constructive reactions to adversity: confidence, obedience, and calm.[7] This chapter then examines what Reddy calls the "ironic effects of mental control" – namely, to quote Biess, "the realization that any attempt to suppress a negative emotion may activate its 'thought-material' and hence prompt an intensified experience of the emotion rather than its avoidance."[8] What resonated with many Canadian children, youth, and their families was not the upbeat rhetoric of containment, but the frightening prospect of a world consumed by nuclear warfare. Finally, this study analyzes the growth of youth activism in the disarmament movement of the 1980s. These young political actors operated on an "emotional frontier," to draw upon a concept developed by historians Karen Vallgårda, Kristine Alexander, and Stephanie Olsen, which existed at the crossroads between "contrasting emotional formations."[9] In the 1980s, fear and angst gave way not only to helplessness or panic, but also to the determined efforts of youth activists to lobby for disarmament, a movement that was nurtured by the existential crises of the Cold War.

As civil defence plans offer an obvious point of contact between strategic government planning, and the acceptance or rejection of these plans by individual families, they provide a rich seam of historical information to judge how children, youth and their families responded to the Cold War and came to live with the bomb in their daily lives, either through conforming to national security expectations or through protesting the status quo. Archival materials from the federal civil defence agency tell us less about the stories of real children and more about the cultural construct of the "symbolic child" that was imbued with national significance. The postwar baby boom led to unprecedented study of children's lives, attitudes, and upbringing, as Marilyn Irvin Holt points out in her study *Cold War Kids*. Popular media was replete with expert opinion about how best to care for and nurture a child, and these often served the dual purpose of ensuring that these children conformed to developing Cold War virtues as they matured to adulthood.[10] As Margaret Peacock describes in her study, *Innocent Weapons*, in both the Soviet and North American contexts, imagery of the "happy, afforded child," secure in access to resources and comforts, was meant to demonstrate each bloc's ideological security. These happy children were expected to defend the systems that ostensibly provided for their happiness. In North America, as Peacock suggests, the ideal child was "patriotic, physically fit, God-fearing, and respectful of authority but also well-educated in the sciences, devoutly anticommunist, defensively mobilized for nuclear disaster ... unperturbed by the possible psychological traumas of the atomic bomb, and dedicated to the maintenance of domestic order."[11] These idealized images, of course, provided a sense of uniformity and equality that was not reflected in the societies they were meant to portray.

Whereas the emotional scripts of civil defence efforts were widely publicized, the emotional practices of Canadian children and youth during the Cold War era have to be pieced together from a wide range of primary sources. Important insights can be gleaned from what Kristine Alexander and Ashley Henrickson in this volume describe as a "child-centred reading" of sources generated by adults. To this end, this study turns to the letters penned by both mothers and fathers who questioned the effectiveness of civil defence efforts and voiced concerns for their children's safety in a world threatened by nuclear annihilation. Echoes of children's voices can also be heard in memoirs, school essays, teacher reports, and letters to newspaper editors, and, more loudly so, in archival documents on the youth nuclear disarmament tour of 1987. It was in exceptional episodes, such as the spontaneous reactions to and reportage of events such as the Cuban Missile Crisis, that we gain a clearer sense of how children, as part of the greater community under threat, reacted to the prospect of annihilation. Much like their older counterparts, children and youth reacted to the nuclear arms race along a spectrum of emotion, from alarm and grief to so-called "what's the use–ism" or apathy, to overt protests in marches against nuclear weapons. Far from being passive recipients of bad news, children assimilated the reality of nuclear weapons in their lives in different and fascinating ways, and, as Cold War orthodoxies gave way to protest, in manners that civil defence planners had not foreseen.

Growing Up in the Shadow of Nuclear War

From the late 1940s to mid-1950s, civil defence planning in Canada was animated by the "self-help" vision. At that time, planners envisioned an attack that would destroy a portion of a city with a single bomb, creating a dire emergency but one not too dissimilar from the damage inflicted by conventional bomber raids during the Second World War. The nominal attack left part of a city in ruins, allowing citizens in other neighbourhoods to rush to put out fires, evacuate and treat survivors, and rebuild. This quaint vision of the impact of an atomic attack was based on air raid precautions adopted during the last war in Europe and North America.[12]

To guard against a potential aerial strike by the Soviet Union, the Department of National Defence identified thirteen cities as most likely target areas and instructed municipal governments to put into place emergency measures. By 1952, as historian Tarah Brookfield writes, "all 13 potential target areas and 543 other municipalities possessed some form of civil defence organizations, while 128 communities had fully developed programs that included a director, various services, and training facilities for civil servants, emergency personnel, and civilian volunteers."[13] Each of these organizations depended heavily on volunteers from the community, usually from extant volunteer and fraternal organizations, to take on training and teach others. To reach the future citizens of the nation, civil defence planners also began involving educators in their campaigns.

According to a 1952 Canadian Institute of Public Opinion poll, between 75 and 85 per cent of respondents agreed that some form of civil defence education should be introduced in public schools; approximately 10 per cent were opposed. The poll did suggest that Canadians' approval was somewhat qualified. The poll report clarified that most respondents were comfortable with preparation, with the provision that the subject be tactfully handled, that it be reserved for older children only, and that, above all, children must not be frightened. This last provision proved most influential over the course of the decade that followed and war with the Soviet Union appeared more likely to occur, and as public knowledge of the risks posed by radioactive fallout took hold.[14]

Canada's foremost advocate for civil defence was its national coordinator, retired Major-General F.F. Worthington. Appointed in 1948, much of Worthington's early efforts were directed at adapting and updating air raid precautions created in the Second World War to suit the nuclear age.[15] For his part, he endorsed youth education in matters of survival – suggesting that all children be taught essential skills of fire prevention and basic firefighting and first aid. He also believed, and this was reflected in most civil defence literature, that responsibility for survival tasks should be divided along gender lines, with men and boys doing much of the "active" work of firefighting and rescue, and women and girls tasked with more traditionally domestic tasks such as home nursing, casualty care, and feeding and billeting of displaced persons. When considering curricular material for schools,

Worthington recognized the value of not alarming children unduly, but also offered that "the average child is elemental and still seems to enjoy such mild-mannered games as cops and robbers, Indians and cowboys and other equally bloodthirsty games. They have been doing this for some thousands of years and will no doubt develop games around ABCW [atomic, biological, and chemical warfare] if their imagination runs in that direction."[16]

The federal government's first guidance directed at schools was a thin volume, the eleventh manual published by Civil Defence Canada: *Civil Defence in Schools* (1952). Addressed to school principals, the booklet offered "basic lines of thought which may be applied according to circumstances and local requirements."[17] School principals asked to align their school's survival plans with municipal civil defence agencies and work with local planners (assuming there were any), but were cautioned: "all matters pertaining to the protection of school children during school hours [should] be considered the immediate responsibility of the principal and his staff."[18] In other words, unless there was specific provision that the local authorities would support the school during or after an attack, the staff and the students were on their own.

Advice about how to speak to children about atomic attack was sparse, save the "imperative" that pupils be prepared for an atomic drill. The booklet's authors suggested that teachers could compare the drills to existing fire precautions, which were already part of the school year routine. They allowed that more senior students could be given more detailed information "particularly in connection with science courses." Teachers and staff should not, the booklet warned, alarm pupils, but in the end "all classes must understand that exact and implicit obedience is absolutely essential."[19] The drills were meant to discourage negative emotional outcomes and encourage positive – that is to say, obedient and calm – behaviour.

Teachers were to prepare for all outcomes, including attacks while children were outside in the play yard or inside in the classroom, with or without warning. If the first warning was a flash of an atomic bomb, the children were told to "duck and cover," to drop to their classroom floor, underneath desks and chairs, using their hands and arms to cover their neck and face. If outside, they would walk to shelter – "a hill, ditch, gutter, or tree will add protection." If there was sufficient warning, teachers would march their children to "shelters" within the school, allotting no less than four square feet to each child.[20]

Some school boards took it upon themselves to practice, instituting drills and evacuations along the lines suggested by federal authorities. The "duck and cover" drill described in Canadian CD documents may or may not have been accompanied by the eponymous American civil defence film featuring the mascot "Bert the Turtle," but it is likely that the cultural phenomenon crossed the border, given that by the early 1950s no Canadian civil defence films had yet been produced for a school-aged audience.[21]

One set of school exercises in St Catharines, Ontario, winked at the film, however. The 1955 drills, dubbed "Operation Turtle," involved fifty-four schools in the region surrounding the city, and 17,000 students. The Turtle drills involved elementary and high schools, and were covered by media. *Globe and Mail* and National Film Board photographers snapped moments of children huddled neatly under their desks or up against concrete basement walls, hands clasped firmly behind their necks. In other photos, children pose with white sand buckets for firefighting.

One clear objective of the exercise was to normalize atomic war preparations for children in schools in the same way that fire and traffic safety lessons were taught as part of the usual curriculum. In a recapitulation of the exercises in the teachers' magazine *School Progress*, St Catharines' civil defence coordinator for schools H.R. Partlow assured readers that the drills "build confidence in the minds of the children and the public. It has been our experience that a feeling of security has developed rather than a feeling of concern." Partlow also mentioned that children participated "with seriousness and interest – they simply take Civil Defence 'in their stride.'"[22] It is, however, questionable whether teachers would have accepted this view, or how eagerly they embraced their forced role as atomic air warden in addition to the other curricular and social development roles they grappled with in the early post-war years.[23]

The federal government did more than just ask schools to educate children in the basics of civil defence; they sought the active peacetime assistance of provincial authorities, youth associations, and civilian volunteers in preparation for an actual wartime role. Civil defence pamphlets were accompanied by an information campaign designed to persuade Canadians of the need for civil defence at home, at work, and, for children, in the schools. Worthington remained the chief proponent of the civil defence gospel at the federal level, but he enlisted allies at the provincial and municipal levels as cities and some provinces responded to the developing threat of atomic war with preparatory agencies of their own.

One of Worthington's allies was J.O. Probe, a former Co-operative Commonwealth Federation member of parliament for Regina who was appointed Saskatchewan's civil defence co-ordinator. Probe's enthusiasm for emergency planning resulted in impressive progress for the only Canadian province the military believed the Soviets would not bother to target with a bomb. Significantly, the

Figure 3.1
Civil Defense, School Scheme. Special Collections & Archives, University of Waterloo Library, GA68-1959-59-12560.

province's future premier, Tommy Douglas, responded positively to federal entreaties in favour of civil defence, remarking: "Our own people have come through difficult times themselves. We have enough of the pioneer spirit left to come to the aid of others in distress. We hope methods of civil defence may not be needed but the only way to be safe is to be ready for it."[24]

Probe translated the support of Douglas and others in the province into accomplishments in education, where he and his staff managed to introduce a civil defence course into the provincial school curriculum. Probe took inspiration from reports of preparedness courses offered in Denmark and Sweden, where youth from between the ages of twelve and sixteen received lessons in fire prevention and fire-fighting, map reading, and what to expect in the event of atomic, biological, or chemical attack. Youth were assigned to a local fire station so that they knew where to go and who to assist during an attack or a major fire emergency. One of Probe's colleagues in the federal government suggested that the courses had assisted Sweden's citizenship training, and had proven quite popular as part of the country's high school curriculum.[25]

Probe managed to arrange the civil defence course for the 1951–52 school year, enlisting the assistance of provincial fire authorities, the St John Ambulance, the Canadian Red Cross, and registered nurses. The thirty-hour course followed federal policy (and gender) prescriptions for civil defence work: "with four sub-topics, namely first aid (boys and girls), fire-fighting and rescue work (boys only), home nursing (girls only), and elementary A.B.C. warfare (boys and girls)."[26] Probe's plan almost failed due to the federal government's unwillingness to spend $2,500 on textbooks and pamphlets for use in high schools, but a plea to Paul Martin, minister of health and welfare, settled the matter in Saskatchewan's favour.[27]

The course, offered as a half-credit elective in Saskatchewan's high schools, resulted in provincial civil defence instructors and service associations offering hundreds of hours of lectures to students, while the province's small civil defence training centre in Fort Qu'Appelle offered more specialized warden and fire-fighting courses for high school students. The curriculum was heavily weighted in favour of firefighting and prevention, with only three hours given over to atomic attack. This bias was in keeping with Saskatchewan's concern about crop fires, as well as their emphasis in planning on civil disaster instead of atomic defence. Canadian civil defence seemed to get a boost when the high school program seemed to pay early dividends, such as when trained high school students assisted during a fire in Kindersley, Saskatchewan, in 1955.[28] Saskatchewan's modest success in training youth did not run into significant opposition, no doubt because the curriculum favoured peacetime preparations instead of atomic war drills.

In 1951, the federal government signed memoranda of understanding with a number of civilian service associations who agreed to provide peacetime training assistance as well as fulfill roles in health, welfare, and warden services in the event of a war. These memoranda involved the Royal Canadian Legion, the St John Ambulance, and the Canadian Red Cross.[29] The Boy Scouts of Canada also officially entered the civil defence fold, with the organization agreeing to train and provide scouts to local emergency efforts in a number of dangerous roles. Their responsibilities would include acting as runners bearing messages where electronic communications had failed, assisting warden services in passing information to the public and fighting fires, directing traffic during evacuations, and damage survey work, among other tasks.[30]

The Boy Scouts' leadership was serious about its new role. In Nova Scotia, the Scouts' provincial civil defence liaison swiftly unveiled a plan to train and make available youth to join peacetime and wartime drills. A Scout chapter in Halifax built mock intersections in its meeting space to help familiarize scouts with traffic direction, and it arranged support from the RCMP to take qualified boys out on road patrol in their cars, after which the boys would be assigned intersections where they were to go and work in an evacuation, "maintaining smooth operation and maximum flow of traffic and especially emphasis will be placed on composure." At first, this work was restricted to King's Scouts and First Class Scouts between fourteen and sixteen years of age, whose parents signed their consent for participation. By October 1951 the local chapter had trained forty scouts in this role, and assigned them in groups to "scramble" on short notice to assist local authorities. In their first, less active assignment, Scouts in the Halifax target area delivered air raid instructions to more than 16,000 homes in less than three hours.[31] In the years that followed, Scouts became fixtures at community exercises and civil defence events, demonstrating fire-fighting skills at the national jamboree in Ottawa in 1953, acting as stretcher bearers and messengers during municipal exercises, handing out literature at the short-lived and happily forgotten National Civil Defence Day proceedings in 1956 and 1957, and providing security and information roles at civil defence displays and events, all presumably with their parents' consent.

Civil Defence Canada did not pursue the support of the Girl Guides of Canada as vigorously as other service associations, but Worthington did receive an initial promise from their leadership to support civil defence measures. In mid-1951, however, the chief commissioner of the Guides reached out to qualify the organization's support: "The executive gave it a great deal of thought and decided that if we promise to do anything too spectacular we would probably not be able to accomplish it when the emergency arose. Our Brownies and guides are nearly all too young to be of use, apart from the family group and therefore, we decided that our training of them would stress this angle in civil defence."[32] The Guides' offer to internalize civil defence training to support the family unit was not far from the role that civil defence officials had already assigned to women and girls in their own literature. Civil defence welfare officials only suggested to the Guides that they consider enhancing their existing cooking courses to include information about emergency feeding for groups of displaced persons, as well as peacetime preparedness measures such as first aid and fire prevention.[33] Despite the limited roles assigned to young women and girls in civil defence (roles that frustrated adult female volunteers eager to do more than cook or perform nursing duties), Girl Guides often appeared alongside Boy Scouts at public civil defence events and exercises in communities across Canada.[34]

Where civil defence policies encountered existing childhood locales, including schools or gatherings of civil societies such as the Scouts or Girl Guides, it was the result of adults planning for children. In these circumstances children had few options to actively resist shelter drills or firefighting and rescue courses unless they were elective. There is little evidence to suggest that the new role for the Boy Scouts, for example, drove down membership or elicited much child or parental protest. Yet absence of protest is not evidence of acceptance or necessarily acquiescence with nuclear survival drills by children. As Kirsi Pauliina Kallio and Jouni Häkli hold, minors "can rarely refuse to adopt the subject positions offered to them." Instead, "children's political agency comes down to young individuals' potential to adopt and negotiate the subject positions that are offered to them by their societies and communities."[35] Children did not, in the absence of adults, organize protests against civil defence policy. But neither, as we shall see, did they assimilate the full messaging that civil defence advocates were hoping that they would absorb.

"Starved Creatures in a Smouldering Pile of Radioactive Ash"

Children growing up in the early Cold War, from 1949 until 1962, were exposed to a steady drumbeat of events that promoted a sense of existential crisis. American monopoly over the nuclear bomb vanished in 1949 when the Soviet Union detonated their own bomb. To overcome the Soviet weapon, the Americans built the more devastating thermonuclear bomb in 1952. The Soviets, too, built their own version of the thermonuclear weapon the same year. The hydrogen bomb, or H-bomb in popular parlance, was an order of magnitude more powerful than the bombs dropped on Hiroshima and Nagasaki. The hydrogen bomb would destroy not only part of a city but its entirety, flattening buildings and causing fires in a destructive radius of dozens of kilometres. Further complicating the survival scenario was the realization that the fatal radioactive contamination, or "fallout" produced by the detonation of nuclear weapons could kill even hundreds of kilometres downwind. The first American thermonuclear test in the Marshall Islands in March 1954 not only obliterated the atoll on which it was detonated, but radioactive fragments of coral also drifted down and poisoned the twenty-six crew of the Japanese fishing vessel the "Lucky Dragon," killing one crew member.[36] With a doomsday weapon in hand, both the Americans and Soviets worked to develop the unstoppable delivery system, the intercontinental ballistic missile, which would send a bomb into orbit and drop it on a target a world away with less than fifteen minutes' warning. The successful Soviet launch of the Sputnik I artificial satellite in November 1957, apart from representing a clear victory in the international space race, was also a demonstration of its rocket capability. As each technological hurdle in the arms race was passed, newspapers and radio broadcasts obliged listeners with dramatized simulations of what these weapons would do to their hometowns, with concentric circles on city maps showing what neighbourhoods would be vaporized, and which would merely be irradiated.[37]

If the weapons themselves produced a source of anxiety, the steady beat of bad news, foreign policy or military crises that could provoke a situation in which these could be used, also contributed to the seething atmosphere of atomic anxiety. From the Korean War to nuclear scares over the Soviet Union threatening Berlin in 1958 and 1961, to the very real war scare over the Soviet decision to install missiles in Cuba in the fall of 1962, and the stand-off that followed, the opportunities for a random event to invoke a world-ending crisis seemed endless. And in these years, any constructive solution to the problem might be seen to be a boon to the well-being of the general populace. Optimism in civil defence plans failed to keep pace with the technological and political developments of the early Cold War. Parents began to demand answers for how to protect their children. Increasingly, children voiced their own concerns in the domestic and public sphere.

Civil Defence Canada was slow to change its plans to reflect the impact of the thermonuclear revolution, but by 1956 it had adopted a policy of evacuating major cities with as little as three hours' warning. Just three years later, the plans changed again, to reflect the possible threat posed by an attack using intercontinental ballistic missiles instead of bomber aircraft, which reduced the window of warning from several hours' time to mere minutes. To reflect the new reality, Ottawa suggested a "shelter in place" program, encouraging families to build fallout shelters in their homes at their own expense, where they could wait out the war and listen to their radio for survival instructions.[38] The so-called "family fallout shelter" combined the family home, which Elaine Tyler May characterized as a psychological fortress against and formed by the anxieties of the Cold War, with real-life domestic fortifications for those fortunate enough to afford them.[39] Yet this family-focused policy change, coming so soon on the heels of others, such as evacuation schemes, exposed obvious flaws, not least of which was the impracticality and expense of private shelter construction and the impossibility of evacuating major urban centres.

Many of the negative reactions to either civil defence evacuation or shelter plans received by Canadian officials were based on practical or political arguments centred on child welfare. The plight of children in schools was particularly challenging, and civil defence officials struggled to answer sharp questions about what parents and children should do in an attack. Notwithstanding the qualified success of a few highly rehearsed city-wide evacuation drills in Halifax, St John's, and Calgary, no new resources were allocated to help major urban centres evacuate in the event of war. Children and women were given priority in evacuation, but children had no practical means to leave their school, let alone the city. Toronto's school board received pamphlets from the provincial and federal agency to instruct children in civil defence but estimated a need for 2,600 to 2,700 buses to evacuate children as well as their parents to avoid family separation. Planners responded lamely that any basic plan for children "must be motivated by school boards."[40]

In their letters to federal officials, both mothers and fathers pointedly criticized civil defence efforts that placed the burden of emergency preparations squarely on individual families. In Ottawa, federal officials spearheaded a letter campaign to the city's mayor that encouraged citizens to lobby for more comprehensive civil defence preparations: "Have we any competent Civil Defence organization? I would like to know what I am to do to save my children? Where am I to go, what is our means of getting there and who will look after us?"[41] Concerned parents used similar logic in the wake of the radio and television broadcast of a national survival exercise in the spring of 1961. As Stephen and Mary Leskard of Vancouver wrote to Prime Minister John Diefenbaker after the broadcast: "we wish to thank the Government and all others concerned for sparing us the unpleasantness of dying unwarned. The sirens were quite loud. With our children we looked for the shelters, since we are not in the income bracket entitling us to our own, but there were none."[42] In her study on Canadian women activists in Cold War Canada, Tarah Brookfield unearthed similar letters that counselled diplomacy instead of futile civil defence efforts (for how were mothers to protect their children from poisonous radiation); that explained the impossibility of a family of seven in northern Quebec to afford a private fallout shelter; and that scolded the government for not investing in large public shelters that would grant even "poorer inhabitants of our big centres" a chance at survival.[43]

Many letter-writers condemned the government's advice that families provide for themselves in a nuclear war as an abdication of its duties to defend Canada and Canadians. Opinion polls suggested that Canadians were not generally opposed to the idea of survival preparations, but favoured the construction of large group shelters managed by the government over unaffordable and cramped shelters in private homes.[44] One New Westminster man's letter reflected some of this opinion: "Deep Community Shelters, or Tunnels are O.K. but not family basement shelters at all. A family would find it too hard, to entertain and be too restless; the mentality would drop to the lowest degree, and many would go berserk, and many would suufocate [sic] to death, and suicide."[45] Others, seizing on the rhetoric of disarmament activists, suggested that they would choose death over survival for themselves and their children: "I have no desire to live in a post-World War III Canada, to grub about among other starved creatures in a smoldering pile of radioactive ash. Nor am I interested in protecting my children so that they can produce misshapen, sub-human offspring."[46] In 1963, official estimates concluded that only about 2,500 shelters existed across the country that would have protected only a tiny fraction of the population of approximately eighteen million Canadians, though more recent research has suggested that some families may not have reported their shelter construction out of fears that their neighbours might attempt to get in should the worst arrive.[47]

If the invention of the hydrogen bomb had rendered obsolete the earnest "self-help" civil defence efforts of the early 1950s, the growing understanding of the risks of dramatic, long-term radiation undermined the appeal of private and communal fallout shelters. Such highly publicized debates could not but affect the young; for every school-based civil defence drill, every ringing of a siren during emergency exercises, indeed, every conversation about the dangers of nuclear testing served as a reminder of the possibility of a devastating nuclear attack.

In the archives, newspaper coverage and personal reminiscences, we encounter children's voices that give a measure of how children and youth reacted to this threat. Often, and unsurprisingly, their reactions matched those of adults – incredulity, anxiety, even panic or anger. Stephen Thorne, a journalist and photographer, recalled nuclear fear "as a constant of my childhood for as long as I can remember. We had regular air raid drills in elementary school in Halifax where we'd line up along the basement walls."[48] Thirty-two twelve-year-olds in a London, Ontario, school selected for themselves in 1961 the essay subject: "Is it better to suffer for two weeks in a shelter and come out to a dead world or die immediately from the blast or from fallout?" The students lamented the need for civil defence, and the majority, perhaps reflecting wider public or parental opinion, criticized the government for not providing shelters for communities.[49] The contrast to school essays written in wartime Britain in the early 1940s is striking. Such normative emotional scripts that sought to instil feelings of patriotism in school-age children and mobilize youngsters for the work of civil defence were popular among Canadian civil defence experts, but failed to hold sway in the Cold War classroom. Contemplating either a quick death or life in a dying world, schoolchildren in 1961 London, Ontario, endorsed a communal vision of civil defence that would offer shelter to all citizens while also echoing the fatalism and cynicism of public debates.

Anecdotal evidence from Canadian public school classrooms points to a similar clash between the stated goals of civil defence – the cultivation of an emotional disposition of calm confidence and patriotic obedience – and the very real fears voiced by the young. According to Tarah Brookfield, "One Montreal grade-school teacher reported to *Maclean's* that many children in her class drew pictures of mushroom clouds and expressed fears of poisonous rain and snow. A survey of high-school students reported that teenage girls were afraid of having deformed babies and that boys were cynical about their futures because they believed them to be non-existent."[50] Children's voices manifested in other ways, particularly in letters from concerned parents to government officials. One such letter, written by Jack Kaufman after the *Montreal Star* ran a magazine feature about the practical challenges of building a fallout shelter, related his son's reaction: "my 12-year-old son called my attention to a feature article in the Montreal Star Weekend Magazine entitled 'Fall-out Shelters Are Not the Answer.' My son's comment was 'I guess you won't be bothering with that shelter business after you've read the article.' He's right! I won't bother. It is a rather futile and negative solution, defeatist rather than defensive on our part."[51] As Biess noted, a fearful or apathetic response like this, once taken to be a sign of defeatism, became more and more the norm by this time in the Cold War, and even became a path to protest.[52]

Children, like their parents, were political subjects whose reasoned commentary on contemporary affairs shaped family conversations. Though disempowered in the sphere of formal politics, they participated in the fallout shelter debates of the early 1960s and resisted the logic of civil defence plans. As the geographer Kirsi Pauliina Kallio suggests, it is by recalibrating the scale on which we search for children's politics that we can locate the "tactical agency" of the young and encounter children who act as "political selves."[53]

The Cuban Missile Crisis of October 1962 seemed to crystallize matters for the place of civil defence and settle Canadian priorities for survival. Most of the public had paid no attention to civil defence instructions, pamphlets, or programs, and during the superpower confrontation flooded the phones with inquiries about what to do. In some cases parents actually learned about what the plans for their cities were through their children, as school boards issued instructions and notices for children to take home with them, sparking outrage. In a memorable visual from the reporting during the crisis, Stan Williams, sixteen and then living in Scarborough, Ontario, began digging a shelter in his backyard with a shovel. Caralee Daigle Hau, in her dissertation about public perceptions of the Cuban Missile Crisis, refers to an account by a paperboy in North Vancouver: "Tall grey sirens appeared among the firs in my North Vancouver neighbourhood, and air raid drills were held at school. I was 12 and having bad dreams. The headlines on the newspapers I delivered had gone from grim to apocalyptic."[54] Peter Kvas, then very young and living in southwestern Ontario in a house with a shelter, recalled little about the shelter or the crisis, but vividly recalled dreams where he was supposed to get to the shelter and could not reach it.[55]

As the dust from the Cuban showdown settled, a nine-year-old girl in Downsview, Ontario, wrote an alarmed letter to the prime minister. She was agitated after seeing newspaper articles about the prospect of nuclear war. The answer from Diefenbaker's office was gentle but revealing: "You are asking a very serious question, so serious in fact that the discussion should be left to grownups while children like yourself should continue to be concerned with their studies and with the process of growing up and enjoying life, its games, and the pleasures of discovering the world around you."[56] Here, then, was the paradox of civilian preparations for war laid bare. Children were expected to be knowledgeable of the risks of nuclear war, yet deprived of the means to survive it if such a thing were possible.

At the same time, those taking direct interest in their own survival were told not to worry, that the adults had a plan. The adults did not.

Fear as a Catalyst for Social Change

The Cuban missile crisis ended. The Soviets withdrew their missiles from Cuba, in return for a similar American reduction of arms in Turkey. But the long shadow of nuclear weapons, and the bitter memory of how close world powers came to using them, lingered. In the 1960s, adult and youth voices were chilled, if only temporarily, by the oppressive anti-communist atmosphere pervading North America and Western Europe. This cloud suppressing dissent was pierced by community activists who wielded public health, and in particular children's health, as a shield against the march of the arms race.

An innocent rite of passage, the loss of baby teeth, assumed a more unsettling meaning when, in a gesture "both tender and macabre," Canadian mothers sent their children's baby teeth to the Baby Tooth Survey, an international investigation to determine the concentration of strontium-90, a radioactive isotope produced by atmospheric nuclear weapons tests, in children's bodies. Dr Ursula Franklin, one of the Canadian participants, worked with more than 45,000 donated baby teeth. The project demonstrated convincingly and irrefutably how nuclear tests had contaminated both the environment and the human race. This enormously successful scientific and public relations "child-centred" endeavour, managed in Canada by the Voice of Women, involved both parents and children, rewarding children for their participation with buttons and other ephemera, while simultaneously proving the immediate, local, and negative effects of nuclear tests, helping to move the needle of public opinion.[57]

The campaign also served to remind Canadian children of the terrifying prospect of nuclear warfare. As the historian Frank Biess has observed, we have to be mindful of "the temporality of emotions." "'Angst,'" he writes, "is defined as the anticipation of an undesirable event in the future that is believed to be likely to occur. This anticipation of the future, however, inevitably arises from memories of the past. Emotions project the past onto the future."[58] For the mothers who donated their children's baby teeth, the dreaded prospect of yet another global war – this one likely to wipe out humanity – likely evoked childhood and family memories of the Second World War. In turn, the children who participated in the campaign learned not only about the fragility of the future, but also the danger of the present. As Dr Franklin would find, there was already a two-fold increase in strontium-90 concentration in young children's bones, due to the increased levels of radiation in soil and milk.[59] In their very bodies and bones, children now carried the traces of radiation.

In the years following the Cuban Missile Crisis, the signature of the Partial Test Ban treaty in 1963, and the according decline of Cold War tensions, federal plans for nuclear war eventually were lumped in with "civil emergency" preparedness measures, and became part of a technocratic emergency preparedness strategy that put infrastructure and systems at its core instead of a dependence on civil participation. This, at least when it came to children's involvement in civil defence, was perhaps a reflection of reality. As the full implication of the arms race became clear, particularly the arrival of the intercontinental ballistic missiles (ICBM) that could deliver death and fallout without warning, the Boy Scouts withdrew the support of their members on practical grounds. Far from marshalling the youth to act as couriers in a nuclear wasteland, the Boy Scouts of Canada National Council concluded that adult Scout leaders would likely look after their families first and last, and as volunteers could not be assumed to be available in time of attack. The Emergency Measures Organization, which replaced Civil Defence Canada in 1958, in turn concluded that there was no need for Cub or Boy Scouts in nuclear attack. Accordingly, the Boy Scouts National Council determined: "as future citizens of the nation, and considering particularly radiation hazards at these ages, they should not be unduly exposed to radiation ... It is unlikely that Cubs and Scouts would be allowed, by their parents, to play an organized role in the event of nuclear attack."[60] With this practical conclusion in November 1962, the organized employment of youth in civil defence was effectively at an end.

Yet concern for children remained a central plank of the civil defence critic and the disarmament supporter throughout the late 1950s and early 1960s. The image of the distressed child, the anxious child, or the child or grandchild mutated by radiation figured heavily in public addresses, opinion editorials, or private correspondence of disarmament activists during this period. Concern for the figurative or symbolic child, as Tarah Brookfield and others have demonstrated, offered women in particular a maternal outlet to enter the traditionally male-dominated space of politics and protest.[61] Margaret Peacock similarly characterized the rhetorical and actual involvement of children in the disarmament campaign as "a revised image of the mobilized American child, prepared not for a war against communism but instead for a struggle against internal governmental forces that had put them at risk."[62] Nicole Marion, in her study of Canada's disarmers, convincingly expands on these arguments, suggesting that "parent-citizens" employed their guardianship of their own children to stake a claim in Cold War politics.[63] As Brookfield discusses in her contribution to this volume, children were frequently present at anti-war or disarmament meetings and protests, in part because their presence was useful in emphasizing the "maternal" nature of opposition to nuclear weapons, or, practically, because no other childcare option was available. Articulated mostly by parents, the role of the mobilized child would grow as Cold War orthodoxies further relaxed through the 1970s.[64]

Youth participation in civil defence schemes fell by the wayside through the 1960s, out of practical concern and largely as a consequence of placing the responsibility for survival on the family unit rather than the community as a whole. It would not be for another generation that youth voices helped shape responses on nuclear weapons in Canada. As Lawrence Wittner recounts in his extensive history of the disarmament movement, the 1970s, termed the "Disarmament Decade" by the United Nations, was anything but. The coherent message and solidarity of activists that had been evident during protests against nuclear testing fizzled in the 1970s, as organizations in North America turned their attention to protesting the Vietnam War. As antinuclear organizations limped along, the superpowers used the breathing space provided by détente to develop more advanced nuclear weapons and delivery systems. The movement against these weapons and their effects did not resume in earnest until well after the spectacular end of the Vietnam War.[65] What likely did not dissipate, however, was the growing sense of futility of preparations and in some cases even daily life among youth confronted with the existential crisis of the bomb. In the United States, the trend towards this feeling of helplessness was articulated by a participant at a 1960 White House conference on children and youth: "I'm part of a generation that is faced with evidence daily that the H-bomb may drop tomorrow. We need something that life is worth something – has meaning."[66]

By the 1980s, youth voices on nuclear issues became more readily discernible, especially amidst the backdrop of the gathering clouds of the so-called "New Cold War" confrontation following the Soviet Union's invasion of Afghanistan, and public demonstrations against the introduction of new missiles in Europe, and the rollout of massively successful (and very frightening) television simulations of nuclear war. These included projects like *The Day After* (1983) and *Threads* (1985), which garnered huge audiences in North America and the United Kingdom respectively. The made-for-television films followed ordinary citizens as they survived the initial stages of nuclear war, with then-realistic depictions of widespread devastation, fires, and destruction. The viewer followed the survivors as they became enfeebled with radiation sickness, or fell victim to roving bands of looters in the post-apocalyptic landscape. As Tarah Brookfield indicates in her analysis of post-apocalyptic film, *The Day After* and *Threads* both were remarkable in that they showed graphic examples of children either dying or suffering, a testament to the very real likelihood that the most fragile among the civilian population would be the first to die as the result of a nuclear exchange.[67] Shows like *The Day After* divided experts about the wisdom of letting children see them. In the United States, a representative of the organization Educators for Social Responsibility urged families to watch the film together: "The threat of nuclear war is real, millions of children are aware of the danger and parents can't reassure children that this is a fictional situation." Kenneth Porter, a family therapist, urged families to discuss these productions, "and not let television do the talking and feeling for them. If they do that, they'll lock feelings of despair and fatalism inside them."[68] In Canada, Physicians for Social Responsibility urged Canadians to sign petitions in support of then prime minister Pierre Elliot Trudeau's so-called "peace tour," citing that *The Day After* would help people better imagine the effects of nuclear war.[69] The film, perhaps serving as a *memento mori*, certainly seemed to serve that purpose. Companies selling fourteen-day emergency food kits saw a sharp spike in demand, officials at Emergency Planning Canada offices screened as many as 110 calls a day from Canadians seeking survival advice in the film's aftermath.[70]

Some children, raised in the era of the televised bomb, had all too little difficulty imagining the effects of nuclear war. In a survey of high school students in Edmonton, Alberta, 71 per cent considered nuclear war a "very important worry." They only feared the death of their parents more. Alexandra Samuel, who was thirteen when she first understood the capabilities of the bomb, was plagued by vivid nightmares. "I am left alive," she described, "to figure out what is left of Toronto and the world ... I have seen the dead bodies of people I really know, but am scarcely able to recognize." Writing for the school newspaper, which she founded, Samuel reflected that surveys suggested that 2 per cent of her peers suffered the same disruption in their sleep. She wondered whether films like *The Day After* or dystopic fiction caused the problem, or whether "the works exacerbate what is already a disproportionately great fear?" She expressed the impact these visions of war had on her psyche with profound insight: "When I wake up after one of these nightmares, I can't simply have a glass of water and go back to sleep. I am haunted by the thought that every horrible moment I have just imagined could be revisited upon me in reality. And it is with real sadness that I consider just what kind of world we live in that a 17-year-old girl can picture the destruction of her friends, family, and society, and nobody can tell her that it is only a bad dream."[71]

Samuel's reflections in her student newspaper were picked up by the *Globe and Mail* in 1988. Samuel found that writing about her nightmares helped cure them, and she worked through her nuclear anxiety by becoming involved in anti-nuclear activism and the disarmament movement. After she graduated she spent six months working with Rosalie Bertell, a sister of the Grey Nuns, and an expert on the effects of radiation whose advocacy gained her the moniker of the "anti-nuclear nun."[72]

Other young Canadians similarly sought an escape from the Cold War deadlock through activism and public education. One of the most acclaimed Canadian productions during this same time frame, the National Film Board's 1982 film *If You Love This Planet*, was, like *The Day After*, hotly debated. Directed by Terre Nash, and featuring a lecture by activist Dr Helen Caldicott to university students against the backdrop of archival footage of the bombing of Hiroshima and Nagasaki, the film received an Academy Award for Documentary Short Subject, and received a wide viewing in schools across the country. The film proved particularly useful for four Montreal youths. In 1986, Bonnie Sherr Klein travelled to London, Ontario, for an Ontario-wide youth peace conference with her film *Speaking Our Peace* (1985), co-directed with Terre Nash, which focused on women's involvement in international peace initiatives. Another panellist at the conference was her eighteen-year-old son, Seth Klein, with his friend Maxime Faille, seventeen, who were youth activists with Students against Global Extermination (SAGE) in Montreal. Inspired by the energy at the conference, Maxime and Seth considered spreading their hopes for disarmament via some kind of tour. They shared their ideas with fellow activists Désirée McGraw, sixteen, and Alison Carpenter, seventeen, and together they worked to raise funds to develop, promote, and carry out the 1986–87 Youth Nuclear Disarmament Tour.[73] The Canadian Institute for International Peace and Security (CIPS), a government-funded think tank established in 1984, provided the seed money for the venture after receiving SAGE's proposal. Though the young activists were surprised that their application was accepted, they perhaps should not have been – as CIPS executive director and former ambassador to the Soviet Union Geoffrey Pearson affirmed, "it is young people who will carry the burden of finding fresh ideas and approaches to peace and security."[74]

After months of preparation, local and national fundraising, and assembling educational material, Klein, Faille, McGraw, and Carpenter set out on 20 September 1986 in a 1980 Ford LTD to begin touring schools across the country to persuade schools to take a firm stance against nuclear arms, and to encourage communities to support efforts to declare a "nuclear weapons free zone," in the style of communities in New Zealand that had done the same. They ultimately visited 162 communities and 350 schools in Canada through 1987, as well as San Francisco and Moscow, speaking to and with some 120,000 students. Their exploits were eventually compiled in Barbara Klein's film: *Mile Zero: The Sage Tour*.[75] Their success in getting into schools, and the positive response their visits purportedly received shows how much the climate had changed from the 1950s, when acceptance of nuclear weapons and their consequences was the predominant norm, to the 1980s, by which time the disarmament movement's young activists were allowed into the schools. In just a short two years following the end of the tour, the Berlin Wall fell, the Cold War ended, and the path forward seemed bright. Children had survived the Cold War. But then, so did the weapons.[76]

Conclusion

As Carolyn Kay and Barbara Lorenzkowski demonstrate in earlier chapters of this volume, children and youth in early-twentieth-century Germany learned about the First World War through the visual language of art-making, while children in 1940s Atlantic Canada made sense of the wartime world through sound. In turn, lessons in civil defence for children in Cold War Canada involved a course in emotional regimes. While much of the civil defence training for adults was built around the idea of preventing panic, which would clog roads and would get people killed in an emergency, defence exercises for children focused on emotional formation. The emotional disposition that civil defence planners sought to inculcate, through advice offered to school principals and teachers, and practised through school or community exercises, was one where obedience, confidence, and calm attributes overcame panic, fear, and apathy. Those who were distraught by the prospect of nuclear war were reassured, in many cases falsely, that matters were under control and that they would be taken care of. But the means for survival were never there. There were no spaces for children to safely run to, be they community fallout shelters or private home shelters, not in any number sufficient to respond to the need. Children and youth were not blind to this disparity – in letters, in discussions at home, in private, they noted that not all would be able to survive. In time, some questioned whether they would even want to, and fear, not obedience or calm or reassurance, was the common response during periods of exceptional and existential crisis such as the Cuban Missile Crisis. Some children channelled this anxiety into more constructive outlets, guided by scientists, disarmament activists and critics of the Cold War arms race. As the détente of the 1970s gave way to the frightening "New Cold War" of the 1980s, children in greater numbers expressed their concern with world events and direction more vocally, and broke out of the emotional regimes set for them by the orthodoxies of the Cold War rivalry, in defiance of the shadow cast over their short lives by the atomic bomb and its depictions in popular media.

NOTES

1 "'Bomb-Blasted' Manor Park Schoolroom for CD Wardens," Ottawa *Evening Journal*, 8 May 1953.
2 See for example Brookfield, *Cold War Comforts*; Boyer, *By the Bomb's Early Light*; McIlroy, "No Interest, No Time, No Money"; McEnany, *Civil Defense Begins at Home*; Barker-Devine, "Mightier than Missiles"; Davis, *Stages of Emergency*; Reilly, "Operation Lifesaver"; and Singer, "Civil Defence in the City."
3 May, *Homeward Bound*, 9–18.
4 Brookfield, *Cold War Comforts*, 66.
5 Biess, "'Everybody Has a Chance': Nuclear Angst, Civil Defence, and the History of Emotions in Postwar Germany," 217. See also Stearns, *American Fear*, Stearns, "Fear and Contemporary History," 477–84, and Boucher, "Anticipating Armageddon," 1221–45.
6 Reddy, *The Navigation of Feeling*, 47. See also the concept of "emotional standards" as developed by Stearns and Stearns, "Emotionology," 813–36.
7 I thank my colleague and co-editor Kristine Alexander for this insight. For more on panic prevention, see Burtch, *Give Me Shelter*, 84–5.
8 Biess, "'Everybody Has a Chance,'" 218.
9 Vallgårda, Alexander, and Olsen, "Emotions and the Global Politics of Childhood," 25.
10 Holt, *Cold War Kids*, 19–20. See also Grieve, *Little Cold Warriors*.
11 Peacock, *Innocent Weapons*, 37.
12 Burtch, *Give Me Shelter*, 26–30.

13 Brookfield, *Cold War Comforts*, 32.
14 "Criticisms of A-Bomb Drill Are Not Shared by Public – Over 8 in Ten in Large Centres Favor School Training." Canadian Institute of Public Opinion, 25 June 1952. Library and Archives Canada (LAC), National Health and Welfare Fonds, RG 29, Volume 56, File 100-5-13 pt.1
15 For more on the early stages of Cold War Civil Defence, see Burtch, *Give Me Shelter*, 17–20. See also Davidson, "Preparing for the Bomb," 29–31.
16 Correspondence from F.F. Worthington to Information Services, 12 May 1952. LAC, National Health and Welfare Fonds, RG 29, Volume 56, File 100-5-1.
17 National Health and Welfare, *Civil Defence in Schools*, 3.
18 Ibid., 4.
19 Ibid., 6.
20 Ibid., 8.
21 For a thorough account of the film's creation and reception in the United States, please see Bill Geerhart, "The Citizen Kane of Civil Defense: Duck and Cover." CONELRAD: *All Things Atomic*. http://www.conelrad.com/duckandcover/cover.php?turtle=01.
22 "The Educational Authorities of St Catharines, Ontario Back Civil Defence," *School Progress* (May 1955): 31–3.
23 Gleason, *Normalizing the Ideal*, 125–39.
24 Report to City Council of Moose Jaw by Louis H. Lewry, Mayor, 4 December 1950, LAC, National Health and Welfare Fonds, RG 29, Volume 704, File 110-7-1 pt. 1.
25 Correspondence from M.P. Cawdron to J.O. Probe, 10 April 1951, LAC, National Health and Welfare Fonds, RG 29, Volume 704, File 110-7-1 pt. 1
26 Ibid., Correspondence from Probe to Cawdron, 14 April 1951.
27 For more information about CD's funding problems, see Burtch, *Give Me Shelter*, 37–57. Correspondence from Study to Martin, 1 August 1951, Library and Archives Canada, National Health and Welfare Fonds, RG 29, Volume 704, File 110-7-1 pt. 1.
28 *Saskatchewan Civil Defence Bulletin no. 24*, 13 May 1955, LAC, National Health and Welfare Fonds, RG 29, Volume 705, File 110-7-1 pt. 2
29 Glassford, *Mobilizing Mercy*, 253–5.
30 Role of National Organizations in Civil Defence, Appendix D, 10 March 1951, LAC, National Health and Welfare Fonds, RG 29, Volume 676, File 108-3-3.
31 Correspondence from H.G. Stevens, Chairman of Provincial Civil Defence Sub-Committee for Boy Scouts to Dewolfe, 20 September 1951, LAC, National Health and Welfare Fonds, RG 29 Volume 696, File 110-2-1 pt. 1

Canadian Children in Civil Defence Planning

32 Correspondence from Mrs D.E.S. Wishart to Worthington, 20 June 1951, LAC, National Health and Welfare Fonds, RG 29, Volume 676, File 108-3-3.
33 Correspondence from Bailey to Wishart, 28 March 1952. Ibid.
34 Burtch, "Armaggedon on Tour," 750.
35 Kallio and Häkli, "Are There Politics in Childhood?," 27–8.
36 Graff, *Raven Rock*, 49.
37 Stearns, *American Fear*, 175–7.
38 Burtch, *Give Me Shelter*, 171–2.
39 Lichtman, "Do-It-Yourself Security," 42–3.
40 "No CD Plan for Pupils If Atom Attack Comes," *Globe and Mail*, 14 November 1956; "No Disaster Plan for City Children," *Globe and Mail*, 7 June 1957.
41 Memo to SAO from Deputy Federal Civil Defence Coordinator, 11 December 1956. LAC, National Health and Welfare Fonds, RG 29, Volume 703, File 110-5-16.
42 Correspondence from Stephen and Mary Leskard to Diefenbaker, 5 May 1961. LAC, John Diefenbaker Fonds, MG 26 M, 7810 Volume 48 File 140 Toscin - Civil Defence–General – Exercise Tocsin 1961, P. 94079-940980.
43 Brookfield, *Cold War Comforts*, 59, 63.
44 Report to Regional Officer 348, 7 December 1962, LAC, John F. Wallace Fonds, MG 30 E211, Volume 3, File 3–4.
45 Correspondence from George Burnham to Diefenbaker, 17 November 1961, LAC, John Diefenbaker Fonds, MG 26 M, 7810 Volume 48 File. 140 Tocsin – Civil Defence – General – Exercise Tocsin 1961: 41826-41829.
46 Ibid., correspondence from Norma Jackson to Diefenbaker, 10 November 1961.
47 See Mushynsky, "Don't Talk about Your Fallout Shelter," 1–35.
48 Stephen Thorne, personal correspondence with author, 24 January 2018.
49 "Pupils Decry Shelter Need," *London Free Press*, 25 November 1961.
50 Brookfield, *Cold War Comforts*, 44.
51 Correspondence from Jack Kaufman to John Diefenbaker, 18 November 1961, LAC, John Diefenbaker Fonds, MG 26 M, Volume 49, File 141 Shelters Civil Defence – Federal Civil Defence Plans and Organizations – Shelters – Nov. 1961–1962, 41736–41740
52 Biess, "Everybody Has a Chance," 242.
53 Kallio, "The Body as a Battlefield," 285, 291–2. For a discussion of children's "political selves" see Philo and Smith, "Political Geographies of Children and Young People," 110.
54 John Moore, "I Was Castro's Paperboy," *Vancouver Sun*, 4 November 2000, as quoted in Hau, "A Challenge and a Danger," 281.

55 Peter Kvas, interview by author, 20 March 2018.
56 Ellen Davis to Diefenbaker and Reply, 11 November 1962. LAC MG 26 M John Diefenbaker Fonds, Vol. 49 file 141 Shelters Civil Defence – Federal Civil Defence Plans and Organizations – Shelters – Nov 1961–62.
57 See Marion, *Canada's Disarmers*, 147–53, and Peacock, *Innocent Weapons*, 164–5.
58 Biess, "'Everybody Has a Chance,'" 218.
59 Brookfield, *Cold War Comforts*, 72.
60 Boy Scouts of Canada National Council Report, November 1962, LAC, John F. Wallace Fonds, MG 30 E211, Volume 3, File 3-11.
61 Brookfield, *Cold War Comforts*, 3.
62 Peacock, *Innocent Weapons*, 161–2.
63 See in particular chapter 3 of Marion, *Canada's Disarmers*, 116–61.
64 Peacock, *Innocent Weapons*, 161–2.
65 Wittner, *Toward Nuclear Abolition*, 13, 33.
66 As quoted in Holt, *Cold War Kids*, 27.
67 Brookfield, "Until the World Deserves Them," 138.
68 Glenn Collins, "The Impact on Children of *The Day After*," *New York Times*, 7 November 1983.
69 "Back PM, Film Viewers Are Urged," *Globe and Mail*, 22 November 1983.
70 Bill MacVicar, "Harbingers of Holocaust," *Globe and Mail*, 17 November 1984; Vincent Blain, "They're Doing Their Best to Prepare for the Worst," *Globe and Mail*, 8 December 1983.
71 Alexandra Samuel, "Now I Lay Me Down to Sleep," *Globe and Mail*, 21 May 1988.
72 Alexandra Samuel, interview by author, 9 September 2019. See also "Rosalie Bertell, Anti-Nuclear Nun (1929–2012)," *Peace Magazine* Oct–Dec 2012, 22. http://peacemagazine.org/archive/v28n4p22.htm. Accessed 9 September 2019.
73 "The Youth Nuclear Disarmament Tour in the Making: May–September 1986," Canadian War Museum, George Metcalf Archival Collection, CWM 19940004-184
74 Pearson, "Canadian Institute for International Peace and Security," 190.
75 In 2015, Désirée McGraw became the president of Pearson College on Vancouver Island, one of the SAGE tour's final stops. At her appointment, the college played the film of her 1987 visit to the college. *Mile Zero: The SAGE Tour*, https://www.youtube.com/watch?time_continue=160&v=Pt4gA_6BUw4. Accessed 8 February 2018.
76 This turn of phrase comes from the Cosford Royal Air Force Museum's presentation on anti-nuclear demonstrations, which ends with this chilling conclusion.

PART TWO
FAMILY AND COMMUNITY

Figure 1.2
Flags of Prussia, Germany, Austria, and the Ottoman Empire. Elfriede Taube, age eleven, Lyzeum Berlin Pankow, 1915.

Figure 1.3
German and French soldiers in combat. Martha Dieckmann, age twelve, Wilhelmsburg III, 1915.

Figure 1.7
Inept French troops face superior German soldiers. W. Bade, age twelve, Wilhelmsburg III, 1915.

Figure 1.8
German soldiers, behind barbed wire, fire on French soldiers. W. Regutzki, age twelve, Wilhelmsburg III, 1915.

Figure 1.12
German airplanes attack. W. Regutzki, age twelve, Wilhelmsburg III, 1915.

Figure 1.14
The caring nurse. Ella Bostelmann, age twelve, Wilhelmsburg III, 1915.

Figure 1.17
A nurse carrying a soldier with a head wound. A. Scharweit, age fourteen, Wilhelmsburg III, 1915.

Figure 1.19
German Zeppelins and aircraft attack and kill civilians in a French village.
G. Gerns, age ten, Wilhelmsburg III, 1915.

Figure 9.1
Drawing by a child in immigration detention. This depiction of a sad crying girl behind bars is striking, and symbolically encompasses the dominant idea of an innocent and vulnerable child.

Figure 9.7
Fenced-in lives. The border of this drawing is also the fence that contains the detention facility, creating a sense of an enclosed and confined site. The two people depicted are sad and crying.

Figure 10.1
"Just a Baby's Letter Found in No Man's Land."

Figure 10.2
"A Message to Daddy."

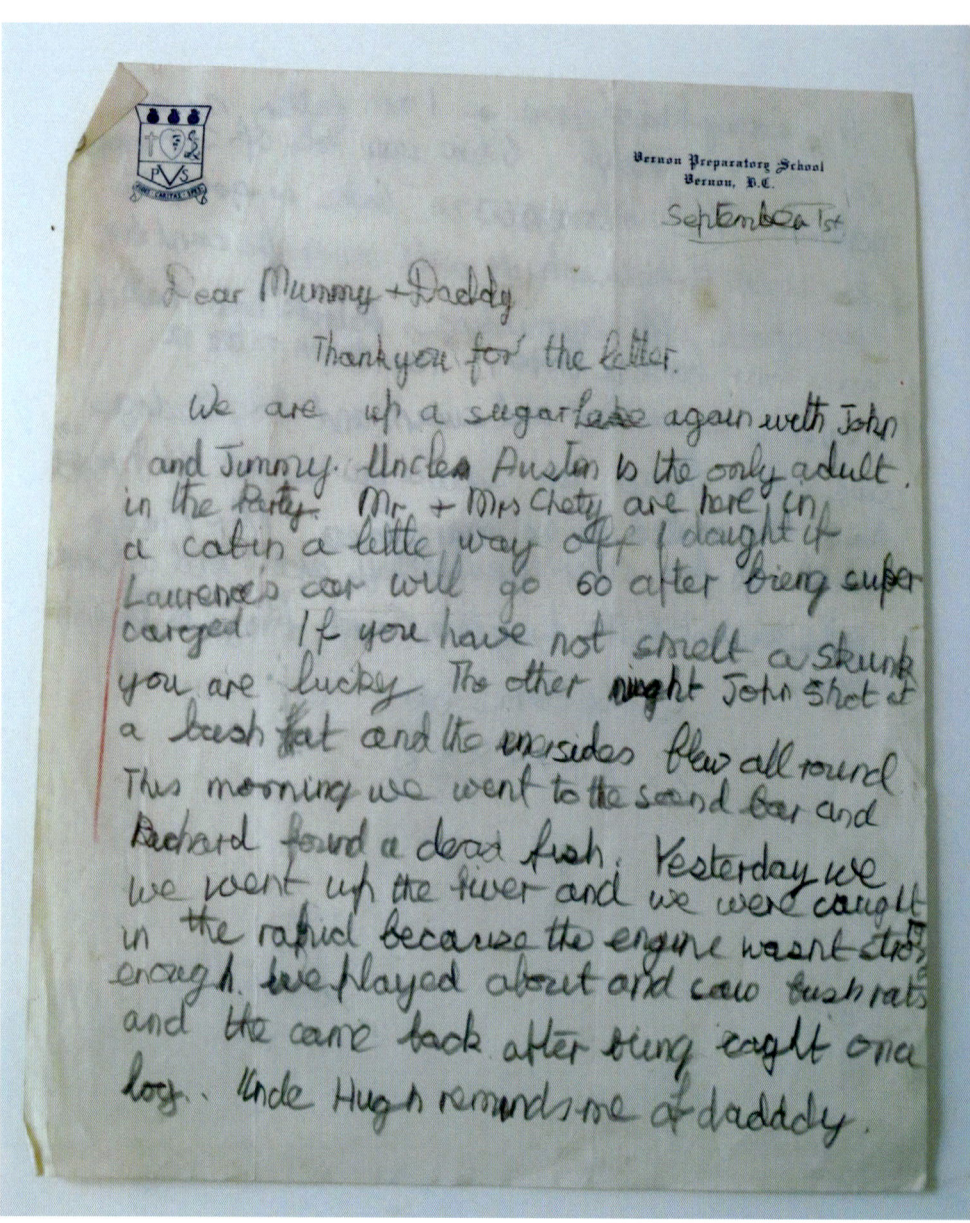

Figure 11.2
Letter from Owen Mackie to his parents, 1 September 1940.

My cough has gone + I am better. Ropers is 10d or a bob!- We've seen lots of chip mongers. The meadow is lake is going to be risen 5 feet which will cover the sand bar and spoil all surrounding. Patrick has made a boat our boat a broken. Term begin on the 12. We went to cousens Burt and swam and lots the dogs and other things. We saw a musk rat. Kit Brays has been visited by us many times. Mr Fraser came up for super yesterday and I had a head ache we went to the Laytons and played Monoply.

Love From Owen

xxx xxxxxxx

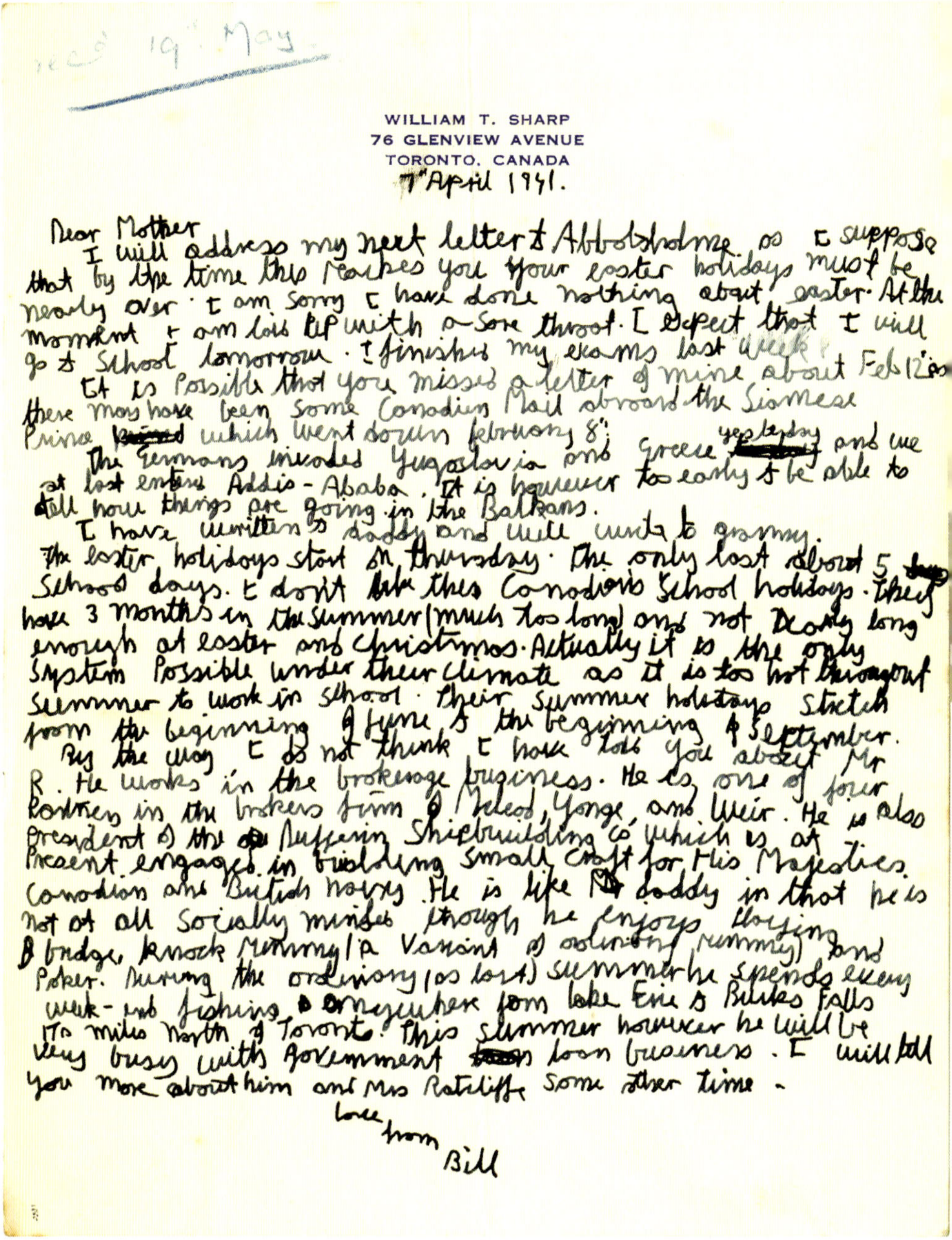

rec'd 19th May.

WILLIAM T. SHARP
76 GLENVIEW AVENUE
TORONTO, CANADA
7th April 1941.

Dear Mother
I will address my next letter to Abbotsholme as I suppose that by the time this reaches you your easter holidays must be nearly over. I am sorry I have done nothing about easter. At the moment I am laid up with a sore throat. I expect that I will go to school tomorrow. I finished my exams last week.

It is possible that you missed a letter of mine about Feb 12 as there may have been some Canadian Mail aboard the Siamese Prince which went down february 8th. yesterday and we

The Germans invaded Yugoslavia and Greece and we at last entered Addis-Ababa. It is however too early to be able to tell how things are going in the Balkans.

I have written to daddy and will write to grammy. The easter holidays start on thursday. We only lost about 5 school days. I don't like this Canadian's school holidays. They have 3 months in the summer (much too long) and not nearly long enough at easter and christmas. Actually it is the only system possible under their climate as it is too hot throughout summer to work in school. Their summer holidays stretch from the beginning of June to the beginning of September.

By the way I do not think I have told you about Mr R. He works in the brokerage business. He is one of four partners in the brokers firm of McLeod, Young, and Weir. He is also president of the Dufferin Shipbuilding Co which is at present engaged in building small craft for His Majesties Canadian and British navys. He is like daddy in that he is not at all socially minded though he enjoys playing bridge, knock (rummy/a variant of ordinary rummy) and poker. During the ordinary (as lost) summer he spends every week-end fishing everywhere from lake Erie to Burks Falls 175 miles north of Toronto. This summer however he will be very busy with government loan business. I will tell you more about him and Mrs Ratcliffe some other time.

Love from
Bill

Figure 11.5
Letter by Bill Sharp, 7 April 1941.

Figure 13.3
"Stabilization Force (SFOR) patrol." Artist name illegible.

Figure 13.4
"We survived the war, survive the peace!" Artist unknown

Figure 14.3
In Memory. Leontine throws petals into the St Lawrence River in memory of her family.

Figure 15.1 This page and following page
"Steven the Donkey" – The Story of Sunday Garang, from *Donkeys Can't Fly on Planes: Stories of Survival from South Sudanese Refugee Children Living in Australia* (Melbourne: Kids' Own Publishing, 2012), 4–5.

Steven the donkey
The Story of Sunday Garang

I was born in a refugee camp named Kakuma, in Kenya. In the camp, our life was difficult. We had no pillows but we all had a blanket. My family also had a very special helper. It was a small donkey named Steven.

The camp was a sad place to be because there was usually no food to eat. When my family and the other families had no food to eat, we would begin to starve. Starving feels like when you are so hungry your tummy hurts. It makes rumbling sounds inside you that can go on for a very long time. We had nothing really to feed Steven either.

When I was starving, I could not cry because I did not have enough energy to make the crying sound or to squeeze tears from my eyes. When we went to bed hungry, my mum would try to make us feel better. She would say, "There is food growing right now while we sleep. It will be ready soon." She was right because we had been given some seeds to grow. There were carrot seeds and some other vegetables. I did not want to go to sleep while the food was growing.

Sometimes I would drink from my mother. She made her own milk for me but she needed to eat food to make the milk. We did have a lot of water in the camp. I would climb on Steven and he would take me to collect the water for the people. I liked to put the water that Steven collected on to the vegetables to help them to grow. Everyone took great care of the growing vegetables

I could go on my own because the well was not too far away. It would take about twenty minutes to get there but I knew a shortcut and I could get there in about five minutes. I always took the shortcut because I would gather water many times in one day. I would give water to people for drinking, for people who were starving and sometimes for cooking.

I tried very hard to always be back in the camp before it got too late. If I got home late my mum would get cross with me because if you are a little girl on your own in the dark, someone might kill you.

When we came to Australia, I had to leave Steven behind. Donkeys can't fly on planes. I miss him but now he is helping my cousin's family to collect water for the people in Kakuma. I hope the people who have Steven remember to take the shortcut.

Figure 15.2 This page and following page
"A Problem for My Mum" – The Story of Nyater, from *In My Kingdom: South Sudanese Parents' Stories for their Children in Australia* (Melbourne: Kids' Own Publishing, 2014), 8–9.

cut my brothers. Every time, I would go together with them when they needed to go into the bush. And I would carry Nyalang all the time on my back and I'm just little.

One day when my mum returned home, I became very upset because I could see a problem for my mum when she put the big bag of corn on the ground, I noticed that all of the hair from the top of my mum's head had gone from carrying the corn. I'm really upset. I see she is bald on top of her head. I cried and cried. I said, "Mum, I'm sorry. Maybe I'm a big girl. Better for me to go next time, not you".

Her hair is gone! Gone!

Mum cooked a little bit of corn and she kept the rest in her room. She would cook a little bit at a time. She said to us, "My children, this corn can never finish. When this corn has finished, we might never get food again. We now must go to Ethiopia. We can't stay here. We need to go."

In 1994, we went back to Ethiopia because the war is always, always, always...

When I read this story about my mum I felt sad because they didn't have any food and I was surprised that my grandma walked 100 miles. I feel proud of her to walk all the way to survive and to do this for her family.
Nyakuan

4

Children, Soldiers, and Correspondence in Canada's First World War

Kristine Alexander and Ashley Henrickson

Throughout the First World War, crowds of men, women, and children gathered at railway stations across Canada to celebrate and bid farewell to groups of newly enlisted soldiers. These departure scenes, captured by professional and amateur photographers alike, represent an instant frozen in time: the last moment of visual contact between men in uniform and their wives, children, siblings, and aging parents.

Images like these are compelling reminders of the optimism and patriotic enthusiasm that swept across many Canadian communities during the early months of the war. At the same time, however, it is also possible to imagine that the soldiers and civilians captured in these photographs were uncertain and fearful about the immediate prospect of family separation as well as the future possibility of injury and death.

The experience of watching fathers and brothers leave for army training and, eventually, the dangers of the trenches evoked a range of complicated emotions in children who were left behind. One young correspondent wrote to the children's page of the *Family Herald and Weekly Star*, a popular Canadian periodical, that his experience at a British Columbia railway station had caused him to take greater notice of the war being fought overseas. "I take interest in [the war]," he wrote, "because two brothers of mine have joined the army. It was hard for us ... to part with them. We may never see them again. At the station the platform was crowded with people. We sang 'Rule Britannia,' 'The Maple Leaf Forever and 'Auld Lang Syne.'"[1]

Historians of the Second World War have shown how civilians who were children during that conflict often remember the war as causing a sudden and

Figure 4.1
Crowds waving goodbye to troops at a Vancouver train station, by James Quiney. Control no. CVA 7-143, City of Vancouver Archives.

irreversible shift in their daily lives and ways of understanding the world.[2] The First World War in general – and the departure of male relatives in particular – was a similar moment of rupture for Canadian youngsters, characterized by disruptions to family life, economic and material hardships, and new emotional and practical responsibilities. Yet despite a recent flurry of publications about how the war shaped Canadian young people's reading, education, and voluntary work, there remains surprisingly little scholarship about the children and families of Canadian soldiers.[3] In part, this imbalance can be explained as a result of the evidential challenges that are often faced by historians of childhood: most archival collections, in Canada as elsewhere, privilege and preserve the perspectives and voices of adults, and it therefore unsurprising that adult-produced and prescriptive sources like children's literature, curriculum documents, and the records of charities and youth organizations continue to dominate historical analyses of young people in wartime.[4]

The particular lack of research about how the First World War shaped Canadian children's emotional and family lives is also a reflection of how past generations of historians understood and approached their primary sources. In the preface to *Fight or Pay*, his valuable 1993 study of the Canadian Patriotic Fund, Desmond Morton wrote that despite his original intentions, he had been unable to produce a book about Great War soldiers' wives and families because "the sources for this story had largely been obliterated."[5] Morton was referring, of course, to the fact that unlike soldiers' letters, most of the correspondence that had been sent to them by their family members on the home front has not survived. His statement is grounded in the assumption that it is impossible to write the history of individuals who did not leave their own written records. Over the past several decades, however, scholars have revealed the limits of this approach to research by reading sources along and against the grain to produce important insights about the histories of (for example) enslaved peoples, women, and the poor.

While a small number of letters written by children to their soldier fathers have been preserved in archives across Canada (see chapter 10, "Dear Daddy: Children, Writing, and the First World War" in this volume), it is possible to paint a longer-term picture of Canadian children's lives during the war by considering a much larger body of archival evidence: the letters that soldiers sent home to their families, thousands of which have been preserved in public archives, online repositories, and private collections across the country. These wartime letters are significant moments where non-elite families enter the historical record. In the context of First World War Canada, this was the result of the convergence of a particular set of circumstances, including high literacy rates thanks to compulsory elementary education in every province save Quebec. Wartime separations also caused people to write who would not normally have done so, and the sense that these letters were important – whether as traces of a lost loved one or because they connected one's family history to national and world events – led families to save them.

At the same time, however, many historians of the war have engaged with epistolary sources in only limited ways, by mining them for facts and anecdotes while insisting that censorship ultimately compromised their usefulness. In his enormously influential 1975 book *The Great War and Modern Memory*, for example, Paul Fussell asserted that most soldiers sought "to fill the page[s] [of their letters home] by saying nothing and offering the maximum number of clichés."[6] Fussell's approach was based on the belief that there was a fundamental and unbridgeable gap of communication and experience between soldiers at the front and their loved ones at home. His work, combined with popular assumptions about official and self-censorship, led a number of late twentieth-century historians to insist that soldiers' letters could only ever be of limited scholarly use. More recent research, however, has undermined this assumption by revealing that wartime correspondence actually offers rich insights about (among other things) gender, subjectivity, and the emotions, as well as about relationships between soldiers and their mothers, sweethearts, and wives.[7]

Less commented on in this recent work, but no less important, are the insights these letters can provide about Canadian soldiers' children – an understudied group of civilians who have been described in one study as "silent casualties of a war fought halfway around the world."[8] One of our aims, then, is to complicate this picture of silence and passivity by using wartime family letters to ask what the experience of "waiting" on the home front actually entailed for young people. Like Michael Roper, we believe in the importance of analyzing both material and linguistic factors to gain a better understanding "of the practices of everyday life; of human experience formed through emotional relationships with others; and of that experience as involving a perpetual process of managing emotional impulses, both conscious and unconscious, within the self and in relation to others."[9]

This chapter takes a microhistorical approach to these questions by analyzing substantial collections of letters written by three Canadian soldiers to their wives and children during the First World War: François-Xavier (Frank) Maheux, a French-Canadian logger from the Ottawa Valley; Lawrence Rogers, an English-Canadian farmer from Quebec's Eastern Townships; and Sidney Brook, an English immigrant who owned a homestead near the central Alberta village of Craigmyle.[10] Unusually, the letters Sidney Brook received from his wife and children have also survived (we suspect he mailed and brought them in person to his siblings in England at various points throughout the war), and our analysis considers these sources as well. All three collections comprise hundreds of pages of handwritten correspondence sent from Canada, England, France, Belgium, and in one case, Russia, during paternal absences that ranged from two to five years. Together, they are examples of what Martyn Lyons calls the "democratization of writing" that took place during the nineteenth and early twentieth centuries: an unprecedented outpouring of correspondence prompted by emigration from Europe and the First World War, global phenomena that separated millions of people from their families for extended periods of time.[11]

In 1914, François-Xavier (Frank) Maheux was a forty-two-year-old French-Canadian logger and veteran of the South African War. He lived in a log cabin (or "shanty") with his wife Angelique – an Odawa woman – and their children in the

Ottawa Valley town of Baskatong Bridge. Frank Maheux enlisted soon after the war began, joining the Second Contingent of the Canadian Expeditionary Force in Ottawa in November 1914. Private (and later Sergeant) Maheux fought at the Somme, Vimy, and Passchendaele, and he travelled to post-revolutionary Russia as part of the Allied intervention in Murmansk before returning to his home and family in 1919. His letters, peppered with improvised spelling and irregular grammar, have been quoted by numerous Canadian military historians, and they appear in the footnotes of books and articles about the battles of the St Eloi Craters and Vimy Ridge, soldiers' stories of the supernatural, the experience of being gassed, self-inflicted wounds, and the killing of German prisoners.[12]

In a 1992 article about Frank Maheux's wartime experience, Desmond Morton wrote that his letters "appear to make reference to" three children.[13] A closer reading of his correspondence, however, reveals that Maheux was actually a father of five. In 1914, Frank and Angelique Maheux's children included two sons, eight-year-old Petuwise and five-year-old Freddy, daughters Condy (seven) and Dolly (two), as well as an infant girl (referred to mostly as "the baby"), who was born shortly before Frank's enlistment. Frank Maheux addressed each of his sons and daughters in writing throughout the war, both individually and in specific passages in letters that usually began with the phrase "To my dear wife and children." His correspondence was carefully preserved by his family after the war, and was donated to the Canadian national archives by Grace Maheux, one of several children born to Frank and Angelique after his return to Canada, in 1977.

The second set of letters on which this chapter is based were written by an English Canadian named Lawrence Rogers. Before joining the 5th Canadian Mounted Rifles in February 1915, when he was thirty-seven, Rogers lived with his wife May and children Aileen (age ten) and Howard (seven) on their farm near the town of Cowansville in southeastern Quebec. He wrote regularly to his son and daughter, both individually and in letters addressed to May, throughout the war. A small teddy bear he took with him to the Western Front – a gift from Aileen – can now be seen in the Canadian War Museum's First World War Gallery. Lawrence Rogers kept his daughter's bear with him during his army training in Canada and while working as a stretcher bearer in France and Belgium, and it was in his pocket when he was killed during the Battle of Passchendaele in October 1917. The bear, along with the letters Rogers sent home to his family, received national media coverage nearly a century later when they were donated to the Canadian War Museum in 2003 through an initiative organized by the Dominion Institute and the *Globe and Mail*.[14] These artefacts and documents have been discussed in several scholarly articles, and are the subjects of two children's books written by Lawrence and May Rogers's great-granddaughter Stephanie Innes.[15]

Third and finally, this chapter also analyzes the letters exchanged between 1916 and 1918 by Sidney Brook and his wife Isabelle and their children. Brook, a forty-five-year-old English immigrant who owned a homestead near the central Alberta village of Craigmyle, enlisted in May 1916, leaving behind four sons: eight-year-old Gordon, six-year-old Arnott, four-year-old Lorne, and two-year-old Glen. Isabelle was pregnant at this point, and she gave birth to a daughter, Alice May, several months after her husband's departure. Sidney Brook wrote regularly to Isabelle and their children throughout the war, and Gordon and Arnott exchanged letters with him individually. All five Brook children appear regularly in their parents' correspondence, and Isabelle's letters also included greetings, reports of milestones, and occasional scribbled drawings from their youngest three children. Sidney Brook survived the war and was discharged in June 1918 because of a wound to his left shoulder and the fact that, at forty-six years old, he was "overage." While his survival and return were undoubtedly a relief, he came home to a family in mourning, as Arnott Brook had contracted diphtheria and died at the age of seven in October 1917. The Brook letters, which have been used recently in studies of gender, work, and marital relationships in wartime, were donated to the Glenbow Archives in 1995 by Irene Brook, the widow of Sidney and Isabelle's son Glen.[16]

The Maheux, Rogers, and Brook letters are material objects as well as pieces of textual evidence. Exchanged across vast distances along with postcards, parcels, and small objects like pressed flowers, they were central to the emotional survival of individuals and families. They were also a primary means through which fathers, mothers, and children all sought to maintain affective ties and a stable sense of self during a time of anxiety and crisis.[17] As David A. Gerber has written of nineteenth-century immigrant letters, wartime correspondence was both a "poor substitute for and an important embodiment of" absent loved ones, and the Maheux, Rogers, and Brook collections provide ample evidence that maintaining intimate relationships in writing over a period of years took effort, and could provoke both tension and tenderness.[18]

The rest of this chapter uses family letters to explore the wartime experiences of Petuwise, Freddy, Condy, Dolly, and "the baby" Maheux; Aileen and Howard Rogers; and Gordon, Arnott, Lorne, Glen, and Alice Brook. While Harrison and Albanese's chapter in this volume focuses on the adolescent children of Canadian soldiers, the children discussed here are younger, ranging in age from infancy to ten years old. Our subjects can therefore be understood as belonging to the age groups that Susan Rubin Suleiman, writing about child survivors of the Holocaust, has dubbed "children 'too young to remember' (infancy to around three years old) … and children 'old enough to remember but too young to understand' (approximately age four to ten)."[19] While we do not fully subscribe to Suleiman's insistence that children under ten are incapable of understanding the context and dangers of total war, we appreciate her point that instead of discussing a monolithic category called "children," it is more productive to pay close attention to the fine-grained distinctions in power and experience that shaped the lives of young people of different ages.

A close reading of these three families' wartime correspondence reveals other differences and similarities, as well. The Brook and Rogers children were Protestant Anglophone settlers, while the Maheux siblings were Catholic children of Indigenous and French-Canadian parentage. All of them were rural youngsters (some of whom, as will be discussed later, also spent parts of the war in urban and town settings), and their experiences were also shaped by regional landscapes, cultures, and economies. All of them, if they were old enough, attended school at least part of the time. The Maheux family was working class, while the Rogers and Brooks children's prewar lives on their parents' farms were marked by a greater degree of material comfort and economic stability.

One additional similarity is also worth noting: while the physical risks encountered by Great War soldiers are well known, reading the letters these men wrote to and about their sons and daughters reveals that it was also dangerous to be a child in early twentieth-century Canada. Frank Maheux, for example, asked his wife about his sons' frequent nosebleeds, and he expressed concern about his daughter Condy's ear problems – while also outlining his own troubles at the front – in September 1916: "it is too bad for Condy ears, I hope she will get better mine they are all right now, I am very lonesome now all my chums they are all, killed, or wounded, how glad I'll be when this war will be done."[20]

Aileen Rogers had contracted polio before 1914; she wore a brace on her leg and had to travel to the United States with her mother for treatment at least once during the war. During the two-and-a-half-year period between their father's enlistment in 1915 and his death in the autumn of 1917, Aileen's brother Howard endured a throat operation and was diagnosed with German measles and St Vitus's dance (now known as Sydenham's chorea and understood as the result of streptococcus infection). Sidney and Isabelle Brook had had a child named Walter who died in

January 1913, and their wartime correspondence includes discussions of their surviving children's experiences with colds, "summer complaint" (diarrhea), and convulsions. Their letters from the fall of 1917, exchanged while Sidney Brook was in England recovering from a shrapnel wound, provide devastating evidence of the dangers faced by children on the Canadian home front, as they describe seven-year-old Arnott Brook's death from diphtheria in late October of that year. (The vaccine for diphtheria was not invented until 1923.)

In addition to providing vivid depictions of the illnesses that afflicted and sometimes killed Canadian youngsters in an era before the development of antibiotics and many vaccines, these sources also reveal information about the wartime lives of soldiers' children that had previously escaped scholarly notice. In this respect, our child-centred reading of adults' wartime letters confirms Joan Scott's claim that the "'discovery' of new materials is actually an interpretive intervention that exposes the terms of inclusion and exclusion in the knowledges of the past."[21] The rest of the chapter combines the historian's focus on close reading with empathic inference to better understand the emotional and material adjustments and readjustments with which the Maheux, Rogers, and Brook children had to contend after their fathers left for the front. Empathic inference, a term coined by historian Mona Gleason, is an analytical technique that invites historians to think contextually, "deeply and critically about how young people might have responded to any given situation in the past."[22] Reading wartime family letters in this way reveals a number of new insights about the immediate changes and more gradual readjustments that shaped the lives of Canadian soldiers' children during the First World War.

Like the early twenty-first-century adolescents discussed in chapter 7, the Maheux, Rogers, and Brook children experienced the absence of their enlisted fathers as an ambiguous loss. While Frank Maheux, Lawrence Rogers, and Sidney Brook were physically absent from their families (and while Lawrence Rogers was alive), they remained emotionally and psychologically present in their lives – in large part through their letters. This "ambiguity of absence and presence," to use the words of psychologist Pauline Boss, could be a source of confusion and anxiety for young people – particularly during the period when Canadian soldiers had left their homes but not yet travelled to Europe.[23] The letters exchanged by Isabelle and Sidney Brook in the immediate wake of Sidney's July 1916 departure for army training at Sarcee Camp (approximately 200 kilometres southwest of the Brook farm) reveal that they both hoped he would be able to return to the farm at least once that summer to help with the harvest. (This did not come to pass, and he left for Europe without seeing his family again.)

Because they had been told that Sidney would likely come back to visit them before going off to fight, the Brook children looked for and asked about him in vain throughout the summer of 1916. When Isabelle's mother visited from Manitoba for a few weeks in July, for example, Gordon Brook, then eight years old, insisted that she "must stay till Papa came home."[24] That August, Isabelle wrote to Sidney: "I suppose you're still in Calgary this evening … I think Lorne thought it queer that Papa did not turn up again to-day. And I'm afraid the next two weeks will seem awfully long ones." She noted that six-year-old Arnott had recently exclaimed "My! I wish Papa'd come home to-night," and wrote a week later that the Brook boys' hopes of seeing their father were partly the result of her own prompting: "I've been promising you to the boys for next Sunday."[25]

By September 1916, it had become clear that Sidney Brook was not going to return to Craigmyle for a final visit with his wife and children. Isabelle wrote to him recalling their moment of parting several months earlier: "I can see you yet as I got a last glimpse of you from the door, as you moved for the train along the platform. Lorne asks so often very pitifully for 'Papa' – he can't seem to understand why you don't come. It's heartbreaking to think of the months & months he must look in vain."[26] While on a train near Montreal on 23 September, Sidney wrote to his wife asking about Gordon, who had assumed that his father would return to the farm at least once before leaving for the front. "Did Gordon feel bad about not saying 'Good bys?' It's likely hard to comfort the little fellows but all will be for the better when the bloody war is over."[27] As Bart Ziino has pointed out in the Australian context, many youngsters "maintained an expectation of the imminent return of their [enlisted] loved ones" during the Great War, especially in the first year after a father or brother's departure.[28] In early 1917, some six months after Sidney Brook had left them, the Brook children continued to ask their mother if their father would be back soon. In January of that year, for example, Arnott told Isabelle that he wanted his father "to get an aeroplane & come over to see us," and several months later Lorne asked his mother to write to Sidney telling him "to come home to see [the] baby."[29]

As the realization dawned that they would be separated from each other for months and possibly years, fathers and children alike began to worry that they might be forgotten or that the physical transformations wrought by growth and combat stress might make their loved ones difficult to recognize. Frank Maheux asked often if his children spoke about him, and expressed anxiety that they had forgotten him and would fail to recognize him when he returned. He also worried about having so few memories of his youngest child, a girl born shortly before he enlisted. In September 1917, for instance, he wrote "now dear wife ... tell me if the kids talks about me, I am away since so long I don't think they remember, I mean, the baby, Baboon and Freddy for my part, I can hardly remember the baby, it is affright to be away since so long."[30] Sidney Brook expressed similar concerns in letters sent from France in December 1916: "I suppose Lorne and Glen are growing fast, likely I would not know them, eh?"[31] While inquiring about Glen's first steps (one of a number of childhood milestones that these fathers missed and sought to mark from a distance), he also noted sadly, "Guess I won't know the family when I return."[32] In a May 1917 letter to Sidney, Isabelle – who, she claimed, was feeling "dissatisfied, [and] unsettled" – lamented the fact that her husband was missing "all of Alice's 'baby ways.'" Lorne and Glen had grown and were particularly changed, she wrote, noting as well that while "Lorne would know his papa," Glen likely would not.[33] Offhand written references to being forgotten also caused misunderstandings among correspondents, and could be especially upsetting for young letter-writers: in October 1916, for example, Lawrence Rogers asked his wife to "tell Howard that I did not mean that he had forgotten me I was only fooling with him as I know he would not forget his old Dad and when I was his age I used to hate to write as much as he dose."[34]

The letters these young people received from their absent fathers were material objects as well as textual documents. Along with the souvenirs that often accompanied them, letters could be manipulated by small hands, hoarded along with other valuable childhood objects, and re-read time and time again. Lorne Brook, for example, liked to play with his father's letters; in February 1917, while his older brothers were at school and his younger siblings were napping, he enjoyed "sorting out 'Papa's letties' from a bundle of letters here on the table, and trying to take the stamps off."[35] At another point, his mother reported that Lorne took one of his father's letters and some Canadian Patriotic Fund paperwork from her dresser and hid them in his bed. Arnott Brook carefully hoarded the cards his father had sent him, a fact that his mother only discovered after his premature death. "On Saturday," Isabelle wrote to Sidney, "I discovered all the cards you had sent him, collected and put in a little cardboard shoe box and left on the bookcase. Laid in there just as his little hands had left them. It must have been when I was in bed he done it I guess, for he did not have them gathered together before, and the little box is one Alice just recently got a little pair of slippers in."[36]

Their parents' wartime correspondence further reveals that the Maheux, Rogers, and Brook children watched their mothers worry about money, moved out of the homes they had lived in before the war, and took on a range of new practical and emotional responsibilities while their fathers were at war. Like many other working-class men, Frank Maheux saw enlistment as an economic opportunity rather than a potential source of hardship: soldiers' wives received a $20 separation allowance each month, and husbands could also choose to assign them up to $15 from their monthly wage.[37] His decision to join up was also likely influenced by some knowledge of Canadian Patriotic Fund, a federally chartered private charity that provided financial support to military wives and children while promoting middle-class values of morality and thrift.[38]

In his letters home, Frank Maheux described the Canadian Expeditionary Force primarily as a reliable employer that would pay him more than logging companies did. "Look at the difference in wage," he wrote to Angelique in October 1914, "working hard in chanty for 22' here you will get 30.0 a month and a fund of the Government side."[39] In another letter, where he also asked Angelique to send a photograph of her and their children ("I like to have one when I am lonesome"), he extolled the physical and economic advantages of his decision by telling his wife "I don't think you will starve so long as I work for this company, it is better than to killed myself making logs."[40]

Despite these assurances, however, the wartime lives of Angelique Maheux and her children were shaped in many ways by material privation and financial worries. Frank's wages from logging stopped early in the fall of 1914, for example, and the first cheques from the Patriotic Fund were not mailed until December of that year. While Angelique's letters have not survived, it is clear that she asked her husband about money regularly – and several of his responses to her questions betray an impatience that was likely linked to his understanding of himself as the breadwinner and head of the family hierarchy. In November 1914, for instance, he wrote angrily: "well you talk about hard time wont get no hard time because you get more money every month than you never got before."[41] He promised several times to send additional funds – "in my next letter I'll try to send a couple dollars so you will be able to watch for the Government pay" – but his letters also show that on a number of occasions, he instead spent this money on drink.

Feeding and clothing five children on an unstable income over a five-year period was a difficult task, made worse by wartime inflation (Canadian food prices, for example, rose 128 per cent over the course of the war).[42] The roof of the Maheux family's shanty in Baskatong Bridge leaked when it rained, it was difficult to afford fuel to heat the house, and Angelique Maheux wanted to find a way to earn extra money to provide for her family. Concerned about his status as the family breadwinner, Frank used one of his early letters, sent from a training camp in Kingston Ontario, to instruct her not to take a job as a cook in a logging camp: "don't go if you are able to help it because you know the way the people talk."[43] In another missive, dated simply "Wednesday" – evidence that he understood but had not yet entirely mastered the temporal conventions of formal correspondence – Frank told Angelique that if necessary, she could "sell Moceasons [moccasins] and Mitts" for cash. At various points between 1915 and 1918, Angelique Maheux and her five children left their home and moved in with her mother. These intervals of mobility on the home front provided Angelique with company, help with childcare, and the opportunity to pool resources with another household.[44]

Thousands of kilometres to the west, the Brook children's daily lives in wartime Alberta were also shaped by economic constraints and geographical mobility. Like Angelique Maheux, Isabelle Brook found that promised cheques from the Patriotic Fund came only intermittently, and she worried about heating their home during a possible coal shortage.[45] The part of Sidney Brook's husbandly advice that was "the hardest ... to follow," she wrote to him at one point, "[was] hanging on to a little money– quite a job eh? I've got a $20 cheque not cashed, but if I paid two of three little accounts here, Thompson, Bell, Setlington, not to mention the Doctor, my funds would be a decided minus quantity."[46] In addition to worrying about bills, heating, and whether her separation allowance and funds from "the Patriotic" would arrive on time, Isabelle Brook and her children watched the farm's crops fail not long after Sidney's departure in summer 1916 because of a combination of hail, rust, and wind storms. That year's wheat, Isabelle wrote, was "awful looking stuff ... shriveled & discolored."[47]

The oldest Brook children, Gordon and Arnott, also took on a number of new household roles during their father's absence. The tasks they performed comprised a different and understudied kind of children's war work: behaving well and conforming to adult expectations was another way that young people could help to support a war that, they were often reminded, was being fought on their behalf.[48] Sidney Brook made his behavioural expectations clear, asking his wife if their children were "Very troublesome? Hope they're good boys? They'll have to be if they want me to come + live with them."[49] Gordon and Arnott Brook regularly picked potatoes, shovelled snow, tended to their younger siblings, and carried messages to neighbours. They also walked long distances to the post office and the local store, to send and pick up letters and to purchase groceries and supplies for their mother.[50] Not long after his departure, Sidney Brook wrote to his wife that it was "very pleasing to hear that Gordon and Arnott are such good Errand boys. Does it tire them much to go into town?"[51] It is easy to imagine that, like their counterparts during the Second World War (as discussed in chapters 2 and 12), the boys might actually have relished the increased autonomy and freedom to roam that these wartime errands afforded them. Other physical tasks assigned by their mother, however, required them to remain closer to home. The basement of family's house in Craigmyle flooded in the fall of 1916 (just as it was becoming clear that that year's wheat crop was irreparably damaged), and Gordon and Arnott spent many after-school hours carrying pails of water up the stairs and outside. "The boys were working again at the cellar after school to-day ... They've taken out a lot of water, but there's still more there. School closes at 3:30 here, so they are home about 4 o'clock."[52] The Brook letters say little about how Gordon's practical and emotional burdens would have increased after his brother's death in autumn 1917, but it is worth pausing to consider this, as well.

Before the shock of Arnott's death, the Brook children had already experienced two significant war-related ruptures: their father's enlistment in mid-1916 and the move, undertaken almost immediately after his departure, from the family farm to a new and still unfinished house in the town of Craigmyle. Memories of their pre-war lives on the farm seem to have loomed large in the minds of the oldest Brook sons, and Isabelle took them back there on several occasions, each of which ultimately proved to be disappointing and unsettling. On Lorne's fifth birthday in October 1916, for instance, she borrowed a horse, buggy, and driver from a neighbor in town and took him to the farm. They had not visited the property since leaving it several months earlier, and Lorne had been eagerly anticipating a visit to what he called "papa's" place. Their homecoming was marred, however, by the property's abandoned appearance – a reminder of what the war had cost them – and by the discovery that a door and all their pitchforks had been stolen.[53] The following summer, Isabelle again borrowed a horse and buggy and took Gordon, Arnott, and Lorne, all of whom had been asking to visit, out to the farm for an afternoon. "To drive into that yard," she wrote to Sidney, "would make your heart sick. I wouldn't like you to see it. There's pig weed as high as me, a regular forest of it. From the kitchen door to the fence – right jammed up to the wall of the kitchen – and of course that stable yard has its supply too. Everything has such a deserted neglected appearance! ... Most everything that could be carried off, and that was worthwhile is gone."[54] Watching their mother discover that more farm implements and wood had been stolen from the yard and cellar, like the sight of a dead horse lying in the ditch of a neighbouring farm, must have been disturbing for the Brook boys. The whole day, it appears, was a difficult reminder of the family's happier prewar lives and the uncertainty that remained about the future.

Like Isabelle Brook, May Rogers was left alone on the family farm with her children when her husband enlisted. She also worried about making ends meet, and tried – and ultimately failed – to find a reliable man who could be hired to look after their livestock. By the early autumn of 1916, when her husband had been gone for over a year, she left the struggling farm and took Howard and Aileen to live in an apartment in Montreal. This appears initially to have been a temporary arrangement, as the family was back on the farm by November of that year. But May Rogers sold their rural property shortly after that point, and the family was living in Montreal when they learned that Lawrence Rogers had been killed in October 1917.

May Rogers sought to cope with her family's straitened finances by reusing items and dressing her children in hand-me-downs. Her husband vehemently disagreed with several of these choices, and his letters reveal a persistent anxiety about how his son's masculinity would develop without direct paternal influence. In January 1917, for instance, he wrote: "Why has Howard to wear an old coat of Aileens? I hope you are not running short of funds if so I would rather go without any myself than have that happen. Let me know and I will see what I can do about it." It was not only the possibility of his son wearing his sister's old clothing that Lawrence Rogers found worrying; instead of buying Howard a new "boy's" bicycle, his wife had chosen to let him ride an older model that used to belong to Aileen. "If I can find a way to send you some money I will do so," he wrote in the same letter, "as my share to-wards Howards Bike as I sure think he aught to have one for himself instead of riding a girls."[55]

The gendered behavioural and emotional norms that influenced Lawrence Rogers's hopes for his son are evident at several other points in his correspondence, as well. A letter to May from August 1916, for example, expressed his expectation that Howard would be "a good real boy not a sissy or anything like that."[56] He praised Howard for showing emotional restraint when he had to stay with an aunt for a few days while his mother and sister travelled to New York to seek specialist treatment for Aileen's leg, which had been damaged by polio. "Howard is a brick," Lawrence wrote, "and I knew he would not make a fuss altho it must have been the hardest thing he ever did in his life poor kiddie but he is too much of a man to show any body what he feels … tell him I am proud of him."[57]

Howard Rogers, who earned praise from his father by hiding any negative feelings he may have experienced during a stressful and unfamiliar situation, was one of many Canadian children who felt compelled to perform emotion work during the war years. Originally explored by sociologist Arlie Russell Hochschild, emotion work is a type of labour that that "requires one to induce or suppress feeling in order to sustain the outward countenance that produces the proper state of mind in others."[58] While Hochschild's initial subject was the emotional labour performed by female flight attendants, looking at children in wartime reveals that young people have also often been called upon to manage their emotions in order to influence the affective states of adults.[59]

Like the adolescent children of Canadian military families during the war in Afghanistan, the Maheux, Rogers, and Brook children experienced the deployment of a parent as an event that negatively affected their quality of life and that burdened them with new emotional responsibilities, including looking after their at-home mothers *and* their absent fathers by masking their fears and acting cheerful in person and in print.[60] It is clear from the remaining sources that Angelique Maheux, May Rogers, and Isabelle Brook regularly expressed feelings like anger and fear in their letters to their husbands, and their emotional states would likely have been obvious to their children, as well. At various points during her husband's absence, for example, Isabelle Brook wrote to Sidney that she felt tired, "dissatisfied [and] half-glum," "sort of upset, [and] unsettled-like," "unrestful, strained [and] anxious," and "pretty nearly like having a little cry."[61] While May Rogers's letters have not survived, it is clear from her husband's responses that she was greatly upset by his enlistment and by the many practical and economic stresses that followed. In August 1915, from Shorncliffe Camp in England, Lawrence Rogers wrote: "I see you are talking nonsense again by saying if you had treated me better I might not have wanted to go to the front."[62] His attempts to console his wife continued as the war progressed: "I know sweetheart just how you feel," he wrote in late October 1915, "picking up the paper every day and reading about all the things that are going on and then putting it away then going around all day trying to smile for the kiddies sake and at the same time worrying your poor dear heart out because I have to sleep on the hard ground but believe me there are worse places than a rubber sheet and some blankets to sleep on."[63]

In letters to his children (which, like the letters sent by Frank Maheux and Sidney Brook, also contained numerous expressions of affection), Lawrence Rogers repeatedly instructed each of them to "look after" their mother. In August 1915, for example, he told Howard to "Be a good boy and take daddies place with mother and see that nothing happens to her just keep her safe for Daddy when he comes home."[64] Several months later, he wrote to Aileen: "Give my love to big sweetheart and tell her not to worry about Daddy and kiss dear old Sunny Jim for me. Your loving Daddy Xxxxxxx X."[65] Another letter, addressed to "Dear Kiddies" in July 1916, ended on a similar note: "Lots of love for you all and take care of mother for Daddy."[66]

While her father and contemporary cultural expectations encouraged Aileen Rogers to perform emotional labour in the service of others, it is clear that there were multiple conflicts between mother and daughter, as well – evidence, perhaps, of Michael Roper's claim that "it was in lived relationships within the home, as much as in public rhetoric or political action, that the war's deepest emotional effects were played out."[67] Lawrence Rogers defended his daughter when May called her a "queer child," writing that it was not Aileen's fault because she had "never had any deasent kids to play with."[68] In April 1916, he again rebutted his wife's criticism by insisting that Aileen was not, in fact, "her own worst enemy." "You must remember, the kiddie has travelled some in fact more than a lot of grown people and has seen things so that like yourself she is kind of fed up with all concerned." "If I had … no better companions," he wrote, "I think I would be a grouch too."[69] Later that year, as Christmas approached, he appealed to May "not to be too hard on poor Aileen you know we are not all built on the same plan and I am affraid she has a large portion of Rogers in her."[70]

The fathers discussed in this chapter used their letters to continue to enact the domestic roles they had left behind, often drawing on idealized images of their own children for inspiration and comfort.[71] Lawrence Rogers wrote to Aileen, for instance: "Daddie can shut his eyes and see you at the little dining table by [indecipherable] stove and then mother and the dear kiddies sitting down at a nice clean table having supper."[72] After describing the human costs of trench warfare ("it will take long before they will be able to beried our boy's who fell in the last battle some are beried in shell holes and some they were not"), Frank Maheux told his wife that he comforted himself by imagining his family: "my only past time now it is my pipe smoke and smoke, first thing in the morning, last at night I am a little happy when I smoke like in the trenches after I visit all the men, I'll sat in a black corner by myself, I'll light my pipe, and then I'll think of dear old sweet home, and the little family I left behind."[73]

Home, as these passages illustrate, was a touchstone for Great War soldiers – a material and emotional ideal that allowed them to link happy pasts with imagined futures while temporarily forgetting the present.[74] Yet while soldiers' letters are testaments to the power of an idealized and unchanging image of home and family, they are also evidence of the ways in which the war in general – and the absence of fathers in particular – marked a dividing line in the lives of young people on the Canadian home front.[75] After their fathers had left, the Maheux, Rogers, and Brook children took on a range of new responsibilities, left the homes they had lived in before the war, and managed their emotions so as not to upset their anxious mothers and absent fathers. Their wartime lives, knowable mainly through their parents' correspondence, are compelling reminders of the importance of the personal, the emotional, and the everyday in the history of Canada's First World War.

NOTES

1 *The Family Herald and Weekly Star*, 18 November 1914.
2 Dodd, *French Children under the Allied Bombs, 1940–45*, and Stargardt, *Witnesses of War*.
3 Glassford, "Bearing the Burden of Their Elders: English-Canadian Children's First World War Red Cross Work and Its Legacies," 129–50; Moruzi, "'A Very Cruel Thing,'" 214–25; Kristine Alexander, "Education during the First World War," *wartimecanada.ca* (2013), http://wartimecanada.ca/essay/learning/education-during-first-world-war (accessed 27 July 2018); Fisher, *Boys and Girls in No Man's Land*; Alexander, "An Honour and a Burden," 173–94; Millar and Keshen, "Rallying Young Canada to the Cause," 1–16.
4 Alexander, "Can the Girl Guide Speak?," 132–44.
5 Morton, *Fight or Pay*, xiii.
6 Fussell, *The Great War and Modern Memory*, 229.
7 Morin-Pelletier, "'The Anxious Waiting Ones at Home,'" 353–68; Hunter, "More Than an Archive of War," 339–54; Roper, *The Secret Battle*; Meyer, *Men of War: Masculinity and the First World War in Britain*; Hanna, "Your Death Would Be Mine"; Hanna, "A Republic of Letters," 1338–61; Hämmerle, "'You Let a Weeping Woman Call You Home?,'" 152–82.
8 Raynsford and Raynsford, *Silent Casualties: Veterans' Families in the Aftermath of the Great War*, 55. The entire sentence reads: "Equally with their mothers, the children, who were orphaned, abandoned, or abused as an aftermath of the war, were the silent casualties of a war fought halfway across the world."
9 Roper, "Slipping out of View," 62.

10 While most members of the Canadian Expeditionary Force were unmarried young men in their twenties, approximately 25 per cent of Canadian soldiers were married. No comprehensive records exist to determine how many of them were also fathers.
11 Lyons, *The Writing Culture of Ordinary People in Europe*, 8.
12 Humphries, "Wilfully and with Intent," 369–97; Cook, "Grave Beliefs," 521–42; Cook, "The Politics of Surrender," 637–65; Cook, *No Place to Run*, 111; Cook, "The Blind Leading the Blind," 24–36.
13 Morton, "A Canadian Soldier in the Great War," 88n6. Morton also notes that Maheux's army paybook listed five dependent children.
14 "It Went to Hell and Back: Mr Rogers's Teddy Bear," *Globe and Mail* Memory Project, http://v1.theglobeandmail.com/special/memoryproject/features/rogers.html (accessed 1 August 2018).
15 Alexander, "An Honour and a Burden," 173–94; Cook and Morrison, "Longing and Loss from Canada's Great War," 53–60; Innes and Endrulat, *Bear on the Home Front*; Innes and Endrulat, *A Bear in War*.
16 Morin-Pelletier, "'The Anxious Waiting Ones at Home,'" 353–68; Brandsma, "'An Honoured Place.'"
17 Roper, *The Secret Battle*.
18 Gerber, *Authors of Their Lives*, 2.
19 Suleiman, "The 1.5 Generation," 283. Suleiman also includes a third age-based category: "children 'old enough to understand but too young to be responsible' (approximately age eleven to fourteen)." Thanks to Lee Talley for introducing us to Suleiman's work.
20 Library and Archives Canada (Ottawa), Francis-Xavier Maheux Fonds, MG30-E297, R5156-0-4-E. Frank Maheux to Angelique Maheux, 23 September 1916. The letters discussed in chapters 4 and 10 include a number of misspelled words. Instead of marking each instance of this with "[sic]," we have opted to leave them as is.
21 Scott, "After History?," 100.
22 Gleason, "Avoiding the Agency Trap," 449n8.
23 Boss, *Ambiguous Loss*.
24 Glenbow Archives (Calgary), Brook Family Fonds. Isabelle Brook to Sidney Brook, 19 July 1916.
25 Isabelle Brook to Sidney Brook, 20 August 1916 and 27 August 1916.
26 Ibid., 12 September 1916.
27 Sidney Brook to Isabelle Brook, 23 September 1916.

28 Ziino, "'They Seem to Understand All about the War,'" 236.
29 Isabelle Brook to Sidney Brook, 6 January 1917, and 21 March 1917.
30 Frank Maheux to Angelique Maheux, 6 September 1917.
31 Sidney Brook to Isabelle Brook, 11 December 1916.
32 Sidney Brook to Isabelle Brook, 26 December 1916.
33 Isabelle Brook to Sidney Brook, 13 May 1917.
34 Canadian War Musuem Archives (Ottawa), Letters from Lieutenant Lawrence Browning Rogers, 1915–17. Lawrence Rogers to May Rogers, 5 October 1916.
35 Isabelle Brook to Sidney Brook, 27 February 1917.
36 Ibid., 29 October 1917.
37 Morton, *Fight or Pay*, 32.
38 Ibid.
39 Frank Maheux to Angelique Maheux, 14 October 1914.
40 Ibid., n.d. (likely 1916).
41 Ibid., 14 November 1914.
42 Heron and Siemiatycki, "The Great War, the State, and Working-Class Canada," 20.
43 Frank Maheux to Angelique Maheux, 14 November 1914.
44 Hanna, "The Couple," 20. "To ease the burden of overwork and oppressive anxiety that beset married women on the home front," Hanna writes, "their husbands [often] encouraged them to move in with parents, in-laws, or other war wives." She notes that this arrangement was also likely appealing to some men because it promised to limit wives' opportunities for infidelity.
45 Isabelle Brook to Sidney Brook, 27 July 1916.
46 Isabelle Brook, *Isabelle Brook to Sidney Brook*, October 4, 1916, Letter, M-9076-21, Glenbow Archives, *Brook Family Fonds*.
47 Isabelle Brook to Sidney Brook, 13 October 1916.
48 This interpretation was inspired by Audoin-Rouzeau, *La guerre des enfants 1914–1918*.
49 Sidney Brook to Isabelle Brook, July 8, 1917.
50 Isabelle Brook to Sidney Brook, 15 November 1917, and 23 November 1917.
51 Sidney Brook to Isabel Brook, 2 August 1916.
52 Isabelle Brook to Sidney Brook, 20 September 1916.
53 Ibid., 13 October 1916.
54 Ibid., 19 August 1917.
55 Lawrence Rogers to May Rogers, 12 January 1917.
56 Ibid., 13 August 1916.
57 Ibid., 12 December 1915.

58 Hochschild, *The Managed Heart*, 7.
59 Alexander, "Agency and Emotion Work," 120–8. See also Dodd, "'Mon petit papa chéri,'" 97–118.
60 See for example Harrison and Albanese, "The 'Parentification' Phenomenon," 1–27.
61 Isabelle Brook to Sidney Brook, 8 October 1916, 7 December 1916, and 3 June 1917. For more on the psychological and emotional stresses experienced by Canadian soldiers' wives, see Hanna, *Anxious Days and Tearful Nights*.
62 Lawrence Rogers to May Rogers, 26 August 1915.
63 Ibid., 29 October 1915.
64 Lawrence Rogers to Howard Rogers, 19 August 2015.
65 Lawrence Rogers to Aileen Rogers, 2 November 1915.
66 Lawrence Rogers to Aileen and Howard Rogers, 8 July 1916.
67 On cheerfulness and femininity, see Alexander, *Guiding Modern Girls*, 88–93, and Kotchemidova, "From Good Cheer to 'Drive-By Smiling,'" 5–37.
68 Lawrence Rogers to May Rogers, 28 January 1916.
69 Ibid., 2 April 1916.
70 Ibid., 14 December 1916.
71 Meyer, *Men of War*, 15.
72 For an examination of how British soldiers imagined domestic spaces to provide themselves with emotional comfort see Roper, *The Secret Battle*, 68–72.
73 Frank Maheux to Angelique Maheux, 3 September 1917.
74 Bourke, *Dismembering the Male*, 23.
75 Kennedy, *The Children's War*, 1.

5
Deconstructing a Canadian Military Family: The Taylor Mother and Son Remember the Cold War

Isabel Campbell

During the Cold War, Canadian military families lived in Belgium, Britain, France, West Germany, and the United States, as well as in communities scattered across Canada. Not only did these families endure long separations from serving members, but they also moved frequently, often to isolated communities located far from their traditional kinship networks. How did family members cope with these demanding circumstances? This chapter will briefly summarize military personnel policies and compare excerpts from oral history interviews with Shelaigh and Paul Taylor, a military wife and son, to show the impacts of these policies on their lives. Their two stories contrast a mother's and a child's perspectives, highlighting differences in personality and age, and demonstrating that family members sometimes challenged the Cold War gender stereotypes. Relishing moves and new friendships as a civilian child, Shelaigh embraced adult life as a military spouse to Jack Taylor. Years later, she concluded: "I think it was a real advantage to be in the military ... it was all moves which I really enjoyed. I found it a very fulfilling life." Her son, Paul, came to the opposite conclusion by age ten. "I knew that no matter [what] I did in my life I would not join the military and I would never uproot my family."[1] As an adult, Paul exercised agency; remaining in Ottawa, enduring sporadic unemployment and poorly paid jobs, he rejected the traditional fatherhood roles that stressed breadwinning. Instead of pursuing career and financial goals, he prioritized family stability and engaged interactions with his wife and children.

After the Second World War, military policies reflected the post-war promotion of the traditional nuclear family with explicitly described and constructed gender roles as an essential component in establishing post-war stability and reconstruction. As a 1945 Liberal election poster declared, "Fathers were to be breadwinners, mothers the 'queens of the home,' children 'the hope of tomorrow.'"[2] Concurrent federal and provincial policies such as the universal family allowance and compulsory education laws bolstered this idealized family lifestyle.[3] Canadian experts normalized a post-war heterosexual, middle class family ideal based upon polarized gender differences.[4] Canadian military personnel policies echoed these notions through newly invigorated post-war measures such as married allowances and the building of military communities. In 1947, for the first time, the military took responsibility for the education of military children and opened schools on military bases where civilian schools were not available. By December 1956, 20,700 children were enrolled in military schools in Canada and another 4,372 in military schools in England and Europe. The military paid school fees for an additional 234 children, while an unreported number of military children attended local public schools in civilian communities.[5]

While the government promoted family-oriented military bases with housing, recreational facilities, and schools, senior army leaders, including the chief of the general staff, Lieutenant-General Guy Simonds, resisted this development, arguing that wives and children distracted male military members from their duties and combat preparation. These leaders opposed sending families abroad to accompany their husbands and fathers.[6] During the early 1950s, more than 26,000 service members, including Jack Taylor, deployed to Korea for combat duties without any dependents; a much higher number rotated to the Air Division and brigade in Europe in a deterrent role.[7] The majority of those deployed were single recruits who had signed up for three years. Married members left their families on Canadian military bases, though with a shortage of married quarters, some were also in civilian housing. Faced with long separations and inadequate housing, members left the services in droves.[8] As described in my study *Unlikely Diplomats: The Canadian Brigade in Germany, 1951–1964*, nearly one-third of the air force and several hundred army families went to Britain and Europe without official approval and most lacked financial compensation.[9]

By their actions, these families forced the government hands, bolstering the case put forward by defence minister Brooke Claxton, chairman, chiefs of staff, Charles A. Foulkes, and chief of the air staff Air Marshall W.A. Curtis as well as some young army leaders who argued that the presence of wives and children improved comportment, deterring venereal disease, drunkenness, and brawling, all behaviours associated with young single males. These pro-family leaders concluded that families helped them retain their best, most experienced members.[10] Curtis also insisted that married men played an important role in raising children, stating that in separated families, "the husband is not available to assist with the day to day family problems and the help of the father is lost during a period when he is often needed to bring up the children properly."[11] And so, in 1953, the Canadian government reversed an earlier decision and allowed families to officially accompany those posted to Europe.[12]

While this result permitted families like the Taylors to live together overseas, it obligated them to relocate more often. Commanders encouraged these families to engage in community activities. In overseas postings, they also carefully instructed them on how to represent Canada in an exemplary manner.[13] Military families, including children, were thus an integral part of creating good military-civil relations, particularly vital in West Germany where the Canadian government hoped to convince the local population to support the western cause. These policies filtered down, and young children, like Paul Taylor, engaged in sports and social activities – all part of a national effort to showcase an idealized lifestyle.[14]

The Cold War conjures up images of a traditional family with bipolar gender roles, dependent upon a father's wage and supported by unpaid female labour with children's voices seldom heard.[15] Peter Grieg's study of Ontario boyhood illustrates how strong, bread-winning fathers were expected to be role models for their sons, shielding them from over-protective mothers who might produce "sissies," while organized activities like sports prepared these lads for the rugged, masculine conformity of the corporate world.[16] Although most military histories ignore the role of families and societal changes on military culture and values,[17] new studies such as Geoffrey Hayes's *Crerar's Lieutenants. Inventing the Canadian Junior Army Officer, 1939–1945* include elements of family life, class, education, region, and ethnicity in their analysis of the masculine characteristics of aloofness, strength, and determination that the military promoted among its junior officer ranks.[18] Other insightful works of feminist advocacy inevitably focus upon adult perspectives, upon how orthodox military thinking trumpets presumptions of masculine superiority, bravery, and toughness – an exaggerated gender polarity to enhance masculine camaraderie, while belittling feminine participation.[19] What emerges is a wide-spread picture of traditional military families which utilizes weak female spouses and obedient children to bolster hyper-masculine military goals.[20] Yet the later Cold War included youth participation in feminist, gay rights, anti-nuclear, and other activism, complicating social changes which impacted Canadian military families among others.[21]

Few studies explore children's voices directly. American scholar Mary Edwards Wertsch draws upon "dark times of struggle" from her military childhood memories combined with stories from eighty other military "brats" in a heartbreaking study, *Military Brats: Legacy of Childhood inside the Fortress*. Written from the distance of adulthood, it details childhood memories of parental alcoholism, abuse, and the horror of possibly losing a parent in a sub-culture of American society marked by rigid discipline and nomadic rootlessness.[22] Wertsch exposes myths about idyllic childhoods which masked loneliness and pain, stoical submissive mothers, and a sense of belonging only discovered later in life through shared experiences with other "military brats" even for those who did not experience neglect or abuse. She concludes that "real roots are about *connection* – the bonding with others who share a similar lived experience" – emphasizing adult bonding among "survivors" of military childhoods.[23] This bonding among the children of American and Canadian service people, does not generally include parents or whole families, but is evident in base reunions, military brat clubs, Facebook pages, and on a variety of internet websites.[24]

Canadian Gil McElroy focuses upon his own adult journey of coming to terms with "the enigma," his absentee, alcoholic father, a Royal Canadian Air Force non-commissioned officer. He opens his *Cold Comfort: Growing Up Cold War* with "sorrow" in the shape of "a glass bottle, green with a grid pattern of ridges" which "my mother used while ironing clothes." That bottle "was for me a primary link to my family's life as itinerants. This bottle, this *thing*, held my family together through moves from one side of a continent to the other, and then halfway back again."[25] The "Cold War, by its very nature, routinely shredded the family to bits."[26] These fractured, dysfunctional revelations from childhood contrast with the idealized Cold War family propagated by leaders and experts.

The Taylor family complicates these opposing historiographic pictures. In most respects, they exemplified the family ideal propagated by the government, experts, and military leaders. Both Taylor parents had an active social life; neither was abusive, mean-spirited, or suffered from addictions. Paul was obedient, good in school, and engaged in sports, Scouts, and other boyhood activities associated with promoting militarism among earlier generations.[27] As Andrew Burtch describes in chapter 3, the Scouts also practiced gendered civil defence measures. However, both mother and son challenged stereotypes, remembering complex, even contradictory gender performances. Paul chafed at his father's absences, strictness, and emotional distance, while revelling in his mother's "cuddling and coddling," especially when he experienced distress before, during, and after deployments.[28] Constructed family memories comparing Paul and his older brother

Don highlight variations in acceptable boyhood performances within this particular family which challenge the norms described in the literature above.

Paul developed his own concept of fathering in direct counterpoint to his father's model, refusing to make breadwinning a priority, and drawing instead upon his mother as a role model. Upon reaching adulthood, he became a new-age, post–Cold War father, insisting on staying in one place and sacrificing his career in order to spend family time with his wife and children.[29] His story throws light upon "the country of fatherhood,"[30] while illustrating agency and demonstrating how even a young child develops critical capabilities and does not necessarily conform to the idealized models propagated by leaders, experts, and the military community. Paul respected his father, but from a young age, he refused to adopt his father's stoical, distant demeanour.

Shelaigh was an exemplary military spouse. While her career as a nurse typified a feminine post-war ideal, she was also the main family breadwinner before the birth of her children and she returned to the workforce when her children entered school and the family returned to Canada. She also challenged military social norms, forming friendships outside tight-knit officer wives groups.[31] She fondly recalls how unrelated military families forged close bonds while posted overseas. This is what anthropologists call "fictive" kin – strong social bonds and dense networks of friendships created through the performance of nurturing acts.[32] While many speak of intense socializing and friendships among military families, especially on bases, only a few transformed from temporary expediencies into intense lifelong bonds. These particular nurture bonds formed among unrelated families mimic extended traditional kinship groups (related by blood or marriage) and are more profound and enduring than the institutional support networks studied in the historical literature which focus upon adult experiences.[33] The nurture relationships described here are distinguished from traditional male-only combat bonding and separate wives networks by the engaged participation and close bonding among all members of the family regardless of age or gender, including children. These family bonds are also distinguished from "military brats" networks found on websites and described in Wertsch's study above. While not all military children formed these bonds with other military families, those that did were transformed by the experience. While Shelaigh initiated and promoted these beneficial relationships, Paul and his siblings learned important nurturing skills from these relaxed and playful family times.

This chapter is based on a series of oral history interviews with Shelaigh and Paul Taylor, highlighting intergenerational and differing perspectives about the enforced mobility experienced by Canadian Cold War service families. These two participants were selected from a Cold War oral history project of forty-six interviews with eight family groups that nuances our historical understanding of military and naval culture, community morale, behaviours, gender performances, and family life itself. During research for this work and for the official histories of the Royal Canadian Navy and Royal Canadian Air Force, colleagues, visiting researchers, friends, and others confided their memories about growing up in military and naval families, revealing widely differing experiences about how service lifestyles and deployments had impacted their childhoods.[34] Some chose to participate in formal whole life oral history interviews. In all cases, I use pseudonyms to protect the privacy of those interviewed, their families, and those they mention during interviews.

Volunteers were recruited by "word of mouth."[35] One interview often led to another, with participants recommending and contacting family members and friends. Most were interviewed separately, though several elderly women, had a daughter present during their interviews. Shelaigh's daughter Annie was present during Shelaigh's interview, but Paul and Annie were interviewed separately. Family members often disagreed with each other, presenting alternative interpretations of the same event. Interviews often lasted several hours, and multiple interviews were sometimes held to fully explore each person's childhood, adulthood, and their differing generational perceptions. New participants join this project each year. None are necessarily representative of Canadian military families, but each sheds light on subtle transformations in gender performances, changing ideas about fathering, and differing modes of coping with militarization and deployments.

This methodology has some obvious advantages and limitations; for example, Paul's stories changed over time.[36] Constructed memories are fluid, reflecting new experiences, incorporating learning, and emphasizing factors that grow more important over time. Annie faced fewer moves, enjoyed them, and had positive memories of her father. Paul considered that his father treated Annie "like his little princess" and was much stricter with his sons.[37] Annie remembers her father as a "reserved" and "very strict," but "more relaxed with me," while she could "tell her [mother] anything."[38] This piece draws slightly on her recollections, but space prohibits a full analysis of her happier childhood experiences. Jack, the father, and Don, the older son, had passed away prior to the beginning of this project. Migration and death fracture families, but whole life methodology allows the family to reconstruct fragments from before, during, and after the Cold War, comparing tales about civilian grandfathers, military fathers, and Paul's post–Cold War hands-on fathering.

The Taylor Family

Paul's father, Jack, grew up in Ottawa. His mother died when he was very young, and his father was a Dominion land surveyor who often worked far from home.[39] Jack and his sister spent their childhood in the care of housekeepers. His civilian middle-class childhood was deeply marked by grief which he confided to his wife Shelaigh, but never spoke about to his own children. Nevertheless this silence transmitted a powerful message to his two sons.[40] Jack joined the officer training corps while studying engineering at Queen's University during the Second World War. In August 1944, he enlisted as a gunner to gain combat experience in Europe.[41] Initially assessed as a "rather fragile looking young man," intelligent, but "not good in the rough and tumble of social contacts [who] may not take easily to Army life," Taylor impressed superior officers with his combat service in the lowest ranks. After the war, they noted his "marked leadership qualities and sincere motivation" and no one minded that he failed his third year at university. Rather, superiors praised his skiing, swimming, and tennis skills.[42] Military leaders wanted tough officers with athletic lifestyles and Jack learned to be "confident, lean, athletic, aloof and unsmiling,"[43] the idealized masculine performances which would later affect his relationship with his family and especially his sons.

Still a student in 1946, Taylor married Shelaigh, who supported him with nursing work in Kingston during the early years of their marriage. During her first pregnancy, she faced discrimination in the workplace. "I had to move out of the hospital because they didn't approve of pregnant nurses. I got a job in a sanitarium where I could wear a coverall. I worked up to my seventh month ... I was very happy to be having a child, but it was worrisome as far as finances were concerned ... He [Jack] was still at university."[44] She gave birth to their first son, Don, in July 1949 a few months after Jack became a full-time military officer, but without her income, their financial situation remained precarious until he received the married allowance in September that year.

The Taylor family moved from Kingston, Ontario, to Shilo, Manitoba, in January 1951, back to Kingston in June 1953, then to Ottawa in December 1956, then to Soest, West Germany, in July 1959, then back to Kingston in June 1961, and then to London, England, in June 1962, and returned to Ottawa in August 1965. Shelaigh left nursing to raise two sons born in 1949 and 1951 and a daughter born in 1957. Apart from moving eight times in sixteen years, Jack was posted away from his family after the birth of his first son during the summer of 1950, and then to Wainwright for training during the summer of 1951, and then to Korea from April 1952 to March 1953, and then to the remote Canadian Forces Station Alert on Ellesmere

Island for seven months in 1961–62. He was also often away on exercises. Shelaigh was athletic, independent, and fun-loving. By the mid-1960s, once all her children were in an Ottawa school, she resumed her nursing career. The Taylors' stories, like others, reveal complicated, evolving gender performances in military families during the Cold War.[45]

Born in Scotland in 1925, Shelaigh had moved to Lachine, Quebec, as a toddler, and to Hull, Quebec, and Ottawa as a young child, and then to Cornerbrook, Newfoundland, in her teens. Her father worked for Domtar in the Canadian pulp and paper industry, reminding us that some civilian children also endured moves. However, she thrived on these adventures. "I was excited. I don't remember being upset at all about the moves. I didn't have trouble making friends." She left Cornerbrook for an Ottawa nursing school at age eighteen. In her words, she had had a "very happy childhood … we could just stand in the middle of a field and call, anybody want to play? And we were all set. We were all tom boys I think in those days. Red rover, anything at all. We just had a wonderful time. I remember being in trouble a lot. I had a lot of fun. I was often in the principal's office. Impish."[46] Her childhood stories dramatized her rebellious, playful streak and her love of adventure. Shelaigh relished her life as a military spouse, enjoying all the moves and the intense socializing. Later she observed: "I think you work at being friends, and I've always kept in touch. It's been important, and it's very satisfying. Yes. It seemed like no matter where we would get posted we would know someone."

At the beginning, Shelaigh's experiences as a military spouse revolved around her friendships with other women: "My husband had been transferred Shilo, Manitoba. And after he was out there several months, we [Shelaigh and her first son, Don] went out … It was dead winter. He was to meet me in a place called Douglas … There was an army truck waiting for me. And then we found that there was no housing for me. And the strangest thing. Someone offered to take us in for a short while, while a house was being completed. And, it turned out it was Bob Marshall from Ottawa and his wife was a school mate of mine. And I didn't know it. I walked in the door and that's Jane Marshall. We were there a couple of weeks."[47] The military wives counted on each other. As the literature on this topic stated, "the extension of combat bonding to wives" helped to offset the "loneliness, continual uprootment [sic], and ceaseless unpaid work."[48] Military spouses enhanced morale, performing reciprocal nurturing acts, including sharing food and even their dwellings in uniquely challenging circumstances.

The Taylors' social life reflected Jack's status as a young officer and the challenges of serving on an isolated army base. "We were invited down to the officer's Mess

Deconstructing a Canadian Military Family 149

quite frequently for dinners or dancing. There wasn't a movie theatre or anything like that. It was mainly social activity. I played badminton quite a bit, but other than that I don't think there was any particular sport."[49] When Shelaigh gave birth to Paul, her second son, in 1951, she made another friend, but this new relationship crossed the boundaries between the officers and the lower ranks and created tension with her husband.[50]

> I made a very good friend in hospital. In the same room, a gunner's wife had a baby girl on the same day. The unfortunate part was we could never really socialize with that couple because they were other ranks. In later years, we had a place in Florida and that couple did come and visit us and that was fine. That [the restriction on socializing with other ranks] bothered [me] a lot. I treasure my friends. I understood it ... but I didn't think I approved of it. Jack said it can't happen. And so it didn't happen. I found it hard to accept ... I did not think it was right ... Officers' wives mainly socialized with each other. The children [of the other ranks] would go to the same school, but that was it.

Her testimony reveals contradictions and nuances with respect to interactions among the military social classes. Officers did not socialize with other ranks and this pecking order often extended to their families.[51] Military housing that grouped families by rank generally worked against developing close friendships outside of rank groupings.[52] The fact that this particular couple from the other ranks visited the Taylors after both men retired speaks volumes about Shelaigh's determination to develop and retain life-long relationships, her unwillingness to comply with military social norms, and the flexibility the men gained after retirement.

During the Korean Conflict (1950–53), camaraderie among military spouses was especially important as many were left alone or with young children. As Shelaigh recounted: "The last year that we were there, he [Jack] went to Korea for a year ... I think I coped very well. I'm a fairly independent person. Jack would write very frequently ... Some other wife would have a letter and share the news. I was part of a group that [was] left behind and I think there's safety in numbers. We played a lot of bridge. That was very handy ... One of my friends had an older daughter who used to babysit."[53] Informal friendships resulted in a feminine *esprit de corps* among those left behind. Far from distracting members from combat, these feminine networks promoted idealized "good mothering" practices, including surrendering their husbands (and grown children) to combat in times of war.[54]

Shelaigh conformed to these expectations, never questioning her husband's service and its demands on her family. Her father's Domtar career prepared her for moves and she insisted that her family benefited from these new experiences.

However, personality differences created tense moments when Jack returned home. Shelaigh enjoyed both her sons, but from birth they displayed nearly opposite traits. "My oldest boy Don was a real devil. And Paul was ... introspective. A quiet child. Their personalities were very different. He [Don] was very active ... Always made friends easily. He [Paul] was a worrier. Paul would very carefully put his things away. Don would erratically grab them and cause problems." Jack was stricter than his wife and when he returned from Korea, family tension grew. "I found it [Jack's return] a little difficult. Because I'd been in charge and now Jack was in charge as it were ... There was a different atmosphere in the house. He was more concerned about the boys' behaviour than I was. I guess I felt that maybe he was blaming me a bit about what was going on. I mean how the boys interacted with each other. I didn't think it was a big deal ... I think it created tension there too. Particularly with Don. He was so exuberant. He [Jack] was used to ordering men around ... He [Jack] wasn't mean but he had expectations that I didn't have. They had to behave the way he wanted them to."[55] Figure 5.1 captures Jack's confident strong appearance along with the children's dubious expressions as they sat in his lap after his return from Korea and his expectations of obedience created tension within the family.

Years later, Paul recalled only distant shadowy memories of his father, contrasted with his warm, protective mother. "Yah I did miss him [my father] when he was gone. I wanted him to be there, but it was well established in our family [that he would be gone]. My mother was completely competent in being the parent ... I was a well-behaved little boy. I thought she did a great job, being the parent. The adult in this family. Mom's fine. Mom's fantastic."[56] Because his father recorded home movies, Paul believed that his earliest memories of Kingston (1954–56) and Ottawa (1956–59) might be derived from these movies, rather than his lived experiences. "I'm not sure if I'm remembering the movie or if I'm really remembering being on that swing ... it's fun. It's family time. I'm playing with my mother and my brother. Family's really important to me. He [Don, his brother] was a lot more outgoing, more adventuresome than me. I tried to be like him. I felt I had to do it. We would play tag, swing on the swings and teeter-totter. She [my mother] was very active. She was the protector, the loving one, the cuddly one."[57]

Despite normative polarized constructions contrasting the masculine role of "tough protectors" and the feminine "protected" role, with a mostly absent father,

Figure 5.1
Jack Taylor with Don and Paul, ca. 1954.
Courtesy of Paul Taylor (pseud.).

Shelaigh emerged as a strong "protector" and the person Paul most wanted to emulate.[58] From their earliest years, Don and Paul performed divergent masculine performances. Paul's obedience caused fewer problems with his father, but he tried to emulate his braver, adventuresome brother. As Shelaigh observed, she and her son Don shared adventuresome, mischievous, and gregarious characteristics as children. Thus relationships and performances within this family did not fit into rigid bipolar gender patterns.

The first move Paul remembers was after three years in Ottawa, when Jack was transferred to West Germany in 1959. He recorded how his father tried to prepare his children for the big move: "We had a blackboard in our bedroom. He [Dad] showed us a map. He wasn't a really involved father, but for some reason, he wanted us to know where we were going. He started teaching us German. He'd come up and each night at bedtime and be like a teacher at a blackboard, teaching us geography and German. My father was actually interacting with us. Something he very rarely did. He explained things in a lot of detail. He had full attention and our respect. There was no doubt there was some excitement there."[59] Jack was likely drawing upon booklets distributed to military families deploying to Europe. These booklets promoted exemplary behaviours, including guidance on German language, culture, and active social engagement to promote a positive image of Canadian lifestyle.[60] With his frequent absences and emotional distance, Jack fit the "workaholic" pattern of fatherhood, but these teaching moments clearly stood out in his son's mind as something to be treasured and memorable.[61] Paul struggled between relishing his father's attention and his regret at leaving Ottawa. His poignant description of this move foreshadowed his subsequent emotional reactions to postings.

> I did not want to move. I had made friends. I went to a great school. I knew that it was matter of uprooting. I find it difficult to say goodbye. My memories are I had good friends, but I honestly now can't remember one friend … I'm anxious about what I'm going to do. What's the house going to look like? What about school? Am I going to make friends? It was pretty scary. I was an emotional kid. My brother wouldn't cry over things because he was tougher than me. I just couldn't hold back the tears. My mother is there. She would do the coddling and the cuddling. My dad didn't get involved. He couldn't cope with it. She'd get me through it and things would look rosy. My mother mentioned it. She thought that I was emotional. It was my personality.[62]

Although the historiography stresses "emotional toughness" and "fearlessness" as idealized boyhood characteristics in the post-war period, no one labelled his crying as girlish, babyish, or proposed punishing him for it.[63] Paul continues: "There was absolutely nothing wrong with it. It was never a negative thing. I never felt badly or guilty about being that way. It was completely accepted." Shelaigh contrasted her two sons' behaviours in respectful terms. "Paul found it [the move] difficult. Don was in sports, the hockey, immediately. He was a valuable player. Paul wasn't as keen. He took things much more seriously."[64] Shelaigh described these divergent behaviours in neutral gender terms, accepting Paul's expressive emotions as a personality trait and not a questionable gender performance. Although Paul compared himself to his "tougher" brother, his crying was not a weakness. Instead, he valued and later adopted his mother's parenting skills.

In Soest, the Taylor family bonded closely with the Nowak and a few other military families who lived in the same apartment building. Shelaigh's earlier stories showcased her feminine friendships, mirroring the normative stories of other military spouses.[65] However, the focus of her European stories shifts to more inclusive interactions among all family members regardless of gender and age, relationships that grew into life-long nurture kinships.

> The Nowaks were across from us, which was great. She had her eightieth birthday the other day. It wasn't until then that I realized there was ten years difference in our ages. I never thought about it. We got along so well together. I guess because the two little girls [her daughter Annie and Susan the Nowak daughter were the same age] got together ... We had a lot of outings. Particularly with Simone and Mack Nowak. We used to go off to all sorts of places, like Hamlin ... I enjoyed my time in Germany. We travelled around a lot. We were really just across the border from Holland. There were so many things to see in Germany. A trip down the Rhine.[66]

Far from their relatives, these families celebrated Christmases, birthdays, and holidays together. As Shelaigh's words suggest, they remained close although the Nowak family racked up fourteen moves in nineteen years. The two families did not share another posting until both families arrived back in Ottawa many years later and their grown-up daughters became best friends again.

Paul, more than five years older than the eldest Nowak child, enjoyed their company and bonded with the entire family group. His stories about these family interactions are some of the few times when he interacted with his younger sister and her friends and not just other boys as he did in Ottawa, Kingston, and London.[67] These special German memories with the Nowaks were commemorated in a childhood photo album Paul created himself.

Referring to his own photos in figure 5.2, Paul described how the Nowaks and another military family became closer to him than his own relatives: "We celebrated Christmas dinner with our very good friends [the Nowaks] who were a military family. And Easter. Sixty years later they are still close friends. There's another family. We see them quite frequently as well. Even aunts and uncles, we would see them once a year or less. These people [the Nowaks and one other military family] we would see all the time. Almost daily or at least weekly. Some of these families were closer than my own kin. Not only would we see them during the week but then we'd plan to do something on the weekend."[68] Such close family friendships evolved into lifelong nurture kinship relations, eclipsing traditional kin who grew distant.[69] Annie also recalled this German Christmas from her father's home movies and from her brother's photos. "One of the things Paul got was this camera and was really excited." She recounts how more than five decades later in Ottawa, Sue Nowak, her best friend, "had our family over to celebrate Paul and my birthdays … Paul brought his album of the first pictures that he took in Soest to show Simone and Mack, Sue's parents, because there were pictures of them, and Sue, and James, Sue's brother … that was something that was really important to him [Paul]."[70] As well as observing and recording family friendships, the Taylor and Nowak children of different ages and genders bonded so closely that decades later they still celebrate together like an extended family.

In Paul's case, life in Germany was also memorable because of the relaxed atmosphere and the subsequent transformation he observed in his father when the families got together. "I remember going on picnics. It seemed to be bubbly and fun. When we had visitors over, the whole atmosphere of the house would change. He [Dad] would relax and have a good time. So I know it was within him to be that way. When other people came in, not only did he look happy, but he had that inside. It was fun. Sometimes you'd think he doesn't [have the ability to be happy]. He [Mr Nowak] is relaxed. He was always a fun guy as far as I could see. And maybe that's why I like him so much. He could bring out the fun in my father. Because I do. Today I like him."[71] While his parents initiated these encounters, Paul was an enthusiastic participant. His German recollections had a nostalgic, enduring aspect which drew upon his own photographic records, his discovery of his father's otherwise hidden capacity for joy, and shared family play time.[72] The posting to Germany became an idealized time of family togetherness, creating romanticized memories similar to those described by Tarah Brookfield in her chapter in this volume about Grindstone Island.

Germany transformed his interior childhood world into one which briefly included his father as a fully engaged person. Jack also relaxed during European holidays with the family and became "a real fun dad," but otherwise his father was "very reserved" and "closed down." "I didn't know much about him. He was very dominant; he was very forceful, he was very strong."[73] These were the idealized masculine personality traits the Canadian military had encouraged among its of-

Figure 5.2
Christmas presents. Bottom left: Mrs Taylor with Mrs Nowak; bottom right: Don and Annie, ca. 1961. Courtesy of Paul Taylor (pseud.).

ficers, straining his relationships with his sons,[74] but after Germany, Paul was more aware that when he grew up, he could choose to be different as the father of his own family.

When the move to Canada came, Paul was so overwhelmed with grief that he tried to avoid discussing the move with his friends. "Leaving anywhere was difficult. As I got older, it got more difficult ... I never talked about leaving. Even my very best friend, I didn't tell him ... I didn't tell anybody because I had a very hard time saying good-bye. He did find out. Military parents talk to each other. He was really annoyed at me. I don't know if I gave him a very good explanation. I was going to simply disappear. That's easier for me than saying good-bye. I was ten."[75] Paul found life in Kingston easier because "I knew where we were going. I could remember being there. It was better than any move I'd done before." Yet, he drew back from friendships and his interior world became smaller. "My brother in contrast to me would go out and make friends and bring people home. I find it so difficult to leave people. I was reserved in terms of making friends. I know friends are temporary. Today, Tomorrow, maybe a year. Not making friends too quickly.

You're going to move again. You're going to lose your friends. My brother just jumps in with both feet. Let's just make friends fast and make as many as you can. We did have a very close-knit family. You relied on your family. I tried to make my brother my best friend. When it was time to come home and you don't go out after dinner, he was mine."[76] The family stayed in Kingston for part of 1961 and 1962, while Jack was posted up to Alert, far away from his wife and children as families were not permitted in this very isolated station located at the northern tip of Ellesmere Island, more than seven hundred kilometres north of the nearest Inuit settlement in Canada.[77] Paul's grief reflected simultaneous losses; he missed his friends in Germany, the close relations with the Nowaks, and the fun father he had just discovered. While Germany had stretched his horizons, multiplying his close connections, the move back to Canada closed them down. Like some of the adolescents interviewed in the chapter about the Afghanistan deployment, Paul's interior world shrunk and became gloomy. The separation was difficult for his mother too. Shelaigh's daughter Annie recalls her mother's tears after her father's weekly "ham radio" calls home on Sunday afternoons.[78]

Then the family moved to London, England. Paul found the timing particularly hard because he had not yet recovered from leaving Germany. "I think we were in Kingston for ten months. It was just disturbing. Here you go again. Very, very disappointing. Something I really didn't want to do. I know I'm a military kid and this is going to happen. It was horrible. I didn't want to go. Every move gets more difficult for me. My mother is always trying to soothe me. I really, really don't want to do this. We have to leave Kingston. We can't stay there. And I know this. I knew that no matter [what] I did in my life I would not join the military and I would never uproot my family. I bought a house in Orleans and I stayed there for twenty-five years. I'm not saying I resent my father. It was a career choice he made. I knew I would never do that [join the military]."[79] More than five decades later Paul's helpless outrage at yet another disruption to his life remained vivid. Yet it also activated his agency. At that moment, he rejected the military lifestyle and his father's workaholic role model – a decision he stood by during his adult years.[80]

In contrast, his mother relished these adventures, "loved London," and reminisced about travelling around Europe. "I got to know Paris quite well and I got to know Brussels quite well. Lots of opportunity to travel. We came back to Ottawa. I like Ottawa." At this point, she decided to go back to nursing. "I wanted to get a car. We couldn't afford to. Then I wanted to get a dryer, I'd be off at 11 p.m. I did some private nursing and I worked in the Civic and I worked at the Royal Ottawa.

This time I was at least fifty years old. I had eight years working at the Royal Ottawa. I felt needed in the work. That was mainly the advantage. I guess I didn't feel as fulfilled until I had done this. Once I had done this, I guess I felt better about myself."[81] The Royal Ottawa was a psychiatric facility and Shelaigh enjoyed this demanding environment. While at first her motivation for working outside the home was financial, she also saw the work as "self-fulfilment" and not just a job. Her career mattered to her. In this regard, her story mirrors the experience of other Canadian mothers who entered the work force in increasing numbers by the 1960s.[82]

In retrospect, she stressed how all the military moves, separations, and challenges were good for the family, despite acknowledging their moments of difficulty and grief earlier in the interview. She believed that overcoming difficulties taught resilience and the lifestyle was worth the moments of sacrifice.

> I don't think my children suffered at all. I'm sure it benefited them. They still talk about it. All three of them have been back. They went separately. I thought that told a tale really. Mostly London. They still had friends there. Comfortable in themselves. A kind of independence. They could handle these different situations. Quite a lot for them to handle but they managed and managed very well and their memories of it are very good. And that's important. I think it made you realize that people lived all over the world. When you're in one place, you're not really aware of other people so much. Same problems and joys as the rest of us. I found it a wonderful experience. If anyone were challenged to do the same things, I hope they would do it. Attack it and enjoy it. So much to learn. I've just had a very happy life.[83]

She was right about the return trips her children had to London – both Annie and Paul recounted happy trips to visit old friends. She dismissed Paul's grief on the basis of what he learned was well worth it. Her determined note of optimism masked her own painful moments; she never mentioned her tears when Jack was in Alert. Shelaigh genuinely thrived on the new experiences and she kept close contact with military friends when her husband retired and after his unexpected death.[84]

Paul clearly disagreed with his mother's positive assessment of military family life. His wife, Sylvia, also grew up in a military family and both agreed to create a stable home life. They met while working with troubled youth in a group home and "we just seemed to click in a lot of areas. Our values were identical." He and his wife worked for the Children's Aid Society for a decade before beginning their own family of four children in 1989 and exploring other careers because they considered that work with troubled children was too demanding to undertake while raising their own children. Paul did not escape traditional masculine breadwinning obligations and a thread of desperate worry runs through his work-related stories. He ran a franchise, did odd jobs in his Orleans neighbourhood, renovation work, computer programming, and then worked in a warehouse for twelve years before retiring. In the meantime, Sylvia ran a home day care and he enjoyed activities with those children as well as caring for his own. He felt obligated to work outside the home, sometimes mowing neighbours' lawns, shovelling their driveways, and accepting short-term contracts that he hated. He enjoyed some of his jobs, but kept the last one only because it was stable. "It was not a fun job. It did not pay much."[85] Both regarded raising their children with both parents present on a daily basis as a high priority: "There were two things we were determined to accomplish and we were in agreement about that. We would not move. That was the highest on the list. We were not going to move the kids around. I knew what that did to me ... I did not want my kids to go through those moves. I wanted the two of us to be home every day. I was not going to be a salesperson or have a job like my grandfather.[86] I was going to have a job in Ottawa and be home every day. And again, I wanted to see my kids every day."[87] Paul rejected the military and the civilian masculine dominant narrative,[88] specifically referencing his paternal grandfather's work which had taken him away from his two children. While Paul worked for money, he did not accord breadwinning the central role that it had played among fathers in previous generations.[89]

Instead he became a "hands-on" parent, a father who regarded engagement as a foremost priority. "I will give them baths. I will feed them. I will change their diapers ... I would play with them in the backyard. I knew what it was like, half the time my father's not there and when he's there, he's not there. He's not engaged. It was all on her [my mother]."[90] The Taylor family stories alternatively reinforce and challenge idealized gender norms. Paul tried to mimic his brave, outgoing brother, but he came to value his own sensitive nature, demonstrating agency in rejecting a military career and in developing a parenting style different from the dominant masculine models he had observed as a child. Instead, he tried to do "a lot more listening, a lot more empathy, getting into that person's shoes and trying to figure out what's going on."[91] He accepted the poor employment and unemployment that plagued his adult years. In retirement he and his wife volunteer as replacement foster parents for abused children – something he recounts with pride and satisfaction, noting that specific children request them as caregivers.[92] His ability to nurture children is undoubtedly his most outstanding life accomplishment.[93]

His mother, Shelaigh, was the main family breadwinner at the beginning of her marriage, and her determination, independence, and outgoing nature contributed to the family's adaptation to military life. Life as a military spouse was something she chose and adored. She became the protector and role model her son most wished to emulate. Both Shelaigh and Paul exercised agency and challenged gender and social norms at key moments in their lives.

They both considered the nurture kinship relations established in Germany as a benefit to their well-being. Paul recounts how these families "were a part of his family" many years later.[94] "There are two military families that we've kept in very close contact with … They both live in Ottawa … They are significant in that they've been there all my life. Definitely the memories. I could phone any of these people any time. And I'd be invited over. And I could invite them over. My mother relied on these people. My father was away so much." These relationships evoked happy memories of playful times and of the experiences Paul wanted most to recreate with his own children when he grew up.[95] While not all military families developed nurture kin, many recount the intense socializing on military bases in Canada and Europe with nostalgia and longing.[96] Whole-life oral history allows us to dissect the interior world of a mother and child; these memories of an inclusive family-based camaraderie challenge the historical veneration of exclusively masculine combat groups and its portrayal of spouses and children as irrelevant burdens or mere support figures with little agency of their own. The Taylor family's golden memories of Germany included men, women, and children of all ages, in contrast to mostly segregated masculine and feminine networks and the childhood groupings also separated by age and gender.

Paul's constructed memories provide a more nuanced picture of Cold War military families than the "survivor" and other historiographies portray. Although rigid bipolar gender roles played a part in his life, he performed a sensitive, emotional boyhood role in this particular family and then developed those traits further as an adult, in caring for his own children and others. His "hands-on" parenting style as father of his own family and as a foster parent came partly from the lessons learned in nurture kinship play. Although Paul rejected the rootless military lifestyle, his constructed memories of Germany reflected an idealized "bubbly" world of family fun when his father became "a real fun dad." The Canadian military encouraged this idealized vision through its provision of housing, schools, recreational facilities, and community programs, but it was family members themselves who made that vision a reality and then constructed and reinforced those idealized memories through home movies, photo albums and reiterations of happy memories in reunions with nurture kin over the years.

NOTES

These are my own personal views and not necessarily those of the Department of National Defence.

1 Author interviews with Shelaigh Taylor and Annie Taylor, 30 November 2015, Ottawa; Paul Taylor, 17 November 2016, 1 December 2016, and 14 May 2018, Ottawa; Annie Taylor, 22 February 2016, 4 May 2016, and 7 November 2016, Ottawa. All names in this text are pseudonyms to protect the identities of family members and their friends. Any possible resemblance to a real Taylor family or others with names used is accidental. References to military personnel files also use pseudonyms and Canadian Access to Information and Privacy legislation applies to all records, including digital tapes.
2 Fahrni, *Household Politics*, 1.
3 Marshall, *The Social Origins of the Welfare State*.
4 Gleason, *Normalizing the Ideal*. These experts included psychologists, teachers, social workers, psychiatrists, and others who promote a highly gendered middle-class version of family values and practices.
5 René Morin, DND *Dependents' Schools, 1921–1983* (Ottawa: National Defense, 1986), 187–9.
6 Simonds to the Minister, 3 January 1952, Directorate of History and Heritage (hereafter DHH), 112.1(d97).
7 Parliament authorized a personnel ceiling of 12,000 for European deployments in 1951. Canada. Privy Council, Order-in-Council, PC 5298, 18 October 1951. The total number deployed from 1951 to 1954 is impossible to calculate because married men rotated annually, while single men stayed for two years. Additionally, air force members who took their families with them to Britain stayed longer, while army members had a high turnover. See Campbell, *Unlikely Diplomats*, chapters 3 and 4. Johnston, *War of Patrols* gives a peak Korean brigade group strength of 8,100, with annual rotations usually about 7,700. Different conditions applied to naval and air members. There is no evidence of any dependents moving to Korea where combat conditions existed.
8 During the Second World War, the idea that single men belonged to families was

more evident because some parents and siblings receiving dependent allowances. This practice ended in 1945. See Isabel Campbell, "The Triumph of the Family," paper presented at the annual meeting of the Canadian Historical Association, Brock University, May 2014.
9 Isabel Campbell, *Unlikely Diplomats*. Chapter 4 discusses different service practices. The term military policy refers to policies that applied to more than one service. While personnel policies and service culture varied, in general Canada developed more uniform policies among its services during the early Cold War until unification in 1968.
10 Ibid., chapters 4 and 5.
11 Curtis to Secretary, Chiefs of Staff, "Movement of Dependents Overseas at Public Expense," 16 September 1952, in DHH, 73/1223, file 888.
12 Campbell, *Unlikely Diplomats*, chapters 3 and 4.
13 Ibid., 115.
14 As discussed in Campbell, "Exemplary Canadians?," 61–93.
15 May, *Homeward Bound*, and Korinek, *Roughing It in the Suburbs*.
16 Grieg, *Ontario Boys*, 1–26.
17 For a recent example, see Kasurak, *A National Force*.
18 Hayes, *Crerar's Lieutenants*.
19 Enloe, *Does Khaki Become You?*; Enloe, *The Morning After*; Harrison and Laliberté, "Gender, the Military, and Military Family Support," 35–7.
20 Harrison and Laliberté, *No Life Like It*, 62–3. See also Campbell, "Exemplary Canadians?," 61–93.
21 Carstairs and Janovicek, eds, *Feminist History in Canada*; Fahrni and Rutherdale, eds, *Creating Postwar Canada*; Kinsman and Gentile, *The Canadian War on Queers*; Duder, *Awfully Devoted Women*. Canada's National Defence Department recently embarked on family studies, which include the perspectives of children and non-traditional families. See Skomorovsky and Bullock, "The Impact of Deployment on Children from Canadian Military Families," 654–73; Fisan Hujaleh, *The Impact of Military Life on Single Parent Families* (Ottawa: National Defence, 2017); Skomorovsky and Bullock, "Children's Positive Experiences Growing Up in Canadian Military Households," 21–6.
22 Wertsch, *Military Brats*. Involvement in the Vietnam War undoubtedly increased the worry of parental loss for American military children. Paul and Annie did not worry about losing their father, perhaps because his participation in the Korean Conflict occurred when Paul was an infant and before Annie was born.
23 Ibid., 426.

24 Military Brats at https://www.mysteriesofcanada.com/military/brats/ is one example (accessed 8 August 2018). There are also numerous Facebook pages and clubs for specific bases or schools.
25 McElroy, *Cold Comfort*.
26 Ibid., 148.
27 Moss, *Manliness and Militarism*, examines the role of Scouts, schools, literature, sports, and other activities in promoting militarism and notions of manliness among young boys. According to Paul's interview, he was exposed to these same influences during the Cold War along with many war movies. Paul Taylor (pseud.), interview by author, 16 November 2016, Ottawa.
28 National Defence studies of Canadian military families since the Afghanistan deployment have found that closeness with the non-deployed parents helps mitigate the negatives impacts of deployments. See Skomorovsky and Bullock, "Children's Positive Experiences Growing up in Canadian Military Households," 21–6.
29 Author interviews with Paul Taylor (pseud.), 17 November 2016, 1st December 2016, and 14 May 2018, Ottawa. See also Doucet, *Do Men Mother?* Doucet conducts in-depth interviews with other post–Cold War men who have chosen to prioritize childcare.
30 For an overview of the international literature on this topic see Ross, "'The Country of Fathers,'" 265–72.
31 In her study *Military Brats*, Wertsch dedicates an entire chapter to the American military class system, demonstrating how children sometimes challenged these boundaries that their parents enforced (see chapter 9).
32 The original anthropological definition of kinship focused upon "a relation between two or more persons that is based on common ancestry (descent or blood) or marriage (affinity)." In the twentieth century, sociologists and anthropologists expanded this definition to include "nurture" kin. My analysis draws upon the theoretical work of American cultural anthropologist David M. Schneider, which highlights the importance of the nurturing acts among individuals for the development of enduring, close relationships. Schneider challenged traditional anthropological theories about the importance of biological and genetic connections, while more recent path-breaking works by Maximilian Holland demonstrates compatibility between the biological and socio-cultural behavioural positions. See Schneider, *A Critique of the Study of Kinship*, and Holland, "Social Bonding and Nurture Kinship."
33 Wienstein and White's *Wives and Warriors* has several chapters that examine the promotion of feminine spousal networks.

34 During these years, I volunteered to teach a "National Alliance for Mental Illness" (NAMI) course, which included families dealing with suicides, murder, addictions, incarcerations, homelessness, and other outcomes of untreated or poorly treated severe mental illnesses. Only a few of these families were military and some disclosed trauma. None of these or others who had been traumatized participated in these formal taped interviews, though the private confidences of these individuals have informed my thinking.

35 Steven High emphasizes the concept of sharing authority and the importance of allowing the community to help shape the project itself. See his *Oral History at the Crossroads*, 8–25.

36 When I interviewed Paul to verify his engagement with nurture kin about eighteen months after his first interviews and after his retirement from a hated warehouse job, he had re-engaged almost full time in replacing foster parents on leave and strongly agreed with the importance of this early bonding experience in his life. However, I noticed other variations in his stories as he touched upon different periods of his childhood. His memories naturally evolved and he talked about engaging closely with troubled children, giving examples of how he and his mother utilized similar techniques to nurture their development.

37 Paul Taylor (pseud.), interview by author, 14 May 2018, Ottawa.

38 Annie Taylor (pseud.), interview by author, 22 February 2016, Ottawa: "The family folklore was that I took a long time to walk because my brothers handed everything to me."

39 The Dominion Land Survey was a massive federal government project. Histories such as Macleod, ed., *Swords and Ploughshares*, focus upon the conflict with Indigenous people over the divisions of land for settlement, but the project also had a largely unexplored impact on labour and families.

40 His daughter Annie recalled that her mother told her that Jack had grown fond of his first housekeeper and was heartbroken when she left his family to get married. Jack also refused to allow his sons to have a dog on the basis that the military moves might be hard on the dog, but Shelaigh told Annie she believed the real reason for his refusal was that Jack had lost a dog as a child and simply could not face the possibility of losing another. See Annie Taylor (pseud.), interview by author, 22 February 2016, Ottawa.

41 Gunner was the lowest rank. Taylor was promoted to bombardier (corporal equivalent) – still regarded as rank and file during service in the UK, Italy, and Northwest Europe. Jack Taylor (pseudonym), Personnel file. LAC. http://www.bac-lac.gc.ca/eng/discover/military-heritage/Pages/obtain-copies-military-

service-files.aspx. (Original paper file accessed with permission of the family and is subject to ATIP).
42 Ibid.
43 Hayes, *Crerar's Lieutenants*, 13.
44 Shelaigh Taylor (pseud.), interview by author, 30 November 2015, Ottawa. Peter and Shelaigh were interviewed separately.
45 Campbell, "Exemplary Canadians?," 61–93. For broader studies of women's engagement in the work force see Sangster, *Transforming Labour*.
46 Shelaigh Taylor (pseud.), interview by author, 30 November 2015, Ottawa.
47 Ibid.
48 Harrison and Laliberté, "Gender, The Military, and Military Family Support," 40.
49 Ibid.
50 The military divides into three broad classes: the rank and file (privates and gunners), the non-commissioned officers (promoted from lowest ranks – corporal and above), and the officer cast (lieutenants and above). Each class has its own messes and social mixing is forbidden.
51 Harrison and Laliberté, *No Life Like It*, 22–5.
52 Ibid. See also Campbell, *Unlikely Diplomats*, 102.
53 Ibid.
54 Ratkovi , "Militarism, Motherhood, and Teaching," 154.
55 Ibid.
56 Paul Taylor (pseud.), interview by author, 17 November 2016, Ottawa.
57 Ibid.
58 In a few cases, children with parents on deployment reported enjoying a closer relationship with the "at-home" parent. See Skomorovsky and Bullock, "Children's Positive Experiences Growing Up in Canadian Military Households," 21–6; Taber, "Introduction: Learning, Gender, and Militarism," xxvi. Wertsch suggests that although military sons are close to their mothers, they learn to devalue females and feminine behaviours. See Wertsch, *Military Brats*, 196–7. Paul's testimony suggests that although his father insisted on a more disciplined home, he valued his mother's nurturing skills all the more.
59 Ibid.
60 *Off to Europe*, Directorate of History and Heritage, National Defence Headquarters, (DHH), Kardex, 410.b27.066(d1).
61 Rutherdale, "Three Faces of Fatherhood as a Masculine Category," 323–48.
62 Ibid.
63 Trepanier, "Building Boys, Building Canada," notes that YMCA workers associated

Deconstructing a Canadian Military Family

emotion with femininity during this period (58). Paul's father withdrew, but did not disapprove of his wife's sympathizing. Mona Gleason found that some postwar experts advised fathers to acknowledge young children's fears with a more sensitive fatherhood role model. See Gleason, "Disciplining Children, Disciplining Parents," 202. This testimony contrasts with the pattern described by Mary Edwards Wertsch who observes that military sons "rarely seem to harbor a lake of tears" in contrast to daughters who display uncontrolled crying. See Wertsch, *Military Brats*, 115–17 and 177.

64 Shelaigh Taylor (pseud.), interview by author, 30 November 2015, Ottawa.
65 Wienstein and White, *Wives and Warriors*. See part 1 for networks among spouses.
66 Ibid.
67 So far, when I asked men about playing with girls when they were children, they denied doing so. Some got defensive, stating that they were "not interested in girls till later," clearly referring to a sexualized interest. All the women recalled at least some playtime with little boys. Gender performance interacts with constructed memories. When closely questioned, most of the men might recall some games that included girls, but women had no difficulty naming these games and recalling them easily.
68 Paul Taylor (pseud.), interview by author, 1 December 2016, Ottawa.
69 Holland, "Social Bonding and Nurture Kinship," examines how nurturing creates long-term bonds among kin groups in different societies.
70 Annie Taylor (pseud.), interview by author, 2 February 2016, Ottawa.
71 Paul Taylor (pseud.), interview by author, 1 December 2016, Ottawa. His sister Annie confided how comforted she was when her own father died suddenly in the early 1980s and Mack Nowak held her and said: "I'll be your father now." See Annie Taylor (pseud.), interview by author, 3 May 2016, Ottawa.
72 McMahan, "Finding Joy in the History of Emotions," 103–19. Historians are just beginning to look at the history of joy, separately from happiness. In this case, joy seems to have impacted Paul's perceptions of his father, of the family dynamic, and later his ideas about what fatherhood might entail.
73 Paul Taylor (pseud.), interview by author, 1 December 2016, Ottawa. Annie similarly described her father as "a closed man," noting that she learned about his childhood from her mother rather than directly from him. See Annie Taylor (pseud.), interview by author, 22 February 2016, Ottawa.
74 Hayes, *Crerar's Lieutenants*, 13. Family interviews revealed a more troubled relationship with the eldest son, Don, who left school and home at age sixteen.
75 Paul Taylor (pseud.), interview by author, 1 December 2016, Ottawa.

76 Ibid.
77 "How to Survive on the Edge: Life at Canadian Forces Station Alert," *Globe and Mail*, 21 May 2015.
78 Annie Taylor (pseud.), interview by author, 22 February 2016, Ottawa.
79 Ibid.
80 Rutherdale, "Three Faces of Fatherhood," 323–48.
81 Shelaigh Taylor (pseud.), interview by author, 15 November 2015, Ottawa.
82 Sangster, *Transforming Labour*.
83 Ibid.
84 Annie Taylor (pseud.), interview by author, 22 February 2016, Ottawa.
85 Paul Taylor (pseud.), interview by author, 1 December 2016, Ottawa.
86 Jack's father, a Dominion land surveyor, was absent much of Jack's childhood. Shelaigh's father had moved, working for Domtar Paper Mills. Note well that these civilian occupations also resulted in moves and separations.
87 Paul Taylor, interview by author, 1 December 2016, Ottawa.
88 See Haraven, "The Search for Generational Memory," 137–49, for a discussion of dominant narratives and intergenerational transmissions.
89 Rutherdale, "New 'Faces' for Father," 241–67, and Rutherdale, "Just Nostalgic Family Men?," http://www.oralhistoryforum.ca/index.php/ohf/article/view/248/323
90 Paul Taylor (pseud.), interview by author, 1 December 2016, Ottawa. According to Paul, his father "hid" behind a newspaper, ignoring his children.
91 Paul Taylor (pseud.), interview by author, 14 May 2018, Ottawa.
92 Paul Taylor (pseud.), interview by author, 1 December 2016, Ottawa. At this point, Paul and his wife had just begun this volunteer work. By April 2018, their work schedule was so full that it was difficult to schedule another interview with Paul; another interview finally took place on 15 May 2018.
93 His sister Annie taught autistic and special needs children for years. Describing herself as "firm, but fair," she credited "both Mom and Dad" as role models for this demanding career. "He was the organizer, focused. Mom not so." See Annie Taylor (pseud.), interview by author, 7 November 2016, Ottawa.
94 Paul Taylor (pseud.), interview by author, 16 November 2016, Ottawa.
95 A retired Paul and Sylvia now work as replacement foster parents with troubled youth and enjoy this work very much.
96 All the participants interviewed within the eight family groups experienced these kinship relations, but several participants from outside these family networks or others who declined to be interviewed indicated that their families did not develop life-long close relationships.

6
From Wartime Refuge to Peaceful Hippie Haven: Generations of Youth on Grindstone Island

Tarah Brookfield

Grindstone Island, a twelve-acre private isle on Big Rideau Lake, has the unusual distinction of twice being used as a sanctuary from war, once by militarists and once by pacifists. Grindstone was first the summer home of Admiral Charles Kingsmill, director of the Naval Service of Canada. After his death, Kingsmill's peace-minded daughter donated the island to the Quakers in 1963 for use as a peace education summer retreat. Attendees included activists, educators, university students, journalists, diplomats, and spiritual leaders. Children and youth were always an important part of Grindstone's landscape and mission. During the Second World War, the island housed British children evacuated from the Blitz. In the 1960s and 1970s, the sons and daughters of Canadian and American peace activists spent their summer vacations exploring the island, and taking part in multi-generational activities, such as the 1965 Grindstone Experiment, an elaborately designed role-playing exercise that simulated a mock invasion of the island that was meant to test the principles of nonviolence. Between 1966 and 1971, an annual workshop for high school students to "Explore the Possibilities of a World Free from War" became a transformative experience for youth concerned about the state of the world.[1]

This chapter will interrogate how the island, as a natural and politicized space, was presented, experienced, and embodied as a refuge for a collective of youth endangered or alarmed by war, be it the Second World War, the Vietnam War, or the Cold War. Drawing on oral history and archival documents, the chapter compares youth's experiences confronting real and imaginary experiences of war, while living away from home in the wild. The island's geographic space, in conjunction with its owners' cultural practices and ideological mission, stimulated young guests' imaginations, allowing the anxieties of war and other forms of violence to seem both distant and present, and in some cases, possible to resist. This particular piece is part of a larger monograph project based on interviews with over forty Grindstone staff or participants, some of whom have asked to be referred to by a pseudonym. I also drew on the manuscript collections of the Grindstone Cooperative and the personal papers of associated activists and Quakers. This chapter focuses on the understudied role played by Grindstone youth as members (willingly and begrudgingly) of politicized families and as independent agents in peace education and activism.

The Kingsmill Era: A Retreat from War

Prior to it becoming a site of peace education, the island was a retreat from war under an entirely different guise. Sir Charles Edmund Kingsmill (1855–1935) served forty years as an officer in Britain's Royal Navy before being chosen to found Canada's naval services in 1908. In the prelude to the First World War, he oversaw the training of Canadian naval cadets and fought unsuccessfully to expand Canada's fleet. When war was declared, he deployed two Canadian cruisers for the purposes of protecting the East and West coasts and refitted government and civilian ships to create an anti-submarine flotilla.[2] It was during his wartime leadership that Kingsmill began to spend summers on Grindstone Island with his wife Lady Frances, and their three children.

Grindstone's main cottage, dominated by a large veranda built to resemble a ship's deck, was finished in 1916. Over the years, twelve smaller buildings were added to the property, including a servants' quarters, guest cabins, a laundry, an icehouse, and a nursery, along with a boathouse, tennis court, and playhouse. Initially much of the acreage remained untamed, full of uncut grasses and bush, beaches and coves for swimming, trees to climb, and wildlife to watch. Electricity was brought over in the 1930s. Still, the island's only form of telecommunication remained a radio until the 1980s. Grindstone was located approximately seventy kilometres from Ottawa and fifty kilometres from Kingston, and was initially accessible via train and ferry. This made Grindstone a conveniently located getaway; close enough to return to the capital when needed, but distant enough to temporarily escape the pressures of war. Historians have characterized spaces such as Grindstone as where modernity and anti-modernity meet. The phenomenon of wilderness tourism, popular in turn of the century Ontario, was rooted in the cultural values of Euro-Canadians, such as the Kingsmills, who had money, leisure time, and freedom of movement. They most likely vacationed, as Patricia Jasen argues, as a "reward for coping with the stressful world of business and social obligation."[3] Spurred by new transportation technologies that made it possible for a comfortable, extended trip to the wilderness, many Canadians believed a short-term stay immersed in nature would rejuvenate the industrialized and urban body.[4]

The wilderness as a transformative space was an enduring myth, one just as appealing to Grindstone's mid- to late twentieth-century visitors. Some guests went so far as to characterize the island in utopic terms. "From the moment the launch motor dies and the craft eases up against the wharf, there is an irrepressible feeling that this is a very different island in the sun," wrote *Ottawa Citizen* reporter Andrew Cohen in 1978. "Weeping willows, maples and pines stencil jagged figures against an ice blue sky. A molten sun sears the landscape. The vision of El Dorado, Shangri-La or any other lost horizon comes to mind."[5] Similarly, oral history participants who visited Grindstone in their youth used terms such as "beautiful," "paradise," "magical," "heavenly," and "amazing" to describe the island. It is quite possible these adjectives are filtered through their adult nostalgia and vocabulary; but certainly, islands have held a special place of enchantment in children's culture and literature, symbolizing discovery and adventure in the case of *Treasure Island* or the danger and uncertainty of *Lord of the Flies* or the sanctuary and romance of *Anne of Green Gables*. Pauline Dewan, a specialist in the art of place in children's literature, classifies islands as representing "for many children their first place of autonomy, spaces free of parental control."[6] She also notes how islands tend to stand apart from the ordinary world, thus allowing not only for a "wondrous adventure" but sometimes "a revaluation of society's values" and "a place of resolution and reconciliation."[7]

In the case of Grindstone, the island was only accessible in summer, a time for school-aged children that symbolized freedom from a certain set of responsibilities. Typical summer days were filled with hours of exploration. Most of Grindstone's visitors, from the elites of the Kingsmill era, and later, the middle-class peace program participants, called cities and suburbs their home, so their exposure to a wilderness landscape would seem somewhat exotic. It was also an opportunity to pretend Grindstone was its own little world where you could practise the principles in which you believed. This might be particularly appealing to youth. "Children, who control little else in their lives," argues Sue Misheff, "have always been drawn to the concept of a place of their own where they can be lords and ladies of their own kingdoms."[8] In the case of Grindstone, the island's natural beauty was seen to be particularly conducive for personal reflection and building relationships. The simple act of leaving home, leaving one's family, and leaving the mainland could allow one to be open to new possibilities.

Admiral Kingsmill retired in 1920, not long after King George V knighted him for his service defending the British Empire. The Kingsmills summered at Grindstone in the interwar years where they hosted many friends and dignitaries, including Prime Minister Robert Borden, Prime Minister Neville Chamberlain, and actor David Niven. In reference to the leisurely days of water sports and nights filled with formal dinners, one grandson described summers on the island containing "a sort of Great Gatsby atmosphere."[9] After the admiral's death in 1935, Lady Kingsmill continued to make Grindstone her summer home. During the Second World War, at Lady Kingsmill's invitation, the island became a welcome retreat for government officials weary of the bureaucratic treadmill in Ottawa, along with members of the Women's Royal Canadian Naval Service and convalescing soldiers.[10]

Seven young family acquaintances, evacuated from Britain to Ottawa during the Second World War, joined the Kingsmill grandchildren on Grindstone in the summer months. As Claire Halstead's chapter in this volume demonstrates, the goal of state-sponsored and private evacuation schemes was intended to shelter children from the physical risks of the war. Unlike unaccompanied children, the Grindstone evacuees came with their mothers or nannies and were not housed with strangers. They also benefited from staying with a privileged family whose resources allowed them to circumvent most wartime shortages and rationing. Keeping with Grindstone's retreat mentality, there was a deliberate effort to leave the war behind, at least in front of the children. The only real tangible reminder was their missing fathers, most of whom were serving overseas or employed in other war service; however, fathers were never a familiar presence in peacetime anyway, since employment usually kept them away until the weekends. "They did not tell us about the awful parts," recalls one granddaughter, Diana Kingsmill-Flynn, in reference to the adults, particularly in regards to her uncle's wartime service in the North Atlantic.[11] Upon reflection, she seemed embarrassed to remember that she spent the war "perfectly happy," a not surprising experience given the children's young ages, the family's socioeconomic status, and their isolated locale.

British children evacuated to Canada likely felt war anxiety and the separation from home and their fathers far more strongly than the Kingsmill's own children and grandchildren. Kingsmill-Flynn has a strong memory of one small British boy who used to perpetually stand at the shore on a big rock and look out to sea, pretending to be an admiral on a ship. It is unclear if this daily game was specifically related to the war or because he was staying in the home of a deceased admiral. Nevertheless, it does call attention to the ways in which a child's imagination could be stimulated by the natural environment.

The surviving Kingsmill children inherited the island after their mother's death in 1956. There was talk of selling the property, but the politically active daughter Diana Kingsmill-Wright "hoped the tranquility of their island can be extended a little into the world."[12] Sent off to boarding school in England and finishing school in Switzerland, Kingsmill-Wright returned to Ottawa to be presented as a debutante in 1929. Her early adulthood involved marriage to the son of a British lord and politician, Victor Gordon-Lennox, international travel, and competing as part of Canada's Olympic ski team. In 1945, she eschewed her life of privilege when she married her second husband, Jim Wright, a prairie socialist, and moved to rural Saskatchewan. Out west, Kingsmill-Wright became active in cooperative, environmental, and peace movements. She worked as the editor of the *Union Farmer* newspaper and campaigned for the Canadian Commonwealth Federation party.[13] As Saskatchewan's provincial representative for the disarmament organization Voice of Women/Voix des Femmes (VOW), ending the threat of nuclear annihilation became Kingsmill-Wright's most critical political cause in the 1960s. At the same time, her son George Gordon-Lennox, a journalist with the *Ottawa Journal*, was also interested in international affairs. When he heard Grindstone might be sold, he suggested the family retain the island but lease it to a university or not-for-profit association interested in "international understanding" and working with young people.[14] The solution came via Murray Thompson, Diana's old friend and the peace education secretary for the Canadian Friends Service Committee (CFSC), the social justice wing of the Religious Society of Friends (Quakers). Kingsmill-Wright leased the island to the CFSC in 1963 for a dollar per year so that they could build a peace retreat there. She explained her decision as such: "While the island has served as a refuge for casualties of war ... the present means of destruction [means] there can no longer be war but annihilation. Thus, we feel there is only one course to follow – to do what is in our power to help build the peace."[15] Kingsmill-Wright felt her father would have approved, explaining that in the last years of his life, Admiral Kingsmill began to question the use of military solutions to resolve conflicts. He felt it was tragic that air warfare put civilians at such great risk.[16]

Building a Peaceful Community

Since the seventeenth century, Quakers have been committed to actively opposing war and committing to peace. They have traditionally worked toward this goal through conscientious objection, civil disobedience, peace education, and assistance to refugees. The CFSC's educational work at Grindstone was both a product of and departure from the broader Canadian peace movement. While the public spectacle of protests, marches, and letter-writing campaigns organized by groups like the VOW or the Canadian Committee for Nuclear Disarmament (CCND) targeted government action and broad civic engagement, Grindstone under the CFSC focused more on social change through education. The CFSC transformed the Kingsmill summer home into a camp that could accommodate approximately fifty overnight guests. Quakers Nancy and John Pocock, who supervised the camp, scheduled fourteen workshops for the first summer on topics as varied as "Creative Alternatives to the Arms Race," "National Interest and International Responsibility," and "Towards a Relevant Christian Peace Testimony."[17] While children, including the Pococks' teenage daughter Judy, accompanied parents to some of the above-mentioned events, the first summer also held one specific multigenerational event. VOW rented out the facilities to host a conference designed to encourage cross-cultural understanding between families from English and French Canada. The conference involves structured meetings, language lessons, cultural exhibitions, and group recreational activities.[18]

By the end of the first summer, Jack Pocock concluded, "Grindstone has already become a concrete and visible symbol of the peace effort in Canada."[19] He attributed this to the centre's ability to attract 377 registered participants in the first summer of operation, followed by 424 visitors in 1964 and 496 in 1965.[20] Most adult guests were members of existing Canadian and American peace, civil rights, and internationalist groups. Grindstone's youngest participants were usually their offspring or teens interested in politics and/or seeking an awakening. The latter was the case of Peter, a high school workshop participant, who recalled: "I'd never been to anything like that [Grindstone]. It ended up being significant to me because I'd grown up in a fairly sheltered, naïve environment ... [I] certainly was not exposed to things politically. At Grindstone I first clued in to Bob Dylan. That was the month Sergeant Pepper Came out, and we had that there. It was a real eye opener ... It certainly affected my life. It was one of the first times I experienced thoughts about social agitation and actually doing political work to make things change."[21] With few exceptions, Grindstone's guests were left leaning and came from white, middle-class households in and around Toronto, Ottawa, and Montreal. Unsurprisingly, Quakers made up a large cohort. There were also a number of Jewish participants and members from Christian denominations, but approximately one-third of participants described themselves as having no religious affiliation.[22] While the gender ratio varied depending on the specific topic of each seminar, high support from VOW meant that women made up approximately 60 per cent of the participants each summer in the 1960s. Between 1963 and 1968 there were a number of international visitors; 12 per cent of the participants were American and 10 per cent came from other countries, including university students on exchange from Asia, Latin America, and Africa. Some of the Americans were young men of draft age and used their visit to make connections with Canadians who could advise them about immigrating to Canada.[23] Among the Canadians, one 1967 survey reports that 67 per cent of Grindstone guests had voted for the New Democratic Party.[24] For some guests, their radicalism extended to lifestyle or fashion choices associated with the counterculture. "Going to Grindstone Island and you could always pick out on the ferry who was hippies and who were the cottagers right?" quipped David Josephy, who visited the island with his parents and brother in the 1960s and later returned to attend the high school workshops.[25]

Practising Peace and Non-Violence as a Family

The Josephys fit the profile of typical Grindstone family: a married couple with young children, active and committed in peace work. Walter and Goldie had immigrated to Canada from England in 1956. Walter was a teacher with the Eastern Ontario Institute of Technology and Goldie focused on raising their two sons, Michael and David, born in the 1950s. The family was Jewish, though non-practising for the most part, and Goldie later converted to Anglicanism. Walter's family fled Nazi persecution in Germany in the 1930s, while Goldie grew up during the London Blitz; both knew firsthand the terror and destruction of war. They became quite active in Cold War–driven peace movements in Ottawa, including branches of the Committee for Control of Radiation Hazards and the Committee to End the War in Vietnam, and they started the Committee for Peace and Liberation. Goldie was also a member of VOW, who on her own, or with her children in tow, participated in anti-war marches and organized the Ottawa visits of Nobel Peace Prize recipient Linus Pauling. As an entire family, the Josephys marched against the installation of BOMARC missiles at the Royal Canadian Air Force base in La Macaza, Quebec, in 1964. The family also opened their Ottawa home to American draft resisters seeking temporary refuge. When asked why she was so active, Goldie replied, "I protest for my children's sake, and for their children. I want the human race to survive. Willfully adding to the peril of the world – nuclear explosions, pollution and the rest – is demonic. We must fight against it."[26]

The Josephys visited Grindstone numerous times together in the 1960s. While Walter and Goldie attended seminars, the sons spent the days hiking, fishing, canoeing, swimming, and reading. Once the high school workshops began, their youngest son, David, visited Grindstone without his parents for two summers. While Grindstone acted as a temporary sanctuary for many families, the participants or island should not be idealized. Like many active families, the Josephys were typical in how the struggle to balance paid responsibilities at work, at home, and in their activism could be insurmountable. The couple divorced in 1975, a decision their sons attribute to their mother's intense commitment to her activism.[27]

The Josephys and other participants who visited as a family attended Grindstone for practical and ideological reasons. The island's setting made it attractive to families looking to combine learning with an affordable summer holiday. It was also a more appealing location than a mainland conference centre.[28] Workshops were usually scheduled during the day, with breaks for shared meals, meditation, and outdoor activities. Children and non-participating spouses were free to spend their entire time on leisure activities. Grindstone also became a family-friendly space for parents wanting to immerse themselves and their offspring in an environment that supported their intertwined political beliefs and parenting goals. Many of these parents believed that being active in the peace movement was part of being a *good* parent, a sentiment expressed by renowned pediatrician and anti-war activist Dr Spock in 1963: "It simply isn't enough today for parents to give birth to a child to feed, clothe and toilet train him and send him to school. They must do their part to see that the world is not annihilated before the child can inherit it. And they must bring him up unwarped by Cold War anxieties. What can we tell our children when they are anxious? We can tell them what we are doing personally in working for peace."[29] While the majority of Grindstone programs approached Spock's advice by attempting to solve global security threats and local inequities, Grindstone also ran a specific workshop for parents and teachers called "Raising Children for a Better World." It orchestrated discussions on how to practise peaceful childrearing in regards to discipline, developing morals, cooperative play, and non-violent toys. More generally, it addressed "concerns for caregivers in a nuclear age."[30]

The Grindstone Experiment

Occasionally, the practicalities of parenting collided with the practices of non-violence and a peaceful ideology. This can be most dramatically seen during the Training Institutes in Non-Violence, which "took discussion about peace issues such as non-violent resistance a giant leap forward by realistically stimulating an actual conflict situation, with participants split into aggressors and defenders."[31] Much like the civil defence training exercises analyzed by Andrew Burtch in this volume, these exercises involved significant role play, a form of experimental learning popular in the 1960s and 1970s in which participants immersed themselves in fictional scenarios to practice decision-making and self-reflection. The goal was to prepare activists and educators engaging in real non-violence activities to most effectively confront resistance to their causes, whether it be police action breaking up a peaceful protest or opening dialogues with those committed to violent action as a means of change or social control. Unlike the infamous role play in the Stanford Prison Experiment or Milgram Experiment, there was no deception involved in Grindstone's role play; however, much like those social psychological experiments, participants in the Training Institutes for Non-Violence deeply immersed themselves in their roles and confessed to having strong emotional reactions to the intense situations they experienced. Unique to Grindstone's role play was the presence of children and youth whose participation added a layer of realism to the fictional scenario, forcing the adults to consider the implications of experimental learning and the ideology they were practising.

Grindstone's most heightened non-violence simulation was the infamous 1965 experiment where fifty-one participants engaged in a mock invasion of the island. Divided into umpires, defenders, and invaders, the simulation was meant to test how well the participants assigned as defenders were able to apply the principles of non-violence resistance in an oppressive scenario. A third of the defenders were young people between the ages of two and fifteen, dependents of the adult participants. These included the four Christiansen family siblings, all but one of whom were high school students from Connecticut. They were on the island with their mother Mary and their father Gordon, a chemistry professor, who was active in the War Resisters League and chairperson of the American Committee for Non-Violent Action. On the younger side were the three Olson siblings from Newborough, New York, who accompanied their mother Lydia and their father Theodore, a Presbyterian minister and creator of the Upland Institute, a professional school

Figure 6.1
Adult and child participants in the Training Institute in Non-Violence known as 31 Hours, 1965. Nancy Pocock Fonds, Clara Thomas Archives and Special Collections, York University.

of social action training in Pennsylvania. Both fathers would later co-author *Thirty-One Hours: The Grindstone Experiment*, a transcript and analysis of the planning, experiment, and debrief of the role play exercise that they had designed.[32] For the Christiansen and Olson families, particularly the mothers, parenting had to continue during the experiment and consequently, decisions had to be made regarding the extent of the children's engagement in the role play. In other cases, the young people's genuine interest or lack thereof in the adults' make believe influenced the experiment's outcomes.

Sometimes the children's impact was a consequence of their schedules, supervisory needs, and attention spans. For example, a late meeting for the defender liaisons was cancelled because a fifteen-year-old liaison had already gone to bed.[33] The experiment's transcript also records a snippet of conversation between the Olson sisters in which they discovered their brother Ernst was somewhere he should not have been, to which Margrit Ann replied, "No! Oh, no," followed by Johanna saying, "He can't go without a mother!" There is no context to this discussion, but it suggests little Ernst was breaking some set of rules, whether out of confusion, apathy, or because the adults were otherwise distracted. During the exercise, there was a meeting for worship, held silently per Quaker principles, in which teenage Scott Christiansen played a practical joke by blasting the Doors song "People are Strange" on the record player in the main lodge. The presence and participation of youth affected the role play's direction in subtle ways, while also demonstrating children's agency to play along or resist the adults' plans.

In more significant ways, Ted Olson believes that "people probably changed how they'd behave because of the presence of the children."[34] Most notably, the well-being of and uses for child defenders were taken into consideration during the planning stages of the exercise. Since people could be "killed" in the game, foster parents were selected in case there was a "loss" of biological parents. Hiding spaces like cubby holes were prepared in advance. Most significantly, meeting minutes show that one idea floated was that "Children may be used spontaneously to break down barriers or in highly defined situations with their parents' consent."[35] In regards to the latter, the use of children in political protest was not a new concept. vow and its American equivalent, Women Strike for Peace, had long used the voices and bodies of real children in their marches and protests as an effective means to reinforce the respectability of their maternal activism and convey the "children are our future" message. For some parents, bringing children along was also due to a lack of other childcare options.[36] Acting on their own or on their parents' initiatives, African American children and teens were on the frontlines of civil rights demonstrations in the American South in the 1950s and 1960s. Michael Sznajderman's study of the youth marches against segregation in Birmingham, Alabama, demonstrates the important presence of young Black activists in the civil rights movement. Not only did it signal a united Black community, but images of Black school children taking to the streets, where they were harassed and arrested by police and brutalized by police dogs and fire hoses, were credited with awakening national public sympathy. Concurrently, civil rights activist parents were criticized for placing their children at risk. In response, these parents argued there were more important, long-term improvements to their children's welfare that only desegregation and equity could bring.[37] No further details were provided in the Grindstone records to illuminate the specific uses of children imagined in the experiment. Given the Quaker mentality, it is unlikely the children were to be used as human shields. Rather, the children may have been expected to consciously or subconsciously charm or trick the invaders with their childish innocence. Alternatively, the presence of children could help the defenders appeal to the emotional nature of the invaders.

In reality, the children made the adult defenders, particularly the mothers, feel more vulnerable than expected, particularly when it came to the main form of non-violent resistance chosen to demonstrate opposition to the invasion, a hunger strike.[38] Most defenders stated they would respect if the mothers and children sat out the hunger strike, though at least one defender thought the cooperation of everyone was necessary since the image of hungry children would give the invaders "a black mark with their superiors and possibly with the world at large, thus bringing pressure for release of the defenders."[39] On the first evening of the hunger strike, Mary Christiansen escorted all the children to the dining hall to eat dinner, though she did not eat herself. Meanwhile in solidarity, her eldest child Steve fasted along with her. He remembers rationalizing his choice: "I wanted to be part of the fasting group. I didn't want to be treated like a kid … I think maybe I was kind of halfway between the life of a child and the life of an adult."[40] Steve's siblings, Scott, Roger, and Cori, confessed by morning they were happy to skip the "lousy" oatmeal breakfast served at Grindstone, and pretended they were participating in a hunger strike too, something Scott remembers the adults praising him for.[41] Meanwhile Lydia Olson, who had experienced real hunger as a child in the Philippines during the Second World War, had "mixed emotions" at including a hunger strike in the role play.[42] Ultimately, the issues of food became moot as the exercise ended after thirty-one hours, several days earlier than planned, due to the emotional distress caused by the "death" of thirteen participants who were "shot" by the invaders for refusing to obey an order to desist their non-violent protests.

In the aftermath of the experiment, many participants classified the role play as a failure for non-violence, while others thought it was valuable in thinking realistically of how one could organize peacefully when confronted with violence. While it had not been a deliberate intent, making the experiment a multigenerational activity with children present impacted the dynamics of the game and forced participants to consider (and in some cases reconsider) the application and style of non-violence resistance. Furthermore, seeing children take on adult-like roles and responsibilities or suffer deprivation likely forced some participants to reflect on the transience of childhood in violent circumstances. Although none of the youth were included in the formal debrief recorded in *Thirty-One Hours*, looking back thirty years later, many mentioned how surprised they were at the adults' intense reaction to a game, and critiqued its value as a learning exercise. Even as a child, Scott Christiansen believed he knew at the time how phony the exercise was, adding, "that's not to say that you couldn't gain some kind of perspective on nonviolence," but that if it had "truly been an occupation of Nazi-type people, it would have been a little more brutal and serious ... I think the fact that we all knew that it wasn't real, that it was a lot easier to ... be a resistor simply because it wasn't real."[43] While some of the youth had harsh words for the experimental learning they witnessed in 1965, many were keen to move from the peripheries of Grindstone programming. In 1966, the development of the high school workshop allowed teenagers to take centre stage at Grindstone for a week each summer.

High School Workshops

Youth visiting Grindstone were part of an exodus of Canadian children trekking far from home each summer to soak in sunshine, fresh air, and the values associated with simple living. While the most extreme expression of this tradition would be hitchhiking, a popular escapade for young men and women coming of age during the counterculture, summer camps remained popular spaces bridging autonomy and collective experiences.[44] In *The Nurture of Nature: Childhood, Antimodernism, and Ontario Summer Camps, 1920–55*, Sharon Wall explains how under the guise of outdoor recreation, camps were designed to imbue a progressive form of education critical to child development. As participants in transformative experiences, campers were expected to graduate with an appreciation and the skills required for becoming productive and well-rounded citizens. Across North America, discerning parents could choose from a variety of camp options emphasizing certain skills, or what particular brand of citizenship would be emphasized. The fact that almost every religious sect and political affiliation hosted a summer camp spoke to the perceived value of camps as important spaces to further inaugurate youth in their parents' belief system. Since the 1930s, Quaker youth had spent summers at Camp Neekaunis on Georgian Bay in youth-only or family camps that combined worship, recreation, and education. Not unlike Grindstone, Neekaunis mixed outdoor education with Quaker principles, including their commitment to peace and non-violence, which meant that campers could spend an afternoon participating in an Underground Railway role play or drive across the US border to bring cash donations to organizations supporting draft dodgers.[45]

Because Neekaunis already served youth, Grindstone did not initially include separate programming for adolescents. "We had no intention of having teenagers," explained Nancy Pocock, "except the odd one who wanted to come. It reached the stage where teenagers were getting too difficult for them to cope with at Camp Neekaunis. It was when kids were first starting to get into drugs and sex. They said: 'Let's send them to Grindstone!'"[46] The psychedelic youth culture emerging within the counterculture in the 1960s and 1970s, some of which ran counter to Quaker principles of abstaining from alcohol and drugs, can partly explain the demand for something less traditional than Neekaunis. More broadly, the new programming at Grindstone addressed adult anxiety about what Mischa Honeck and Gabriel Rosenberg have dubbed the "Atomic Generation," the cohort of baby boomers who grew up in the shadows of Hiroshima and the Cuban Missile Crisis. This generation were by no means the first to reflect on their vulnerability, but the dangers specific to that period prompted an urgency for the development of political programming "accessible to youth, directed toward youth, and expressed by youth."[47] As high school workshop participant Mary Newberry recalled, "I don't remember a time that we weren't afraid of nuclear war … My generation all remembers the day Kennedy died and, and I remember the tension around the Cuban Missile Crisis and the Vietnam War."[48] The Pococks' own daughter Judy experienced this restlessness. Raised as a Quaker, by the time her parents were wardens on Grindstone, she had begun to drift away from Quakerism and was "moving towards Marxism, moving towards Communism," where she wrestled with the principles of pacifism alongside the possibility that a revolution might be needed to bring about social and political change. "We fought a lot," Judy recalls, over her new influences. At Grindstone, she bunked with the kitchen staff and experienced more independence as she mingled with the other guests. "So the nice thing about Grindstone was … although I was with them [her parents] … I had some independence and people related to me independently of them."[49]

The high school workshop began in 1966 and ran for five years. Students in their last three years of study were eligible and the cost was $15 or $20 for one week. Often, the young participants had already been to Grindstone with their families before or heard about the program through friends or faculty in alternative schools in Toronto, Ottawa, Montreal, and New York. Unlike Neekaunis, the high school workshops were non-denominational, had a significant portion of time led by the youth themselves, and prioritized a semi-structured curriculum based on non-violence, civil rights, and disarmament over traditional camp activities. "I was aware that Grindstone Island wasn't a camp," recalls Eve Schmitz-Hertzberg, "it wasn't a place where you just went and had fun, that you were expecting that you would be doing some work, intellectual work, thinking."[50] The day began at 7:00 a.m. with a swim, followed by meditation, and a time set side aside for a creative activity. In the afternoon and evening there were three time slots for work groups and community meetings, plus another swim break and free time. Questions addressed in the work groups included "Can we honestly respond to social problems and still make a living, please our parents and live in suburbia – do we want to?" and "How are social issues confronted today by non-violence confrontation, flower-power politics, dropping out, working groups for change, and traditional politics?" Facilitators, referred to as "resource people" to avoid an authoritarian perception, were typically under twenty-four years of age. They included David DePoe, de facto leader of Toronto's Yorkville community of hippies, diggers, and other counterculture youth, or "young thinking" adults like the Pococks.[51] While there were rules against underage drinking, oral history recollections from youth and staff suggest some resource people turned a blind eye when some kids engaged in pot smoking or alcohol consumption during free time.

As with most camps, the friendships, romances, rivalries and pranks, and sense of place stand out the most thirty years later. As Mary Newberry recalls, "my memories are really around developing my own personality and not so much about developing political ideas or social justice ideas even though that was the stuff at the background."[52] For others the trip to Grindstone was indeed life changing. Such was the case for Ted Hill, an African American young man from New Jersey who in a letter to the Pococks asked if he could come back because "I had never enjoyed myself so much in such a complete way as I did last year on Grindstone, and I had a lump in my throat the size of an apple the morning I left." According to his letter, his time at Grindstone and meeting the Pococks inspired him to immigrate to Canada where he would be safe from the draft.

In other cases, youth left Grindstone disappointed, feeling the program was too tame. "I'm stifled in school and in a similar way here," expressed one participant in anonymous evaluation of the 1967 workshop. Harsher criticism came from another youth who called the program "bureaucratic" claiming the organizers tended to manipulate consensus in meetings.[53] Other feedback included complaints about the presence of cliques, accusations that the girls were not being serious enough or the boys were too hostile. In 1969, there were recurring tensions between American and Canadian youth that played out on the volleyball court. The escalating aggression resulted in the triumphant American volleyball team replacing Grindstone's United Nations flag with their own handmade USA flag. In response a group of Canadian boys torn it down and burnt it, an event that caused multiple attempts at reconciliations by facilitators with lacklustre results.[54]

Figure 6.2
Players on Grindstone volleyball court, 1976. Canadian Yearly Meeting Archives and Library, Pickering College.

While internal discord could make for powerful teaching moments, it could also spark pessimism at humanity's capacity for conflict and violence. "I still don't understand people," one youth reflected at the end. "I mean the hatred, killing, stupidities and goddamn blindness. I find myself hating mankind and wishing I was dead and other times trembling at the thought of the A-bomb and wishing all the hate in the world were changed into love."[55] As with the adult programming, often the sessions at Grindstone exposed individual and group imperfections, prejudice, and biases which participants acknowledged were barriers toward building a culture of peace not only in the wider world, but also on the island.

In the early 1970s, participation in all of Grindstone's adult and youth programs declined, a change attributed to less public engagement in the peace movement, as well as CFSC's attention and resources being split between Grindstone and Neekaunis. Paired with a financial crisis that meant Diana Kingsmill-Wright had to sell the island, the early to mid-1970s represented a period of disillusionment. The 1974–75 shift from CFSC leadership to a cooperative model, with former participants buying shares and managing governance, saved Grindstone from financial ruin and revived its programming. It lasted for another decade and half, during which time youth once again became critical players, as participants in an alternative children's camp, as well as taking on roles as staff and co-op board members.

Conclusion

While there was no universal experience of children and youth at Grindstone, the young people drawn to the island commonly viewed it as a sanctuary. Whether it literally offered protection from war, as in the case of the British children escaping the Blitz, or acted as a safe space for the Canadian and American hippie youth to grapple with the causes of and solutions to war in the 1960s and 1970s, the island represented possibility. This is best summed up by David Josephy: "Growing up in suburban Ottawa, I very much felt in the late 1960s that a revolution was going on and I was missing it. Because all these incredible things were happening, but they were happening somewhere else … and then suddenly you went into this place where you just felt like you were part of this revolution of change in the world." Grindstone might have been miles away from Woodstock or Birmingham in terms of geography and urgency, but for the young people who spent time on the island, it was a transformative space that allowed them to feel they were somewhere safe, somewhere special. Not only were their futures valued, they were considered valuable members of their families, communities, and nations.

NOTES

1 This research was supported by the Social Sciences and Humanities Research Council of Canada.
2 Sarty, "Admiral Kingsmill and the Early Years of the Royal Canadian Navy," 75–7.

3   Jasen, *Wild Things*, 20.
4   Stevens, "Cars and Cottages," 26–56; Wall, *The Nurture of Nature*.
5   Cohen, "Sticking to the Grindstone for Peace," *Ottawa Citizen*, 16 August 1978.
6   Dewan, *The Art of Place in Literature for Children and Young Adults*, 99.
7   Ibid., 102–3.
8   Quoted in ibid., 99.
9   George Gordon-Lennox, quoted in MacAdam, *Making Waves: The Grindstone Story*, 9.
10 MacAdam, 11.
11 Diana Kingsmill-Flynn, interview by author, 9 May 2013.
12 Barrie Zwicker, "Quakers Lease Island for Peace Conference," *Globe and Mail*, 3 July 1963, 10.
13 Carroll Allen, "Making a Little Go a Long Way," *Homemaker's Magazine* 9, no. 5 (September 1974): 85–7.
14 Quoted in MacAdam, *Making Waves: The Grindstone Story*, 16.
15 Archives of Ontario (AO), Grindstone Cooperative Fonds (GCF), Minutes of the Advisory Council for Grindstone Island Peace Centre, 2 June 1963
16 MacAdam, *Making Waves: The Grindstone Story*, 7.
17 Zwicker, "Quakers Lease Island for Peace Conference," 10.
18 Library and Archives Canada (LAC), Voice of Women Fonds, MG 28, I 218, Vol. 7, File 17.
19 MacAdam, *Making Waves: The Grindstone Story*, 19.
20 Ibid., 18–22.
21 Quoted in MacAdam, *Making Waves: The Grindstone Story*, 22.
22 AO, GCF, "1967 Quaker-UNESCO Seminar, Written by Dr Hanna Newcombe and Dr William Eckhardt, F4326-2 Archives 1967.
23 Clara Thomas Archives, Nancy Pocock Fonds, 1998-041 1017 (26), Letter from Ted Hill III to Nancy and John, 7 April 1968.
24 Ibid.
25 David Josephy, interview by author, 17 June 2013.
26 Bruce Ward, "'I Am a Bit of a Fossil,' Says City's Habitual Protester," *Ottawa Citizen*, 12 June 1974.
27 Author interviews with Michael Josephy and David Josephy, 7 June 2005.
28 Workshops ranged from weekend to weeklong events, costing $6 per day per adult, $5 per day per couple, and $3 per day for children under twelve and students. It was slightly cheaper in the non-peak months of June and September. AO, GCF, "1965 brochure," F4326-2 Archives 1965.

29 LAC, VOW Fonds, "What, How, Why?" Pamphlet, NA, MG 28, I 218, Vol. 7, File 17.
30 AO, GCF, F4326-6-0-4, Raising Children for a Better World Part III Poster, no date.
31 MacAdam, *Making Waves: The Grindstone Story*, 23.
32 Olson and Christiansen, *Thirty-One Hours: The Grindstone Experiment*.
33 Ibid., 7.
34 Ted and Lydia Olson, interviews by author, 21 October 2014.
35 Olson and Christiansen, *Thirty-One Hours: The Grindstone Experiment*, 8.
36 Brookfield, *Cold War Comforts*, 14.
37 Sznajderman, "A Dangerous Business," 27.
38 Olson and Christiansen, *Thirty-One Hours: The Grindstone Experiment*, 90. It should be noted that at points in the text people are not identified by name, though sometimes they are described as a "mother" or "child" narrowing down the list of potential people belonging to the Olsen or Christiansen family.
39 Ibid., 13.
40 Steve Christiansen, interview by author, 18 September 2014.
41 Scott Christiansen, interview by author, 22 September 2014.
42 Ted and Lydia Olson, interview by author, 21 October 2014.
43 Scott Christiansen, interview by author, 22 September 2014.
44 Mahood, *Thumbing a Ride*.
45 Author interviews with Nora Newcombe, 15 October 2014 and Eve Schmitz-Hertzberg, 25 April 2015.
46 Quoted in MacAdam, *Making Waves: The Grindstone Story*, 22.
47 Honeck and Rosenberg, "Transnational Generations," 237.
48 Mary Newberry, interview by author, 13 July 2013.
49 Judy Pocock, interview by author, 23 September 2014.
50 Schmitz-Hertzberg, interview by author, 25 April 2015.
51 AO, GCF, F4326-3-0-14, Grindstone Reports, High School Workshop "Theme: Man as a Creative Force?" July 2–8 1967, 1–3.
52 Mary Newberry, interview by author, 13 July 2013.
53 AO, GCF, F4326-3-0-14, Grindstone Reports, High School Workshop 1967, 4–5.
54 AO, GCF, F4326-3-0-14, Grindstone Reports, High School Workshop "Theme: No Man Is an Island," 2–8 July 1969.
55 AO, GCF, F4326-3-0-14, Grindstone Reports, High School Workshop 1967, 5.

PART THREE

TELLING DIFFICULT STORIES

7
Adolescents during Canada's Afghanistan Mission

Deborah Harrison and Patrizia Albanese

The war in Afghanistan (2001–14) represents, to date, the longest military engagement in Canadian history. This engagement was also the first occasion since the Boer War that Canadian troops participated in a counterinsurgency, and the first time since the Korean War that Canadian military members sustained a significant number of casualties. More than 40,000 Canadian Armed Forces (CAF) members served in the twelve-year campaign, and 165 Canadians – 158 soldiers and 7 civilians – lost their lives.

During the Afghanistan mission, the Canadian public heard from the media daily about the deployment of troops to volatile areas, coverage that intensified when CAF members were killed by roadside bombs or in combat. But they heard almost nothing about the impact dangerous deployments had on the members of military families, especially children. As a result, Canadians who were not members of the military community learned very little about how the Afghanistan mission affected members of military families.[1]

By 2006 this chapter's first author had completed two large research projects on CAF spouses.[2] Harrison and other researchers from across Canada shifted their attention to CAF adolescents, realizing that research on CAF adolescents could potentially capture some of the intergenerational aspects of the impact of military life stressors, especially deployments, on the civilian members of military families. As opposed to very young children, military adolescents possess a full understanding of the dangers of a volatile deployment. They are also often required to become family caregivers for siblings and/or struggling parents at a time when their own developmental needs are strong.

In the meantime, 800 soldiers from the CAF base in Armyville, Canada (a pseudonym), were scheduled to deploy to Kandahar early in 2007. More than forty staff members and 1,600 students in the Armyville School District (ASD; also a pseudonym) had a close relative serving in the CAF. In response to feedback from teachers who had warned her that the Afghanistan deployment would be "different," the superintendent of the ASD began to implement an action plan that included assembling a multidisciplinary emergency response team that would be in a position to provide support to principals and the affected students who attended their schools, in the event of an incident in Kandahar involving casualties. During the process of implementing this plan, the superintendent became aware that her staff knew little about what the ASD students experienced at home during even a routine overseas deployment. She agreed to enter the ASD into a partnership with our team because she believed that reliable Canadian research data could lead to an improved, evidence-based Armyville School District response.

This chapter discusses some of the survey and interview findings of the research project that emerged from this collaboration. It provides some insight into how the students attending Armyville High School (AHS) were affected by the Afghanistan mission – at home, at school, among their friends, and when their parents returned suffering from post-traumatic stress disorder (PTSD).[3]

Our first step was to compare the well-being, family functioning, attitudes toward school, and peer relationships of adolescents from CAF families with those of (a) their civilian peers at the same school, and (b) their peers in Cycle 7 (2006–07) of the National Longitudinal Survey of Children and Youth (NLSCY). To this end, we administered a quantitative survey to most of the students attending AHS (1,066 out of a total of circa 1,200) on 7 October 2008.

The NLSCY is a national study that began in 1994 to collect information on Canadian children's development and well-being. The NLSCY followed its initial cohort of over 22,000 children (zero to eleven years) every two years until Cycle 8, the last cycle, which was collected between September 2008 and July 2009.[4] The NLSCY sample was selected in such a way that children from military families were excluded. In addition to NLSCY measures, our survey included selected measures from (a) the Children of Alcoholics Screening Test (CAST)[5] and (b) the Juvenile Victimization Questionnaire (JVQ)[6] in order to address specific stressors associated with military life that are not included in the NLSCY. Our survey also added questions that were designed to elicit each participant's "CAF status."

We defined a CAF *adolescent* as someone who had at least one parent or stepparent who either (a) was a current regular or reservist CAF member or (b) took their release from the regular or reserve CAF during the previous five years *and* had been a member for at least four years prior to release. In our view, a CAF adolescent's parent or stepparent needed to have been a member of the CAF long enough to have experienced the impact of CAF membership upon family life. We considered four years to have been long enough. If the parent was a former CAF member, we believed that they needed to have been released during the five years before our survey so that their CAF experience was recent and could be remembered by the adolescent offspring we studied. Adolescents with parents who met these criteria were counted as CAF adolescents. A *civilian youth* had no parents or stepparents who had ever belonged to the CAF. Fifty-two adolescents fell into neither category (e.g., they had parents who had been CAF members for two years twenty years ago) and were excluded from our quantitative analyses. About half (481) of the participants who answered the survey questions about CAF status were CAF adolescents. Forty-five percent (436) were civilian youth.[7]

During the fall/winter of 2009–10, we conducted semi-structured, two-hour interviews with sixty-one of the CAF adolescents, on the impact of deployments and other military life stressors on their lives. We recruited these sixty-one participants by inviting the students in each classroom who had participated in the survey to volunteer by filling out the contact information sheets attached to their surveys. From the pool of 450 volunteers, we constructed a quota sample, consisting of fifteen CAF adolescents from each grade (sixteen from grade 9), with gender proportions reflecting our volunteer pool demographics, and an attempt to include youth with parents representing all ranks, and both regular and reservist status.[8] We interviewed thirty-five girls and twenty-six boys who, among them, had sixty-nine parents who were current or recently retired CAF members. Only sixteen (23 per cent) of these parents were other than current regular members, and all of these sixteen parents were recently retired regular members, retired regular members who now worked as reservists, or regular members who had been medically released. None of them had ever been career reservists. Seven (10 per cent) of the sixty-nine parents were present or former commissioned officers (captains, majors, or lieutenant-colonels); the remaining sixty-two (90 per cent) were present or former non-commissioned members (warrant officer, sergeant, corporal, and private ranks). This ratio varied from the 20:80 ratio of officers to non-commissioned members that currently exists in the CAF.[9]

All sixty-nine parents were present or former army members, except for four who were from the air element or the navy. Since we carried out the interviews a year following the survey, the interviews were with students who, when interviewed, were in grades 10, 11, 12, and recently graduated. The interviews covered a range of topics unique to military life that had not been covered in the survey, including relocations, deployments, deployment-related PTSD, family functioning, the participants' perceptions of the impact of military life stressors on their families and lives, their perceptions of how they and their families had been supported by the school and the local Military Family Resource Centre (MFRC), and their perceptions of their own resilience.

All the interviews were audio-recorded. After they had been transcribed, we organized the responses to our open-ended questions thematically, via an inductive process of generating categories from data, which resembled (but was not synonymous with) grounded theory methodology.[10] We developed a range of codes to begin compiling our strongest evidence. Once our descriptive codes had been created, three team members worked independently, eventually merging their work in order to arrive at the set of "subcodes" within each code that best reflected the interview data.

Since our interview participants were relatively few in number, and self-selected, what they told us cannot be considered representative of the experiences of military adolescents, CAF adolescents, or even the CAF adolescents who attended Armyville High School in 2009–10. However, much of what they told us was rich and insightful, and consistent with other, mostly American-based, research. We therefore consider it suggestive.

Our survey findings were possibly more than suggestive because almost all the students attending AHS on 7 October 2008 actually filled out the survey. As well as comparing the mental well-being of CAF students with that of their civilian peers at the same school (there was no significant difference), our analysis of survey data compared all the students at AHS with their age peers across Canada. A somewhat disturbing finding that emerged from this comparison was that *all* AHS students – CAF and civilian alike – were significantly more likely than their national peers to experience depression, to suffer from low self-esteem, and to have thought about suicide.[11]

Huebner and colleagues recently applied Boss's *ambiguous loss* theory to adolescents living through parental deployments.[12] According to this theory, the combination of (a) the *loss* of the parent as they were (e.g., because they are away on the deployment) and (b) the *ambiguity* inherent in the fact that, despite this loss, the parent is still "there," very much present in the adolescent's life, is a potent emotional brew. According to Boss, the confusion inherent in loss coupled with ambiguity erects a barrier to effective coping and grieving, and leads to mental health problems such as depression and conflicted relationships.[13]

According to both Reed[14] and Jensen,[15] boys' well-being may be more negatively affected than that of girls by the loss of their father during a deployment, and by the fact that they are more likely than girls to respond to the diminished supervision at home with risky behaviours. On the other hand, the school staff who participated in the focus groups organized by Anita Chandra and colleagues reported that older and female adolescents are more emotionally challenged during deployments than male adolescents because they are more frequently required to assume increased household responsibilities, take care of younger siblings, and become co-parents with their undeployed parents.[16]

One of the most important themes to emerge from our interviews was isolation, an outcome that is characteristic of both internalizing and externalizing mental health symptoms. As "Zoe," a senior girl, eloquently told us, "you feel isolated. You can't talk to anybody, or no one's giving you the chance to talk to anybody."[17] As we will see below, much of the isolation experienced by the adolescent children of deployed parents inside the family is a product of family dynamics. Outside the family, they experience the feeling that too few people at school and within the community understand what they are going through.[18]

Our participants identified same-aged friends – especially those from other CAF families – as their most important sources of extrafamilial support. As Shanda put it: "There's definitely something that you can't talk about with civilian kids that aren't really close to you, that military kids would know about ... Stuff like how you feel when your parents are posted, or on a mission for six months, or they're gone living in [Training Base] for two years. They don't get it. They're like, 'Oh, why can't they just come back?' Or, you know, 'It's not that bad in Afghanistan.' It's like, well, it kind of *is*. It kind of sucks when you can't talk to your dad for four weeks." However, other participants were more cynical, to the point of expressing disappointment even in friends from CAF families whose parents had also been deployed to Afghanistan. For example, Amanda's father's situation in Afghanistan had seemed so uniquely dangerous that Amanda had refrained from confiding in her peers. "There's a lot of people whose parents did go to Afghanistan, but ... they were on base. A lot of the guys that were with my dad's troop or my dad's platoon or whatever, they didn't have kids my age. My dad was one of the older guys there, so of course he had older kids in the family. Whereas a lot of them were younger guys, early twenties ... So, no, there wasn't a lot of people in my situation. So that's why it's so hard to find people who understand to talk to." Support received from the school was also often disappointing. This is unfortunate, since researchers in California found that military adolescents who perceived themselves to be in a positive school climate – operationalized as relationships with caring adults, school connectedness, and feeling safe – were more likely than their peers to have a high level of mental well-being, to be free of depressive thoughts, and to be free of thoughts of suicide.[19] Despite having participated in the district's strategy for dealing with casualties of the Afghanistan mission, Armyville High School appeared to lack the expertise and resources to be sufficiently supportive to its students during the mission. For example, Amanda noted that the teachers had not been sufficiently trained to recognize how deployments affected adolescents' states of mind. She explained: "Teachers being untrained, they don't know how to deal with the situations. A lot of the times, my mom ended up calling the school and explaining what was going on. They knew for a fact, because my brother was never like that before. They weren't understanding; they just saw him as a troublesome boy, a typical boy who was causing disturbances in class." Brad told us that the school had represented the Afghanistan deployment to its student body in such an upbeat fashion that civilian students had not been sufficiently informed and mobilized to offer support to their affected peers: "The school is kind of sugar-coating it ... saying it's nothing too bad. Like, [the civilian students] don't quite understand what's going on there."

Zoe told us that the school had significantly failed to address the students' deep experiences and feelings around their parents' deployments.

> We have, like, "Support the Troops." Or we'll have an assembly. We'll be like, "Raise your hand if your father's over there." So 400 kids will stand up: "Yeah, my dad's over there." Or "My mom's over there." Or "Raise your hand if your mom or dad have ever been deployed." Almost everyone stands up. We have a situation in our school like so many other schools in military towns, but we all have the same problems ... We'll have kind of a rally for "support the troops." And we all had "Support the Troops" stickers. We all wear red on Friday, and all that. But the real stuff that's making these kids sad, it just gets pushed under the table.

She added an eloquent description of how students who had been affected by the Afghanistan mission had responded to the "denial" climate they perceived to be surrounding them by retreating into themselves: "Like, kids that I would usually see smiles on their faces, the next year if there's, say, two hundred people from Armyville going, and you see that kid maybe with their hood up, or their iPod always in their ears, or never smiling or never answering the teacher ... There are kids who act superficial, or act like they're not the same person they were before, just to hide the fact that no one's talked to them about it ... You want to be alone. You feel isolated. You can't talk to anybody, or no one's giving you the chance to talk to anybody." The contrast between the opinions of these students and the content of Carolyn Kay's chapter in this collection will remind readers that concern on the part of schools with students' emotional and psychological well-being has become a societal expectation in Western countries only recently.

Feeling isolated among friends or at school served to magnify isolation that the deployment had already created at home. At home, anxiety about the deployed parent's safety was experienced differently by every family member, and the shared fate of being compelled to live through this anxiety often wedged family members apart instead of bringing them closer together. Louanne recollected: "We never spoke, really ... 'Cause like if one person starts crying, then the next person will start crying, and the next person will start crying, and we're all going to be crying. So everyone, I think, just kind of kept to themselves about it. I never really spoke to anyone. At the time I didn't have anyone to speak to. 'Cause me and my brother weren't that close. And me and my mom didn't talk. Me and my mom didn't get along, really. And me and my sister didn't talk." In contrast, Amanda berated herself for having communicated with her mother too much. Amanda had shared her fears about her father's safety with her mother, and she believed that, as a result, her mother had reverted to hiding her own feelings and being protective again (as if Amanda had reverted back to being a child) and had stopped confiding in her. Knowing that she had been her mother's only conversational outlet, and having become proud of the close communication that had developed between them, Amanda regretted this episode for the new barrier it had erected: "I was the one person she could talk to, really, and trust. Because I never talked about stuff that we talked about with anybody else ... I kind of wish that I didn't tell her that I was scared. Because then she wouldn't have felt stuck – that she didn't have anybody else to talk to." Stoicism during deployments has long been recognized as a military family practice.[20]

The parents who were not deployed (mostly mothers) struggled to juggle full-time jobs with housework, caring for their children, and maintaining their children's participation in extracurricular activities and friendship networks. Some of them were unable to live up to the last two of these expectations; those who "went the extra mile" did so under duress. As well as having insufficient time to perform their tasks, these parents were stressed by having to make decisions by themselves that they normally made jointly with their partners, or that their partners normally made by themselves. They also often found their emotional aloneness overwhelming. Sometimes the parent who remained at home was stressed to the point of being emotionally unavailable to their children. Alluding to what he had missed from his mother (who worked full-time), Zachary described a typical "bad" day during his father's Afghanistan deployment: "You're really missing [your dad]. And then you go to school and nothing's really working out for you … And then you go home and your mom has to work late, and you have to get yourself a sandwich for supper." When her mother spent almost a year on an unaccompanied posting, Bridget found herself living with a father whose loneliness for his wife made it hard for him to provide any nurturing to his children. She described her daily life: "It was pretty much leave for work, come back for dinner, go to bed, leave for work, come back for dinner. That was it. We didn't really talk. It was just 'Here's your dinner. I'm going to go watch TV now' … That was it. I didn't talk to anybody. I was really, really lonely." Bridget's mother and father were sent on long, back-to-back deployments. When they returned, Bridget thoughtfully reacted by allowing them to focus on re-establishing their own relationship, repressing her need to communicate with each of them: "We started getting really distant, and not telling him as much – and same with my mom. I didn't hide stuff from them. I just didn't tell them as much, so they could get back to being them again and not have to worry about me."

Parental emotional unavailability is often accompanied by the parentification of the older children and adolescents in a home.[21] Parentification is a set of interactions in which children are assigned roles and responsibilities that are typically considered the responsibility of their parents but which the parents have relinquished.[22] Parentified children tend to be expected to fulfill caretaking and emotional roles, including the care of siblings and the provision of comfort, advice, or protection to a parent.[23] Military adolescents indeed carry out emotional (as well as instrumental) work during deployments and/or, as can be seen in Bridget's case above, also post-deployment.[24] Some do so to the extent of being expected to co-parent both younger siblings and the undeployed parent.[25]

One part of our participants' (mostly girls') emotional work had to do with helping the parent remaining behind (usually a mother) – both instrumentally and emotionally – for the explicit purpose of helping them to manage the stress they were experiencing. Some of the girls became their mothers' best friends and/or confidantes. Heather, for example, reorganized her social life in order to prioritize her mother's social needs while her father was away on an unaccompanied posting: "I don't like going out with my friends, so I usually bring my friends over. 'Cause I don't like leaving my mom home ... She says it's fine when I go out, but I think she'd be bored ... She has friends, but she doesn't go out much." Petra spoke up similarly about the months her father was in Afghanistan: "She's going through a lot right now with my dad being gone and her mom [has a serious illness] ... And things are going wrong at work, and she has all this stress, and she doesn't really have anyone to talk to about it. So I sit there and talk to her about her problems." Another part of "taking care of Mom" involved a form of self-censorship similar to the self-censorship that surrounds the information that is conveyed by civilian family members to military members who are on a deployment. Participants of both genders (but mainly girls) reported having kept their own problems to themselves, in order to minimize the stress to which their mothers were being exposed. Marilee, whose father deployed frequently and whose mother was chronically ill, did not tell her parents for four years about the severe bullying she had been subjected to in elementary school. She explained: "I think it's because [of] how independent I had to be once my dad had to constantly go. When he was in the military, he wasn't home till late at night some nights. So, to be honest, it was kind of just like Mom was dealing with all this stuff, so I'll just deal with my stuff alone." Stewart tried to help his mother, who was chronically depressed, by forgoing sports practices, in order to avoid having to ask her for transportation: "Like, if I needed a drive to a certain sport I didn't want to ask my mom, because I didn't want to make her do that. Because it's not her daily schedule. It's not what she's used to, and my dad's used to doing it. And it almost makes her grouchy because she's not used to doing it. So it's a different ritual. It's almost like getting in a certain schedule. It's hard. I tried to make it easier." For Cindy, self-censorship became a pervasive way of life during the Afghanistan deployment, and she commented on the energy that it exacted from her: "I have days where I break down and just want to cry all day ... It's like a buildup, and then I just need to cry it out, and then I'm all good. Until something big happens, and then I need to talk to somebody. I don't usually talk about my feelings with people because ... I'm the one who listens to people's problems. So when I cry, it's my way of letting my stress out, instead of talking about it or getting mad." When asked, "Who is the mom for you?" Cindy replied, "Nobody really." A recent study of youth in US

National Guard families found that some of these youth withdrew emotionally from their undeployed parents during a deployment, after arriving at the conclusion that these parents could no longer provide them with nurturing.[26]

Some of our participants grew and developed as a result of the extra responsibilities they took on at home during the Afghanistan mission, and they were justifiably proud. For example, Brady commented on his newly close relationship with his mother: "Over the last few years, she's seen me grow into the boy or man that she didn't expect me to grow into at the time before Dad left for Afghanistan. We grew a lot closer. I mean, we were close before Afghanistan as a mother is to her oldest son. But not that close. She needed me a lot when Dad was gone." Nevertheless, our findings suggest that these young people endured major struggles with stress, anxiety, and aloneness, as a result of the changed situations within their households and the resulting changes in the needs of family members and in family dynamics. Adolescence is normally a time of growth and development, absorption in peers, new interests, new skills, and the beginnings of imagining life as an adult. During the Afghanistan mission, Armyville CAF adolescents put many of these normal adolescent preoccupations on hold in order to co-parent younger siblings, take care of their undeployed parents, keep their worries to themselves and, in many instances, forgo extracurricular activities and the companionship of their friends. The girls in particular tended to take on these roles and become parentified.

If the deployed parent had returned home with a physical injury with chronic implications, and/or with PTSD, the long-term situation for the adolescent, and for the "healthy" parent, became even harder.[27] In the case of a parent returning home with PTSD, both previous research literature and our own findings have identified isolation as an adolescent mental health outcome.[28] The PTSD of a returning parent has the effect of weakening relationships both inside and outside the family. PTSD is a mental health issue, and a stigma continues to surround mental health issues in the CAF and civilian communities.[29] The number of mental health care providers currently available to CAF members is also between 15 and 22 per cent short of the level of mental health care that would have been adequate for CAF members, had the Afghanistan mission never happened. The mental health care shortage, post-Afghanistan, is therefore much larger than the 15 to 22 per cent figure would indicate.[30]

Participants whose fathers had returned home suffering from PTSD continued to feel isolated, as they struggled to provide emotional caregiving to both of their parents and to take responsibility for some of their parents' feelings. Paula, for example, wanted to leave home and move in with her boyfriend, but was in the process of deciding, instead, to remain at home to protect her mother from having to live alone with a husband who had become verbally abusive: "I just see me having my own life, like anything regular, you know. Come back to visit every Sunday, maybe, to have supper with the parents and everything. But it's a little scary moving out from home, thinking that my mom's going to have to deal with him all by herself. That's the thing I'm very worried about. 'Cause out of all of us, the one who gets the most heat is her. Like, the most painful things that get said are to her ... I don't want her to have to be alone." Huebner's *ambiguous loss paradigm*, described above, also applies to adolescents whose parents suffer from PTSD. Since previous research has established that living with parental PTSD creates emotional difficulties for adolescents, the dearth of mental health services in communities affected by current or recent military deployments is a significant problem. In March 2007, the Ontario ombudsman felt compelled to launch an investigation into the unacceptably long wait times for mental health services that were being endured in Pembroke, Ontario, by the children of CAF members stationed at CFB Petawawa.[31]

Armyville High School was the first school in Canada to initiate a PTSD peer support group. This group, which meets once a month during the school day, is facilitated by the guidance counsellor who started it during the 2007–08 school year. The counsellor was moved by what he was hearing in the media about "invisible wounds"; he advertised his new initiative during the school's morning announcements, through posters, and through conversations with other guidance counsellors. Paula explained how being a member of the group counteracted some of the social isolation she had been experiencing: "It's one of those things that when you find out your dad has post-traumatic stress disorder you keep it secret. 'Cause you don't know what people are going to think, and you just try to keep it confidential. But when we got into that group last year, it felt like you could finally breathe. And you could tell people, 'It really sucks' ... It [had been] really traumatic telling my friends about it." Louanne added: "The guidance counsellor can talk to you, but really they won't understand. They can say, 'I understand,' but they really don't. And it's different talking with an adult than it is with somebody your own age who knows exactly what you're going through." The Armyville High School PTSD peer support group has been resoundingly successful; several of its 2009–10 members came forward to be interviewed for our project. The success of the group is consistent with previous research that has found the egalitarian structure of peer support to be effective in mobilizing adolescents to deal with their problems and to feel at ease.[32]

In March 2011, the relevant stakeholders attempted to put the key findings of our project into practice by collaboratively organizing a two-day symposium in Armyville. The objectives of this event were to discuss the team's findings, and to make recommendations aimed at improving school-based services to adolescents who are affected by military deployments. The thirty attendees included most research team members, personnel from Armyville High School, other school and district staff from the ASD, and a representative from Canadian Forces Base (CFB) Armyville. The final event of the symposium was a plenary session to condense the symposium's breakout groups' findings into eighteen recommendations that were agreed upon by all, considered important, and deemed suitable for follow up. One of these recommendations was that the AHS Guidance Department start a monthly pre-deployment and deployment peer support group for interested eligible students during the school day. If implemented, this recommendation would have extended the model of small-group peer support to a broader range of students living through deployment-related issues than those students who were eligible to belong to the PTSD peer support group.

For two reasons, only a very few of the recommendations from our symposium ended up being implemented. First, Canada began withdrawing its troops from Afghanistan in 2011, and by the spring of 2014 the last of the Canadian troops had returned home. The end of Canada's combat involvement in Afghanistan marked the end of the sense of urgency that had surrounded the issue of military deployments in the town of Armyville and in the offices of the Armyville School District. Second, on 1 July 2012 a major amalgamation occurred among the school districts in the province in which Armyville is located. With almost no prior warning, fourteen districts were reduced to seven. The old Armyville School District, consisting of eighteen schools, became part of a much larger school district, consisting of seventy-four schools, and the province no longer contained a school district that was dominated and driven by a military family presence. All the Armyville School District personnel now worked in a larger school district which had a different name and a broader set of priorities than the needs of military families.

Despite this disappointment – especially about the recommendation that would have established a deployment peer support group – our project was a stellar example of collaborative action research, which was structured from its beginnings to lead to action outcomes.[33] While discrepancies existed among the respective

Adolescents during Canada's Afghanistan Mission

agendas of the academic team, the ASD, and CFB Armyville, the three entities were sufficiently able to focus on the convergences amongst their agendas to work cooperatively to carry out the research, the symposium, and some useful post-symposium follow-up. Our school district–affiliated team members bought into the research project to an enormous extent, and made major contributions to every phase of its work.

Our findings were consistent with research carried out in other countries about the challenges of being an adolescent during a parental deployment.[34] At a crucial developmental point in their lives, many of our interview participants were struggling with overwork, anxiety, and aloneness, and stress. All the adolescents in Armyville – civilian and military alike – were experiencing more suicide ideation and struggling with more depression and low self-esteem than were their same-age peers across Canada. The Armyville civilian adolescents were included in this "military effect" trend, possibly because Armyville is a geographically isolated single industry community.[35] These findings are alarming, and the fallout from future volatile deployments will add to, rather than subtract from, the problems that they reflect.

In deciding to collaborate with a school district, we assumed that schools are crucial aspects of military adolescents' lives because they comprise the main way that these geographically mobile youth manage to forge meaningful connections in a community into which they have newly moved. Schools also often assume heightened importance in the lives of youth whose parents are participating in an overseas deployment. By the end of the project we had not changed our minds about the importance of schools. We know from previous research that military adolescents who perceive themselves to be surrounded by a positive school climate experience a higher level of mental well-being.[36] One result of our quantitative survey was that youth who have experienced a parental deployment are more likely than their peers to have a positive attitude towards school, to talk to their teachers, and to refrain from skipping school. In addition, our interview participants expressed both appreciation for the school support they received, and regret regarding the school support they lacked.

Our and previous findings – plus the continual need for children's mental health services in locations such as CFB Petawawa, as documented by the CAF ombudsman and the media – suggest that school-based mental health support for adolescent offspring of CAF members and veterans might make a positive difference. The ideal solution would be a deployment support program, including both staff training and support services that would permanently exist in every military community and would require all school staff to possess at least a minimal level of deployment-related expertise. The advantages of this policy would include the availability of mental health support for CAF adolescents who had been affected by deployments, and the maintenance of a culture of deployment-related expertise within the school district that did not rapidly have to be reinvented whenever the district was faced with a crisis of the magnitude of Afghanistan. The most effective way to create and maintain a school-based culture of expertise would be through the provision of a form of federal financial support to school attendees from military families, of the kind that now exists in England and in the United States.[37]

We believe that these initiatives would be reasonable to hope for. We owe them to the adolescents of the future whose lives will be altered by military deployments.

NOTES

1 For a more detailed discussion of the subject matter of this chapter, see Harrison and Albanese, *Growing Up in Armyville*. We would like to thank the other members of our research team: Rachel Berman, Angie Deveau, Danielle Kwan-Lafond, Lucie Laliberté, Marg Malone, Mary Mesheau, the late Christine Newburn-Cook, Karen Robson, Chris Sanders, Shanyn Small, and, in particular, Jennifer Phillips, our site coordinator, and David McTimoney, superintendent of the Armyville school district. We also owe appreciation to Marilyn Ball, Peggy Blackwell, Sharon Crabb, Greg Lubimiv, Gary Nason, and Joy O'Neill.
2 Harrison and Laliberté, *No Life Like It*; Harrison et al., *The First Casualty*.
3 The CAF community is quite small. Using these pseudonyms was one of the steps we took to protect the privacy of our research participants.
4 The text of this survey can be found at http://www2.unb.ca/youthwellbeing. Statistics Canada, *National Longitudinal Survey of Children and Youth 1994–1995: Public Use Microdata Files User's Documentation* (Ottawa: Statistics Canada, 1997). See also Statistics Canada, *National Longitudinal Survey of Children and Youth (NLSCY)* (Ottawa: Statistics Canada, 2014).
5 Clair and Genest, "The Children of Alcoholics Screening Test," 414–20; Jones, *Children of Alcoholics Screening Test*; Lease and Yanico, "Evidence of Validity for the Children of Alcoholics Screening Test," 200–10.
6 Finkelhor et al., "The Juvenile Victimization Questionnaire," 383–412; Sherry L. Hamby, David Finkelhor, Richard Omrod, and Heather Turner, *The Juvenile*

Victimization Questionnaire (JVQ): Administration and Scoring Manual (Durham: Crimes against Children Research Center, University of New Hampshire, 2004).

7   Some of our survey findings have been discussed elsewhere. See Harrison et al., "The Impact of Shared Location on the Mental Health of Military and Civilian Adolescents in a Community Affected by Frequent Deployments: A Research Note," 550–60; Robson, Albanese, Harrison, and Sanders, "School Engagement among Youth in Canadian Forces Families," 363–81; Harrison and Albanese, *Growing up in Armyville*.

8   A quota sample is a non-probability sample of self-selected individuals, which takes into account and captures some of the stratification or diversity within the population under study (in our case, the various high school grades).

9   Treasury Board of Canada, *Expenditure Review of Federal Public Sector, Vol. 2: Compensation Snapshot and Historical Perspective, 1990 to 2003* (Ottawa: Treasury Board of Canada, 2007).

10 Charmaz, "Grounded Theory," 496–521; Strauss and Corbin, *Basics of Qualitative Research*.

11 Harrison et al., "The Impact of Shared Location," 550–60. See also Harrison and Albanese, *Growing Up in Armyville*.

12 Huebner et al., "Parental Deployment and Youth in Military Families," 112–22; Boss, *Ambiguous Loss*.

13 Boss, *Ambiguous Loss*.

14 Reed, Bell, and Edwards, "Adolescent Well-Being in Washington State Military Families," 1676–82.

15 Jensen, Martin, and Wantanabe, "Children's Response to Parental Separation during Operation Desert Storm," 433–41.

16 Chandra et al., "The Impact of Parental Deployment on Child Social and Emotional Functioning," 218–23.

17 All participants' names, as reported in this chapter, are pseudonyms.

18 Chandra et al., "The Impact of Parental Deployment," 218–23; Chandra et al., *Views from the Homefront*; Krause-Parello, "Loneliness in the School Setting," 66–70, and Harrison and Albanese, *Growing Up in Armyville*.

19 De Pedro et al., "School Climate, Deployment, and Mental Health among Students in Military-Connected Schools," 1–23.

20 Harrison and Laliberté, *No Life Like It*; Wertsch, *Military Brats*.

21 Hooper, "Expanding the Discussion Regarding Parentification and Its Varied Outcomes," 322–37.

22 Barnett and Parker, "The Parentified Child," 146–55; Broszormenyi-Nagy and

Spark, *Invisible Loyalties*; Hooper, Moore, and Smith, "Parentification in Military Families," 123–34.

23 Earley and Cushnay, "The Parentified Child," 163–78.

24 Chandra et al., "The Impact of Parental Deployment," 218–23; Richardson et al., *Effects of Soldiers' Deployment on Children' Academic Performance and Behavioral Health*; Kwan-Lafond, Harrison, and Albanese, "Parental Military Deployments and Adolescents' Household Work," 161–88. See also Harrison and Albanese, *Growing Up in Armyville*.

25 Angela Huebner and Jay A. Mancini, *Adjustments among Adolescents in Military Families When a Parent Is Deployed* (Lafayette, IN: Purdue University Military Family Research Institute, 2005); Richardson et al., *Effects of Soldiers' Deployment*; Harrison and Albanese, "The 'Parentification' Phenomenon," 1–27; Harrison and Albanese, *Growing Up in Armyville*.

26 Thompson, Baptist, Miller, and Henry, "Children of the US National Guard," 1–17.

27 Post-traumatic stress disorder (PTSD) is considered to be an appropriate diagnosis if two conditions have been met: (1) experiencing or witnessing an actual or threatened death or serious injury; and (2) responding to this trauma with intense fear, helplessness, or horror. Cited in Gifford, Hutchinson, and Gibson, "Lifespan Consideration in the Psychological Treatment," 204–15. See also Arrabito and Leung, "Combating the Impact of Stigma," 25–35.

28 Beckham et al., "Minnesota Multiphase Personality Inventory Profiles," 847–52; Westerink and Giarratano, "The Impact of Posttraumatic Stress Disorder," 841–7; Glenn et al., "Violence and Hostility among Families," 473–89; Ahmadzadeh and Malekian, "Aggression, Anxiety, and Social Development," 231–4; McFadyen, *A Long Road to Recovery: Battling Operational Stress Injuries. Secord Review of the Department of National Defense and Canadian Forces' Action on Operational Stress Injuries* (Ottawa: Department of National Defence and Canadian Forces Ombudsman, 2008); Grant Charles, Tim Stainton, and Sheila V. Marshall, *Young Carers in Canada: The Hidden Costs and Benefits of Young Caring* (Vancouver: Vanier Institute of the Family, 2012); Harrison and Albanese, "The 'Parentification' Phenomenon," 1–27.

29 André Marin, *Special Report to the Minister of National Defense on the Systematic Treatment of CF Members with PTSD* (Ottawa: Department of National Defence and Canadian Forces Ombudsman, 2001); André Marin, *Follow-Up Report: Review of DND/CF Actions on Operational Stress Injuries* (Ottawa: Department of National Defence and Canadian Forces Ombudsman, 2002); André Marin, *Off the Rails – Crazy Train Float Mocks Operational Stress Injury Sufferers* (Ottawa: Department

of National Defence and Canadian Forces Ombudsman, 2003); King et al., "Directionality of the Association between Social Support and Posttraumatic Stress Disorder," 2980–92; McFadyen, *A Long Road to Recovery*; Baker and Norris, "The Experiences of Female Partners of Canadian Forces Veterans Diagnosed with Post-Traumatic Stress Disorder," 175–85; Chapin, "Family Resilience and the Fortunes of War," 527–42; Pierre Daigle, *Fortitude under Fatigue: Assessing the Delivery of Care for Operational Stress Injuries That Canadian Forces Members Need and Deserve, Special Report to the Minister of National Defence* (Ottawa: National Defence and Canadian Forces Ombudsman, 2012); Blais, Renshaw, and Jakupcak, "Posttraumatic Stress and Stigma," 116–19; Harrison, Albanese, and Bernan, "Parent-Adolescent Relationships in Military Families," 81–103; Harrison and Albanese, *Growing up in Armyville*.

30 Daigle, *Fortitude under Fatigue*.
31 Mary McFayden, *Assessing the State of Mental Health Services at CFB Petawawa*. (Ottawa: Department of National Defence and Canadian Forces Ombudsman, 2008).
32 Seiffge-Krenke, "Adaptive and Maladaptive Coping Styles," 379.
33 Abraham and Purkayastha, "Making a Difference," 123–41; Byers and Harrison, "Building Collaborative Action-Oriented Research Teams," 21–52; Small, "Action-Oriented Research," 941–55; Weiner, "Critical Action Research and Third Wave Feminism," 631–44.
34 Chandra et al., "The Impact of Parental Deployment," 218–23; Davidson and Mellor, "The Adjustment of Children of Australian Vietnam Veterans," 345–51; Evans et al., "Chronic Posttraumatic Stress Disorder," 765–72; Frederikson, Chamberlain, and Long, "Unacknowledged Casualties of the Vietnam War," 49–70; Huebner et al., "Parental Deployment and Youth in Military Families," 112–22; Knobloch et al., "Experiences of Military Youth during a Family Member's Deployment," 319–42; Mmari et al., "When a Parent Goes off to War," 455–75; Morris and Age, "Adjustment among Youth in Military Families," 695–707; Richardson et al., *Effects of Soldiers' Deployment*; Thompson et al., "Children of the US National Guard," 1–17; Westerink and Giarratano, "The Impact of Posttraumatic Stress Disorder," 841–7.
35 Harrison et al., "The Impact of Shared Location," 550–60, and Harrison and Albanese, *Growing Up in Armyville*.
36 De Pedro et al., "School Climate, Deployment," 1–23.
37 Personal communication from Joy O'Neill, founder and chair, Service Children's Support Network, United Kingdom.

8

The Intergenerational Effects of Wartime Sexual Violence: Children Born of Wartime Rape in Northern Uganda

Myriam S. Denov

Historically, sexual violence has been routinely committed against females[1] during armed conflict and was prevalent in the wars of the ancient Greeks, Romans, and Hebrews as well as in the Trojan War. Mass sexual violence has been documented during the First World War, the Second World War, the Vietnam war, and in contemporary armed conflicts around the globe.[2] Although sexual violence during armed conflict has garnered increased scholarly and media attention, its *intergenerational* impact and legacy remain poorly understood. While individual rape survivors have been the major focus of most research, policy, and practice, sexual violence also and invariably affects families and communities.[3] As the UN secretary-general has noted: "systematic sexual violence, without a doubt, can be every bit as destructive to communities as more conventional weapons."[4] Moreover, conflict-related sexual violence may leave a multi-generational impact, with its legacy being passed down in multiple forms – whether in word, writing, body language, or even in silence. Here, the cumulative effects of trauma may be passed down along generations and often amplifying or causing other unpredictable impacts.[5] Regardless of how such trauma is transmitted, conflict-related sexual violence has a powerful and devastating impact.

Children born of conflict-related sexual violence are powerful reminders of the intergenerational legacy of conflict-related sexual violence and face important challenges as a result of their birth origins. As the World Health Organization has noted: "Children born of rape may be neglected, stigmatized, ostracized or abandoned. Infanticide may occur."[6] Indeed, research has uncovered the similarity of the experiences and realities of these children born of conflict-related sexual violence across time and contexts.⁷ In their study of Bosniak adolescent girls born of wartime rapes, Karmen Erjavec and Zala Volcic found that girls suffered from internalization of guilt as well as physical and psychological abuse from families and communities.⁸ Drawing on the context of Rwanda, Jemma Hogwood et al. found that young adults born of genocidal rape in Rwanda experienced challenging parent-child relationships, discrimination, stigmatization, and identity issues.⁹ Similarly, Myriam Denov et al.'s study of Rwandan youth born of the genocide found that youth struggled with issues of identity and belonging, ambivalence in the mother-child relationship, and a desire to learn of their biological origins and heritage.¹⁰ Historical analyses have found similar realities and themes in populations born as a result of conflict-related sexual violence during wars in the twentieth century.¹¹

The context of northern Uganda is one where the intergenerational impact of conflict-related sexual violence is of critical importance. Northern Uganda emerged from a twenty-year war lasting between 1986 and 2007. During those two decades, the region endured brutal violence characterized by mass killings, sexual and physical assaults, abductions, torture of civilians, the use of child-soldiers, and the forced displacement of entire communities. More than 1.4 million people were displaced by the war, and an estimated 60,000 to 80,000 children were abducted and forced to become child soldiers and forced wives.¹² Although the war initially developed as an armed conflict between northern-based armies – most notably the Lord's Resistance Army (LRA) – and the national government, it ultimately took the greatest toll on civilians in the north. The seemingly endless violence tore at the social fabric of families and communities, led to the erosion of economic infrastructure, health and education systems, and fuelled changes in cultural and social norms that condone, if not support, violence and brutality.¹³

The abduction, forced marriage, and impregnation of females was a key military strategy of the rebel Lord's Resistance Army. As a critical part of his military and ideological operations, LRA leader Joseph Kony organized and implemented a forced wife system.¹⁴ Abducted girls – with a preference for those who had reached age twelve to thirteen – were forced to "marry" male commanders and were victims of repeated sexual violence. While girls and women abducted into the LRA held multiple and complex roles as soldiers, commanders, porters, cooks, and spies, forced marriage and motherhood represented key functions within the LRA's war machine. The forced wife system had among its objectives to produce a new clan and the next generation of LRA fighters.¹⁵ Roughly 10,000 abducted girls became pregnant from sexual violence, giving birth to two or more children each.[16] While not all of these children survived war, hunger, violence, and deprivation, thousands of children born in LRA captivity are currently living in northern Uganda.[17]

This chapter will explore the post-war experiences of children born in Lord's Resistance Army captivity. Conceived and raised in contexts of violence, brutality, and deprivation, children born in LRA captivity continue to be deeply affected by their biological origins and subsequent treatment by their families, communities, and society in general. Highlighting the intergenerational realities of conflict-related sexual violence and drawing upon the voices and perspectives of sixty children born in LRA captivity, the chapter will address the psycho-social effects of the war on these children, and the challenges and opportunities in the post-war period, including issues of identity, belonging, coping mechanisms, and hopes for the future.

Funded by the Pierre Elliott Trudeau Foundation, the Social Sciences and Humanities Research Council of Canada, and the Canada Council for the Arts,[18] this study received ethical approval from two research ethics boards: the first from the Uganda National Council for Science and Technology, and the second from the Research Ethics Board of McGill University, Canada. Data collection was carried out between June and October 2015 in Gulu, Pader, and Agago districts of northern Uganda. Interviews were conducted with sixty children born in captivity.[19] All participants were engaged in the research through local research partners who had ongoing contact with women and children formerly in the LRA as a result of their ongoing work and advocacy for women and children born in LRA captivity. Child and youth participants (thirty-three male and twenty-seven female) were between the ages of twelve and nineteen at the time of the data collection and were living in Gulu (twenty), Pader (twenty), and Agago (twenty) districts of northern Uganda. Participants had often spent their formative years in captivity, ranging from a few months after being born, to seven years. All interviews for the study were conducted in Acholi,[20] audio-recorded with permission, and then translated and transcribed into English.

As the realities and circumstances of children born of conflict-related sexual violence have been predominantly overlooked and under-researched, the goal of this chapter is to highlight the voices of participants, privileging their direct perspectives and experiences as they related to the impact of the war, their strategies of coping and resistance, and their hopes for the future.

The majority of child and youth participants spent their formative years in LRA captivity and "grew up" in a context of war, perpetual violence, fear, and being constantly on the move. Living within the LRA meant being surrounded by a culture of violence. Participants reported directly experiencing and/or witnessing severe and brutal forms of violence and cruelty. Child participants vividly recalled their experiences as victims and witnesses to extreme forms of violence during captivity:

> I had been shot in the leg … the LRA soldiers came and they were shooting. Then my brother's bag that he was carrying [on his back] was shot at from the plane above. The bag started burning his back and he dropped the bag with all his shirts inside. There was also the child of our stepmother whose stomach was shot and the intestine came out. My mother was the one who pushed the intestine back in and tied that child's stomach … Then another thing that I remember was when our mother escaped from the bush … she left me in the bush with three other siblings with our father. My father lay me on the ground and he lifted a panga [machete] towards me. He wanted to cut me because I was crying.

For those who were old enough to remember, the context of war remained etched in participants' memories. However, while there was initial relief when participants transitioned from life in the bush to rehabilitation centres once they had been demobilized, the post-war period proved less than ideal. Transitioning into civilian life, participants re-entered into extended families and communities scarred by their own losses, who often bore anger, resentment, and mistrust towards the LRA and all those who had been affiliated with them. Participants' heritage and former association with the "enemy" LRA had a very direct impact on the treatment of children born in captivity and their long-term social integration.

Many of the children and youth interviewed suffered physical injuries during their time in captivity that continue to affect their health today. They suffered physical injuries such as burns and gunshot wounds during the war, and some participants reported still having bullets or shrapnel lodged in their body which continued to cause pain. As a result of the high cost of having the bullets surgically removed, they often went untreated. Children reported chronic eye and ear problems resulting from bomb blasts and explosions, as well as head and body pains. Because of widespread malnutrition during their time in the bush, some children born in captivity reported suffering from chronic kidney, liver, and stomach problems. Further linked to their post-war poverty and marginalization, participants also reported frequent and chronic illnesses such as malaria, typhoid, TB, and chronic pneumonia, some of which required hospitalization. Due to participants' socioeconomic marginalization and geographic isolation, families had severe difficulty accessing and affording basic healthcare services, leaving the majority of these illnesses untreated. This was even more pronounced in isolated rural regions – particularly Pader and Agago – that had limited healthcare resources.

In terms of psychological impacts, children and youth interviewed for the study reported experiencing important mental health issues related to their time in captivity. Separating what is as a result of the traumas they endured in the bush from what is due to the effects of their post-conflict marginalization and lack of social support is difficult, as they are inextricably linked. A young person highlighting how the impact of his experience in the LRA affected him in multiple ways – physically, mentally, and spiritually – described it thus: "Sometimes I feel sharp headache as if I am insane. I also shout a lot when this happens ... I was taken to the hospital and I was given medicine to take ... [At night] I usually get bad dreams about dead people (Youth, male)." The most common mental health complaint reported was nightmares. The youth participants disclosed that they experienced frequent nightmares related to their wartime experiences that were disturbing and debilitating. Children born in captivity reported dreaming about the violence and bloodshed of the bush, demons coming to torment them, or spirits of lost family members who were angered that the child was being mistreated in the post-war period: "I dream about my mother. She appeared to me one night in an ugly form saying that she wants to kill us all because we are not being taken good care of. I woke up from my sleep and I started praying. I also dreamt about the bad things that were happening when we were in the bush (Youth, female)." "Sometimes the other children that were sleeping with me would tell me that at night I always dream and talk and shouted with very loud voice about the bad things from the bush. And sometimes I could see my mother and father and other bad things in my dreams that always disturb me (Youth, female)." "I had a bad dream one night that we went and slept along the path leading to our garden. Some people came and asked us why we were lying down there. We answered that we were waiting for something. They tied our hands and told us that they were going to shoot us with guns. They shot us. I felt a cold bullet going through my body, but I was still alive. That is when I woke up from my sleep (Youth, female)." Children and youth also described invasive memories from the bush that continue to haunt them. This participant discussed her invasive memories: "I sometimes have a flashback of the experience of life in the bush. When I am being beaten and crying, sometimes I see red flashes in my vision. I then tremble and scream more (Youth, female)."

Critical to understanding the context of northern Uganda, the Acholi people traditionally conceptualize two types of disease – the "normal" disease and "spirit-related" disease.[21] "Normal" diseases represent physical ailments such as old age, malaria, and fungal infections, which tend to be treated with herbs, natural medicines, or visits to health units/hospitals.[22] "Spirit-related" illnesses originate from ancestors sending mild illness as a response to the misconduct of clan or family members and require Acholi rituals and ceremonies performed by local clan leaders in order to be healed.[23] In northern Uganda, children's traumatic distress resulting from war may be manifested as spirit possession, a dissociative phenomenon that involves "experiences of being under the control of a powerful entity, such as a god, a demon, a devil or a ghost."[24] It is said to be especially common among children born in captivity.[25] In the post-war context, children complain of being haunted by spirits of people who have been killed during the war, referred to as *Cen*.[26] Cen has been described as the revenging of spirits of those who were killed during the war and not given a proper burial. It manifests by haunting the sufferer (usually the perpetrator of the killing) as well as their family, via nightmares, disturbing visuals, sickness, and physical pain.[27] The healing of such ailments are normally performed through Acholi-specified cultural rituals or ceremonies, which are conducted through spirit mediums (ajwaka) or local clan leaders.[28] These participants explained their experiences: "When the sickness attacks me, it makes me keep my head lowered down. It was found out that it was because of the human bones we used to skip over when I was in the bush. [This is] causing a blockage in my chest and also giving me a heavy head. It is demonic in nature (Youth, female)."

> When I came from class, I was lying with my head intact with a bible, and it came like a sleep with my eyes closed. But I was not sleeping. Then I could hear a drum being beaten on my head and many people had surrounded me. I don't see those people but only their loud voices singing, shouting, ululating, blowing other materials and others were dancing. Then what came into my eyes that I saw at that time was, I saw a short soldier who was fat who came to me and told me: "You girl, when you came from the bush, you refused cultural rituals to be done on you. You will see what we shall do to you. Then I just responded to that soldier that "You are lying nothing will

happen on me." Then he just disappeared from my sight and all other sounds and voices continued playing. I was not sleeping and I knew what was taking place. When I tried to get up, they pushed me back on the bed. I could not get up and even my voice – even if I speak it cannot be heard. Then I started praying hard from my heart and I think my prayers were touching them. They opened my mouth and I continued to pray. I got up and sat on the bed. Then I found there were no soldiers. I said to the demons "Jesus is greater than you" and I continued to pray and they went away. Then my friend came to me and asked me if I was sick. I said no, but she said I looked like someone who was sick. But sometimes demons keep tempting me. I think of my father and that if he was around, I would not be suffering like this. I often cry so loud that other students fear staying around me. Whenever I think of my father, at night demons disturb me to the extent that I may not sleep. (Youth, female)

While the war has long been over, its direct repercussions continue to impact the long-term well-being of participants. Concurring with the findings of Harrison and Albanese in the volume, this research highlights not only that young people's struggles and challenges do not necessarily cease when war has ended, but also that participants have to deal with the complex transition from war to "peace." This is not only related to physical, spiritual, and mental health realities, but also related to stigma, identity, and belonging, which are addressed further below.

Identity, Stigma, and Belonging

Given their varied ages when participants left the bush (ranging from a few months to seven years of age), as well as whether their mothers shared information with their children about their histories, the level of knowledge that children born in captivity had of the circumstances surrounding their conception, their biological origins, and past histories varied widely across the sample. Within the family, levels of communication varied, where some mothers were reported to have an open and honest communication with their child about the past and origins. In many other cases, however, participants reported that their mother or caregiver kept the details of the child's identity secret, in an attempt to protect themselves and their children from stigma. In many of these latter cases, children reported learning about their identity and origins from stigmatizing insults from peers, neighbours, or family members: " I didn't know that I was a CBC [child born in captivity] ... [My mother] did not tell me ... I started knowing that am a CBC from my grandmother who always keep insulting me that am a CBC (Youth, male)."

> [Who told you that you were born in captivity?] The first person was my uncle who insulted me that am a CBC and am useless then I went and asked my grandmother about it and to tell me the truth about where I was born. Then she called me she told me that I was born in captivity and at that time I was still very young only seven years old. And she told me that my mother died also from the bush there. (Youth, female)

> I overheard my uncle and my mother insulting each other. My uncle said; "Aunty, they have brought home only rebels." ... I asked my mother that; "mother, earlier my uncle said to you that, they brought home only rebels; where were we born?" Then she told me. (Youth, female)

Participants reported having pieced together bits of information to try and make sense of their identity. Many of the children born in captivity described wanting to know more about their identity and heritage, but not wanting to hurt their mothers by triggering bad memories from the past. Those children who had little or no information about their fathers reported wanting to find out more, but not knowing where to start in the search.

Within the LRA, children produced through rape and forced marriage were understood to belong first and foremost to their fathers and these fathers lavished great attention on them.[29] Children born in captivity represented an important status symbol in the LRA, which the children often internalized. However, in the aftermath of the war, participants were forced to transition and adapt to new family and communal structures post-conflict, without their father (or sometimes mother). Moreover, they were often rejected within these new family structures and told that they did belong to that family or home. This drastic shift in status and social identity was especially difficult for the children to make sense of. Interviews with children born in captivity revealed that stigma and social marginalization, based on their biological origins and identity as children born in captivity, were pervasive factors that extended into every aspect of their daily lives at the individual, family, school, and community levels. In the home, children born in captivity reported being stigmatized by their mothers, stepfathers, caregivers, and siblings. Within their extended family networks, they faced stigma by grandparents, cousins, aunts, uncles, and in-laws. Outside of the home, when their identity and former affiliation with the LRA was known, they reported facing discrimination from neighbours, community members, community leaders, peers, teachers, and school administration. The effects of stigma were reported to be pernicious and cumulative, with implications for the overall physical, psychological, and social wellbeing of the child, their family, and the community. As these participants explained: "At home where I am staying, I do not get enough food. We are normally told to leave to go to where our father is. They say that we do not belong at home where we are staying. They also tell it to our face that we were born in the bush, and we are useless. Sometimes we are sent away from home and we end up spending a night in a nearby bush (Youth, female)." "When I do something wrong, they would beat me and tell me that 'Your father is now dead, and no one will take care of you from here; go follow your mother and stay with her' (Youth, male)." "When I do something wrong they tell me that I am not a child of that home and that I should go and follow my father (Youth, male)." "Sometimes when I return from school in the evening, my grandmother behaves well towards me; we chat and she would seem friends; but that is usually for a short time. All of a sudden, she begins assuring me how she does not like boys. She also sometimes mistreats my sister [also born in captivity]; so with all this, we sometimes feel like we do not belong there. She likes my sister more than me; she tells me that we boys have no place in her home. She says that she hates us the boys and that one day she will decide to send me away to my mother's place (Youth, male)." The stigma and rejection that participants experienced often led to a profound sense of isolation: "Life is very hard for us especially for me who is heading the family and caring for the young siblings because our mother and father are all dead. So I'm the one acting as the parent to other siblings at home. So life is very hard when it come to the issues of feeding, medication and many others which are left on the young me. We do also have an uncle but he is totally committed to his family and he never thinks about us, in terms of caring and help (Youth, female)." "There is no one. We just give support among ourselves [three children born in captivity] in our family ... My mother is dead. It hurts me and I always cry whenever I remember her face (Youth, male)."

Given the profound stigma they faced, a key theme that stood out in the interviews with children born in captivity was the emphasis and effort placed on keeping their identity secret wherever possible: from community members, neighbours, peers, and even from their closest friends. Children and youth were creative and adept at disguising their identities. For example, they have a "code word" for the bush when they refer to the bush with other children born in captivity. Participants reported that concealing their identity protected them from stigma, allowing them to learn and exist freely, and helped them avoid thinking about the past: "It is not easy because sometime when you are chatting, you are always careful not to say anything that will create suspicion about you. The problem is when you tell one person, he may again tell another person and within a short time it will have spread through the entire school. They may even go ahead to nickname you 'Olum!' 'Olum!' Literally meaning a rebel (Youth, female)." "Sometimes I get the urge to tell my friends that I was born in the bush, but my conscience keeps holding me back from telling them. This happens when I now feel I can trust a friend to an extent of confiding in them. The problem is if I tell a friend, he may in turn tell another friend of his … that is my fear (Youth, male)." In some cases, children were told by their mothers to keep their identities secret from siblings born from home or even from their caregivers (especially in cases where the father was a high-ranking commander, which carries a heavier stigma): "We stay with our mother the six of us. Our mother sat us down explaining to the six of us that we are children from one family, thus the need to live together peacefully. She didn't tell the rest of the four children. We found at home that we were returnees from the bush. She told us that we should live peacefully as one family and also love each other (Youth, female)." "I was in the house and she called me and said; 'look! Here in this picture is [Joseph] Kony. Do not tell anyone that I am the one who told you.' Then I asked her; 'How about this other person in the picture?' She told me that he is also Kony's son. I asked her: 'How about my father; where is he?' Then my mother told me that this is Kony. 'He is your father.' Then I kept quiet. [How did you feel when your mother told you that you were Kony's son?] … I felt bad because Kony is a murderer. (Youth, male)." As demonstrated by other authors in this volume, the intergenerational legacies and memories of war and their links to identity cannot be understated. War, trauma, and memory became part of a (sometimes secret) family narrative, sometimes creating a sense of belonging within the family, while at other times creating sharp chasms within families.

Gender Differences

In Acholi culture land is traditionally inherited along patrilineal lines, handed down from fathers to sons. Male children born in captivity have sometimes lost their father, are estranged from him, or have been rejected by the father's family.

The absence of their father is a significant source of concern for boys, especially in rural areas where access to cultivatable land is crucial, with subsistence farming as the main source of livelihood and survival. The absence of land rights leads to a deep insecurity that they have nowhere to settle, and often gives way to a lack of hope for future social and economic stability. The situation, unfortunately, does not change if a child's mother marries another man. All stepfathers in the study sample refused to offer land to their stepsons: through their eyes, children born in captivity are not considered to be part of the family. Often male youth are left with no choice but to work as labourers on other people's land. However, the income generated from such activity is meagre, making it difficult for these young people to ever acquire, or even rent, their own land. Even then, many of these youth are refused as labourers in light of the stigma attached to their identity and lived experiences. For youth who cannot attend school because of poverty, an anguish and hopelessness for the future can be even more pronounced. "I do not think my stepfather will give me land because he hates me so much … I will have nowhere to go, so the only thing will be for me to die and leave this world (Youth, male)." "I am worried about my future. I worry of how my future will be like if I am not educated. I also worry that my siblings will be given land in future while I will be left out. So, that means I will not have land of my own to cultivate and also live on (Youth, male)." Girls, in contrast, do not traditionally inherit land. Moreover, girls also face other societal pressures complicated by their identity as a result of having been born in captivity. Traditionally, girls will marry and move out of the home to the husband's home. The husband's family pays a "bride price" to compensate the girl's family (most often paid to her stepfather). Because girls born in captivity are frequently unwanted in their homes by stepfathers or relatives who consider them a financial and social burden, they may be under pressure for early marriage and forced from the home. Once with their husband's families, they face stigma and are forced into strict caregiving and labour roles so the family can "get their money's worth." In cases where the girl is being abused, returning to her maternal family for refuge is not usually a viable option, as the family will be reluctant to jeopardize the payment of the bride price. Especially in rural areas, girls are more often prevented from completing their education, where the stepfather or relative is less invested in paying school fees for a child who can be married off.

Managing Stigma and Adversity

Over their years of exposure to adversity, children born in captivity have developed a myriad of creative coping and resistance strategies to survive and transcend their realities of extreme hardship. These strategies include distractions and ignoring, and religious faith. They also attempted to challenge stereotypes community members held about them through resistance strategies including hard work, academic achievement, self-sufficiency, and resourcefulness. These strategies are explored further below.

Searching for Their Heritage

The paternal clan holds significant socioeconomic and cultural importance in Acholi society. Feeling they did not belong in their post-war family and communities, the issue of identity and heritage was of great concern to children born in captivity. The interlocking themes of identity, belonging, and sense of "home" frequently emerged in the data, revealing the complex questions and struggles in the everyday lives of the participants. In families where participants were treated as unwelcome and out of place, many longed to search for and (re)connect with their biological father and paternal families, with hopes of being cared for and finding land they have a right to settle on, and where they were welcome: "I think my mother should open up to tell me about my father or his family. I do not mind whether he is dead or alive, but I deserve to know about him. So, that when someone asks me about him. For example, questions like; 'What is your father's name?' I can be in position to answer them confidently (Youth, male)." "Yes, I want to know because it is important for a child to know where you come from. A person always belongs to the name of their family. And in the future, they may ask me, 'Where is your family?' And I should be able to tell where I come from. It is also important for people from our family to know that we [children born in captivity] are also there even if they are not giving us anything (Youth, female)." "I think I should put them to task to tell me if they have information about my father's home or where his relatives are. I think it is important to know, because in the event that my uncle passes on, his children could turn against me and chase me away from their land. So, my uncle should tell me if he knows where my father's or relative's homes are so that in future even if he may be dead, I will still know [my father's] home (Youth, male)."

Distraction and Ignoring

The children and youth interviewed consistently referred to *distraction* and *ignoring* as strategies to help them to "forget the past," to de-escalate feelings of frustration, and calm themselves in situations where they faced hostility or abuse. For example, when they began to "overthink" about their difficult lives or if they were reminded of traumatic experiences they suffered in the bush, they chose to socialize with friends, or to go play soccer. Singing, dancing, and working were other methods participants reportedly used to occupy their minds and manage their stress. In other situations, many children born in captivity confronted with aggression and abuse purposefully made the choice to "turn the other cheek" and ignore the insults and mistreatment. The following participants explain their various coping mechanisms: "I was having dreams because we were still in the period of insurgency and we were confined in a camp. We always heard gunshots, which made me scared and worried. I would worry that we would be abducted and taken back to the bush. So, to avoid all these worries I would make sure I am always in company of friends as a way of pre-occupying my mind (Youth, female)." "If I have some work to do I would go to it. And when I'm free I would go and play soccer with my fellow friends and it helps relieve me from that stress (Youth, male)." "Singing helps keep me busy and forget many things, especially those songs that make me happy (Youth, female)." "I feel education is very good. Because in school, I can forget my past and even other challenges that I normally experience at home (Youth, male)." "Sometimes, I hurt inside, but I decide to ignore anything that I would be thinking about … I do not share it with anyone (Youth, female)." "People also keep talking ill about me, but since I am a man, I choose to ignore those comments (Youth, male)."

Religious Faith

Religion, faith in God, and prayer were reported as playing a particularly powerful role in helping children born in captivity to endure their difficult circumstances and make sense of their suffering. Many participants were Christian and discussed the suffering they endured as a part of "God's plan," and that it was by God's grace that they survived the war and its aftermath. Through faith in a greater meaning, participants reported drawing strength to carry on and had hope that God would help them through their difficult times towards a brighter future: "I don't need to blame anyone for me being born in captivity, I feel that is what God had planned for me though it is what is making my life hard now (Youth, female)." "I could say a problem is what God has made that when you are born in the world, that if you are lucky, or if you are unlucky, then you pass through it. So I could say it wasn't being in the bush that is making me to suffer like this but it was God's plan for me to be like this (Youth, male)."

Challenging Stereotypes through Hard Work and Resourcefulness

Children born in captivity generally perceived themselves as strong, having passed through times of great difficulty. Although their wish was to be treated equally to children born from home, they were acutely aware of the obstacles they were up against. Ultimately, out of necessity, they learned that they had to work harder than other children at school, at home, and in the community in order to contend with multilayered obstacles. They developed a strong work ethic, and had to become self-sufficient, resourceful, and determined in getting their basic needs met. Participants valued hard work and took their domestic chores, labour, discipline, and their studies all very seriously. They saw themselves as individuals who had an influence over how they were perceived in their community. They spoke of resisting stigma and dominant attitudes, by deliberately challenging stereotypes of them that they were "useless," "not needed," or "mentally disturbed": "What people say about you depends on what you do. For example, some people say that a child born from the bush works even harder than a child born from home and they give the example of me … For me I just talk to them freely but some of them when I meet them on the way and I greet them, they don't respond and the next time I meet them again I would still greet them and talk to them freely, though at the beginning they used not to like me (Youth, female)." Although not all participants were able to attend school because of their financial situation, above all else, children born in captivity viewed education as their fundamental priority. As such, they took their studies very seriously, often walking long distances to reach their school. Despite the barriers they faced to education including hunger, forced absences, violence at home, and social exclusion, many of the children and youth interviewed excelled at school and in the community: "She [mother] appreciates me. For example, I became 2nd in [my] class and she was happy. She said: 'So I am not wasting my money.' One day I dug our field seriously and she appreciated me. She was very happy. She gave me praises, she was happy (Youth, male)." "I am so hard working. We normally do 'Aleya' [This is a practice of digging, and preparing land for planting seeds] in a group of 10. So, since I do my work very fast and well, they use me as an example to other children to learn from (Youth, female)." Children born in captivity had to be resourceful in order to get their basic needs met. Children and youth tended to be self-reliant and enterprising in the ways they worked to support themselves, including contributing to the family by working to generate income. Predominantly in the rural areas, children and youth, either alone or alongside their mothers, engaged in casual labour in the mornings, after school, and during weekends and holidays in order to pay for their school fees and to provide for themselves and their family. The casual labour that they were engaged in included cultivating land, selling charcoal and mangoes, raising goats, and rearing livestock: "The best thing that has happened to me at my aunt's place was when I was about eleven or twelve years when I started feeling good about myself. My aunty taught me how to dig well, and as I speak I am able to cultivate crops and raise some money to buy clothes, soap and other necessities necessary for life. So, I am happy that she taught me how to dig well (Youth, male)." "Am the only big child in that family, and I always go to the garden and dig with my grandmother. In the dry season, I can go and lay people's bricks for money and I can go to construction site where I can collect water for the construction, and they pay me. The money that I get I can give to my grandmother to help her in paying for my school and for my transport (Youth, female)." "Even when it comes to buying necessities like soap for washing our uniforms, I have to first look for casual work like digging in people's gardens in order to raise money for soap; the same applies to raising money for school fees; I have to work to raise money for my school fees on my own (Youth, male)."

Despite the relentless obstacles, most children born in captivity held hope for a bright future and goals and dreams for their lives. While many have been prevented from attending school or have had to drop out due to economic hardships and lack of school fees, they dreamed of being doctors, nurses, medical professionals, teachers, lawyers, tailors, sisters, politicians, and mechanics. They hoped that by working hard at what they did, and contributing to their families, communities, and society, they would be able to transcend their situations of marginalization and bring themselves and their families out of poverty: "If I am supported to complete my studies, and God willing, I manage to get a job, I could act as an example to the people in the community to compare their children with me and also encourage them to work hard the way I have done. This will make them understand that we children born in the bush are not any different from the rest who were born from home after all. We can also achieve something in life as well ... If the community I live in could treat me in the same way as the rest of the children born from home, then I would feel accepted (Youth, female)." Children born in captivity were very clear in identifying their greatest needs, and what specific forms of support would most benefit them. They have typically been an invisible war-affected population and have received little to no support following their initial transition from the reception centres to civilian family life. As part of this project, children were asked what they believed was critical to their protection and long-term security and well-being. They identified education and training and access to land and livelihood as the key pathways to protection, prevention, and well-being. Their needs included very basic access to healthcare, education, land, livelihood, and employment, in addition to follow-up and support for improving the relationship between children born in captivity and their parents, families, and communities, and for fostering equality.

In addition to the above-noted pathways, participants also noted the need for community sensitization to combat stigma. According to participants, sensitization should include programs and workshops with school administration and with students at the schools, as well as targeted workshops with their mothers, their caregivers, family members (including stepfathers), and local leaders and community members. Sensitization should centre on (a) the history of children born in captivity, and formerly abducted persons and how it was not their parent's choice to be abducted nor their choice to be born in the bush, and (b) the challenges faced by children born in captivity and how to communicate with and guide them rather than fearing and punishing them. They suggested radio talk-shows, music, drama, and dance as effective ways to engage and sensitize the community to their plight.

Child and youth participants also suggested that the government could institute bylaws to protect children born in captivity from stigma, as well as inform people in the community of the effects of stigmatization. They desired equality, to be treated like the other children within the community, and to be treated with dignity and respect. They wanted to be afforded protection from harm when their right to physical and psychological well-being was being threatened. As it stands, no formal avenues exist in the way of child protection. As such, participants expressed the wish for official policies or by-laws against discrimination to afford them some security and possibility for recourse when their rights are being violated. Children born in captivity believed that by being supported in these fundamental ways, they will grow the capacity to be good citizens and earn the respect of their families and communities.

NOTES

1 It is important to note that during armed conflict, males are also victims of sexual violence. This article, however, is focusing solely on conflict-related sexual violence against females.
2 Denov, "Children Born of Wartime Rape," 61–8.
3 Cohen and Nordas, "Sexual Violence in Armed Conflict," 418–28; Nicola Jones, Janice Cooper, Elizabeth Presler, and David Walker, *The Fallout of Rape as a Weapon of War* (London: Overseas Development Institute, 2014); Henry, *War and Rape*.
4 Ban Ki-Moon, *Report of the 63rd Session of the UN General Assembly, Agenda Items 44 and 107* (12 January 2009), https://unispal.un.org/DPA/DPR/unispal.nsf/0/ EEF9DE1F698AA70D8525755100631D7C (accessed 20 July 2018).
5 Evans-Campbell, "Historical Trauma in American Indian/Native Alaska Communities," 316–38.
6 World Health Organization, *Reproductive Health During Conflict and Displacement: A Guide for Programme Managers* (Geneva: World Health Organization, 2000), 114.
7 Lee, *Children Born of War in the Twentieth Century*; Mochmann, Lee, and Stelzl-Marx, "The Children of the Occupations Born during the Second World War and Beyond," 263–82.
8 Erjavac and Volčič, "'Target,' 'Cancer,' and 'Warrior,'" 524–43.
9 Hogwood et al., "'I Learned Who I Am,'" 549–70.
10 Denov et al., "The Intergenerational Legacy of Genocidal Rape," 1–22.
11 Lee, *Children Born of War in the Twentieth Century*; Mochmann and Lee, "The Human Rights of Children Born of War," 268–98.
12 Shanahan and Veale, "How Mothers Mediate the Social Integration," 72–86.
13 Khristopher Carlson and Dyan Mazurana, *Forced Marriage within the Lord's Resistance Army* (Medford, MA: Feinstein International Center, Tufts University, 2008).
14 Ibid.
15 Denov and Lakor, "When War Is Better Than Peace," 255–65.
16 Akello, "Experiences of Forced Mothers in Northern Uganda," 149–56.
17 Denov and Lakor, "Post-War Stigma, Violence, and 'Kony Children,'" 217–38.
18 This research was a partnership between researchers at McGill University and Watye Ki Gen. Watye Ki Gen is made up of a collective of women who were abducted by the LRA and held in captivity. In the post-conflict period, the organization is working to strengthen the rights, needs, and collective voice of former abductee women and their children, particularly within mechanisms of transi-

tional justice. While this chapter provides a summary of some of the research findings, our team's collective work can be found elsewhere: Denov and Lakor, "When War Is Better Than Peace"; Denov and Lakor, "Post-War Stigma, Violence, and 'Kony Children'"; Denov et al., "Complex Perpetrators."

19 "Children born in captivity" is the local term used in northern Uganda to refer to children who were born in Lord's Resistance Army captivity. It should be noted that children use this term to refer to themselves, as a group, especially its short-form acronym – "CBC."
20 Interviews conducted by non-Acholi speakers included Acholi-English translation.
21 Bilotta, "Uprooting the Pumpkin," 384–95.
22 Harlacher, "Traditional Ways of Coping."
23 Bilotta, "Uprooting the Pumpkin," 384–95.
24 Neuner et al., "'Haunted by Ghosts,'" 548–54.
25 Ibid.
26 Akello, Reis, and Richters, "Silencing Distressed Children," 213–20.
27 Ibid.
28 Bilotta, "Uprooting the Pumpkin," 384–95.
29 Denov and Lakor, "When War Is Better Than Peace," 255–365.

9
Politics and Emotion in Drawings by Children in Australian Immigration Detention

Mary Tomsic

A drawing, mostly in grey lead pencil, shows a girl behind bars with red tears covering the cheeks of her circular face (figure 9.1). The bright tears, dripping from her blue eyes, dominate the image. The girl is looking out from behind bars, which are drawn as thin grey vertical lines and fully cover the page. The bars have been drawn against a support, maybe a ruler, and it looks like the person doing the drawing found it difficult to keep the support still.

A child in immigration detention created this drawing in 2014. The Australian Human Rights Commission collected this drawing and many others as part of their inquiry into the impact of immigration detention on children and an assessment of detention practices and policies in relation to Australia's international human rights obligations.[1] These drawings entered an ongoing, highly charged, and fractious public debate about people seeking asylum in Australia. The debates rarely included voices from asylum seekers themselves. Advocacy groups, the commission, and the media have all circulated detained children's drawings as evidence of the harm detention causes children, but the political voice that the children express in the drawings usually goes unexamined. Here I argue that these drawings should be recognized as more than proof of children's victimhood – instead they should be seen as serious representations of children's understandings of forced displacement and their responses to their detainment.

The drawing in figure 9.1 has been shared widely in reporting on the commission's work in publications, in print and online by those opposed to the government's treatment of people seeking asylum, as well as on placards in political protests.[2] In these reproductions the drawing becomes a stark visual symbol against detaining children. Yet the collection of drawings from which figure 9.1 is

Drawings by Children in Immigration Detention

Figure 9.1
Drawing by a child in immigration detention. This depiction of a sad crying girl behind bars is striking, and symbolically encompasses the dominant idea of an innocent and vulnerable child. National Inquiry into Children in Immigration Detention 2014, Australian Human Rights Commission (AHRC) Flickr Album, https://www.flickr.com/photos/23930202@N06/sets/72157645938124048/.

derived has received limited scholarly attention and no historical analysis.[3] This chapter, like others in this collection, takes a microhistorical approach and will focus on the drawings made by children who were held in Australian immigration detention facilities in 2014. They have been examined in published and digitized forms so the material nature of the art is not part of the analysis presented here.

This drawing of a child, by a child, can be read as one that fits within a dominant Western understanding of children as archetypal figures of innocence and beings who are entirely apolitical.[4] Anthropologist Miriam Ticktin has examined the operation of innocence as it regulates notions of purity and subsequently limits the ways a person can be "a thinking, engaged, active, or informed subject."[5] This is crucial when considering the specific position of children seeking asylum who are generally presented as the most innocent victims. In the Australian context, historian Jordana Silverstein has shown how emotionally laden constructions of children seeking asylum have rendered them "as innocent victims requiring state aid."[6] But as cultural studies scholar Carly McLaughlin has shown, the experiences and treatment of children seeking asylum often directly contradicts this as children seeking asylum can be rapidly transformed from children into non-children when they do not neatly fit within notions of young apolitical innocence.[7] Reading children's drawings against this dominant construction of innocence, and following the developing body of scholarship in this area, we see that children's narratives are nuanced, and not governed solely by external constructions of innocence. Children's active political understandings, expression and engagement can be seen in their drawings.[8]

The children who created the drawings collected by the Australian Human Rights Commission were consciously responding to their displacement, whether caused by war, conflict, or persecution. They are also responding to Australian immigration policy. Through their creative expression we can see the children's political engagement. As Carolyn Kay has shown in the first chapter of this book, looking at artwork by children in German schools during the First World War, historians can access children's perspectives and voices from artwork. In this chapter, in a different time and context, we can similarly see children speaking for themselves and explaining how they see the world. A fuller analysis of the images created by children in immigration detention requires contextualization within the history of refugee resettlement and of people seeking asylum in Australia.

Child Refugees and Immigration Detention in Australian Refugee History

Between 1901 (when Australia was federated as a nation) and June 2014, an estimated 823,000 forcibly displaced people resettled in Australia.[9] These people came to Australia from various countries of origin, most under specific international refugee-humanitarian schemes. Only a small proportion arrived first in Australia (by air or boat) to then claim asylum. Despite this, people arriving in boats on Australian shores have dominated the national conversation about asylum seekers in Australia resulting in substantial political and public attention.[10]

Australia did not have a specific and comprehensive refugee policy until May 1977, after the arrival of large numbers of Vietnamese refugees, following the end of the Vietnam war.[11] Australian policy has become increasingly punitive in terms of administration and treatment of people seeking asylum. Policy formalized in

1989 resulted in the establishment of immigration detention camps in remote locations.[12] In 1992, Australia made detention mandatory for all people who arrived in the country without a valid visa seeking asylum.[13] Although this policy has been brutal and costly, it remains in place and the time period for detention is indefinite.[14] The mandatory detention regime, part of a longer history of administrative detention in Australia, is presented as protecting national borders, discouraging practices of people smuggling, and stopping people seeking asylum drowning en route to Australia.[15]

In 2001, the Australian government began detaining people seeking asylum in "offshore" detention facilities on Manus Island (Papua New Guinea) and the island nation of Nauru. The facilities were paid for by the Australian government and run by private companies (some of which also operated prisons).[16] There was a brief stop to this system of offshore detention when facilities were closed in 2008. They reopened in 2012 when the number of boats carrying refugees to Australia increased and many boats capsized, sank, or went missing.[17] This coincided with an increased number of people seeking asylum worldwide, when the United Nations High Commissioner for Refugees estimated there were forty-seven million forcibly displaced people worldwide, the highest number on record since 1994.[18] The offshore, indefinite mandatory detention policy remains in place. A 2016 addition ruled retrospectively that people who had arrived in Australia by boat, seeking asylum after July 2013, would never be allowed to enter Australia regardless of their refugee status determination.[19] In addition to immigration detention facilities, there are a range of sites that the government now uses to detain people. These can include hotel accommodation or hospitals that are identified as "alternative places of detention." Detention centres, or parts of them, have also been reclassified as "alternative places of detention."[20] Unaccompanied minors, families, and so-called vulnerable adults may also be moved into "community detention" while they are awaiting the processing of their applications. Though living in the community in assigned places of residence, they remain subject to rigid restrictions, including curfews, and may be moved back to detention at any time without judicial review. At the end of 2022, two children were reported as being held in immigration facilities, and 1,527 children as living in Australia with limited rights and supports.[21] There are at least thirty-eight stateless children who were born to stateless mothers in Australia's immigration system.[22]

The numbers of children and adults in Australian immigration detention facilities (excluding offshore facilities in Nauru and Manus) has been recorded since 1989–90. At that time sixty-two children were in immigration detention, comprising 25 per cent of the total detention population. The lowest number of children detained was in 1992–93 (seventeen children or 6 per cent of the total detention population) and peaked at 6,264 in 2012–13 (16 per cent of the total detention population).[23] While the majority of children seeking asylum have been accompanied by family, the numbers of unaccompanied children has fluctuated considerably, and it reached 1,788 in 2011–12 (which comprised 62 per cent of the total number of children in detention) and 1,900 in 2012–13 (comprising 30 cent of the total number of children in detention).[24] At the time of the 2014 Australian Human Rights Commission inquiry there were 1,068 children in detention: 584 in immigration detention on mainland Australia, 305 on Christmas Island, and 179 in Nauru.[25] The largest group of children were born in Iran, the second largest were of Rohingya ethnic origin, and others were from Sri Lanka, Vietnam, Iraq, Afghanistan, and Somalia.[26]

The countries these children came from have different histories of political conflict and violence leading to displacement. Not all movement, however, was directly caused by war. Some forced movement is more clearly linked to discrimination, persecution, and violence. Violence, conflict, and political unrest in the bordering countries of Iran, Iraq, and Afghanistan over a long period has forced the movement of many people within the region and outside of it. Massacres and human rights abuses of Hazara people, an ethnic minority in Afghanistan, prompted the forced movement of many. In the commission's report, a child from Iran said he and his family were forced to leave "because we had no freedom, no free speech and we have [a] dictatorship."[27] Civil war and ongoing political conflicts in Somalia have forced people to leave since 1991. The civil war in Sri Lanka that ended in 2009 resulted in the forced displacement of many Tamil people, which is depicted in the child's drawing in figure 9.2.

Stateless people of Rohingya ethnic origin have been violently persecuted in their home country of Myanmar, as well as experiencing violence in places they fled to in the region. One child in detention described his situation: "I am a person who came from Myanmar … Our Muslim people were killed, tyrannised, persecuted and treated unjustly."[28] Current Vietnamese refugees have fled political persecution under the communist government.

Journeys of forced displacement are often over long distances, taken over many years and through many different countries and conditions. Some families travel together, while others decide to move separately. Some people make multiple attempts to seek asylum in Australia, with most who take a dangerous boat journey coming through counties in Southeast Asia.[29] An unaccompanied child

Drawings by Children in Immigration Detention

Figure 9.2
Comparison between being in immigration detention and life in Sri Lanka. The confinement and prison-like conditions of detention are presented against violent acts of the army in Sri Lanka. National Inquiry into Children in Immigration Detention 2014, Australian Human Rights Commission (AHRC) Flickr Album, https://www.flickr.com/photos/23930202@N06/sets/72157645938124048/.

said of the journey, "I saw death on the way here. I wouldn't be here if I didn't have to be."[30]

People are, and have been, detained in facilities that primary school–aged children described as like a "prison," a "sad place," and a place of "no freedom."[31] The majority of the facilities are in remote locations; children and adults are housed in cramped conditions, most with severe restrictions on their movements, with four head-counts per day and checks at 11 p.m. and 6 a.m. that disrupt people's sleep. People detained have limited access to medical care, education, and recreation.[32] What is available and possible changes over time; for example, some children were able to attend school outside of their detention facility (as shown in figure 9.3), while others were provided with limited education within the facility. An eleven-year-old child said: "The most important thing is my study. I want to be a doctor. I need to go out of the centre to study." Another crying child said: "Our friends are going to school in Iran and we are not … This was a mistake to come to Australia."[33] On Christmas Island in 2013–14, school-aged detained

Figure 9.3
Sad children returning to the Wickham Point Detention Centre on a school bus. National Inquiry into Children in Immigration Detention 2014, Australian Human Rights Commission (AHRC) Flickr Album, https://www.flickr.com/photos/23930202@N06/sets/72157645938124048/.

children received two hours of daily education.[34] The sadness of children on their return to detention after school was drawn by an eight-year-old.

Many people are also moved between different detention facilities.[35] At the end of 2003, the majority of children had been in immigration detention for more than two years and in March 2014 children had been detained in Australian detention centres for 231 days on average.[36] The length of time and desolate nature of detention is seen in drawings such as figure 9.4.

Self-harm by children and adults occurs, and is included in a number of children's drawings (such as figures 9.5 and 9.6). The Australian Human Rights Commission described children in Nauru as "suffering from extreme levels of physical, emotional, psychological and developmental distress."[37]

Children in Nauru have reportedly said they were "just a number" and also referred to themselves by the identification number of the boat on which they ar-

Figure 9.4
Time standing still in detention centre. The drawing is devoid of people and shows the repetitiousness and isolation of detention. National Inquiry into Children in Immigration Detention 2014, Australian Human Rights Commission (AHRC) Flickr Album, https://www.flickr.com/photos/23930202@N06/sets/72157645938124048/.

rived, rather than their names.[38] More than 30 per cent of the drawings by children on Christmas Island were signed with boat identification numbers. One child said that the "[boat] number has [be]come like our first name."[39]

Drawings by Children and the Australian Human Rights Commission

Drawings and artwork by children in immigration detention have been collected and used as part of awareness raising, political lobbying, and activism in Australia in the twenty-first century. Examples of this include a 2001 Adelaide exhibition of six drawings by children of the riots by detainees in Woomera Detention Centre (in operation between 1999 and 2003) by a group called Volunteers in Support of Asylum Seekers (VISA).[40] Another was an exhibition titled *Innocent Victims: Children's Drawings from the Woomera Detention Centre*, which toured Melbourne, Sydney, Darwin, and Adelaide in 2004 and 2005.[41] In 2013 there was a successful

Figure 9.5
Actions of self-harm in detention centres. This drawing conveys a strong sense of despair from all of the people whose tears are clearly shown and collecting on the ground around them. National Inquiry into Children in Immigration Detention 2014, Australian Human Rights Commission (AHRC) Flickr Album, https://www.flickr.com/photos/23930202@N06/sets/72157645938124048/.

campaign to remove children from detention on Manus Island and drawings by detained children featured in this. Greens senator Sarah Hanson Young held up drawings in federal parliament (and also posted them on her Flickr page) and a campaign run, in part, by ChilOut (children out of immigration detention) used children's drawings in an online exhibition and video. The campaign aimed to collect voices from inside the detention facilities and raise public awareness of the situation when a total medial ban and restrictions on visits by non-governmental organizations was in place.[42] Children in offshore detention on Nauru established a Facebook page, "Free the Children NAURU," in November 2015. One child, known as M, posted their art on this page and people have responded to it on social media.[43] These examples reflect a number of ways drawings by children in immigration detention facilities have been created, collected and circulated.

At the heart of this chapter is the specific collection of 327 children's drawings,

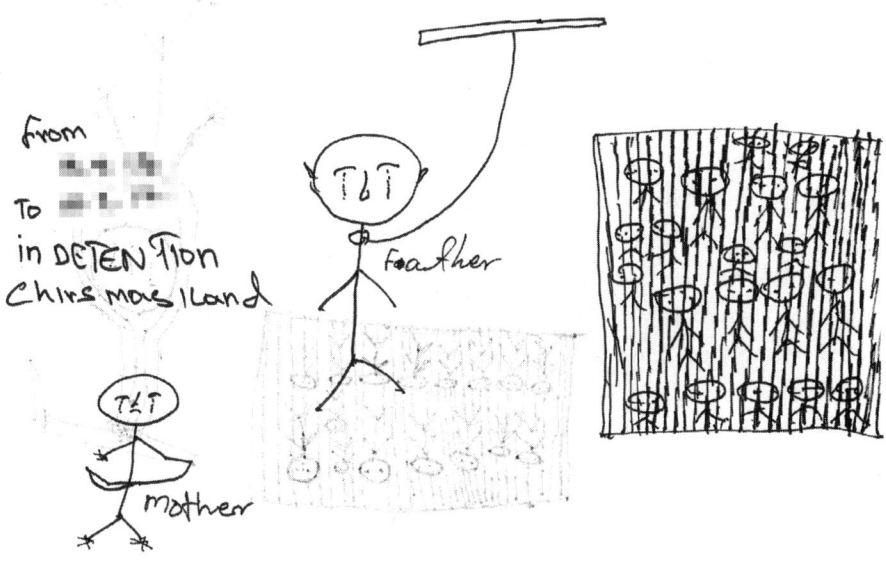

Figure 9.6
Adults' self-harming and suicidal acts. The adults shown in this drawing are separated from a large group of people enclosed behind bars, almost shown as held in a cage. National Inquiry into Children in Immigration Detention 2014, Australian Human Rights Commission (AHRC) Flickr Album, https://www.flickr.com/photos/23930202@N06/sets/72157645938124048/.

which the Australian Human Rights Commission gathered as part of its second major inquiry into children in immigration detention centres in 2014 and published as *The Forgotten Children*.[44] The commission's role in seeking children's voices directly is an explicitly political act, and places children's voices through drawing, a form of creative expression, within a regulatory and official framework. The commission carried out 486 separate interviews involving 1,129 individuals for the inquiry.[45] From March to July staff from the commission and inquiry consultants visited eleven detention centres across mainland Australia (three in Darwin and one in each of Sydney, Melbourne, and Adelaide) as well as five sites on Christmas Island. Two centres on Christmas Island were revisited after people protesting their detainment began self-harming.[46] No visits were made to Nauru as the commission's powers do not extend to that nation, but the commission obtained evidence from children and adults detained there as well as people who had worked there.[47] The inquiry held public meetings and also took 239 written submissions from a range of individuals and organisations, including thirty-five submissions by children.[48] The commission framed their published report as "[giving] voice to these 1,068 children" (the total number of children detained at the time of the inquiry).[49] These sources are ones created with the aim of hearing directly from children but must also be read with an understanding of the institutions and social relations involved in their creation.

Inquiry staff also collected drawings when they visited to conduct interviews. The staff gave children "paper and textas [felt-tipped pens] and asked them to draw something about their life." The children were asked for their permission to publish the pictures and the Australian Human Rights Commission has said: "These drawings are the children's submissions to the inquiry."[50] Asking children to draw about their lives was linked to the Convention on the Rights of the Child (1989), to which Australia is a signatory, which, among other rights, defines children's right to express their own views freely.[51] This particular aspect of the Convention of the Rights of the Child, described broadly as children's right to public participation, expands on earlier articulations of children's rights. It has been described by ethicist John Wall as the most controversial but groundbreaking and empowering aspect of the 1989 convention.[52]

The Australian Human Rights Commission used thirteen of the images in the formal report of the inquiry *The Forgotten Children*. A drawing is reproduced at the start of each of the chapters and over half of these are accompanied by quotes from children and others. The images starkly punctuate the report's text, and place representations by children within the pages of a formal inquiry.[53] As Caroline Lenette and her co-researchers note, this inquiry was one of the first to use children's drawings to "effectively highlight the failures of Australia's immigration detention policies."[54] The images themselves, however, are used for emphasis in the report, and not analyzed. Following the Convention of the Rights of the Child, these asylum-seeking children can be seen as "legitimate public participants in their own right," as individual subjects, with ideas, demands, and thought.[55]

Digitized versions of twenty of the collected drawings were placed on the Human Rights Commission website in August 2014, before the full report's release, and a larger collection of 327 drawings was published in an album on the commission's Flickr page.[56] Many of these drawings by children in detention have been circulated online and in the press. The widespread use of social media, particularly Flickr, Facebook, Twitter, and Instagram, has enabled the easy sharing of these images online.[57]

In the context of the strict limitations placed on people in immigration detention, these drawings circulate predominately as digital artefacts of the creative expression of children and young people who have been forcibly displaced and subjected to incarceration due to Australian government policy. There is value in examining these sources carefully. And, as Kay notes in chapter 1, being able to study a large collection of drawings provides the possibility of understandings children's attitudes. I too see it as instructive to read images collectively, to examine the themes and ideas represented. This is a way to understand how these children who were detained express themselves, and to see children as full human rights-bearing subjects, rather than only victims and human rights objects.[58] Taking seriously this creative expression counters the dominant construction of refugees being "habitually portrayed as if they are without agency."[59] Following this, I consider how these possible understandings are not taken up when the images are circulated more widely through the media and in online environments.

Reading Political Claims in Children's Drawings

There is a history of collecting, circulating, and examining drawings by children affected by war and conflict, with these drawings serving a host of political, social, and therapeutic purposes. Large collections of drawings by children displaced during the Spanish Civil War (1936–39), children in the Theresienstadt concentration camp, Terezín (1942–44), and more recently children who had survived genocide in Darfur (from 2003) have been mobilized in distinct ways.[60] This creative expression, as with any historical source, needs to be examined within its context, but often with children's art, there is a distinct lack of information and established methodology to facilitate analysis.[61] In light of this it is important to think carefully about how the Australian Human Rights Commission's collection and others capturing children's creative expression can and should be used. In chapter 1, Kay examines children's art as a social and cultural dialogue as well as artifacts of lived experience.[62] Here I have drawn on historian Nicholas Stargardt's work on children's drawings from the Holocaust as he constructs a valuable framework from which historians can read such material. Through his analysis of collections of art work he reminds us to carefully consider the context of the creation of the drawings, which can reveal a "sense of time and place" and "clarify the emotional content of these pictures as a whole."[63] He reads images collectively, "as the frozen moments of a social history lived in a very particular time and location," and finds in them "the faint lines of a moral and emotional map."[64] This approach, distinguishing between individual and collective reading, and thinking about drawings as maps, defines my reading of these drawings. This collection of drawings by children in detention can be read for political expression rather than solely as emotional productions of victimhood to be circulated to generate sympathy or policy change. There are three features in this collection of 327 drawings that reveal the children's political understandings: a focus on people; images as representations of confinement; and finally the comparisons made between people detained and those who are not.[65] I will now look at each of these in turn.

This collection of drawings is full of people. Almost all the drawings have one or more people in them. There is great diversity in how the children draw people: sometimes they are only faces; in other cases they are more conventional busts (showing a face and shoulders); while other drawings show people with complete bodies in a range of ways and with varying degrees of detail. The children created these drawings when asked to draw something of their lives, and from this I make the assumption that many of the drawings are of themselves. Some people are explicitly identified with words "me" and "I."[66]

In interviews with Australian Human Rights Commission staff, children in detention were asked to identify how they felt at three specific times; first, before they came to Australia and were living in their home country; second, when they first arrived in Australia; and finally, how they felt that day of the interview. They were asked to respond using a scale of 0 to 10, which included six emoji facial expressions that ranged from happy and smiling (0) to sad and crying (10). Children were asked to identify their face on that scale for each of the three times.[67] In some of their drawings, children use similar representations to this visual scale, providing another way of seeing these drawings as self-representations.

The majority of the people drawn have their faces clearly depicted. Faces in photographs have been analysed by historian Vera Mackie as a significant way of representing and recognising humanness in people.[68] In the Australian immigration system, where children and adults are known by numbers rather than names, a child depicting themself and others with a face can be read as a way of claiming an individual identity. The children portrayed a majority of people in the drawings as sad and confined, but there are at least thirty where sadness is not shown, and clear and happy faces are present. The faces are mostly on human forms but also on a cat and butterflies.[69] We can read these apparently more benign images too as an active assertion of humanness directly (as well as through anthropomorphosis). We should read these children's drawings as visual expressions of their own humanness. This feature of the drawings marks a stark contrast to what is seen in other public spaces such as newspapers and the media. Scholars have identified the trend in Australian newspaper depictions of "dehumanising visual patterns" of representations, showing anonymous groups of refugees in preference to identifiable individuals.[70] The creation and subsequent circulation of identifiable individuals in these images by children can be seen as a material and visual response to broad reaching visual dehumanizing trends.

People are crying in about a quarter of the drawings. Tears are seen in a wide variety of shapes: some are drawn as dots, circles, or short lines. Others are droplet shaped (such as in figure 9.1) and some like a small letter u. Most are in the dominant colour of the drawing, but others stand out in red, blue, green, and orange. Some of the tears are large and others small. Some are presented singularly and others in a stream. In some cases, they are drawn almost as a line scarring the face. Some of the tears are accommodated on the face, while others extend well beyond the face of the person crying (such as in figure 9.7). In some pictures where there is more than one person, all people are crying, while in others, only one or some of the people have tears on their faces. Some of the children have included written text addressing the viewer of the drawing with declarations and desires including "Pleaze help!!!!,"[71] "I Want Freedom,"[72] "WE WANTS DAD,"[73] and "Take me out the prison."[74] The tears depict an individual's sadness as well as a political demand for help and change in their situation.

Representations of confinement and containment are present in almost half of the images. In many of the drawings a fence or bars dominates the illustration, often taking up all, or the majority, of the page (such as in figure 9.1). Representations of isolation and containment are also clearly conveyed when bars and cages are not the dominant part of the image. For example in one case a child drew a three-dimensional border which is also a wire fence. An orange-coloured building takes up almost all the space inside this border and two people towards the front of the drawing have large tears that spill from their faces (figure 9.7).[75] While the fence is on the outside of the image, a sense of containment and isolation is readily conveyed. Another drawing from an overhead perspective is more directly map-like, showing a high-walled compound with people inside, separated from people, water, a road, tall buildings, and cars.[76] Another drawing, sparser in design, also effectively conveys separation with a face obscured but peeking over a large zigzag, which may be read as a fence. The jagged and large triangular fence segregates the person from what is outside it, possibly the ocean.[77]

Fences and cages separate people in detention from people and life outside. Direct comparisons are made between people in detention and those outside who

Figure 9.7
Fenced-in lives. The border of this drawing is also the fence that contains the detention facility, creating a sense of an enclosed and confined site. The two people depicted are sad and crying. National Inquiry into Children in Immigration Detention 2014, Australian Human Rights Commission (AHRC) Flickr Album, https://www.flickr.com/photos/23930202@N06/sets/72157645938124048/.

are depicted as free, often smiling and playing.[78] Some drawings include written text as well as questioning the distinctions between those on either side: "what the differenc?"[79] Others explicitly show birds outside of the space where individuals are confined.[80] The children sometimes named places: for example a fenced-in sad face is labelled as Christmas Island and presented in comparison to a smiling person, with a complete body, labelled as Australia; another distinguishes between being in the camp and being free; between the camp/detained and Australia, and "No Nauru" and "free" outside the camp.[81] Another drawing incorporating written text asks, "We are in detention … Is anyone in Australia to help us."[82] In another, a child drew a person with tears covering her face and behind bars that cover the whole page saying: "I Come for Australian Not Come for Camp."[83] These drawings demonstrate the ways in which people are controlled and confined, and what the impact this has on individual children. They also show children questioning why they are treated differently.

It is not surprising that confinement and containment is a clear theme in the drawings as it is a feature of daily life for these children as well as the purpose of detention. In terms of the perspective presented in these drawings, almost all are shown from the outside, looking in on the detention centres and the people inside of them. This means that viewers of these images rarely share the same view with the people inside the image. "Looking in" at the image is significant. Historian Nicholas Stargardt, reading children's drawings of gas chambers and barracks during the Holocaust, suggests this perspective was used as a means "to locate what is happening within them."[84] Here too we can read many of these drawings as children showing those outside what is happening in these particular spaces of detention. It is a claim against those who are free and look at the children. They are saying to viewers: Here we are. Here are the conditions in which we live.

The systematic dehumanizing nature of the Australian government's treatment of people seeking asylum and the policies of mandatory detention cannot be underestimated. When reading these images by children collectively, and seeing the individuals that populate them, what is revealed is a stark response to a political system that does not treat them as human. If these drawings illuminate a map, we can see people in places where they are confined, tears are a protest against this confinement and political comparisons are made between people in detention and people who are not. The map articulates a deep understanding of the place of people seeking asylum in the Australian context and the rigidly policed borders of the nation. The drawings reveal a clear understanding of freedom and confinement.

Circulation of Children's Drawings

The drawings collected by the Australian Human Rights Commission were circulated in the media to oppose the policies and practices of mandatory detention of people seeking asylum and specifically the mandatory detention of children. The drawings are often publicly presented in emotional terms as "heartbreaking" and "disturbing" proof of the damage detention does to children.[85] For example, in an essay by pediatrician and academic Karen Zwi, the images are captioned with commentary on the long-term physical and mental impact of detention on children. The drawing that opens this chapter, of the girl behind bars with red tears on her cheeks (figure 9.1), is captioned with "Deprivation and trauma and [*sic*] early childhood can affect the developing brain"; another that shows a sad person behind bars next to smiling people labelled Australian has the caption "Children who spend time in immigration detention centres are often plagued by nightmares, anxiety and depression." Another shows a girl holding a sign saying "we want freedom." We see the girl's back but she is holding the sign towards the viewer who can read it. A black mesh fence covers the whole drawing and obscures our direct vision of the girl and her sign. This drawing is captioned with a statement about the physical impacts of chronic stress in childhood.[86] The text frames these drawings in terms of the harm and damage that detention can do to children, but that was not necessarily all that the children have chosen to tell with these images. We can also read them as creative expression that maps their feelings, awareness, and active political demands.

The power of the political meanings of these drawings was recognized by conservative newspaper columnist Andrew Bolt, who took issue with the circulation of the drawings in Australian media. Bolt argued that the *Daily Mail*'s online publication of the drawings and the paper's indictment of "the treatment of the young detainees" amounted to a plea: "Let them free." If these children were freed, Bolt held, "we'll soon see boats loaded with yet more children to smash our resolve" because "how many millions do we really want, and how will they change this country?"[87] Here, Bolt was advocating against engaging with the drawings; the children's political expression was acknowledged but dismissed. For Bolt these drawings represented a distraction from the significant issue, which was the (supposed) danger of having more non-European people seeking asylum in Australia.

Of the thirty-five formal submissions children made to the Australian Human Rights Commission inquiry most are written text, but six of the submissions include illustrations and four are predominately visual presentations (which also include written text that has been translated into English).[88] Like the larger collection of drawings, these images also depict people, portray conditions of confinement, and make comparisons between people in detention and those who are not. Three of the visually dominant submissions also include explicit representations of violence, with depictions of children hanging themselves, children protesting by sewing their lips together, and children dying by suicide. These drawings have not been circulated widely through social or standard media avenues.[89] The lack of public attention paid to the formal submissions in written and visual form can be explained by the difficulty of presenting and understanding children outside of dominant Western understandings of an apolitical childhood. Scholar Margret Meyhew has identified drawing as a socially acceptable "safe and therapeutic activity for children to engage in, akin to play" and not "tainted with the coercive implications of written or oral testimony."[90] These submissions that depict violence could also be read as tainted and therefore not as useful in advocating for change as the children who created them cannot be so readily seen as apolitical and innocent.

Conclusion

Tracing the creation, collection, and circulation of drawings and artwork by children seeking asylum is a significant contribution to historical research about children and war. It gives us access to how some children have represented and understood their experiences of forced displacement in the past and present. Through this we can see the times and spaces in which children's opinions and understandings are asked for, in this case for official inquiries and medical interventions as well as by political activists. These drawings have then been shared in many ways in concrete and digital forms, online, in news reports, in official documentation, as well as on social media and in museums and galleries.

The particular drawings examined in this chapter are children's voices from immigration detention in Australia that have been actively sought and shared. Children's creative expression has been used to represent the impact of detention on children, and as evidence of the need to stop this practice. These pictures have been used to show children's victimhood, to demonstrate the personal and mental health impacts of these experiences. The drawings are presented as showing sadness and horror during childhood, which is conventionally idealized as a time of innocence. Understanding children primarily as innocent precludes the presence of the children's own political understanding and demands. Consequently, what has not been seen in these drawings is the political engagement of the children who have created them. The human subjects these children have drawn, the tears on their faces, and the confinement of the people they represent all make political claims. When we consider the images collectively we can see the maps that the children created, showing that children seeking asylum present themselves, their families, and fellow detainees as fully human and political subjects.

NOTES

1 "National Inquiry into Children in Immigration Detention 2014," Australian Human Rights Commission (AHRC), 10 September 2018, https://www.human

rights.gov.au/our-work/asylum-seekers-and-refugees/national-inquiry-children-immigration-detention-2014.

2 "National Inquiry into Children in Immigration Detention 2014"; Sarah Whyte, "Number of Children in Nauru Detention Centre Set to Increase after Being Returned from Australian Mainland," *Sydney Morning Herald*, 23 February 2015, http://www.smh.com.au/federal-politics/political-news/number-of-children-in-nauru-detention-centre-set-to-increase-after-being-returned-from-australian-mainland-20150223-13m6ib.html; Sarah Whyte, "Government's Medical Health Provider to Be Proved over Treatment of Children in Detention," *Sydney Morning Herald*, 2 July 2014, http://www.smh.com.au/federal-politics/political-news/governments-medical-health-provider-to-be-probed-over-treatment-of-children-in-detention-20140701-3b6le.html; Mowe SJ, "What Are the Limits of Our Generosity?," 1; Photograph of placard by M4R (activist group Mums 4 Refugees) posted on Instagram by @hurricane.melissa (Melissa McLeary, handle now @tired_ize), 6 March 2016.

3 Exceptions are Mares and Zwi, "Sadness and Fear," 663–9, and Lenette et al., "What Is It Like Living in Detention?," 42–60.

4 Ticktin, "A World without Innocence," 577–90; Higonnet, "Child Witnesses," 1565–76; McLaughlin, "'They Don't Look Like Children,'" 1757–73; Fass, "The World Is at Our Door," 16.

5 Ticktin, "A World without Innocence," 579.

6 Silverstein, "'Because We All Love Our Country,'" 544.

7 McLaughlin, "'They Don't Look Like Children,'" 1758.

8 Eldén, "Inviting the Messy," 66–81; Kallio, "The Body as a Battlefield," 285–97; Habashi, "Palestinian Children," 421–33.

9 "Refugee Arrivals to Australia since Federation," Refugee Council of Australia, 17 May 2016, archived at https://web.archive.org/web/20180515155431/https://www.refugeecouncil.org.au/getfacts/statistics/aust/historical/refugee-arrivals-australia-since-federation/.

10 According to Australian government statistics, 71,155 people arrived in boats between 1976 and 2013. See Janet Phillips, "Boat Arrivals in Australia: A Quick Guide to the Statistics," Parliamentary Library, Parliament of Australia, 23 January 2014, https://www.aph.gov.au/About_Parliament/Parliamentary_Departments/Parliamentary_Library/pubs/rp/rp1314/QG/BoatArrivals.

11 Neumann et al., "Refugee Settlement in Australia," 6; Barry York, "Australia and Refugees, 1901–2002: An Annotated Chronology Based on Official Sources," Parliamentary Library, Parliament of Australia, 16 June 2003, 18, http://www.aph.

gov.au/About_Parliament/Parliamentary_Departments/Parliamentary_Library/ Publications_Archive/online/Refugeescontents. A Special Humanitarian Program was established in 1981. For pre-1970s history see Neumann, *Across the Seas*.

12 *Migration Legislation Amendment Act* (1989) in York, "Australia and Refugees," 3–5.
13 *Migration Reform Act* (1992) in York, "Australia and Refugees," 52.
14 The Australian Border Deaths database records all known deaths associated with Australia's borders since 1 January 2000, and the total stands at 2,026 in February 2020. Most of these deaths are at sea, while others are in immigration detention facilities. See "Australian Border Deaths Database," Border Crossing Observatory, accessed 28 April 2020, https://web.archive.org/web/20200303171754/https://www.monash.edu/arts/border-crossing-observatory/research-agenda/australian-border-deaths-database.
15 Hartley et al., "'The Situation Is Hopeless; We Must Take the Next Step,'" 24. See also Nethery, "'A Modern-Day Concentration Camp,'" 73–7.
16 York, "Australia and Refugees," 51–5; Stivens, "Gendering Cosmopolitanisms," 87–8.
17 For detailed analysis from 2012 to 2016 see Gleeson, *Offshore*. For an estimated number of deaths at sea, see Hutton, "Drownings on the Public Record of People Attempting to Enter Australia Irregularly by Boat since 1998," *sievx.com*, 2 February 2014, http://sievx.com/articles/background/DrowningsTable.pdf.
18 United Nations High Commissioner for Refugees (UNHCR), "Displacement, The New 21st Century Challenge, Global Trends 2012," 19 June 2013, https://reliefweb.int/sites/reliefweb.int/files/resources/UNHCR%20GLOBAL%20TRENDS%202012_V05.pdf, 3.
19 Detention facilities in Nauru and Manus Island were named "Regional Processing Centres" in 2012. Nauru became an "open" residential site in October 2015 and the facility on Manus Island formally closed in November 2017 (after the Papua New Guinea court ruled detention illegal in 2016) and the men there were forcibly moved to other sites. Gleeson, "Protection Deficit," 3, 8; Australian OPCAT Network, "The Implementation of OPCAT in Australia Report to Subcommittee on Prevention of Torture and Other Cruel, Inhuman or Degrading Treatment or Punishment (SPT) and United Nations Working Group on Arbitrary Detention (WGAD)," January 2020, https://www.refugeecouncil.org.au/wp-content/uploads/2020/02/Implementation_of_OPCAT_in_Australia.pdf, 68–70.
20 "Statistics on People in Detention in Australia," Refugee Council of Australia, 24 May 2022, https://www.refugeecouncil.org.au/detention-australia-statistics/3/. See also https://www.refugeecouncil.org.au/detention-australia-statistics/3/;

https://humanrights.gov.au/our-work/asylum-seekers-and-refugees/publications/health-and-well-being-children-immigration.

21 "Statistics on People in Detention in Australia," Refugee Council of Australia, 26 December 2022, https://www.refugeecouncil.org.au/detention-australia-statistics/4/.

22 Asher Hirsch, "Children Born in Australia's Asylum System," Statelessness Working Paper Series, No. 2017/06, Institute of Statelessness and Inclusion, December 2017, https://files.institutesi.org/WP2017_06.pdf.

23 Phillips, "Immigration Detention in Australia," Parliamentary Library, Parliament of Australia, 21 March 2017, https://www.aph.gov.au/About_Parliament/Parliamentary_Departments/Parliamentary_Library/pubs/rp/rp1617/Quick_Guides/ImmigrationDetention, 2–3.

24 Ibid., 2–3.

25 Australian Human Rights Commission (AHRC), *The Forgotten Children: National Inquiry into Children in Immigration Detention* (Sydney: AHRC, 2014), 21.

26 Ibid., 22.

27 Thirteen-year-old, Nauru, May 2014, quoted in ibid., 53.

28 Child, Nauru, May 2014, quoted in ibid., 53.

29 "Asylum Insight Facts and Analysis," Asylum Insight, March 2017, https://www.asyluminsight.com/countries-of-origin-asia-pacific-1?rq=transit%20countries#.XqktsC-r1aI.

30 Unaccompanied child, Christmas Island, 4 March 2013, quoted in AHRC, *The Forgotten Children*, 53.

31 Quoted in ibid., 129.

32 Ibid., 129–30, 138, 149.

33 Human Rights and Equal Opportunity Commission (HREOC), *A Last Resort? National Inquiry into Children in Immigration Detention* (Sydney: HREOC, 2004), 130.

34 AHRC, *The Forgotten Children*, 146.

35 Ibid., 57.

36 HREOC, *A Last Resort?*, 2 and AHRC, *The Forgotten Children*, 56. This time limit excludes offshore detention and community detention.

37 "Tell Me About: Children in Immigration Detention in Nauru," AHRC, accessed 10 September 2018, https://www.humanrights.gov.au/our-work/asylum-seekers-and-refugees/publications/tell-me-about-children-immigration-detention-nauru.

38 AHRC, *The Forgotten Children*, 187.

39 Thirteen-year-old, Darwin, 12 April 2014, quoted in AHRC, *The Forgotten Children*, 73.

40 "Children Draw Hardest Lines," *Australian*, 26 November 2001, 7.
41 "South Australia Twenty Fifth Annual Report of the History Trust of South Australia for the Year Ended 30 June 2005," History Trust of South Australia, accessed 10 September 2018, http://history.sa.gov.au/wp-content/uploads/2017/05/annual-report-2004-05.pdf; McErvale, "A Chance to See Detention through the Eyes of Children," 8; "Museums Board of Victoria Annual Report, 2003/04," Museum Victoria, accessed 10 September 2018, https://museumsvictoria.com.au/media/3684/annual-report-2003-2004.pdf, 51; "Art Attack," *Northern Territory News/Sunday Territorian*, 19 November 2004; Liveris, "Through a Child's Eyes," *Northern Territory News/Sunday Territorian*, 8 October 2004; Goodnow, "Traditional Methods and Now Moves," 45–6.
42 Bianca Hall, "Manus Island Children Draw on Desolation of Detention," *Sydney Morning Herald*, 5 February 2013, 3; Greens MPS, "Sarah Hanson Young: Drawings from the Manus Island Detention Centre," Flickr, accessed 10 September 2018, https://www.flickr.com/photos/greensmps/albums/72157632692940532; "Out of Sight, In Our Minds," Get Up! And ChilOut collaboration, accessed 19 September 2017, archived at https://web.archive.org/web/20170301093920/http://www.outofsight.org.au/, http://web.archive.org/web/20170216162701/http://outofsight.org.au/about.php, http://web.archive.org/web/20170216162616/http://outofsight.org.au/letters.php, and http://web.archive.org/web/20170216162550/http://outofsight.org.au/.
43 "Free the Children NAURU" (now "Human Rights Visual Story Telling Place"), Facebook, 11 November 2015, https://www.facebook.com/childrennauru/posts/pfbid0jQP2gdfnvcxpxTn7gZHJVwPXyLbRHaMHdoXQ6y867HMZG3yYkRg5eaz8JufLMXBYl, 20 November 2015, https://www.facebook.com/childrennauru/photos/a.840306886086838/847183342065859?type=3; and post from 29 August 2016 explaining that the children no longer run the "Free the Children NAURU" Facebook page, https://www.facebook.com/childrennauru/posts/1029190563865135.
44 AHRC, *The Forgotten Children*. HREOC, *A Last Resort?* focuses on the legal status of Australian Immigration Detention laws.
45 AHRC, *The Forgotten Children*, 11, 251.
46 Ibid., 248–50.
47 Ibid., 12.
48 Ibid., 259–66. Two submissions did not identify location of detention and another two were from children who had previously been in detention.
49 Ibid., 51.

50 "Drawings by Children in Immigration Detention," AHRC, 29 August 2016, https://www.humanrights.gov.au/news/photos/drawings-children-immigration-detention (link defunct). Some of children's formal written submissions to the inquiry also included illustrations. See "Submissions made to the inquiry," AHRC, accessed 10 September 2018, https://www.humanrights.gov.au/our-work/asylum-seekers-and-refugees/national-inquiry-children-immigration-detention-2014-0, submission no. 60, 61, 62, 64, 144, 191, 194, 195 and 228; also AHRC, *The Forgotten Children*, 252.

51 AHRC, "Drawings by Children in Immigration Detention," Flickr Album, accessed 14 September 2017, https://www.flickr.com/photos/23930202@N06/sets/72157645938124048/.

52 Wall, *Children's Rights*, 57–8.

53 "National Inquiry into Children in Immigration Detention 2014." The report was provided to the attorney general on 11 November 2014, and tabled in Federal Parliament on 11 February 2015.

54 Lenette et al., "What Is It Like Living in Detention?," 49.

55 Wall, *Children's Rights*, 62.

56 "Drawings by Children in Immigration Detention."

57 Facebook founded 2004 (open to anyone over thirteen since 2006); Flickr 2004; Twitter 2006; Tumblr 2007; Instagram 2010.

58 Wall, *Children's Rights*, 4. See also Higonnet, "Child Witnesses," 1565–76.

59 Gatrell, *The Making of the Modern Refugee*, 9. Only in recent years have scholars begun to turn to children's own perspective on the experience of forced displacement. See, for example, Hammel, "Authenticity, Trauma and the Child's View," 201–12; Williams, *The Forgotten Kindertransportees*.

60 Keren, "Autobiographies of Spanish Refugee Children at the Quaker Home in La Rouvière," 5; Roith, *Memory and Critique*, 123–46; Huxley, *They Still Draw Pictures!* More recent publications include Geist and Carroll, *They Still Draw Pictures*; Aradau and Hill, "The Politics of Drawing," 368–87; and Volavkova, ed., *I Never Saw Another Butterfly*.

61 Higonnet, "Child Witnesses," 1571, and Stargardt, "Children's Art of the Holocaust," 197.

62 Ivashkevich, "Drawing in Children's Lives," 56–7.

63 Stargardt, "Children's Art of the Holocaust," 224.

64 Ibid., 234.

65 Themes of confinement, sadness, childhood, suffering, and community have been identified by Lenette et al., "What Is It Like Living in Detention?"

66 "Me" is used in CI2-PIC-2, CI-PIC-3, CI-PIC-23, CI-PIC-24, CI-PIC-79, CI-PIC-116, D-PIC-74, G-PIC-78, G-PIC-170, G-PIC-274 and "I" in CI-PIC-3, CI2-PIC-2, D-PIC-72, G-PIC-77, and G-PIC-78 in AHRC, "Drawings by Children in Immigration Detention," Flickr Album. Please note, individual drawings are referenced by their file name in Flickr.
67 Form included in AHRC, *Forgotten Children*, Appendix 6, 286–300, detailed methodology, Appendix 2, 248–58.
68 Mackie, "Putting a Face to a Name," 213–36.
69 AHRC, "Drawings by Children in Immigration Detention," Flickr Album, G-PIC-293 and G-PIC-229.
70 Bleiker et al., "The Visual Dehumanisation of Refugees," 398–416.
71 AHRC, "Drawings by children in immigration detention," Flickr Album, G-PIC-277.
72 Ibid., G-PIC-276.
73 Ibid., CI-PIC-18.
74 Ibid., CI-PIC-116.
75 Ibid., D-PIC-32.
76 Ibid., G-PIC-4.
77 Ibid., G-PIC-268.
78 Ibid., including CI-PIC-128final, CI-PIC-122-a, CI-PIC-23, CI2-PIC-3, CI2-PIC-11, CI2-PIC-22, D-PIC-31, D-PIC-56, D-PIC-58, and D-PIC-84.
79 Ibid., CI-PIC-26.
80 Ibid., G-PIC-192.
81 Ibid., G-PIC-76; CI2-PIC-22; CI(2)-PIC-3, CI-PIC-7, and CI-PIC-126.
82 Ibid., CI2-PIC-7.
83 Ibid., CI-PIC-21.
84 Stargardt, "Drawing the Holocaust in 1945," 31.
85 Melissa Smith, *Mail Online*, 2 July 2004; "Heartbreaking New Drawings by Kids in Detention," *Australian Women's Weekly* website news story, 21 August 2014, http://www.aww.com.au/latest-news/news-stories/sad-drawings-by-kids-in-detention-9509; Sarah Mares and Karen Zwi, "Sadness and Fear: What the Drawings by Children in Detention Showed Us," *Guardian*, 12 May 2014, https://www.theguardian.com/commentisfree/2014/may/12/sadness-and-fear-what-the-drawings-by-children-in-detention-showed-us.
86 Karen Zwi, "Detained Children Risk Life-Long Physical and Mental Harm," *Conversation*, 19 February 2015, https://theconversation.com/detained-children-risk-life-long-physical-and-mental-harm-37510.

87　Andrew Bolt, "Lethal Cost of Kindness to Asylum Seekers on the High Seas," *Herald Sun*, 2 July 2014.

88　"Submissions Made to the Inquiry," AHRC, accessed 10 September 2018, https://www.humanrights.gov.au/our-work/asylum-seekers-and-refugees/national-inquiry-children-immigration-detention-2014-0, see submission no. 60, 62, 64, 91, 144, and 228. Predominantly visual submissions include no. 61, 191, 194, and 195. Those under eighteen identified as nos 15 and 21(A) and 21 (B) (by unaccompanied child); 20 (seventeen-year-old); 34 (former child in immigration detention); 42 (child who lived in immigration detention previously); 59–64 (child in Nauru); 91 (sixteen-year-old old in Nauru); 92–4 (unaccompanied child in Nauru); 95 child in Nauru; 96 (sixteen-year-old in Nauru); 97 (seventeen-year-old in Nauru); 98 (child in Nauru); 132 (child in Nauru); 141 (unaccompanied child in Nauru); 142 (twelve-year-old in Nauru); 143 (unaccompanied child in Nauru); 144 (child in Nauru); 145–7 (unaccompanied child in Nauru); 148 (fifteen-year-old in Nauru); 149–51 (child in Nauru); 191 and 192 (child in Nauru); 193 (fifteen-year-old Nauru); 194–5 (child in Nauru); 215 (boy in immigration detention); 228 (child in Nauru). See also Tomsic, "Children's Art," 137–58.

89　Exceptions includes news article Louise Cheer, "Shocking Drawings Emerge from Nauru Detention Centre – Including Depictions of Suicide and an Unflattering Caricature of Tony Abbott," *Daily Mail*, 15 August 2014, http://www.dailymail.co.uk/news/article-2725665/Shocking-drawings-child-emerge-Nauru-detention-centre.html. Drawings are also included in the documentary *Chasing Asylum* (2016) as well as reports connected to it such as Brigid Delaney, "Eva Orner on Chasing Asylum: 'Every Whistleblower That I Interviewed Wept,'" *Guardian*, 30 April 2016, https://www.theguardian.com/australia-news/2016/apr/30/eva-orner-on-chasing-asylum-every-whistleblower-that-i-interviewed-wept.

90　Margaret Mayhew, "What Can We Draw from Pictures by Detained Child Asylum Seekers?" *Conversation*, 23 February 2015, https://theconversation.com/what-can-we-draw-from-pictures-by-detained-child-asylum-seekers-37647.

PART FOUR
IN THE SPOTLIGHT

Editors' Introduction

This final section of *Small Stories of War* features chapters that focus closely on epistemology and evidence, wrestling with what Saidiya Hartman calls "the power and authority of the archive and the limits it sets on what can be known."[1] In prising open archival documents and inviting readers to look at the lives of young, Black, urban women in early twentieth-century United States on their own terms, Hartman's *Wayward Lives, Beautiful Experiments* constructs both a compelling narrative and an intricate mosaic. By juxtaposing fragments of photographs, official records, diary excerpts, and newspapers with her own fictionalized interjections, she shines a spotlight on the quotidian and radical experiences of young women who dared to live and imagine otherwise, in conditions shaped by the structural forces of racism, surveillance, and economic exploitation.

In inviting our readers into an archive of youthful voices in wartime, we, too, seek to demonstrate how primary sources as varied as letters, oral histories, memoirs, children's wartime drawings, digital stories, and intergenerational picture books can offer insights into the making of the subjectivities of children and youth. These narrative sources differ in their provenance and discursive conventions from institutional records such as, for instance, court proceedings, state welfare reports, case histories of children's homes, refugee reception records, or state welfare reports that social historians have examined to such excellent effect.[2] These narrative sources were not produced by modern authorities invested with the power to collect and organize knowledge and regulate and discipline subaltern groups such as children and youth.[3] Instead, these varied life writings constitute rich and complicated source materials that we may well conceive of as "genres," governed by their own social dynamics, conversational narratives, and the historical conditions of their production. Here, our debt to oral historians who have reflected on voice and subjectivity with such sophistication and imagination for several decades will be readily apparent.[4]

In pairing lengthy primary source excerpts with brief analytical essays on the historical production and preservation of young people's voices, part 4, "In the Spotlight," offers a kaleidoscope of experiences of children and youth in wartime. This part of the collection opens the door to a "history workshop" in which scholars examine the interpretive richness, nuance, and epistemological complexity of different kinds of evidence generated by children and youth in times of armed conflict and warfare.

The first three chapters in this section foreground the voices of a handful of young people who lived on the Canadian home front during the First and Second World Wars. They do so by looking carefully at two particular types of evidence: letters exchanged between parents and children in wartime, and oral history interviews recorded decades after the fact. These sources offer distinct but complementary perspectives about how young people understood and experienced home, identity, family separation, and conflict during the first few decades of the twentieth century. Letters and interviews provide valuable information about children's relationships and experiences on the Canadian home front during two total wars. They are also performances of self that work across multiple temporalities: wartime letters are often preserved and revisited across generations, for example, while interviews about childhood memories are always at least partly about the relationship between the interviewee's adult self and the child they used to be.

Chapter 10, by Kristine Alexander and Ashley Henrickson, begins by analyzing sheet music and picture postcards to highlight the significant symbolic roles children played in the global culture of correspondence that connected combatants and their distant kin during the First World War. It then looks

In the Spotlight

more closely at the correspondence exchanged by one of the families discussed in chapter 4: British-born Canadian soldier Sidney Brook, his wife Isabelle, and their children Gordon (b. 1908), Arnott (b. 1910), Lorne (b. circa 1912), Glen (b. circa 1914–15), and Alice (b. 1916). Whereas this collection of family correspondence includes only a handful of written records produced by three of the five Brook offspring, in their letters to each other Sidney and Isabelle discuss all their children regularly. These parental acts of inquiry, description, and translation, when read alongside their children's wartime writings, allow us to imagine and "hear" parts of their children's wartime lives.

During the First World War, thousands of Canadian families like the Brooks depended on writing to keep their relationships alive across vast distances. The long and complex trajectories of their letters, postcards, and parcels were linked to global postal networks and infrastructure that, as Laura Ishiguro has recently written, were central to the expansion and administration of the British empire.[5] Ishiguro's work on family letters and settler colonialism in nineteenth- and early twentieth-century British Columbia provides another important frame through which to view the Brook family's letter-writing: Sidney Brook himself was a British settler, who left his mother and siblings in England to move to the Canadian prairies in the early twentieth century. He maintained epistolary relationships with these family members during the years when he married and established a homestead in Alberta, and his wartime enlistment added to and reconfigured what was an already-dense trans-imperial network of family correspondence.

Family ties between Britain and the settler empire are also at the heart of chapter 11, in which Claire Halstead examines the letters that British child evacuees like Owen Mackie (b. 1929) exchanged with their parents during the Second World War. In 1940, Mackie's father, a British Army officer and physician who had spent much of his career in India, sent Owen and his older brother Richard to live with his brothers Hugh and Austin Mackie in Vernon, British Columbia.[6] The elder Mackie brothers ran the Vernon Preparatory School, an elite boarding school whose aim, in Jean Barman's words, was to encourage boys to "grow ... up British in British Columbia."[7] Owen and Richard Mackie were private evacuees: upper-middle class children whose paths were determined by pre-existing networks of family and friendship across the British empire. At the same time, their experience also needs to be seen as part of a broader global pattern during the Second World War: the large-scale, state-supported evacuation of young people (in countries that also included Japan,

Finland, and France) in an attempt to protect children as vulnerable and valuable national human capital.

The letters Owen Mackie sent to his parents in England during his four years in Canada included detailed descriptions of exciting new environments, sensory experiences, and daily activities. His wartime experience appears to have been a positive one – a marked contrast from the separation-related trauma and abuse suffered by many working-class evacuee children who remained in Britain.[8] While adhering to standard epistolary conventions (and likely composed under the watchful eyes of his uncles), his largely optimistic correspondence also occasionally hints at possible conflicts and disappointments in his long-distance relationship with his parents. We can only imagine, for example, how his mother would have felt when she read, three years into their separation, that he "would just as soon stay" in British Columbia. These textual traces of one British boy's wartime life come to a stop in the spring of 1944, when fourteen-year-old Mackie returned to live with his parents in England. The archive is silent about the emotional tenor of this particular family reunion, but it was likely not entirely smooth: for many British evacuees, as Matthew Thompson has written, "the return home was in fact invariably recalled as at least as difficult as the initial separation."[9]

The importance of place in experiences of home front childhood during the Second World War is explored in more detail in chapter 12, which focuses on Barbara Lorenzkowski's oral history interview with seventy-eight-year-old Gordon Perks. Born in 1931, Perks spent the war years exploring and playing in the streets and parks of Halifax, Nova Scotia, with his friends, and these experiences come to us filtered through the lenses of memory and temporal distance. In many locations, and especially for boys, wartime meant excitement and new freedoms to explore and occupy public space. Gordon Perks and his friends made places like Point Pleasant Park their own by naming them, telling stories about them, and making detailed mental maps that retained a hold on their memories over more than six decades. Unlike Owen Mackie, who was sent back to England in 1944, Perks (whose father had died before the war) remained in Halifax and continued to revisit the spaces of his wartime childhood in person and in memory throughout his adult life.

Chapters 13 and 15, by Andrew Burtch and Mary Tomsic, respectively, shift the spotlight toward children's drawings – a compelling type of non-textual evidence that has attracted the attention of a number of scholars. During the First World War, schools in Paris, Berlin, and Vienna, to name a few, collected drawings from children for publication and exhibition, frequently selecting those from children who had witnessed the devastation of war personally.[10] In the Spanish Civil War (1936–39) as well, the American Friends Service Committee and the Canadian Committee to Aid Spanish Democracy collected children's drawings from Republican teachers to raise funds overseas to support the fight against Franco. In the years after the war, divorced from their immediate contexts, these children's drawings were taken as a narrative on their own and regarded as a more reliable account of the impact of war on the most vulnerable than either official histories or statist propaganda. Literary scholar Anthony Geist, curator of a travelling exhibition of the Spanish Civil War collection, comments: "In the drawings ... the children depict their own experiences. Their self-representation gives them a subjectivity and agency as historical subjects that they cannot achieve as objects of adult artists. The drawings offer us a view of children as participants in the historical drama of the civil war ... a collective testimony of children's experiences of the war."[11]

In considering the ways in which scholars can interpret children's artwork, Tomsic suggests treating "children's drawings as both aesthetic and social objects."[12] Indeed, among the most fruitful approaches are those studies that offer a close reading of the visual language of children's drawings as well as an analysis of the historical context in which the artwork was created. In his study of children's artwork from the ghetto of Terezín during the Holocaust, the historian Nicholas Stargardt, for instance, seeks to render visible "the faint lines of a moral and emotional map" that emerges from a reading of children's drawing. Taught by Friedl Dicker-Brandeis, an artist and former member of the Bauhaus school who regarded "art as a form of creative release," the boys and girls in the ghetto's voluntary children's homes in Terezín learned "how to break away from mechanical copying and to develop their own forms of self-expression."[13] Their drawings speak to children's recollections of life before the war, their hopes for survival, and their efforts to transcend the emotional and physical traumas of the ghetto. As Stargardt argues, taken collectively, these drawings constitute important historical artifacts, even though we may know nothing more of the young artists than their name, age, and gender.[14]

Turning in chapter 13 to the drawings that Bosnian schoolchildren produced as part of a mine education course in the aftermath of the Yugoslav Wars (1992–95), Andrew Burtch investigates how the child, made victim by the circumstances of war, is given the added burden of truthful witness. Children have some grace period extended to them in this regard, their views not considered tinged by ethnic hatred or strategic agenda (though this too is blurred when considering child soldiers or military education of youth), and so their drawings have historically been used by adults to bolster existing narratives. Yet Bosnian children, much like the young people whose artwork Kay and Tomsic examine elsewhere in this volume, appropriated and translated pedagogy and expectation and reproduced it in their own terms in these drawings, blending propaganda and lived experience to produce something unique that expressed memory and feeling (pride, trauma, fear, anxiety) rather than being a literal reproduction of events.[15]

In chapters 14 and 15, Elizabeth Miller and Mary Tomsic offer multimodal explorations of how refugee children, youth, and their families created spaces for the mediation and transmission of difficult knowledge in the early twenty-first century. The Canadian and Australian initiatives featured in these chapters are underpinned by a shared ethos of storytelling as a creative and collaborative practice. As a practice of everyday life, storytelling has allowed survivors of war and genocide to remember the families they lost and the social worlds they once called home. As an act of bearing witness, storytelling has served as a means by which youth and adult survivors have shared their experiences beyond the more intimate circles of family and peers. As a process of cultural translation, storytelling has transformed the ways in which we tell, and listen to, stories of war, violence, and social dislocation.

Such narrative sources, as Lindsey Dodd and Wendy Michallat write, have "profound generative value," and can be constitutive of new relationships.[16] The digital story crafted by Leontine Uwababyeyi, a survivor of the Rwandan genocide, as discussed by Elizabeth Miller in chapter 14, was meant to emphasize the resilience of young survivors and destabilize tropes of victimhood. At the same time, the act of storytelling brought together a community of young adult refugees in Montreal who decided to form families of choice. As a scholar and documentary filmmaker, Miller was an integral member of the Montreal Life Stories Project (2005–12), a collaborative enterprise that explored the experiences and memories of Montrealers who had been displaced by war, genocide, and human rights violations and made the city home. The project was remarkable not only for its many and varied research outcomes that comprised scholarly publications, public performances, exhibitions, art installations, creative writing classes, radio programs, audio tours, and pedagogical programming, but also its careful attendance to an ethos of collaboration and its profoundly democratic conception.¹⁷ Over the span of the seven-year project, the line between "researchers" and "participants" became increasingly blurry as community members, including a host of young people, joined the project as researchers, leaders, and affiliated members.¹⁸ This kind of participatory research, as lead investigator Steven High would later write, is deeply invested in the "co-creation, co-curation, and co-diffusion" of stories.¹⁹ For Miller, this meant curating a safe space for storytelling in which youth participants could share (or choose to remain silent about) their experiences of war, genocide, and displacement and together develop a "mobile memoryscape" that took the form on alternative city bus tour, replete with audio soundscapes, music, storytelling in situ, and pre-recorded audio stories.²⁰ It was in a community of peers that Leontine Uwababyeyi told, and re-told, her story of loss and survival, searching for a form that would make it safe for her to go public with difficult and sensitive memories. As writer, painter, and scholar Stéphane Martelly reflects, such collaborative storytelling de-centres – in productive and often poetic ways – the authority invested in the oral historian: "Interpretation itself was not the interviewers' or speakers' prerogative, as everybody chimed in to finish each other's sentences; to offer strength and care through yet another narrative, emerging from the previous one, consolidating it or breaking it apart, and, in a way, anticipating the next one and legitimizing it."²¹

In chapter 15, Mary Tomsic examines how storytelling and publishing helped knit together refugee families in Australia in an extended, intergenerational conversation about wartime rupture, belonging and the meanings of home. Tomsic traces the process by which generations of South Sudanese families in Australia began exchanging – and listening to each other's – stories of war, forced mobility, and displacement that were captured in illustrated children's books, produced by a community arts-based publisher. Their stories took the place of tangible objects of memory, which had to be jettisoned in the rushed flight to safety and the long, wary years spent in refugee camps. These stories, much as Martelly found in her collaborative work with Haitian narrators in Montreal, could not be contained in individual narratives but merged, as Martelly writes, in "a chorus of voices" that were mingling and overlapping, sounding re-assurance and shouting support, all the while "propelling" each other "into the unchartered territories where the subject, the destination, and the very form of the narrative, were profoundly transformed."²² Whereas the first book *Donkeys Can't Fly on Planes: Stories of Survival from South Sudanese*

Refugee Children Living in Australia (2012) features the stories and artwork of South Sudanese children, two follow-up volumes are the products of intergenerational exchanges, in which refugee children, their parents, and other adults in the community shared in the process of oral and visual storytelling.

The evidence of experience produced by young people during and following war and displacement thus exists in variety of mediated, relational forms: actions and words described by a mother, handwritten letters intended to inform and please distant parents, childhood recollections recounted to a historian of childhood, drawings made in a classroom, and memory fragments shared, at times searchingly and hesitantly so, in storytelling circles and then translated into digital stories, storytelling bus tours, and picture books. As such, these chapters, drawn from rich narrative and visual source materials, provide scholars and students with greater understanding of how to find and think about young people's voices in wartime. They are also compelling evidence of the enormous range of ways in which war shaped the lives of children and youth across the twentieth century in Canada and beyond.

NOTES

1 Hartman, *Wayward Lives, Beautiful Experiments*, xiii.
2 Historians Tamara Myers and Elizabeth Alice Clement, for instance, have produced exemplary studies on the policing and disciplining of adolescent girls (in Canada and the United States respectively) by drawing on the rich case files of juvenile courts and reformatories. See Myers, *Caught*, and Clement, *Love for Sale*.
3 For an extended exploration of the theoretical and methodological questions raised by historians' work with a broad range of different case files, see, in particular, Iacovetta and Mitchinson, eds, *On the Case*.
4 Alessandro Portelli, "Oral History as Genre," from his *The Battle of Valle Giulia*, 3–23. For a discussion of young people's wartime subjectivities see also Stargardt, "Moments of Rupture," 37–56.
5 Ishiguro, *Nothing to Write Home About*, 39.
6 George Owen Mackie, "Mackie Men and the Empire" (2006). http://web.uvic.ca/~mackie/MME.pdf. Accessed 22 March 2020.
7 Barman, "Growing Up British in British Columbia," 303–18. See also Barman, *Growing Up British in British Columbia*.
8 For more on the experiences of evacuees who remained in Britain, see Thompson, *Lost Freedom*, ch. 2; Welshman, *Churchill's Children*.

9 Thompson, *Lost Freedom*, 56.
10 Higonnet, "Child Witnesses," 1569–71. See also Pignot, *La guerre des crayons*, and Pignot, "Drawing the Great War," 170–88.
11 Geist and Collins, *They Still Draw Pictures*, 24. See also Roith, "They Still Draw Pictures," 1–20.
12 Tomsic, "Children's Art: Histories and Cultural Meanings of Creative Expression by Displaced Children," 138.
13 Stargardt, *Witnesses of War*, 204 and "Children's Art of the Holocaust," 191–235.
14 Ibid., 197–225. See also Volavkova, ed., *I Never Saw Another Butterfly*.
15 Higonnet, "Child Witnesses," 1565–76, 1569.
16 Dodd and Michallat, "Hidden Words, Hidden Worlds," 7.
17 The project's rich publication record includes, among others, High, *Oral History at the Crossroads*; High, ed., *Beyond Testimony and Trauma*; and Miller, Little, and High, *Going Public: The Art of Participatory Practice*.
18 High, *Oral History at the Crossroads*, 121–44.
19 Miller, Little, and High, "Introduction," 20.
20 Miller, "Going Places," 113–27.
21 Martelly, "'This Thing We Are Doing Here,'" 189.
22 Ibid., 188.

10

"Dear Daddy": Children, Writing, and the First World War

Kristine Alexander and Ashley Henrickson

"Dear Daddy." During the First World War, thousands of children used this simple greeting while writing to their fathers fighting on distant fronts. In Canada as in other combatant countries, children were active participants in the popular culture of correspondence that developed during the war: they read and wrote letters and postcards, sent care packages to the front, and received gifts (pressed flowers, embroidered handkerchiefs, and even small war trophies) from enlisted fathers, brothers, uncles, and cousins. Letter-writing was often discussed as a patriotic duty, and it gave young writers many opportunities to practice the literacy skills and epistolary conventions they were beginning to grasp at home and at school.

Written correspondence was crucial to the emotional survival of enlisted men and their families on the home front throughout the First World War, and the thought of children worrying about and crafting letters to their fathers in the trenches packed a particularly powerful affective punch.[1] As popular symbols of home, nation, innocence, and hope, young people were central figures in wartime propaganda and popular culture, and a number of these cultural products focused on children and letter-writing.[2]

The archival collections at the Canadian War Museum include several examples of this phenomenon, such as the sheet music for "Just a Baby's Letter Found in No Man's Land," a 1918 song with words by American lyricist Bernie Grossman, whose other patriotic wartime offerings included "We're Going Over the Top," "Say a Prayer for the Boys 'Out There,'" and "There's a Service Flag Flying at Our House."

The song's lyrics and cover art depict a single soldier amidst the aftermath of a battle on the Western Front. Surrounded by barbed wire and a ruined trench

Children, Writing, and the First World War 259

Figure 10.1 *Left*
"Just a Baby's Letter Found in No Man's Land," Canadian War Museum, accession no. 19810333-001.

Figure 10.2 *Right*
"A Message to Daddy," Canadian War Museum, accession no. 19990037-004.

landscape, he stands holding his bayonet and a single piece of paper: a letter that says "Dear Daddy I love you" in what Grossman described as "a simple baby hand." Was the father of this young correspondent still alive? Had he been killed or wounded? By raising these questions and focusing on a letter by a young child, the song – like wartime correspondence more generally – reminds us that for combatants and their families during the Great War, concepts of home, safety, and love were always intertwined with threats of violence, danger, and death.

Intensely affectionate epistolary relationships between soldiers and their children were also represented visually and textually on mass-produced postcards that were purchased and sent by family members on both sides of the home/front divide. A number of these postcards used photomontage – a technique that, as Marie-Monique Huss notes, made it possible to bring together in a single frame

Figure 10.3
Lorne's letter to Papa, 8 February 1917. Glenbow Archives, Canada.

"people or concepts which would otherwise be separated" – to depict young boys and girls putting pen to paper to write to their absent soldier-fathers.[3]

The emotional intensity of wartime correspondence, highlighted in postcards and sheet music, is also evident in archival collections of family letters. As Manon Pignot has recently written about soldiers and their children, "absence stimulated the expression, often for the first time, of feelings of affection and love: from this perspective the war brought people closer as much as it separated them."[4]

For very young children like Gordon, Arnott, Glen, Lorne, and Alice Brook, discussed in chapter 4, adjusting to their father Sidney's absence after he enlisted in May 1916 happened just as they were beginning to master the physical and intellectual practices of literacy. The Brook children, in other words, were developing writers for whom the processes of learning to read and hold a pen were temporally and materially intertwined with their father's wartime absence.

In the letters she wrote to her husband from their home in Craigmyle, Alberta, Isabelle Brook described how their children used the physical practices and material culture of letter-writing to imagine their father and engage with his absent presence in their everyday lives. On 8 February 1917, for instance, she wrote "Lorne [who would have been four years old at this point] is sending you a letter he has written. You may possibly need an interpreter for it. He says it's 'papa's name – S. Brook, papa's name.'"[5]

In another letter, dated "Sat. 4 p.m. Feb 17th [1917]," Isabelle wrote to Sidney that just as she had sat down with her paper and pen, "Lorne came along enquiring 'Letty, Papa?' I said, 'Yes.' Then, 'Me yite letty, Papa.' He thinks every letter that comes is maybe one from Papa, and all I write are to Papa. He hasn't stopped to write a 'letty' to Papa just now tho', he's off outside to play."[6]

Ten days later, Isabelle wrote that Lorne was "chattering away about his Papa" and "sorting out 'Papa's letties' from a bundle of letters here on the table, and trying to take the stamps off now. With the boys [older brothers Gordon and Arnott, ages nine and seven] at school, and Glen [b. 1914 or 1915] having his afternoon nap he feels so much alone he scarcely knows what to do with himself."[7]

While the oldest Brook children, Gordon and Arnott, wrote to their father throughout the war, only two of their letters have survived. On one level this is unsurprising, as textual sources produced by adults vastly outnumber child-authored ones in most archival collections. This is because children often wrote less, but it also reflects broader ideas about national and regional "importance" that continue to privilege the collection and cataloguing of adult-produced sources in many different repositories.[8]

Sidney Brook's correspondence reveals him to have been an engaged and affectionate father, and we contend that it was also the intense sentimental value of the letters he received from his children that has led to their underrepresentation in the Brook Family Fonds (donated by Glen Brook's widow Irene in 2005) at the Glenbow. His letters to Isabelle regularly mention the cards and notes he had received from Gordon and Arnott. They also tell us that, unlike the letters he received from her and other adult family members (which he mailed and hand-delivered to his sister in England), Sidney often kept letters written by his children on his person, in the pocket of his uniform. Here they were literally close to his heart: folded and unfolded, read and reread, tattered and torn – to eventually be replaced with new ones. In March 1917, for example, Sidney wrote to Isabelle about a letter in which Gordon had called him "very brave." This "beauty," he wrote, was stored in his left breast pocket, beside his Bible.[9]

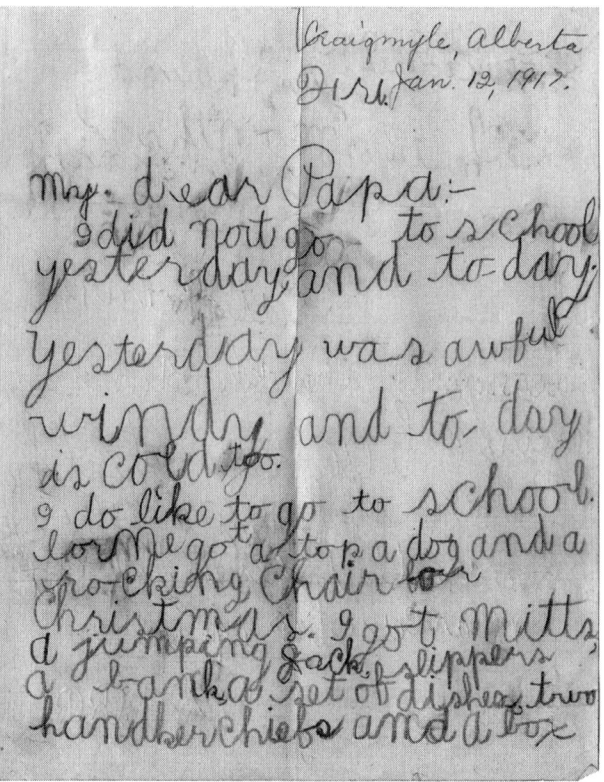

Figure 10.4 Gordon Brook, letter to Sidney Brook, 12 January 1917. Glenbow Archives, Canada.

Letters, as Martyn Lyons reminds us, are "highly coded forms, obeying generally accepted conventions and applying and adapting unspoken formulas."[10] Throughout the First World War, children like Gordon and Arnott Brook worked hard, often under adult supervision, to adhere to these conventions and formulas in the letters they wrote to their father. Their two surviving letters, both written in mid-January 1917, include formal salutations ("My Dear Papa") and acknowledge a Christmas card and photograph they had recently received from him. They describe the weather in Craigmyle ("awful windy"), their and their siblings' health (Arnott was "getting better of a cold," while two-month-old Alice had grown to weigh "nine pounds"), and provide lists of their recently received Christmas presents — the latter of which may also be read as evidence of Isabelle Brook's concerted efforts to maintain a sense of normalcy in her children's lives despite straitened financial circumstances and their father's absence. The Brook boys' letters, with their uneven cursive characters and not-entirely-straight lines, clearly

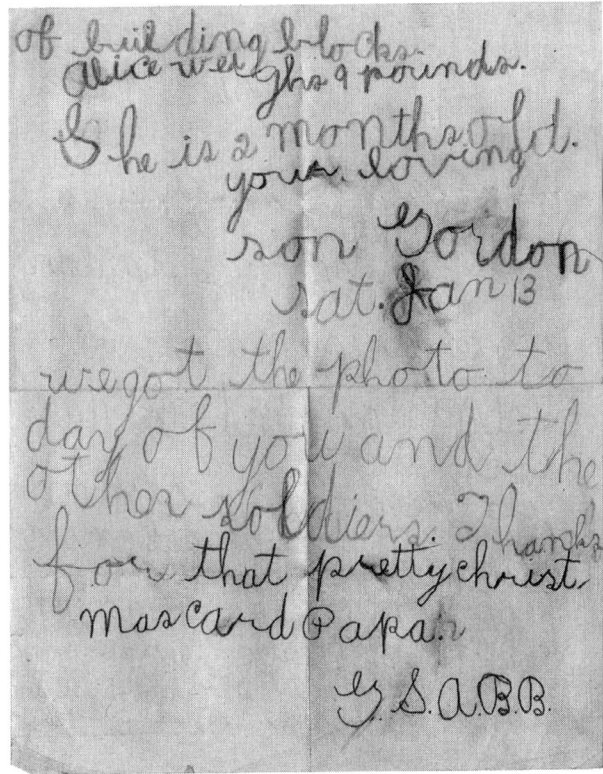

took time and concentration to produce. They close with expressions of affection: "Your loving son Gordon" and "Come home soon. Lovingly Arnott," the latter of which must have become even more poignant after seven-year-old Arnott died from diphtheria in October 1917.

The Brook family's wartime correspondence is a rich and compelling fragment of a conversation that historians will never fully "hear." It is also composed of material objects that were treasured, hoarded, and reread throughout the First World War – and that were carefully preserved by family members for nearly a century afterwards. Like the popular cultural representations of children's correspondence that were produced throughout the conflict, the letters written by Sidney and Isabelle Brook and their children provide evidence of young people's active participation in wartime epistolary culture – while revealing the impact of the war on individual young lives.

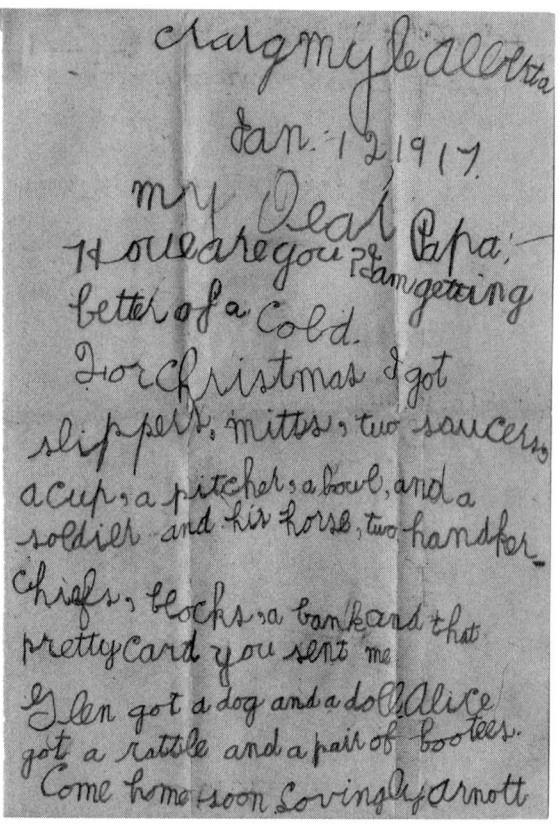

Figure 10.5
Arnott Brook, letter to Sidney Brock, 12 January 1917. Glenbow Archives, Canada.

NOTES

1 See for example Hunter, "More than an Archive of War," 339–54; Roper, *The Secret Battle*; Hanna, *"Your Death Would Be Mine."*

2 Olsen, "Children's Emotional Formations," 643–58. It is worth pointing out here that the image of innocent childhood represented in these cultural products was racialized as white. For more on this see Alexander, "An Honour and a Burden," 176–7, and especially Bernstein, *Racial Innocence*.

3 Huss, "Pronatalism and the Popular Ideology of the Child in Wartime France," 337. See also Alexander, "An Honour and a Burden," 177–8, and Fraser, "Propaganda on the Picture Postcard," 39–47.

4 Pignot, "Children," 30.

5 Glenbow Archives (Calgary). Isabelle Brook to Sidney Brook, 8 February 1917. We suspect that this is the drawing to which Isabelle's letter of 8 February 1917 refers, but it is catalogued not with the letters she and her children sent to Sidney during

Children, Writing, and the First World War

that month; instead, it appears (though is not mentioned in the description of) File M-9076-13 of the Brook Family Fonds: "Letters from Sidney to Isabelle. – June 28–September 17, 1916."

6 Glenbow Archives, Isabelle Brook to Sidney Brook, 17 February 1917.
7 Ibid., 27 February 1917.
8 Alexander, "Can the Girl Guide Speak?," 132–44.
9 Glenbow Archives, Sidney Brook to Isabelle Brook, 18 March 1917.
10 Lyons, "Love Letters and Writing Practices: On Ecritures Intimes in the Nineteenth Century," 233.

11

Writing "Home":
Letters from British Child Evacuees Sent to Canada during the Second World War

Claire L. Halstead

In July 1940, ten-year-old Owen Mackie wrote a letter to his parents in Britain while in the mid-Atlantic aboard the *Monarch of Bermuda*. "Dear Mummy and Daddy We have been sick for the last three days and have just got up ... we are going under convoy. We did have another Liner, a trader, the battleship Revenge, and a Cruiser. The trader was to [*sic*] slow so it left us accompanied by the cruiser ... we have two A.A. guns and another 6″ ones. We are going to fire them for practice at 4 o'clock. We discovered a lady called Mrs Henly or Henry who is very kind to us and helps us when sick. We have had two lifeboat practices so far ... Lots of love from Owen."[1] Owen closed his letter with drawings of two boats, visually illustrating his ocean voyage for his parents. Despite the matter-of-fact tone in which it is written, Owen's letter offers a profound glimpse into the wartime experiences of British child evacuees and signals how children relied on letter writing to communicate their perceptions of evacuation.

The advent of total war in the twentieth century inescapably changed the ways that children were exposed to and affected by war and conflict. No longer were wars fought by men on distant battlefields while the family waited at home for their return. Around the globe, the Second World War caused an unparalleled level of destruction, civilian displacement, and familial disruption; children were no longer immune from the shadow of war. In Britain, this new warfare manifested itself as an intense fear that Britain's children, previously protected from distant European battlefields except for limited Zeppelin raids, would no longer be safe on the "home front." At the outbreak of war, nearly one million British children were consequently separated from their parents and evacuated to "safe zones" across the country.² In the spring of 1940, when an invasion of Britain became ever more likely after the fall of France and the Low Countries, the anxiety of British parents prompted an overseas evacuation movement through both privately organized auspices and the state-sponsored Children's Overseas Reception Board (CORB). With the view that children were vulnerable and in need of being protected during conflict, overseas evacuation led thousands of children to be separated from their families and sent to homes in Canada, Australia, New Zealand, South Africa, and the United States.³ Canada received the most British evacuee children.⁴

As an unprecedented non-permanent relocation of children, the evacuation of British children to Canada is a unique case study for the separation of children from family and home due to war. Unlike child migration or adoption schemes which often caused a permanent separation and disconnection between children and their biological families, overseas evacuation was established as a strictly temporary movement. Consequently, this meant that British families aimed to maintain contact and remain connected with their evacuee children throughout their evacuation. In a time without readily accessible telephone, telegraph, or airgraph contact, letter writing was the main mode of communication for British families, their evacuated children, and the children's Canadian foster families. The surviving correspondence provides a valuable yet underestimated perspective on the evacuation experience for the child, family, and foster family. While children do not tend to create documentary sources during childhood, evacuation created unique circumstances whereby evacuee children, between the ages of three to fifteen, wrote letters home about their lives routinely, even if sometimes with encouragement. Correspondence between evacuees and their families in Britain presents an alternative to the narrative of children's experiences of war dominated by a disruption of family life due to the father's departure for war service. Instead in this instance, it was the children who were moved, had to readjust to new surroundings, and wrote "home" about their new living conditions. While evacuees, as innocent young souls, were intentionally whisked away from danger and violence, evacuation became a wartime experience that came with its own trials, tribulations, and potential harm. Exacerbating this is that childhood is a crucial time for emotional development; letters, therefore, provide an often-hidden window into the children's world.⁵ Evacuees' letters, like those from Owen Mackie, illustrate that the children had to cope with the emotional and psychological (and sometimes physical) toll of being sent away from home. Yet of equal importance is that the letters also reveal in the children's own words, their perspectives of their evacuation to Canada. For evacuees, war and evacuation brought an opportunity to create their own narratives of both their wartime experience and childhood.

Destined to stay with his uncles in Vernon, British Columbia, Owen Mackie set off for the seventeen-day, six-thousand-mile journey across the Atlantic and then Canada, with only his thirteen-year-old brother.[6] Travelling without an adult escort meant that the boys had to navigate much of the voyage themselves. Not dissimilar to many other evacuees travelling unaccompanied to Canada, Owen and Richard were met with spontaneous care and kindness by random strangers along their trip. "Mrs Henly or Henry," as Owen wrote, was one such person who stepped in and cared for the boys, particularly when they were indisposed, like many other evacuees, with seasickness. Owen's letter also reveals other aspects of the evacuation ocean journey such as ships travelling in convoys, mounted guns, and lifeboat drills which many evacuees wrote about with excitement but, to parents, highlighted the intense danger that lurked beneath the water. Owen, his brother Richard, and 147 other unaccompanied private evacuee children aboard the *Monarch of Bermuda* safely arrived in Halifax, Nova Scotia, on 12 July 1940.[7] Not all were as lucky; on 17 September 1940, the SS *City of Benares* carrying ninety CORB evacuee children was torpedoed and sunk.[8] Seventy-seven evacuees perished. The tragedy proved that crossing the Atlantic was too dangerous and brought an end to the state-sponsored overseas evacuation program and reduced private evacuation to a trickle by the end of 1940.

The just over 3,000 evacuees who did arrive safely in Canada were instantly met with a new life that required acclimatization.[9] Once evacuees arrived at their destination, which was either with foster homes that were selected by local childcare authorities in each Canadian province, or, as in Owen's case, with distant family members or relations, they had to recuperate after the long and often arduous journey. For Owen, as he recorded in his first letter from Canada, this meant going "straight to bed with a hot water bottle and aspirin." Owen used the space of the letter to create his own narrative of his immediate perceptions of life in Vernon as he recounted that the next day was "spent in exploring." Owen also reported that there was "1 large car, 1 van, one lorry and one old fas^{h}oned [*sic*] car (all Chevrolets)" and "a swimming bathe which ~~pump~~ gets its water by having it pumped up from a stream by an electric pump."[10] For Owen, the unfamiliar presence of Chevrolets (a North American brand) and an electric pump swimming pool were new and noteworthy. In this way, Owen's letters resemble other letters from newly arrived evacuees as they too tended to spend much of their correspondence explaining to their parents the new sights, spaces, and experiences of Canadian life. This often extended to "new" Canadian terminology. Eight-year-old Patricia Cave, who also sailed aboard the *Monarch of Bermuda* but settled in Toronto, wrote to her parents shortly after arrival: "I have got a very small but very 'cute' mouth organ … everything is 'cute' in Canada." Paddy's use of quotation marks was a gentle way of poking fun at the constant use of the term by Canadians to describe almost anything. She later described, "There is arithmetic and geography. In Canada geography is called natural science. Funny name. In ENGLAND we have gears on the floor in the car but in Canada the most of them are attached to the steering wheel. I think it is very funny but the Canadians do not – they say that England still keeps the old way. I think so to [*sic*] because of all the new things in Canada."[11] Evacuees in a literal sense mobilized the trope of Canada as the "new world."

In their letters, evacuees tended to provide detailed descriptions of their new physical surroundings. For Owen, this meant explaining to his parents that "[their] room [was] at the corner of the house with 4 windows." Then, more days spent "chiefly exploring" led to other new experiences. In scripting out a narrative, Owen wrote to his parents about the Canadian wildlife: "Yesterday I had my first adventure with a skunk. It was a baby one, it looked like a squirrel [*sic*] only black with a white stripe on its back. It ran away & I saw it this morning." Since the majority of evacuees arrived in Canada in the summer of 1940, many had their first introduction to Canadian life and holiday customs at summer camp or at a lake or cottage. Owen and Richard were whisked off with their uncles and aunt to Sugar Lake, fifty miles north of Vernon, which provided many opportunities for exploring the Canadian wilderness that contrasted with the manicured British countryside and tradition of going to the seaside. From Sugar Lake, Owen told his parents that they were "going to the sand bar continuously and riding down rivers on logs" and "adventured to Sip Sap creek." Owen carefully recorded how the adventure peaked: "We saw a storm coming so we turned the engine to full speed and took cover. When we did land after a 6 mile ride at full speed we I produced some maches [*sic*] and set a good fire going. Later we returned."[12] Owen completed his letter and adventure narrative with a large drawing of them in a boat during the storm and then on the shore with a fire. When reading these letters today, one must be careful not to undervalue these letters and overlook the importance of their descriptions. Rather than relying on adult retrospective views and accounts

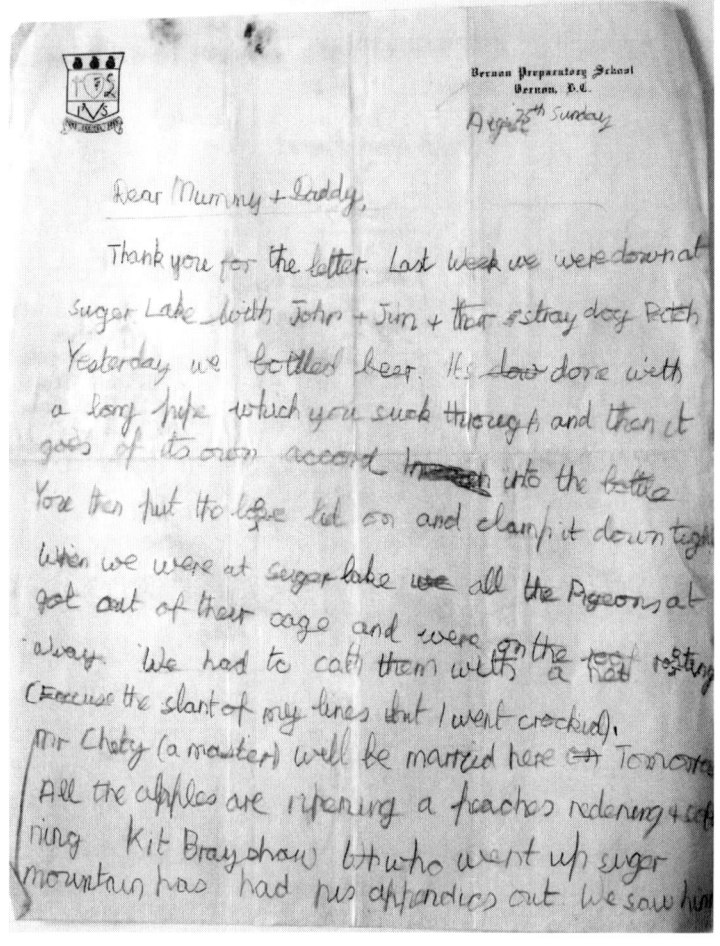

Figure 11.1
Letter by Owen Mackie to his parents, 25 August 1940.
Courtesy of the George Mackie Collection.

formed many years after the war, evacuees' wartime letters illustrate how evacuees experienced and concurrently recounted their experiences as *children*.

Evacuees' wartime letters should also be valued for their importance as the only real means of communication with their families back in Britain. For parents, such letters provided a much-desired link to their children and enabled a cherished, if sometimes nerve-wracking, insight into their children's new lives in Canada. Parents responded to their children's letters with comments, instruction,

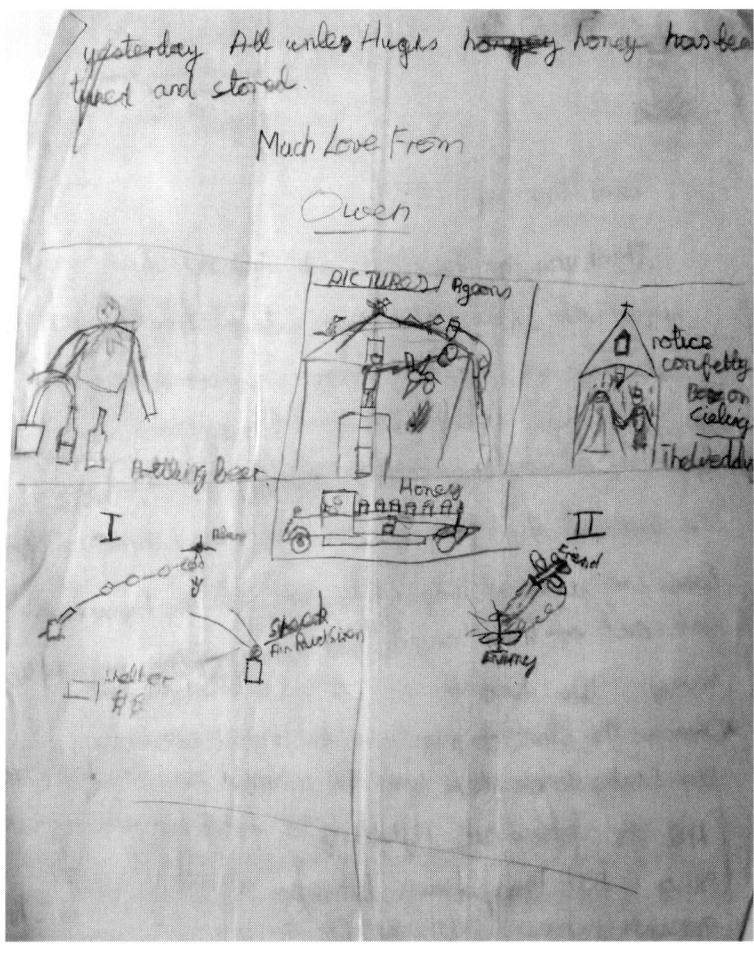

and words of love and encouragement. It is not often however that both letters from evacuees and letters from parents to evacuees survive; that the George Owen Collection contains his own letters as well as some from his parents makes the correspondence even more valuable to historians. On 14 August 1940, Owen's mother replied to his letter and wrote, "we are interested in your meeting a skunk, and seeing other strange animals. Do they smell?" Responding to Owen's mention of harvesting twelve gallons of cherries to make cherry wine, she noted her envy for his cherries as she had tried to make a cherry pie for a luncheon with only one bottle of cherries that was not sufficient to prevent the pastry from sagging. With concern, Owen's mother also took the opportunity to ask if his cough was better

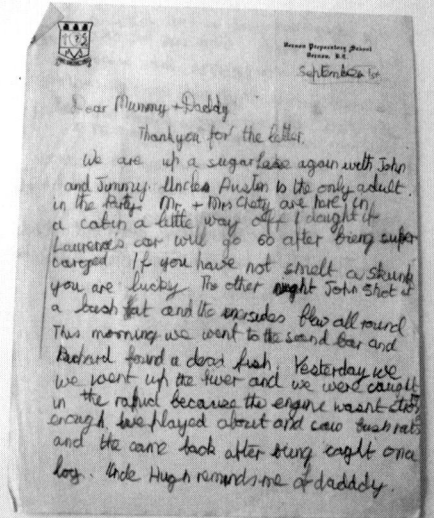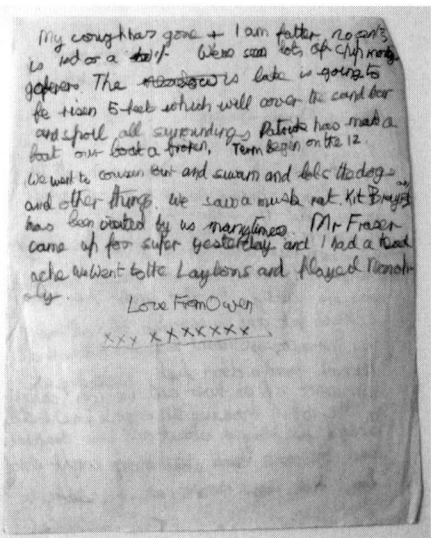

Figure 11.2
Letter by Owen Mackie to his parents, 1 September 1940. Courtesy of the George Mackie Collection.

and if he was fatter. Evacuees' weight featured often in letters as parents rejoiced that their children were receiving a near-endless supply of healthy, fresh food in Canada. Reflecting that Owen would have already become accustomed to Canadian currency, his mother asked, "how much is 20 cents, the cost of your boats? I don't know the dollar coinage yet. I expect you do."[13] Parents also used letters to provide evacuees with updates from home. Sometimes this included mention of relatives, pets, and in Owen's instance, siblings who were serving or enlisting. Even this mode of communication was not always reliable since letters were often infrequent, delayed, or even lost as they crossed the Atlantic. As a remedy, some families took to numbering their letters to prevent misunderstandings and help recipients determine if a letter was lost.

On 1 September 1940, Owen replied to his mother's letter writing "if you have not smelt a skunk you are lucky" and explaining that his cough was gone and he was fatter. While these seem like monotonous reports of daily life, such topics like health and school were often employed by both evacuees and parents to keep up discussions. Later in the war as life in Canada became their daily norm, many evacuees found that they had less to write "home" about. In this 1940 letter however, it is evident that Owen was still thinking very much of his family. Mid-letter, Owen included a line that seemed out of place from the letter's context: "Uncle Hugh reminds me of dadddy." The line illustrates that Owen was subconsciously comparing or relating his father with his foster father. That Owen spelled Daddy with a lower-case letter and with three letter d's also reflects his young age at the time of evacuation.

Owen's correspondence with his parents continued throughout the war. While Owen arrived as a young ten-year-old boy, by 1943 he had matured into adolescence. This is immediately apparent from his penned cursive writing – no longer childlike squared-off cursive writing in pencil with some errors, his writing transformed into even penmanship that slanted with his own unique style. Attending Vernon Preparatory School, Owen decided to write on 10 October 1943, "Our class room is decorated now by beautiful girls – Every inch of space not occupied by posted is utilized in glamor girls, I sit facing the black board above which repose Ida Lupino."[14] In late 1943, as Owen approached the age at which he foreseeably could return to Britain, his mother proposed that he go back sometime in 1944. Owen's response, which he penned on 17 October 1943, was practical yet not devoid of emotion: "Apart from wanting to see you so much and realizing the expense to Uncles, I would just as soon stay here. Of course I would like to go back to England very much, and see you most of all." Quite strategically Owen proposed that if he stayed, he would academically remain a year advanced whereas if he returned to England, he would be behind because his evacuation had interrupted his education. He responded with his own proposal asking, "I suppose you couldn't come out here? I have got all settled down here and have adopted their speech to a certain extent and their methods of education." He concluded that "Much as I'd like to come back & live at Mark with you and go to such a well-known school – well anyway – I suppose I don't really mind, as long as we can be together again."[15] Such hesitant sentiment was shared among many evacuees. Although they wanted to be reunited with their families, they had spent between three and five formative years in Canada, had established friendships, grown attached to their foster families, become accustomed to traditions and cultural "Canadianisms," and become fond of the Canadian landscape.

As the tide of war changed after D-Day in June 1944, the first exodus of private evacuees left Canada and sailed "home." Owen Mackie returned to England in the spring of 1944 and went on to study zoology at the University of Oxford. Many evacuees experienced a tumultuous return to their families and Britain, which

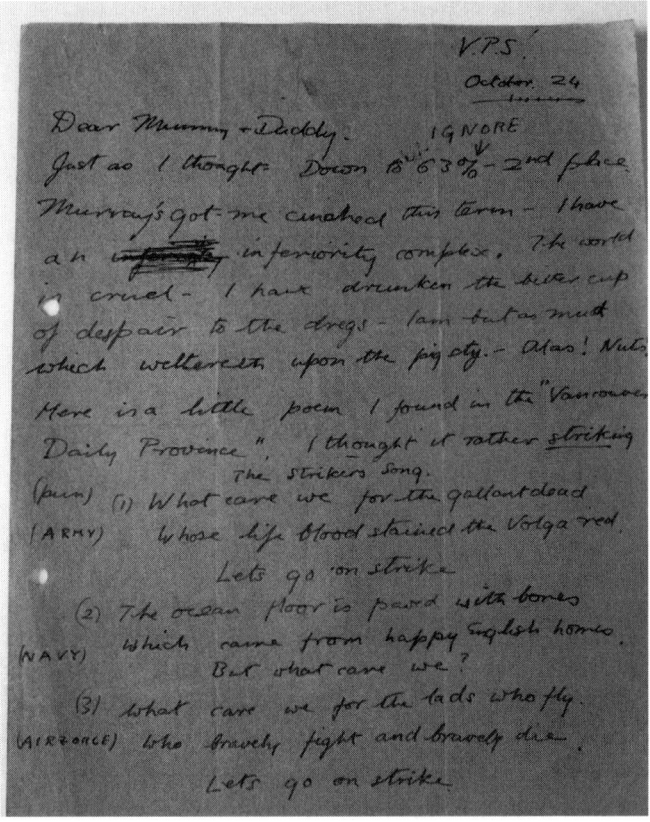

Figure 11.3
Letter by Owen Mackie to his parents, 24 October 1940.
Courtesy of the George Mackie Collection.

had both been changed by war and time and become unrecognizable. Back "at home," a phrase which brought confusion to many of the children, evacuees often felt alienated from their families. Evacuation left permanent and irreconcilable scars on the family dynamic, as was the case with Owen and Richard Mackie. Many eventually returned to Canada for visits or emigrated permanently either immediately after the war or later in life. Owen returned to Canada in 1956 to teach at the University of Alberta and later returned to British Columbia to become a professor of biology at the University of Victoria.[16]

The experience of British children who were evacuated to Canada may be seen as a vastly different story to children who witnessed violent conflict first-hand.

What care we?
The bells of death are tolling, tolling.
What care we?
The only loyalty we know
Is to are own self interest, so
Lets go on Strike". (J. F Turner).
I think its just typical of strikers now.
It should be cut out + framed and put in
every factory in the province.
Rain, slush + mud is the weather mans war
cry now. It has been raining since the day
before yesterday evening.
It stopped in time for the football tournament.
We tied with Vernon X and Vernon Y. [illegible]
and were beaten by two by Oyama.
I was on duty this week with Murray.
Oh yes! On my birthday I was given a box
of chox. by Aunt G + Mrs Orwell & also a camera
from Aunt G. Mrs Atkinson a wrench for my carpentry
And from you - well I've told before. Thank you very
much for them all. As no ice cream was obtainable in
town, The sixth form went to "7th moon is down"
It was very good. Much Love Owen.

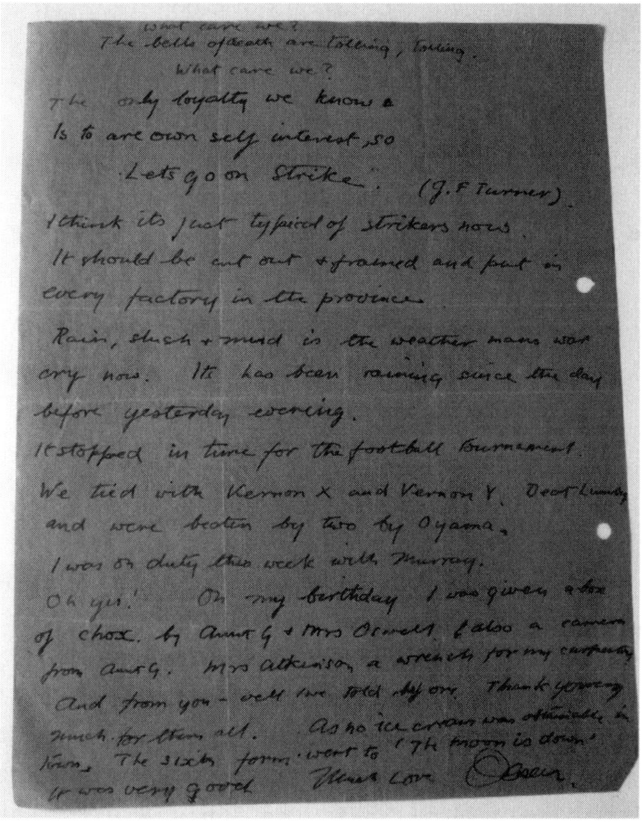

Yet evacuees had to navigate their own emotional and sometimes traumatic war experience. Evacuees muddled through their dangerous ocean journeys but also had to emotionally cope with being removed and separated from their families and their country for an extended period of time. They were then expected to seamlessly reintegrate into their former lives despite all their Canadian experiences and self-development and maturation. As some evacuees had to transition between foster homes during their time in Canada, not all evacuees were as fortunate as Owen, who stayed with relatives and received consistency in home life and education. The correspondence between evacuees and their parents reveals much about these struggles and successes, yet there was still much more, like intense homesickness, that remained unwritten. One must not forget that even at a young age, children were still capable of dissimulation and could tailor their narratives for their parents. Yet still, the letters and accompanying drawings composed by evacuees provide an effective yet historically overlooked access to their wartime experiences. Whilst hindsight has the benefit of reflection, the letters capture children's quotidian feelings and reflections and for that, we must give them the credit they deserve. While children are often perceived as incapable of constructing thoughtful and meaningful historical sources, evacuees' wartime letters boldly illustrate that children do create narratives of their experiences through letter writing. As a concluding example, one of Owen's final letters from Canada was written in 1943 to his brother Richard who had gone to boarding school outside Toronto; their fondness and cheekiness are apparent as Owen signed his letter: "Yours till the Borders cows come home."[17]

The Sharp Brothers

In 1940, Marie Williamson was living in Toronto with her husband and two small children. With the plight of children on their minds, Marie was one of the thousands of women in Canada who wanted to help British children through overseas evacuation. Marie wrote to her cousin Margaret Sharp in England and offered to take care of Margaret's three sons for the duration of the war.[18] In one short sentence, Marie summed up the sentiments of a nation when she wrote, "it will just be a little larger family and the more children we can have out of England the better we will be pleased."[19] In the summer of 1940, nine-year-old Tom Sharp and his brothers, eleven-year-old Christopher and thirteen-year-old Bill, arrived in Toronto from Cumbria. Tom and Christopher joined the home of Marie, her husband, and their children, seven-year-old Mary and eleven-year-old Peter, while Bill being older, went to stay with the Ratcliffes, who were friends of the Williamsons.

Over the course of the following four years, the Sharp boys wrote to their mother and father (who were divorced) as well as their "Granny."[20] Their letters record their explorations of their new Canadian environments, both in urban Toronto and in rural Muskoka, their successes at school, their perceptions of Canadian culture (including holidays), as well as more day-to-day experiences. At different times in the war, the boys used small drawings embedded in their letters to emphasize and share their perspectives. In 1941, Christopher illustrated the way he was able to comprehend his separation from his parents and his homeland through a visual depiction.[21] He made sure to even include the cat Gypsey in his list of loved ones left behind in England. With a surprising amount of accuracy, Christopher also drew his father in London. While his biological family remained

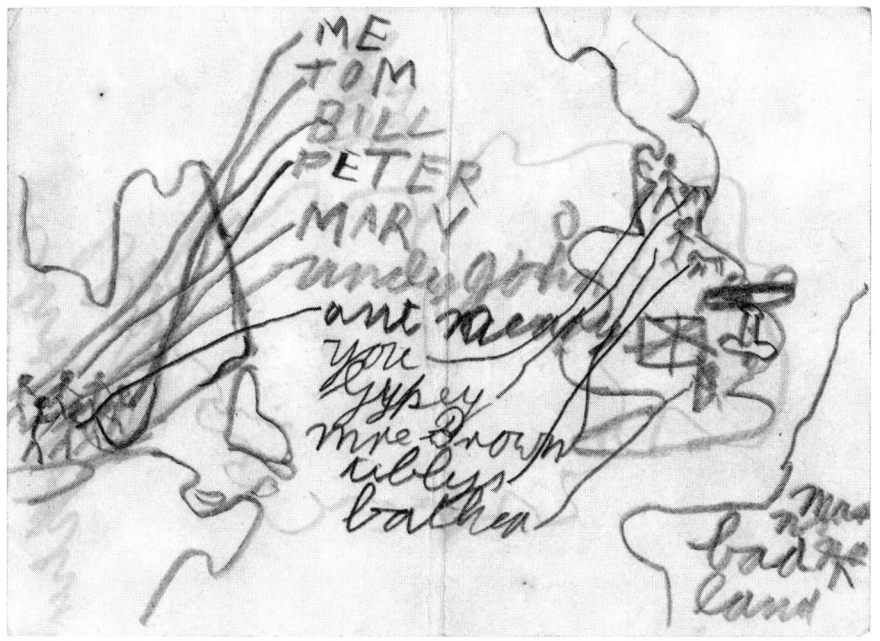

Figure 11.4
Letter by Christopher Sharp, 1941. Canadian War Museum, "Letters of Marie Williamson and the Sharp Family," accession no. 58A.1.273.47.

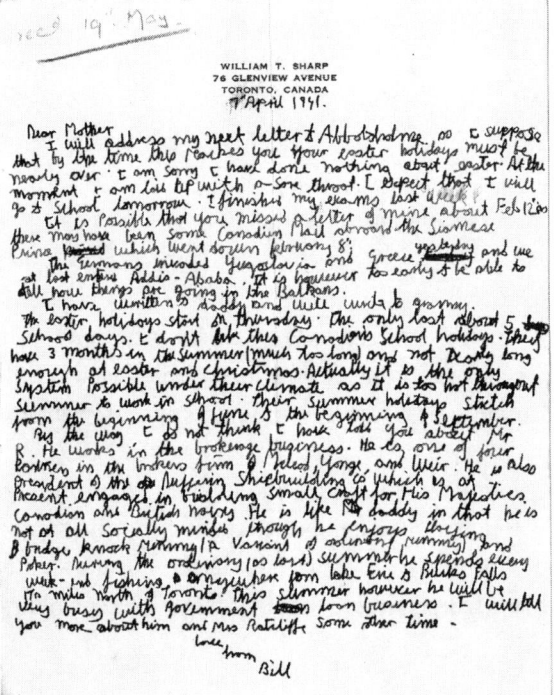

Figure 11.5
Letter by Bill Sharp, 7 April 1941. Canadian War Museum, "Letters of Marie Williamson and the Sharp Family," accession no. 58A.1.273.47.

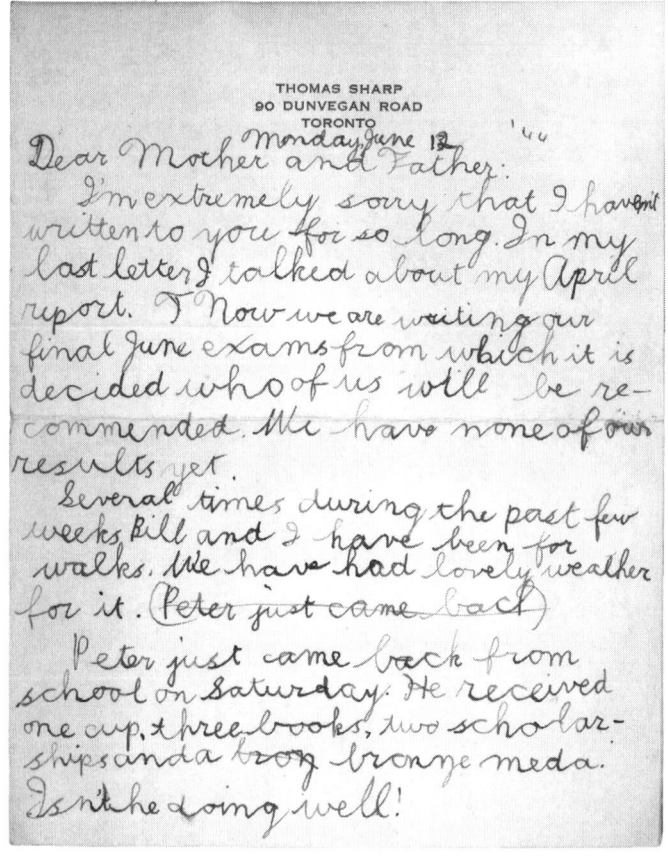

Figure 11.6
Letter by Tom Sharp, 12 June 1944. Canadian War Museum, "Letters of Marie Williamson and the Sharp Family," accession no. 58A.1.273.47.

an ocean away, Christopher's inclusion of Peter, Mary, Uncle John, and "Ant Marie" [sic] in his picture reflects his emotional connection to his foster family and suggests that he perceived himself to be a part of this new, temporary wartime family unit.

Bill Sharp also used visual depictions to communicate his new surroundings but instead of little drawings, he often included detailed maps such as one depicting the floor plan of the Ratcliffes' house. In an April 1941 letter, Bill decided to discuss the war (which did not always happen in evacuee letters). With a sprinkling

> I'm glad you are now going to be history mistress at Ulverston Grammar School. Does that mean that you will teach me?
> Our choir is in rather a mix up now. Our leading 1st tenor soloist died a few days ago and another tenor left to be organist of another church leaving one tenor. This means that the only anthems we can sing are all boy's anthems. To make matters worse our leading boy is sick!
> Love,
> From Tom.
> P.S. Our I hope they will be able to spare one ship from the invasion to take me back to England.

of criticism over Canadian school holidays, Bill also reflected the unreliability of wartime mail as ships were frequently sunk.[22]

By 1944, the Sharp boys had spent a significant proportion of their childhood in Canada. Tom, for instance, was no longer a shy nine-year-old but a more self-assured thirteen-year-old. His letter from June 1944, however, illustrates that despite the four years of living in different homes, Tom and Bill still made an effort to share some sibling time together. Tom's open apology for not writing to his parents was not unique as many foster parents had to remind evacuees to write "home." In some instances, it is understandable that hidden beneath apologies are deepening feelings of emotional distancing from their biological parents still in Britain. This letter is also significant because it marks the end of Tom's correspondence with his parents. His postscript hopes that a "ship from the invasion" could be spared to take him "back to England." That he wrote England instead of home may suggest that his feelings for "home" may have been relocated, much like him, to Canada. Not long after his last letter, Tom's hope was met and he sailed back to Britain.[23]

NOTES

1. The author wishes to give special thanks to George Owen Mackie for allowing me to use his private collection of letters. Letters will hereafter be cited as "Correspondence from the George Mackie Collection."
2. See also Inglis, *The Children's War*; Jackson, *Who Will Take Our Children?*; and Titmuss, *Problems with Social Policy*.
3. Overseas evacuation was completely voluntary and no children were forcibly removed from their families by the state. See Halstead, "Dangers Behind, Pleasures Ahead," 163–80.
4. For more on how evacuation functioned and how children were selected see Halstead, "From Lion to Leaf."
5. Vallgårda et al., "Emotions and the Global Politics of Childhood," 12–34. See especially page 13.
6. Mary Elizabeth Mackie, "Children Venturers," in *Okanagan History: Fifty-eight Report of the Okanagan Historical Society* (1994), 49.
7. Author's British Child Evacuee Database. See also Claire L. Halstead, "Digitising Childhood Evacuations: A Serendipitous Pursuit of Active History," Active History, 15 June 2016, https://activehistory.ca/2016/06/reports-from-new-directions-in-active-history-digitising-childhood-evacuation-a-serendipitous-pursuit-of-active-history/.
8. Ralph Barker, *Children of the Benares*.
9. Halstead, "From Lion to Leaf," 25.
10. Correspondence from the George Mackie Collection.
11. "Private Papers of Mrs P. Cave," Documents 10034, Imperial War Museum, London, England, United Kingdom.
12. Correspondence from the George Mackie Collection.
13. Ibid.
14. Ibid.
15. Ibid.
16. For more on Owen Mackie's story, see: George Owen Mackie, "Mackie Men and the Empire," last modified 2006, http://web.uvic.ca/~mackie/MME.pdf.

17 Correspondence from the George Mackie Collection.
18 To read more of Marie Williamsons letters, see Williamson and Sharp, eds, *Just a Larger Family*.
19 Canadian War Museum (CWM), 20110125-001, 58A.1.273.47, "Letters of Marie Williamson and the Sharp Family."
20 In 1944, Margaret Sharp wrote to Bill (as the eldest) explaining that their father had remarried. She noted that when she had initially divorced their father, the boys had been so young that they called it "getting unmarried." The Sharp boys therefore returned to Britain and had to adjust to having a new "mother."
21 CWM, 20110125-001, Letters of Marie Williamson and the Sharp family, 58A.1.273.26, Christopher Sharp to Family, 1941.
22 CWM, 20110125-001, Letters of Marie Williamson and the Sharp family, 58A.1.273.22, Bill Sharp to Mother Margaret, 1941.
23 CWM, 20110125-001, Letters of Marie Williamson and the Sharp family, 58A.1.273.20, Tom Sharp 1944.

12
Charting the Social Spaces of Childhood in 1940s Halifax

Barbara Lorenzkowski

In 1940s Halifax, the spectacle of the street and the theatre of war proved far more alluring to youngsters than the highly prescriptive environment of the city's few remaining playgrounds. Born on 20 January 1931, Gordon Perks grew up "right across the street" from Point Pleasant Park, the "backyard" of his childhood. "When we would come home from school," he recalled in our two-hour-long conversation in August 2009, "first thing we would do, four or five of my friends, we would roam through the park."[1] In the cadences of a seasoned storyteller, Gordon Perks remembered his favourite boyhood places: the Quarry Pond where the boys learned to skate in wintertime, the dance hall in adjacent Franklyn Park where Gordon and his friends played pranks on unsuspecting servicemen, the park's wooded areas where servicemen retreated to "snuggling nests" with their girlfriends, and Sandy Beach Park, a sliver of land along the North West Arm that was made into a beach each May with the help of a few truckloads of sand. "I learned to swim there; we all did," Gordon Perks described the beach on which servicemen mingled with neighbourhood folks. "My mother couldn't swim, but still, she went there at the odd time, lay a blanket down, you know, because it was like it was *our* beach. We literally owned the beach."[2]

Recalled in vivid detail, Gordon Perks's wartime memories are bound up with the geographies of his childhood – the spaces he roamed, the places he found meaningful, the physical shapes and tactile quality of the environment in which he took delight. His recollections belong to a genre that human geographers call "environmental autobiographies."[3] He vividly evoked both the stories and adventures of his wartime boyhood and the places in which these memories unfolded.

As the environmental historian Bernard Mergen has remarked, "places have 'official' stories told on historical markers and in guidebooks, but they also have vernacular versions told orally or in unauthorized texts."[4] Spending long hours in Point Pleasant Park, Gordon Perks and his friends amassed "a detailed child's-eye local knowledge" of the sounds, smells, sights, and textures of their local world.[5] To them, the park was "*a practiced place*," to quote the French philosopher Michel de Certeau, a landscape made "knowable" in the rhythms of daily life and play.[6] It was a space the boys claimed as their own by virtue of the stories they told and the mental maps they made.[7]

The largest public park on the crowded Halifax peninsula, Point Pleasant Park, offered neighbourhood children a space of sensory stimulation and the opportunity to interact creatively with the environment.[8] As Albert Eide Parr asserts, "our minds have needs of sensory intake quite similar to our bodily appetite for food."[9] The park's winding paths and foot trails, its varied flora and diverse topography, the tactile sensation of sand, rocks, and water, the rustle of leaves, the quiet of hidden places, the salty taste of ocean spray, and the more gentle waves of the Northwest Arm, rippling onto Sandy Beach, provided a rich sensory diet. Children imbued the landscape with meaning of their own, as did Gordon Perks and his childhood friend Charles Grantham when they built warship models out of scrap wood from nearby construction sites and let them float on Quarry Pond, its small waters momentarily transformed into the oceans of the world.

As the human geographer Doreen Massey holds, places are "constructed out of articulations of social relations," with even the small spaces of childhood fashioned by "the geographical beyond, the world beyond the place itself."[10] To the boys living across the park, who proudly referred to themselves as "Tower Roaders," war literally marched into their local world when platoons of soldiers paraded through city streets and into the park. Children's ears were attuned to the "clack, clack" of soldiers' "heavy hobnailed boots as they hit the street while parading all in step," a distinctive sound that carried over half a mile and announced a platoon's arrival well in advance. Whereas young girls' interaction with servicemen was carefully circumscribed, boys darted up and down the columns of marching men, selling soft drinks and snacks.

The park also offered boys an alluring space of transgression, namely the opportunity to steal out of their bedrooms at night to play tricks on the young servicemen, just a few years older than themselves.[11] In the nocturnal and hidden spaces of Point Pleasant Park, boys observed outbursts of drunken violence and received an informal sex education as they secretly observed servicemen with their girlfriends. Such recollections speak to the gendered nature of children's knowledge of public places. Indeed, the comparison with the childhood memories of my female interview partners is instructive. When young Jeanne Hill walked to her elementary school in 1940s Dartmouth, just across the harbour from Halifax, she wondered about the mushrooms dotting the grass of Dartmouth Park. "And they were French safes!," she laughed some sixty years later. "The park was *full* of them!" While Jeanne Hill always felt safe on her journey to school ("Nobody ever bothered us"), she did not leave the path to investigate the "mushrooms" more closely, much less collect the two unused condoms in each pack as ammunition for future water-fights.[12] Boys enjoyed a freedom of the city that girls did not.

But to juxtapose the female world of the home with the rough-and-tumble of boyhood culture is to miss some of the most intriguing aspects of Gordon Perks's tribute to Point Pleasant Park.[13] Though not included in the excerpts that follow, his recollections also paint a vivid portrayal of his mother and the domestic spaces of his childhood, as did, in fact, many of my male interview partners when recalling their wartime experiences. Gordon Perks was not the solitary explorer of boyhood lore, but, rather, a narrator enmeshed in the webs of family and friendship. What made the "backyard" of his childhood so special was the time spent, and the relationships forged, with his tight-knit group of friends. If the meanings of places are made in social interaction, the story Gordon Perks told of Point Pleasant Park was that of a site of boyhood friendship that would last into old age.

In our interview, I invited Gordon Perks to describe to me his friends who had formed part of a group of eight that, in his words, "hung around together and did mischief." Reflecting for only a moment, he launched into a tribute, both funny and tender, to his childhood friends that would run over two single-spaced pages in the final interview transcript. There was "Benny, a red-headed fellow ... full of the devil!" and the brothers "Rudy and Howard," a study in contrasts. Whereas Rudy was "stocky, quiet, and smart, and neat as a pin," his brother Howard was a larger-than-life storyteller, indeed the "*scheming*-est actor you'd ever met in your life! Even at the age of eight, nine, ten, he could look you in the eye and tell you the *damndest* story." There was Ted, a passionate fisherman. "We loved calling him Clumsy Ted because he would trip over something, but, oh, he was a good guy, I was very close to Ted; he loved to fish. I think he had the very first lobster licence ... Ted was basically, and still is *today*, the fisherman." There was young Jack on whom his mother kept a close eye, and Bud. "He was just a solid guy. He loved to sing and even when we were little kids, just young boys of eight, ten, or somewhere around there, Bud would sing." There was Sonny with whom Gordon sneaked out of the apartment building and into Point Pleasant Park at night, and Charles, more solitary and self-contained, his playmate at Quarry Pond where the two boys launched their model warship into the water once the ice had melted.[14] These intimate portrayals speak to a kind of close-knit and long-lasting friendship not commonly associated with the world of boyhood culture. Indeed, scholars are only now beginning to write the history of "emotionally intimate male friendships" that take into account the "complexity, emotional nuance, and depth" of these relationships.[15]

At the conclusion of our interview, Gordon Perks entrusted me with a copy of his memoir – a "'coal scuttle' full of true stories and adventures" featuring 136 stories, all unfolding during the war years and set in Point Pleasant Park or the streets bordering the park. As I started reading these snapshots of a 1940s Halifax childhood, I quickly noted that the stories Gordon Perks has shared in our interview faithfully echoed the words on the page. These were oft-told tales, consistent in their content, narrative arc, rhythm, and phrasing. Whereas most oral history interviews constitute "a 'text' in the making" that "has hardly ever been told in sequence as a coherent and organized whole," to quote oral historian Alessandro Portelli, these were stories that had been performed frequently until they settled into just these words.[16] As I would later learn, Gordon Perks and his childhood friends, now men in their late seventies and early eighties, still saw each other regularly.

In its conversational tone and lively rhythms, the memoir bears the imprint of oral culture: it is a document honed in the act of collective remembering. It represents a vernacular history of Point Pleasant Park as well as an act of collective memory whose purpose is not only to recall the past, but also to affirm the present, namely the bonds of friendship between now elderly men who might well have added bits and pieces of their own to Gordon Perks's tales over the course of the decades. In so doing, Point Pleasant Park, once a place for play and exploration, has become a landscape of memories. Perhaps, as the historian Melanie Tebbut has suggested when examining her late father's geographical exploits in inter-war Britain, "as the space he inhabited shrank when he was in his seventies, so the meanings of these early spatial experiences expanded."[17]

As geographer Doreen Massey reminds us, places are "set in time as well as space." Places, she adds, "stretch through time. Places as depicted on maps are places caught in a moment; they are slices through time."[18] When revisiting the sites of his childhood, Gordon Perks's memories settled on the park's environment

Figure 12.1
Memories of Quarry Pond, Point Pleasant Park, Halifax.
From Gordon Perks, "My Backyard: Point Pleasant Park."
Unpublished manuscript, Halifax, 2008, 28.

like an old photograph superimposed upon the present. Deftly drawn by hand, a model of one of the warship toy boats that young Gordon and Charles liked to pull around the pond has been inserted into a photograph of Quarry Pond.

To his detailed map of Franklyn Park, Gordon Perks has added a cautionary note: "Not to scale." His is a map of memories. Unlike official maps of Point Pleasant Park, this hand-drawn map is preoccupied with children's microgeographies rather than scale. It depicts an alternate world, invisible to most adult eyes, in which children named place-markers and gathering spots such as "Flat Rock" and meandered like "cats" through the night-time park. Scale is a poor measuring unit to capture these childhood memories, set in places that appear so small to the adult eye. "I don't know what happens to you when you get older," Gordon Perks mused in our conversation when recalling Sandy Beach. "But when you're a kid, everything is so *big* ... And you get there now, and it's only a little tiny, a little tiny spot."[19]

Just as past places linger in present ones, so, too, do life-narratives contain within them multiple temporalities. In echoing what many of my interview partners told me, young Gordon Perks did not yet understand the meaning of war. "Being just children, we had absolutely no understanding about what terrible occurrences were taking place in the world," he wrote in his memoir.[20] To his younger self, the servicemen marching into Point Pleasant Park were tall, young men – adults who danced and drank, fought and loved, and eagerly snatched moments of normalcy by taking their girlfriend for a boat ride on the Northwest Arm. At the time of our interview, Gordon Perks was nearing his eightieth birthday and wistfully remarked on the heartbreaking youth of the servicemen. "My God, they were so *young*! You know, just kids, eighteen, nineteen, there were probably seventeen-year-olds in there," he said.[21] This inherent tension – the weaving back and forth between the "now" and "then" and the corresponding re-fashioning of memories – is what Alessandro Portelli has called "shuttlework."[22]

Gordon Perks's memoir is a written document that has been forged in a culture of oral storytelling. Its vivid narrative vignettes have been performed and honed many a time when the circle of friends – the "Tower Roaders" – came together to visit and share stories of both present and past. The memoir also carries us into the small spaces of childhood, while reminding us that the meanings of places are made in the interaction between the local and the global; the war arrived even on the "little tiny spot" that was Sandy Beach. Though written in the tradition of boyhood adventures, the memoir's narrator is embedded in dense social networks of both family and friends, offering an intimate portrayal of male friendship. Finally, this memoir depicts children who are drawn to the flexible landscapes of public spaces and parks that offered sensory stimulation, social interaction, and the opportunity to engage imaginatively with the environment. Whereas historians of childhood often turn to institutional spaces (for spaces that held children captive also generated rich archival records about the young), there is much we can learn about the geographies of wartime, children's voices, and the texture of childhood memory by searching for children in public outdoor spaces instead.

◆ ◆ ◆

Gordon Perks, "My Backyard: 'Point Pleasant Park': A 'Coal scuttle' full of true stories and adventures that I experienced in and around the two parks; Franklyn and Point Pleasant during my childhood days of World War 2, 1939–1945." Unpublished manuscript, Halifax, 2008.

Our Apartment House

Those of us who were fortunate enough to live on the south side of the railway bridge, were commonly known as "Tower Roaders." We wore our imaginary badge with great pride! To the rest of the city folks however; we were simply the "South Enders."

I lived on the third floor of number 4 Tower Road. It was a kind of puzzling address in that there was a small grocery store on the first floor of this building and it was number 2 and we were number 4. I guess it was to separate the commercial store from the household living, apartments. The building is still the first house at the start of Tower Road and is also one of the oldest in the area. Because it is next to the park it truly was "My Back Yard!"[23]

The Quarry Pond

This very small rock quarry pond is located just about 150 yards inside the park at the south end of Young Avenue. The blasted rock from the quarry was used in the construction of the nearby army house and also in the building of Fort Ogilvy.[24]

When the Ice Melted

The quarry pond in spring, summer, and fall was my favourite place to play. But I think I will only mention some of my fondest treasured memories I experienced there and not the many times I slipped off the rocks or accidentally tramped in the slimy mud and got my camp shoes full of crap and had to meet my mother again. Yep, my two lower cheeks were made sore again, and another solemn promise was broken.[25]

The Warships

One of my friends who liked to play with toy boats in the pond as much as I did was Charlie Grantham. We used to make warships from pieces of wood that we would just happen to remove from one of the new houses that was being built on the road. And we did all right for a couple of kids who had no good tools and a lack of skills for that sort of thing. I recall very vividly of the time we made two destroyers and got some gray paint, probably taken from his father's workshop and painted them. We thought they looked great. And they did!! We would pull them around the pond tied with a six-foot piece of string to a five foot stick, similar to a fish on a fishing pole. To go all around the pond without stopping, meant that we sailed all around the world. Our home port was in a groove in the rock located on the east side of the pond at the base of a nice pine tree. A couple of big pieces of rock were forced out of the bedrocks by us using a couple of metal pipes. The spaces they left were just perfect docks for our warships.

Just as a matter of note;

I went for a walk in the park in October of 2007 and those play docks are still there, just as we left them, sometime about the year of 1944.[26]

The Troops Poured into Halifax

I cannot remember the year when the Canadian troops in great numbers started to converge on the City of Halifax, but they came here by the thousands. It was a time of great excitement for everyone especially for us kids! Being just children, we had absolutely no understanding about what terrible occurrences were taking place in the world and would change our way of living forever.

As soldiers, sailors, and airmen began pouring into our city by troop trains from all across Canada, they required exercise. One method was to have these troops take route marches through the city streets. Since Point Pleasant Park was so spacious with many roads and as its name suggests "Pleasant" it was the ideal place for these brave young fighting men to go. We kids of course were only too happy to march right along with these military people. It was just a great "Happening!"[27]

Our "Highly Sensitive Ears" Told Us

When the times came that I would hear that very distinct, but far off sound of the soldiers' "marching noise," that was made from their heavy hobnailed boots as they hit the street while parading all in step; I would drop everything I was doing and make a bee-line toward the bridge in time to catch the lead platoon as it clack, clack, clacked over the concrete bridge. It was loud enough to hear all the way up to our house at number four, right at the entrance of the park. It was a rhythm that was engrained in one's pea brain and we could pick it up like it was sent to us away ahead of all other sounds. We were truly attuned to that sound and I swear we could pick it up when the soldiers turned the corner at Englis Street and Tower Road, a half mile away.

I don't mean to be mean or nasty here; but as you walked alongside of these sweaty men; they sure use [sic] to smell awful. I guess it was a combination of sweat and the wooden material in their uniforms. But as soon as they handed us coins to get pop and stuff; they smelled pretty damn good!

While all this was going on; out in front of Mr Ryan's Store, Mrs Romo was on the street shaking hands with the soldiers and kissing some as they passed by. She did this with every platoon that marched by through-out the war years. She was a nice lady.[28]

Sneaking out the Fire Escape Window

One good thing about sleeping in the back room of our apartment was; the window opened out to the fire escape. Quite often in the summer when Mom would send me off to bed at night, I would wait for awhile then at a predetermined time I would gently open the window and sneak down the steps till I reached Sonny's window. A few secret taps and out he would come. Like two cats we would bee-line-it across Miller Street, through the corner woods and make our way to the tramfield, then worm our way around the big dance hall and soon join forces with our buddies …

There were many places to dance throughout the city but I believe the most favourite spot had to be the dance hall in Franklyn Park. It had a nice large hardwood dance floor, a dry canteen but no liquor bar. A beautiful big field on one side, the wooded park on the other side and a wonderful view of the Northwest Arm. Dance night was always crowded with servicemen. It was a very popular spot!

When we arrived there, if there was no activity around we would climb up the wire fencing to watch the people dancing. In fine weather the window shutters were opened and we had a good view of the inside. One thing I must say is; "we all agreed that Sailors were the best dancers." The American Sailors were best at Jitter Bugging!

There was a wire fence strung around the railing so no one could get in without paying the fifty-cent entry fee. The fencing was a great help to us for climbing up to get a good look inside! We always had to keep a sharp look out for Gerry the Cop! If he saw us on the fence he would shout in his loud voice; "You kids get the hell down from there and fly the hell home!" We would get down real fast all right but we didn't fly the hell home, like he demanded; "Oh no, we had things to do!" Our mission was to see how much money we could make. This dancing thing was just to size up the evening by looking over the crowd.

One maneuver was to spread out and position ourselves on the path that leads from the tram stop to the dance hall. When the tram would arrive and the crowds of servicemen and girls would head for the dance, we would single out

Social Spaces of Childhood in 1940s Halifax   291

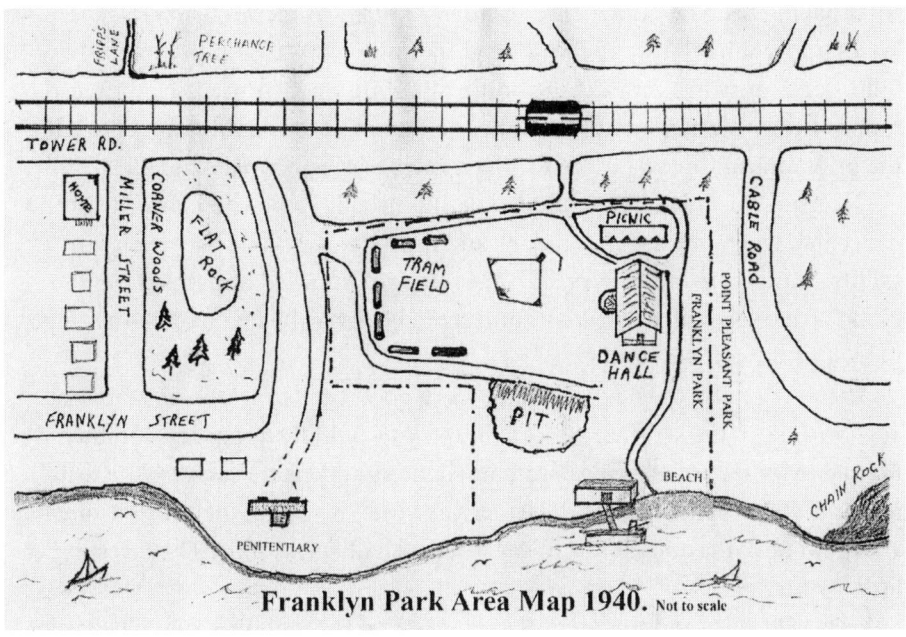

Figure 12.2
"Franklyn Park Area Map 1940. Not to scale." Courtesy of Gordon Perks, "My Backyard: Point Pleasant Park" (unpublished memoir, Halifax, 2008, n.p.).

certain sailors, the ones with a bulge in their jumper. They were dead giveaways. "cuz sailors could not hide a bottle of rum under their jumpers!"

We would approach one of the "jumper bulging sailors" with this awe-inspiring but convincing story about the "Cops being on the lookout for guys carrying booze into the dance hall," so they should hide it in the woods and go get a drink; but whatever you do don't take booze into the dance or they could put you in jail! The reply from them was usually the same; "Thanks kid!"

Occasionally a nice guy would fork out a dime for us, then head for the woods near the entrance to find a good hiding place, but not before taking a big swig first, then hiding it behind a tree that he thought he would remember. "Oh My!"

Unbeknown to him; a couple of our lads were lurking in there with acclimatized eyes watching every move. The ball was now in our court, we knew that wooded area like the back of our hands and had the added advantage of having the lights of the dance hall in foreground so we could see all movements clearly from our darken position. "Sneaky eh?" No one could hide anything from us!

After having been laid down, the "hidden" bottle was picked up so fast the leaves under it hadn't stopped moving! In no time it was sold to some other sailor for twenty five cents. If the bottle was about half empty, it was often topped up with water and then sold as being full, so we could now get double the price amounting to fifty cents. Big money was being made here!!!

Occasionally a big fight would break out, usually somewhere outside of the dance hall where it was kind of dark and mostly it would be between two sailors. Some were quite spectacular as teeth got knocked out, noses were bloodied and eyes blackened cuts and scratches over the face and clothes torn to hell. At times it was quite scary! …

After a big fight, the next morning was a good time to search around that area because in the scuffles, all sorts of things would fly out of the combatant's pockets. Money, wallets, rings, watches, lighters and cigarettes were the usual things that we would find. If the Americans were involved; their little white hats always went flying and all the Tower Roaders had at least one. They were a neat little hat …

V packets and condoms were always scattered through the park. They were issued to the servicemen and I am sure everyone who went into the park carried them. We would see them in all the "snuggling nests" and usually if one condom was used; then the pack containing the unused other two, was lying on the ground nearby. Yes they came in packs of three. Why? I can't answer that! Anyway; we always picked up the two in the pack to be used as ammunition for a water fight that was bound to take place sooner or later! They were great toys for us! We had many great wet fights with them! Sometimes we would blow up a bunch of them and see how long we could keep all of them in the air. Invariably one of us would trip on a rock and go ass-over-kettles; then all of them would fall to the ground, followed by great laughter![29]

NOTES

1 Gordon Perks, interview by author, 5 August 2009, Halifax.
2 Ibid. and Gordon Perks, "My Backyard: 'Point Pleasant Park': A 'Coal Scuttle' Full of True Stories and Adventures That I Experienced in and around the Two Parks; Franklyn and Point Pleasant during My Childhood Days of World War 2, 1939–1945" (unpublished manuscript, Halifax, 2008), 26 and 32–7.
3 Moore, *Childhood's Domain*, 19.
4 Mergen, "Children and Nature in History," 655.

5   Philo, "'The Corner-Stone of My World,'" 249.
6   de Certeau, *The Practice of Everyday Life*, 117.
7   As the human geographer Robin Moore holds, "children spend more time wandering outdoors than most adults, and their patterns of interaction are more intimate, fluid and intense." See Moore, *Childhood's Domain*, 57.
8   See also Hart, *Children's Experiences of Place*; Philo, "'The Corner-Stone of My World,'" 245; and Sleight, *Young People and the Shaping of Public Space in Melbourne, 1870–1914*.
9   As quoted in Ward, *The Child in the City*, 9–10.
10 Massey, "Places and Their Pasts," 183.
11 Gordon Perks, interview by author, 5 August 2009, Halifax.
12 Jeanne Hill, interview by author, 12 August 2009, Halifax.
13 For an influential formulation of boy culture see Rotundo, "Boy Culture," 337–62.
14 Gordon Perks, interview by author, 5 August 2009, Halifax.
15 Way, *Deep Secrets: Boys, Friendships, and the Crisis of Connection*, 3.
16 Portelli, *The Battle of Valle Giulia*, 4–5.
17 Tebbut, *Being Boys*, 251.
18 Massey, "Places and Their Pasts," 188.
19 Gordon Perks, interview by author, 5 August 2009, Halifax.
20 Perks, "My Backyard: 'Point Pleasant Park,'" 32.
21 Gordon Perks, interview by author, 5 August 2009, Halifax.
22 Portelli, *The Death of Luigi Trastulli and Other Stories*, 65 and 50 (emphasis in original).
23 Gordon Perks, "My Back Yard: 'Point Pleasant Park,'" 7.
24 Ibid., 24.
25 Ibid., 27.
26 Ibid., 27–8.
27 Ibid., 32.
28 Ibid., 32–3.
29 Ibid., 34–7.

13
Surviving the Peace: Mine Awareness Education in the Former Yugoslavia

Andrew Burtch

During the war in the former Yugoslavia from 1992 to 1995, militias expelled, terrorized, or murdered rival ethnic groups in desired territory. The euphemistically titled "ethnic cleansing," a tactic employed by all sides in the conflict, did not differentiate between civilian and military targets, or children and adults. In addition to the waves of internally displaced people produced by the Yugoslav Wars, factions on all sides also indiscriminately employed hidden killers, landmines, to deny lands and infrastructure and make it difficult for the local populations to return once the conflict was over. The drawings reproduced in this section highlight how children interpreted the threat left behind from the war in Croatia.

Canada's National Defence Demining Action Center summarized the landmine problem in its June 1997 report on affairs for Bosnia-Herzegovina: "Mines laid by professional armies are normally laid as part of an overall obstacle plan or to deny access to particular locations. They are employed sparingly ... Mines laid by terrorists and paramilitary forces often follow no pattern and may seem to serve no tactical purpose. In many cases they have been placed to cause the most disruption to civilians and effect [*sic*] day to day life as well as transportation and the economy of the country involved."[1] In Bosnia-Herzegovina, Croatia, Cambodia, Rwanda, and elsewhere, the problem of indiscriminate mining posed enormous problems for post-conflict resettlement and reconstruction. In the 1990s, an international mission arose to mitigate the impact of landmines, the United Nations Mine Action Service (UNMAS).

One of the five pillars of mine action favoured by UNMAS and adopted by its local coordinators or NGOs is "mine risk education," a preventative measure to teach those living close to mines or refugees returning to landmine-contaminated territory how to recognize legacy munitions, the basics of mine safety, similar to fire prevention programs taught in schools outside former conflict zones. The goal of these programs is to reduce the incidence of mine-related injury or deaths, and the resulting hardships on the individual survivor and their communities. In Bosnia the problem was particularly pronounced, as belligerent factions routinely set traps to inconvenience, intimidate, or kill the targets of ethnic cleansing during the war, and these remained when the war ended. Children in the fourth and fifth grades produced the sketches featured in this chapter during mine education in local schools in the Bihac region of Bosnia-Herzegovina after the Yugoslav Wars. Sergeant Bernie Kuhn, a combat engineer with 31 Combat Engineer Regiment (The Elgins), deployed to the NATO Stabilization Force (SFOR) as a mine monitor. During the winter months, when minefield work was difficult, he taught mine awareness to students in local schools. Kuhn, seeing in the school corridors children's drawings about their wartime experience, asked teachers if they would have students draw their experiences with landmines and mine safety instruction. The selection below is drawn from forty drawings later donated to the Canadian War Museum. Kuhn reflected on the paintings when he offered them for donation: "I received something more than what I was expecting. The pictures were very clear to me ... what the kids saw through their eyes."[2]

Kuhn's observation is true to an extent, as some of the children in their drawings appear to have drawn on personal accounts and lived, local experiences of the war that raged in the area seven years before Kuhn arrived. Yet, their drawings were also mediated through the lens of the mine education curriculum. In the classroom, children received prompts about risk, danger, and the need for constant caution as they navigated their surroundings. Of the 161 drawings offered to the museum by Kuhn, the forty drawings selected for acquisition tended to represent unique or personalized interpretations of the experience of living with landmines. Many of the other drawings depicted scenes that strongly resembled mine awareness pamphlets distributed through NATO and NGOs. Figures 1 and 2, for example, show the gruesome aftermath of a minestrike on a football pitch, a common scene, along with the warning "Don't remove mine tags, it's the same as setting up a new minefield!"

Children repeat this scene or theme in other drawings in the collection. As Kuhn was inspired to ask for these artistic reflections after having seen other expressions of wartime hardships posted in school hallways, it is suggestive that these drawings are an outlet through which a reader can assess childhood memories of war.

Figure 13.1
"Don't remove mine tags." Almira Ramić, Druga Osnova Škola.
Canadian War Museum, accession no. 20130650-003.

Figure 13.2
"Never touch mine signs." Sanel Pilipovic. Canadian War Museum,
accession no. 20130650-001.

Mine Awareness Education in the Former Yugoslavia

Figure 13.3
"Stabilization Force (SFOR) patrol." Artist name illegible.
Canadian War Museum, accession no. 20130650-002.

It is worth observing how children chose in their drawings to represent not just the implements of war, but everyday objects, environments, and settings.[3] While their drawings go some distance to communicate the dangers of everyday life in post-conflict Bosnia, they also speak strongly to the child's sense of environment, community, and home. These environments, the roads, fields, and forests, in bounds or out of bounds, provide evidence of what the children value just as much as the depictions of danger. See figure 13.3, where the child has drawn clear borders between their home, their play area, and the minefield, the road between patrolled by green NATO vehicles.

Of course, the scourge of landmines in the Kuhn series is such that places meant to be safe and a refuge can, in a tragic instant, be transformed into no-go zones, so their drawings communicate both safety and danger at the same time. Living in a former warzone, children had to contend with danger on a daily basis. They were schooled in risk both formally, in the mine education lessons they received at school, and informally so, in the stories about landmines that circulated in their

Figure 13.4
"We survived the war, survive the peace!" Artist unknown.
Canadian War Museum, accession no. 20130650-008.

communities. Child refugees given paper and crayons to occupy themselves while their parents were interviewed by NGOs, too, might capture parts of their parents' stories to portray along with their own memories in ways they would not be able to articulate verbally.[4] These drawings are children's statements, which like any other historical document, carry private meanings and agency worthy of critical study to better understand what the child has to say about war. The children are fearful of the risks from legacy munitions and landmines, and cautious about their future. As one child expressed in their drawing of a child looking on the crater left behind from an explosion on a soccer pitch, "We survived the war, survive the peace!"

NOTES

1 Canadian Department of National Defence Report, *National Defence Mining Action Center: Mine Report for Bosnia-Herzegovina, 23-Jun-97*, 20030091-005,

George Metcalf Archival Collection, Canadian War Museum, Ottawa, Ontario, Canada.
2 Correspondence from Bernie Kuhn, "CWM Collections Acquisition Form Offer AL2013032, April 2018," Corporate Records, Canadian War Museum, Ottawa, Ontario, Canada.
3 Aradau and Hill, "The Politics of Drawing," 382. See also Tuneu et al., "The Spanish Civil War as Seen through Children's Drawings of the Time," 478–95, 479, 481.
4 Ibid., 1574–5.

14
"My Two Families": Experiences of Refugee Youth

Elizabeth Miller

I first met Leontine Uwababyeyi during a workshop that I developed as the director of Mapping Memories, a participatory media project for youth with refugee experience.[1] We offered participants a safe space to create short films about their experiences of violence and displacement. Over several years we reached more than one hundred youth and offered support and training in storytelling, writing, video, audio, and public speaking. Mapping Memories was the youth arm of a larger research initiative, the Montreal Life Stories project that brought together researchers, artists, educators, human rights activists, and survivors to record and disseminate the oral histories of survivors of mass violence.[2] Both of these initiatives emphasized partnerships, shared authority, collaborative processes, and an intention to create with rather than about.

A critical part of the project was to offer participants like Leontine an opportunity to take their story public, and we shared the resulting work in museums, in schools, and on walking and bus tours. To do this we involved policy advocates, service providers, and teachers. Stereotypes and anxieties about immigrants and refugees were escalating throughout Canada and we wanted to use these stories to build understanding. Our method was to emphasize resilience rather than focus on victimization, and we wanted the stories to communicate what it takes to adapt to a new country. Leontine's long-term involvement in the project actively shaped the direction of Mapping Memories and informed my own understanding of working with sensitive stories. Together we wrestled with complex questions such as: When is someone ready to share a difficult story? What does it mean to *learn with* rather than *about* refugee youth? And what is the power and potential of using personal stories to shift public discourse?[3]

Figure 14.1
Elizabeth Miller (foreground) and Leontine Uwababyeyi (background). A still from Leontine's video. Photo by Anne-Renée Hotte.

When Is Someone Ready?

Leontine was one of seven participants who enrolled in the media workshop "Going Places." The other participants were from Zimbabwe, Palestine, Congo, and Rwanda. The objective of this workshop was to create an alternative city bus tour of Montreal, an immersive mobile storytelling space. The group met for four hours a week over a three-month period to develop audio stories for the tour. Each audio story would connect to a location in Montreal. The idea was to illuminate personal geographies of the city, places that were important for individuals with refugee experience but invisible for other residents of the city.

Leontine was initially ambivalent about getting involved in the workshop and sharing her story publicly. She had lost her family in the Rwandan genocide and was relatively new to Montreal. Getting involved meant working through difficult questions. What part of her story did she want to share with others? Whom did she want to reach? What did she want to achieve? Leontine did not want to fuel ongoing tensions between the Hutu and Tutsi ethnic groups at home or abroad, and she did not want to risk her refugee status in any way. Telling her story also meant that she would have to revisit painful memories. Finally, Leontine worried that after telling her story, people would see her differently. At the same time, as the sole survivor, she felt a responsibility to honour her family. In *All I Remember*, a short documentary about her involvement in Mapping Memories, she explains, "Once upon a time there was a little girl, she was eight years old … if she wasn't alive – who could tell this story. Who could remember her family?" Leontine's motivation to honour her family ultimately determined her decision to go public with her story for the first time. Peer support was also a critical factor, and she had the support of other participants in the group who were wrestling with their own complex stories.

Learning Together

As an educator and documentary maker, I have experience facilitating participatory media projects with youth and human rights advocates, but I had my own set of concerns. Would I know how to navigate the complex issues that emerged as youth participants shared and then went public with highly sensitive stories? How could I help ensure that the stories did not fuel perceptions of refugees as victims? And given that we were also sharing our work on the Internet, what were the possibilities for unintended exposure in an environment where stories circulate quickly and often without sufficient context? What gave us all the courage to proceed was in large part due to our shared mission to challenge stereotypes and to build understanding about the underlying causes of migration and displacement.

Over seven years, I learned a great deal especially about the value of creating safe and supportive environments in both the creation and the dissemination of a project. For example, in the production of the stories, we incorporated meals into our workshops. In each class a participant was asked to bring in a dish from home and share a story. Sharing meals was a way to develop cultural understanding and to build intimacy. We referred to the food stories as our "back-up" stories in case anyone got cold feet about sharing a more personal story about displacement. Another approach was to ensure that technological tools did not outweigh the emphasis on connecting to each other. I made sure that participants had support from our cadre of students and media trainers who helped teach and negotiate software tools. And importantly we made time to rehearse before any public presentation. For the "Going Places" tour we did a trial run before the actual tour, which helped foster confidence and group cohesion. We also made time to debrief

Experiences of Refugee Youth

together after public presentations. Structuring time for rehearsal and reflection helped us negotiate the thorny questions and concerns we were working through together. Being vulnerable together, taking risks together, and reflecting on the process were key methods in our collaborative endeavor.

Taking Stories Public

The bus tour was a great success. In addition to the pre-recorded stories, there was music, impromptu dance, and five stops throughout Montreal. We also made a point of linking the personal stories to current debates on immigration rights in Canada. The tour ended in the Old Port area of Montreal, where visitors were invited to throw flowers into the St Lawrence River in memory of those who lost their lives in the Rwandan genocide. We made this stop to honour a commemoration that Montreal's Rwandan community holds each year to mark the anniversary of the 1994 genocide.

Figure 14.2
Going Places. Leontine shares her story during the bus tour. Photo by Anne-Renée Hotte.

Figure 14.3
In Memory. Leontine throws petals into the St Lawrence River in memory of her family. Photo by Anne-Renée Hotte.

The success of the bus tour influenced our decision to organize a series of school visits to facilitate dialogue about refugee rights and about safe spaces in schools for all newcomers.[4] With the support of the Montreal Life Stories project Leontine's story gained even more exposure and she witnessed the potential of her story to make change. Her story was part of a year-long exhibition at the Centre d'histoire de Montréal, *We Are Here*; it was incorporated into a curriculum module for grade eleven high school students across Quebec; and it was also part of a subway initiative that enabled commuters to download and listen to one of nine life stories including Leontine's story.

While the Mapping Memories and Life Stories projects did come to an end, Leontine has continued to use her story to make a difference. She has been invited to speaking tours, she has joined several film and research initiatives, and she has completed a degree in social work. Leontine continues to negotiate the risks of being vulnerable, of taking a personal story public, and in doing so she continues to inspire others.

My Two Families
Leontine Uwababyeyi

Leontine was eight years old when she lost her family to the Rwandan genocide and twenty years old when she applied to become a refugee to Canada during Rwanda's truth and reconciliation process. As part of the Rwandan diaspora in Canada, she participated in the Mapping Memories and the Montreal Life Stories project, which helped to tell her story of how she lost her family, and how she later created a second family with students who were also survivors of the genocide. Below is a transcript of Uwababyeyi's video that is hosted on the Mapping Memories website.[5]

I want to tell you a story, a true story. My story. It's about how quickly your life can change in just three days, and then three months.

Day one: 9 April 1994. It's dark out when my story begins. My father tells us to put on our jackets because it is cold and rainy, and we must leave the house and go to sleep at our neighbour's. I don't understand what is going on, but I am happy to go to sleep at my friend's.

Day two: 10 April 1994. In the morning we return home, nothing's left in the house, windows and doors are broken. There are many people around, talking to each other. I am eight years old, and for me, it's exciting. Everyone is wondering what happened. My mother prepares something to eat; my brother and I are sitting outside. The rest of my family, my father, mother, sister, and brother are inside. A lady comes running towards us, she seems crazy. She tells us that they are killing people. We started running, I follow my brother. We go into woods, we stay there for hours, then we move to another forest, and we find our father. But he tells us to leave. It is not safe. When we return we try to find him, but we cannot find him. We stay there the whole night, awake.

Day three, 11 April 1994: In the morning, we move again, we meet someone who tells us that our mother has been killed. I start crying, I tell my brother that I want my mother, and he tells me that if I continue crying, they will kill us. So I stop.

A home for three months: My brother and I, we find a banana plantation where we hide in a bush for three months. This bush is our bed, our salon, our toilet; it is everything. The first few days, a person brings us food twice a week.

But then, he stops. I ask my brother, why are we here? He tells me, "Because we are Tutsi." I ask him why are we Tutsi? I ask him, why can't we go home? "Our home is demolished," he answers. Why can't we go to our neighbours? Sometimes he has no answers. I have so many questions. One day the owner of the plantation comes and tells us now the killers are hunting with dogs, that it's better to go away. Each night we try to leave, we start and then come back because we see lights or we hear children crying.

On the fourth day, we manage to leave, but on the way, we meet a man with a bowl of blood and a knife in his hands. He sees us and screams out to the others, to the Interahamwe.[6] They have knives, they chase us, I fall down, they chase my brother, and three weeks later, he is gone also.

Three days, three months, three weeks; so much has changed. I have found myself alone. I am the only survivor of my family. But I am a survivor, and today I am twenty-two-years old, and I am no longer alone. I have a new family, I am the mother of this family, and I have sixteen children, girls and boys. Some of my children are older than me. You can ask yourself, how is this possible? This is my adopted family, the family who adopted me. My family is made up of orphans, students at my school, who are also trying to fight loneliness. Together we make groups and choose the father and the mother. When you are chosen as a mother, you cannot refuse, even if you are shy. I was once shy, but over time, I have learned how to be a mother, to take care of my children. I love my family because if you are in a family like this, you share a lot and you are not alone. We visit each other often and share the problems that we have. When one of the family members is happy, we are all happy. If one is sad, we are all sad. You have a lot of things inside you, you cannot just share with anyone, but they understand, even without words.

In our family, we say: it is better to live twice than to die twice. This is the first time I am sharing this story, and this story is for both of my families. In our family, we say: it is better to live twice than to die twice.

NOTES

1 Miller et al., *Mapping Memories*. See also the project's website, "Mapping Memories: Experiences of Refugee Youth," http://mappingmemories.ca.
2 For an introduction to the Montreal Life Stories project see High, *Oral History at the Crossroads*.

3 On the ethics of collaborative storytelling and participatory practice see Miller, Little, and High, *Going Public*.
4 See Luchs and Miller, "On Tour with Mapping Memories," 235–53.
5 *Mapping Memories: Experiences of Refugee Youth.* http://www.mappingmemories.ca/going-places-memoryscape-bus-tour-montreal/video/my-two-families-leontine-uwababyeyi.html. Accessed 8 March 2018.
6 The Interahamwe, translated as "Those Who Attack Together," were the militias supporting the Hutu-led government of Rwanda during the genocide, and were supplied with large quantities of machetes and other weapons and equipment before the genocide in Rwanda began on 6 April 1994. The Interahamwe were responsible for most of the killing during the three months that followed. For more information, see the United State Holocaust Memorial Museum, *Confront Genocide: Rwanda*. https://www.ushmm.org/confront-genocide/cases/rwanda/rwanda-violence. Accessed 8 March 2018.

15
"Donkeys Can't Fly on Planes": Intergenerational Storytelling and Artwork

Mary Tomsic

While images of refugees readily circulate in the media and in humanitarian publications, refugees are often dehumanized in these contexts and rarely presented as active subjects with a voice of their own. Children's voices are even less likely to be heard.[1] This chapter introduces a collection of four books – *Donkeys Can't Fly on Planes* (2012), *In My Kingdom* (2014), *All the Way Home* (2015), and *This Is My Home* (2021) – that work against this dominant trend. The books introduce readers to the stories of men, women, and children who were forcibly displaced from South Sudan and are now living in Australia. The most recent book is based on the stories and artwork of Australian-born children who are part of this community. The books were published by Kids' Own Publishing, a community arts organization committed to fostering children's self-representation, self-expression, and visibility in books by children and for children.[2] The stories reproduced here constitute vital primary sources that speak to the history of displacement, forced mobility, war, and violence as well as resettlement. These books encompass children and adults' storytelling as a social activity by sharing personal experiences through narrative and artworks and engaging in an intergenerational dialogue. As the historian Joan W. Scott holds, "narrative is a way of making human experience meaningful."[3]

The process of creating and illustrating these books began in 2006.[4] Initially, the stories in *Donkeys* were collected by the children's school, the Latrobe English Language Centre, and the Liddiard Road Primary School in the Victorian regional city of Traralgon. The stories were recorded and collated by Sharon Sandy, a student well-being coordinator, along with her colleagues Sue Sleswick and Sue

O'Rouke.⁵ Artist Lisa Gardiner ran workshops with the children to create the illustrations for the book. The twenty-two children involved in the production of *Donkeys* had initially been reluctant to share their stories publicly, but agreed once they "realised people weren't going to laugh at them, that people were really interested," as Sharon Sandy recalls.⁶

Following the publications of the children's book *Donkeys Can't Fly on Planes*, parents and adults in the community recounted their own stories in two collections – *In My Kingdom* and *All the Way Home* – that were written primarily for their children.⁷ Two adult community leaders, who have reflected on the experience of creating the books, are Abraham Malual and Abraham Maluk. Both men lived in Bor in South Sudan as children and were twelve and fourteen years old respectively in 1987, when the Second Sudanese Civil War forced them to flee. Many members of their families were killed.⁸ They initially fled to Ethiopia and later to the Kakuma refugee camp in Kenya.⁹ They first met in Kakuma in 2005 when preparing to come to Australia with their families.¹⁰ In 2008, they met again, coincidentally, when both moved to Traralgon. The act of sharing their own stories was transformative, Abraham Malual said: "The storytelling has increased in our homes and we feel like our children now respect our stories and understand finally who we are and where we have been. People didn't know where we came from or why we came here. Now they understand."¹¹ As Abraham Maluk reflected, "We have to share our histories, so the children in the school know where we came from … So the people around – our neighbours – will understand our struggles and our issues."¹²

Collectively, these books speak to children's and their parents' understandings of displacement, war, and violence as well as cultural differences and cultural heritage. In *Donkey's Can't Fly on Planes*, children recount the day-to-day life in refugee camps alongside their encounters, both friendly and dangerous, with animals in various parts of Africa. Their stories also describe physical hardships and the lack of food.¹³ Almost all stories convey a range of emotion, as narrators recall the impact of violence, processes of resettlement and family separation, often juxtaposing their lives in Africa and Australia.

The story that has given the collection its title is "Steven the Donkey," written by Sunday Garang. In this story, Sunday describes the refugee camp in Kenya where she was born, the hunger she and her family experienced, and the stories her mother told to comfort her children: "She would say, 'There is food growing right now while we sleep. It will be ready soon.'" Several times a day, Sunday would ride her donkey, Steven, to a nearby well to fetch water for drinking, cooking, and watering the vegetables. The collage that accompanies her story shows food growing in the soil and a smiling person watching over the plants.[14]

While *Donkeys Can't Fly on Planes* offered children a space to share their stories, the next two collections – *In My Kingdom* and *All the Way Home* – provided a forum for intergenerational exchanges. In these collections, children shared their reflections upon hearing their parents' stories, some of which they had never heard before. The joint creation of these books thus became an occasion for intergenerational storytelling. Children responded to the personal histories the adults told and the cultural practices their elders described. One of the stories in *All the Way Home*, for example, describes initiation practices for boys in Bor communities, illustrating gender-specific roles that people play. "The ceremony would be hard," Gugeui reflected, adding that "I think it would be cool, having my sister wait on me!" His sister Angeth responded: "That would never happen!"[15] In this short and light-hearted exchange, children learned about, and responded to, cultural knowledge and cultural practices. Such intergenerational exchanges are rarely captured in published writings; they reveal how cultural dislocations are experienced and handled and constitute important historical evidence. Another story, "A Problem for My Mum," tells of Nyater Chuol's childhood in 1992, when her mother would be away for days, collecting corn for her family to eat. "My country was broken," Nyater recalled when describing her family's separation and dislocation. The accompanying illustration depicts the broken ground. Walking across it is a woman, standing tall and carrying corn on her head.[16]

The final book in the series, *This Is My Home*, was created in the context of the many challenges of the first two years of the COVID-19 pandemic. Agum Maluach was the storyteller who worked with the children and their parents in creating a book about their homes. Maluach shared childhood games she played growing up in Makuar, South Sudan, which feature in the published book, as do all the activities the children enjoy today alongside their parents' stories of the childhood homes they left in South Sudan.[17]

While the stories in these four books cover many themes, both of the stories reproduced here primarily focus on the history of war, violence, and forced displacement. Yet, in doing so, the narrators cast themselves and their families not as "victims," but, instead, as active subjects with life experiences to share. As anthropologist Ghassan Hage posits, memories of migration form part of a "construction of the future."[18] The memories, personal histories, and cultural practices

Figure 15.1
"Steven the Donkey" – The Story of Sunday Garang, from *Donkeys Can't Fly on Planes: Stories of Survival from South Sudanese Refugee Children Living in Australia* (Melbourne: Kids' Own Publishing, 2012), 4–5. Permission to reproduce this story was granted by the publisher, Kids' Own Publishing, Abbotsford, Australia.

Figure 15.2
"A Problem for My Mum" – The Story of Nyater, from *In My Kingdom: South Sudanese Parents' Stories for their Children in Australia* (Melbourne: Kids' Own Publishing, 2014), 8–9. Permission to reproduce this story was granted by the publisher, Kids' Own Publishing, Abbotsford, Australia.

conveyed in these books are primary sources created in an effort to record and share both past and present lives. In intergenerational storytelling and artwork, both children and their parents present themselves as active and capable people, expressing their emotional and physical responses to the lived experiences of conflict, displacement, and cultural change.

NOTES

1 Bleiker et al., "The Visual Dehumanisation of Refugees," 398–416, and Malkki, "Speechless Emissaries," 386.
2 See Kids' Own Publishing website, "About Us," at http://kidsownpublishing.com/about/.
3 Scott, "Storytelling," 203–4.
4 Sarah Hudson, "Turning the Page on Sad Beginnings," *Weekly Times*, 5 March 2014, 61.
5 *Donkeys Can't Fly on Planes: Stories of Survival from South Sudanese Refugee Children Living in Australia* (Melbourne: Kids' Own Publishing, 2012), 3.
6 Quoted in Benjamin Press, "Sudanese Students Offer an Insight into Their Other World," *Age*, 2 May 2013, 17.
7 *In My Kingdom: South Sudanese Parents' Stories for Their Children in Australia* (Melbourne: Kids' Own Publishing, 2014) and *All the Way Home: South Sudanese Parents' Stories for their Children in Australia* (Melbourne: Kids' Own Publishing, 2015).
8 Arnold Zable, "The Two Abrahams," *Monthly*, September 2015. https://www.themonthly.com.au/issue/2015/september/1441029600/arnold-zable/two-abrahams.
9 International Rescue Committee, "The Lost Boys of Sudan," 3 October 2014. https://www.rescue.org/article/lost-boys-sudan.
10 Zable, "The Two Abrahams."
11 Quoted in Margaret Robson Kett, "Kids' Own Publishing," *Horn Book*, 9 September 2015, https://www.hbook.com/?detailStory=kids-own-publishing.
12 Quoted in Andrew Bell, "Stories from South Sudan: Parents Living in Regional Victoria Tell Stories, Inspired by Children," ABC News, 27 June 2015, https://www.abc.net.au/news/2015-06-27/south-sudanese-parents-living-in-regional-victoria-tell-stories/6577162.
13 See also Gardner, "Transnational Migration and the Study of Children," 905.
14 Sunday Garang, "Steven the Donkey," in *Donkeys Can't Fly on Planes*, 4.

Intergenerational Storytelling and Artwork 313

15 Malual, "The Luak and the Razor," in *All the Way Home*.
16 Nyater Chuol, "A Problem for My Mum," in *In My Kingdom*.
17 Australian families of South Sudanese heritage, *This Is My Home* (Melbourne: Kids' Own Publishing), 2–3.
18 Hage, "Migration, Food, Memory, and Home-Building," 419.

Figures

1.1 Austrian forces attack 36
1.2 Flags of Prussia, Germany, Austria, and the Ottoman Empire 39
1.3 German and French soldiers in combat 46
1.4 French and German soldiers fire at each other 47
1.5 Battle scene of the First World War 47
1.6 German troops use cannons to kill French soldiers 48
1.7 Inept French troops face superior German soldiers 49
1.8 German soldiers, behind barbed wire, fire on French soldiers 49
1.9 German troops on the move against French soldiers 50
1.10 German soldiers fire cannons against the French – cover of a popular wartime colouring book for children 51
1.11 Caricature of the French soldier, in a children's picture book on the war 52
1.12 German airplanes attack 53
1.13 The German U9 submarine hits a British warship 53
1.14 The Caring Nurse 54
1.15 Nurses and the soldiers' hospital, the "Lazarett" 54
1.16 Soldier, nurse, and horse-drawn ambulance at the Red Cross hospital tent 55
1.17 A nurse carrying a soldier with a head wound 56
1.18 A nurse cares for a severely wounded soldier 56
1.19 German Zeppelins and aircraft attack and kill civilians in a French village 57
2.1 Convoy in Bedford Basin, Halifax, Nova Scotia 68
2.2 Norwegian MV *Kronprinsen* awaiting repairs at Halifax dry dock 70
2.3 View of the Halifax Dockyard during wartime 75
2.4 The Bedford Magazine Explosion, 18 July 1945 76

2.5 Cloud hovering over Halifax in the wake of the explosion at Bedford Magazine 83
3.1 Civil Defense, School Scheme 100
4.1 Crowds waving goodbye to troops at a Vancouver train station 122
5.1 Jack Taylor with Don and Paul, c. 1954 151
5.2 Christmas presents 155
6.1 Adult and child participants in the Training Institute in Non-Violence 176
6.2 Players on Grindstone volleyball court, 1976 182
9.1 Drawing by a child in immigration detention 225
9.2 Comparison between being in immigration detention and life in Sri Lanka 229
9.3 Sad children returning to the Wickham Point Detention Centre on a school bus 230
9.4 Time standing still in detention centre 231
9.5 Actions of self-harm in detention centres 232
9.6 Adults' self-harming and suicidal acts 233
9.7 Fenced-in lives 238
10.1 "Just a Baby's Letter Found in No Man's Land" 259
10.2 "A Message to Daddy" 259
10.3 Lorne's letter to Papa, 8 February 1917 260
10.4 Gordon Brook, letter to Sidney Brook, 12 January 1918 262–3
10.5 Arnott Brook, letter to Sidney Brook, 12 January 1918 264
11.1 Letter by Owen Mackie to his parents, 25 August 1940 270–1
11.2 Letter by Owen Mackie to his parents, 1 September 1940 272
11.3 Letter by Owen Mackie to his parents, 17 October 1940 274–5
11.4 Letter by Christopher Sharp, 1941 277
11.5 Letter by Bill Sharp, 7 April 1941 277
11.6 Letter by Tom Sharp, June 1944 278–9
12.1 Memories of Quarry Pond, Point Pleasant Park, Halifax 286
12.2 "Franklyn Park Area Map 1940. Not to scale." 291
13.1 "Don't remove mine tags" 296
13.2 "Never touch mine signs" 296
13.3 "Stabilization Force (SFOR) patrol" 297
13.4 "We survived the war, survive the peace!" 298
14.1 Leontine Uwababyeyi 301
14.2 Going Places 303
14.3 In Memory 304
15.1 "Steven the Donkey" – The Story of Sunday Garang 311
15.2 "A Problem for My Mum" – The Story of Nyater Chuol 312

Bibliography

Abella, Irving, and Harold Troper. *None Is Too Many: Canada and the Jews of Europe, 1933–1948*. Toronto: Lester & Orpen Dennys, 1982.

Abraham, Margaret, and Bandana Purkayastha. "Making a Difference: Linking Research and Action in Practice, Pedagogy and Policy for Social Justice: Introduction." *Current Sociology* 60, no. 2 (2012): 123–41.

Ahmadzadeh, G., and Azadeh Malekian. "Aggression, Anxiety, and Social Development in Adolescent Children of War Veterans with PTSD versus Those of Non-Veterans." *Journal of Research in Medical Sciences* 9, no. 5 (2004): 231–4.

Akello, Grace, Ria Reis, and Annemiek J.M. Richters. "Silencing Distressed Children in the Context of War in Northern Uganda: An Analysis of Its Dynamics and Its Health Consequences." *Social Science & Medicine* 71, no. 2 (2010): 213–20.

Akello, Grace. "Experiences of Forced Mothers in Northern Uganda: The Legacy of War." *Intervention* 11, no. 2 (2013): 149–56.

Alexander, Kristine. "Agency and Emotion Work." *Jeunesse: Young People, Texts, Cultures* 7, no. 2 (2015): 120–8.

– "Can the Girl Guide Speak? The Perils and Pleasures of Looking for Children's Voices in Archival Research." *Jeunesse: Young People, Texts, Cultures* 4, no. 1 (Summer 2012): 132–44.

– "Domestic Demobilization: Letters from the Children's Page." In *Canada 1919: A Nation Shaped by War*, edited by Tim Cook and J.L. Granatstein, 177–89. Vancouver: UBC Press, 2020.

– *Guiding Modern Girls: Girlhood, Empire, and Internationalism in the 1920s and 1930s*. Vancouver: UBC Press, 2017.

– "An Honour and a Burden: Canadian Girls and the Great War." In *A Sisterhood of

Suffering and Service: Canadian and Newfoundland Girls and Women and the First World War, edited by Sarah Glassford and Amy Shaw, 173–94. Vancouver: UBC Press, 2012.

Alexievich, Svetlana. *Last Witness: An Oral History of the Children of World War II*. New York: Random House, 2020. First edition published 1985.

Aradau, Claudia, and Andrew Hill. "The Politics of Drawing: Children, Evidence, and the Darfur Conflict." *International Political Sociology* 7, no. 4 (2013): 368–87.

Arrabito, G. Robert, and Anna S. Leung. "Combating the Impact of Stigma on Physically Injured and Mentally Ill Canadian Armed Forces (CAF) Members." *Canadian Military Journal* 14, no. 2 (2014): 25–35.

Ashwin, Clive. *Drawing and Education in German-Speaking Europe 1800–1900*. Ann Arbor: UMI Research Press, 1981.

Audoin-Rouzeau, Stéphane. "Children and the Primary Schools of France, 1914–1918." In *State, Society and Mobilization in the First World War*, edited by John Horne, 39–52. New York: Cambridge University Press, 1997.

– *La guerre des enfants 1914–1918: essay d'histoire culturelle*. Paris: Armand Colin, 1993.

Audoin-Rouzeau, Stéphane, and Annette Becker, *14–18: Understanding the Great War*. New York: Hill and Wang, 2014. First edition published 2002.

Backhouse, Constance. *Colour-Coded: A Legal History of Racism in Canada, 1900–1950*. Toronto: Osgoode Society for Canadian Legal History by University of Toronto Press, 1999.

Baker, Sandra Pickrell, and Deborah Norris. "The Experiences of Female Partners of Canadian Forces Veterans Diagnosed with Post-Traumatic Stress Disorder." In *Shaping the Future: Military and Veteran Health Research*, edited by Alice B. Aiken and Stéphanie A.H. Bélanger, 175–85. Kingston: Canadian Defence Academy Press, 2011.

Barber, Brian K. "Making Sense and No Sense of War." In *Adolescents and War: How Youth Deal with Political Violence*, edited by Brian K. Barber, 281–312. New York: Oxford University Press, 2009.

Barker, Ralph. *Children of the Benares*. London: Methuen, 1987.

Barker-Devine, Jenny. "Mightier Than Missiles: The Rhetoric of Civil Defence for Rural American Families, 1950–1970." *Agricultural History* 80, no. 4 (2006): 415–35.

Barman, Jean. "Growing Up British in British Columbia: The Vernon Preparatory School, 1914–1946." In *Children, Teachers, and Schools in the History of British Columbia*, edited by Jean Barman and Mona Gleason, 303–18. Edmonton: Brush Education Inc., 2003.

– *Growing Up British in British Columbia: Boys in Private School*. Vancouver: UBC Press, 1984.

Barnett, Bryanne, and Gordon Parker. "The Parentified Child: Early Competence or Childhood Deprivation?" *Child Psychology and Psychiatry Review* 3, no. 4 (1998): 146–55.

Baron, Nick, ed., *Displaced Children in Russia and Eastern Europe, 1915–1953: Ideologies, Identities, Experiences*. Leiden: Brill, 2016.

Beckham, Jean C., Loretta C. Braxton, Harold S. Kudler, Michelle E. Feldman, Barbara L. Lytle, and Scott Palmer. "Minnesota Multiphasic Personality Inventory Profiles of Vietnam Combat Veterans with Posttraumatic Stress Disorder and Their Children." *Journal of Clinical Psychology* 53, no. 8 (1997): 847–52.

Bell, Amy Helen. "Heroes or Hooligans? Children in English War-Scarred Landscapes 1940–1953." *Journal of the History of Childhood and Youth* 10, no. 1 (2017): 89–95.

Bentley, D.M.R. "Simile, Metaphor, and the Making and Perception of Canada." *Studies in Canadian Literature/Études en littérature canadienne* 42, no. 1 (2017): 66–83.

Bernstein, Robin. *Racial Innocence: Performing American Childhood from Slavery to Civil Rights*. New York: New York University Press, 2011.

Biess, Frank. "'Everybody Had a Chance': Nuclear Angst, Civil Defence, and the History of Emotions in Postwar West Germany." *German History* 27, no. 2 (2009): 215–43.

Bilotta, Neil. "Uprooting the Pumpkin: Neo-Colonial Therapeutic Interventions with Formerly Abducted Young People in Northern Uganda." *Children and Society* 30, no. 5 (2016): 384–95.

Blainey, Geoffrey. *The Tyranny of Distance: How Distance Shaped Australia's History*. Melbourne: Sun Books, 1966.

Blais, Rebecca K., Keith D. Renshaw, and Matthew Jakupcak. "Posttraumatic Stress and Stigma in Active-Duty Service Members Relate to Lower Likelihood of Seeking Support." *Journal of Traumatic Stress* 27, no. 1 (2014): 116–19.

Bleiker, Roland, David Campbell, Emma Hutchinson, and Xzarina Nicholson. "The Visual Dehumanization of Refugees." *Australian Journal of Political Science* 48, no. 4 (2013): 398–416.

Boddice, Rob, and Mark Smith. *Emotion, Sense, Experience*. Cambridge: Cambridge University Press, 2020.

Boss, Pauline. *Ambiguous Loss: Learning to Live with Unresolved Grief*. Cambridge: Harvard University Press, 1999.

Boucher, Ellen. "Anticipating Armageddon: Nuclear Risk and the Neoliberal Sensibility in Thatcher's Britain." *American Historical Review* 124, no. 4 (2019): 1221–45.

Bowen, Zazie, and Jessica Hinchy. "Introduction: Children and Knowledge in India." *South Asian History and Culture* 6, no. 3 (2015): 317–29.

Boyden, Jo. "Children under Fire: Challenging Assumptions about Children's Resilience," *Children, Youth, and Environments* 13, no. 1 (Spring 2003): 1–29.
- "Anthropology under Fire: Ethics, Researchers and Children in War." In *Children and Youth On the Front Line: Ethnography, Armed Conflict and Displacement*, edited by Jo Boyden and Joanna de Berry, 237–61. New York: Berghahn Books, 2004.
Boyer, Paul. *By the Bomb's Early Light: American Thought and Culture at the Dawn of the Atomic Age.* New York: Pantheon, 1985.
Bragin, Martha. "Editorial: Special Issue on Children Affected by Armed Conflict: Views from the Global South." *International Journal of Applied Psychoanalytic Studies* 9, no. 3 (2012): 179–86.
Brandsma, Michelle. "'An Honoured Place': Gender, Work, and the Brook Family on the Western Canadian Homefront During the First World War." Master's thesis, University of Saskatchewan, 2017.
Brookfield, Tarah. *Cold War Comforts: Canadian Women, Child Safety, and Global Insecurity.* Waterloo: Wilfrid Laurier University Press, 2012.
- "Until the World Deserves Them: Representation of Apocalyptic Childhoods in *The Day After, Testament*, and *Threads*." In *The Child in Post-Apocalyptic Cinema*, edited by Debbie Olson, 129–52. New York: Lexington Books, 2015.
Bourke, Joanna. *Dismembering the Male: Men's Bodies, Britain, and the Great War.* Chicago: University of Chicago Press, 1996.
Broszormenyi-Nagy, Ivan, and Geraldine M. Spark. *Invisible Loyalties: Reciprocity in Intergenerational Family Therapy.* Hagerstown, MD: Harper & Row, 1973.
Burtch, Andrew. "Armageddon on Tour: The 'On Guard, Canada!' Civil Defence Convoy and Responsible Citizenship in the Early Cold War." *International Journal* 61, no. 1 (2011): 735–56.
- *Give Me Shelter: The Failure of Canada's Cold War Civil Defence.* Vancouver: UBC Press, 2012.
Byers, E. Sandra, and Deborah Harrison. "Building Collaborative Action-Oriented Research Teams." In *Understanding Abuse: Partnering for Change*, edited by Mary Lou Stirling, Catherine Ann Cameron, Nancy Nason-Clark, and Baukje Miedema, 21–52. Toronto: University of Toronto Press, 2004.
Cabanas, Bruna. "Negotiating Intimacy in the Shadow of War: New Perspectives in the Cultural History of World War I." *French Politics, Culture, and Society* 31, no. 1 (Spring 2013): 1–23.
Campbell, Isabel. "Exemplary Canadians? How Two Canadian Women Remember Their Roles in a Cold War Military Family?" *Journal of the Canadian Historical Association* 27, no. 1 (2016): 61–93.

– *Unlikely Diplomats: The Canadian Brigade in Germany, 1951–1964*. Vancouver: UBC Press, 2013.
Carden-Coyne, Ana, and Kate Darian-Smith, eds. "Special Issue: Young People and the World Wars: Visuality, Materiality and Cultural Heritage." *Cultural and Social History* 17, no. 5 (2020).
Carstairs, Catherine, and Nancy Janovicek, eds. *Feminist History in Canada*. Vancouver: UBC Press, 2013.
Casey, Edward S. "How to Get from Space to Place in a Fairly Short Stretch of Time: Phenomenological Prolegomena." In *Senses of Places*, edited by Steven Feld and Keith Basso, 13–52. New Mexico: School of American Research, 1996.
Cave, Peter, and Aaron William Moore, eds. "Japanese Children amid Disaster and War, 1920–1945: Special Issue." *Japanese Studies* 36, no. 3 (2016).
Chandra, Anita, Sandraluz Lara-Cinisomo, Lisa H. Jaycox, Terri Tanielian, Bing Han, Rachel M. Burns, and Teague Ruder. *Views from the Homefront: The Experiences of Youth and Spouses from Military Families*. Arlington: RAND Corporation and National Military Family Association, 2011.
Chandra, Anita, Laurie T. Martin, Stacy Ann Hawkins, and Amy Richardson. "The Impact of Parental Deployment on Child Social and Emotional Functioning: Perspectives of School Staff." *Journal of Adolescent Health* 146, no. 3 (2010): 218–23.
Chapin, Mark. "Family Resilience and the Fortunes of War." *Social Work in Health Care* 50, no. 7 (2011): 527–42.
Charmaz, Kathy. "Grounded Theory." In *Approaches to Qualitative Research*, edited by Sharlene Nagy Hesse-Biber and Patricia Leavy, 496–521. New York: Oxford University Press, 2004.
Chatani, Sayaka. *Nation-Empire: Ideology and Rural Youth Mobilization in Japan and Its Colonies*. Ithaca and London: Cornell University Press, 2018.
Chickering, Roger. *The Great War and Urban Life in Germany: Freiburg, 1914–1918*. New York: Cambridge University Press, 2007.
Clair, David J., and Myles Genest. "The Children of Alcoholics Screening Test: Reliability and Relationship to Family Environment, Adjustment, and Alcohol-Related Stressors of Adolescent Offspring of Alcoholics." *Journal of Clinical Psychology* 48, no. 3 (1992): 414–20.
Classen, Constance. "Foundations for an Anthropology of the Senses." *International Social Science Journal* 49, no. 153 (1997): 401–12.
Clement, Elizabeth Alice. *Love for Sale: Courting, Treating, and Prostitution in New York City, 1900–1945*. Chapel Hill: University of North Carolina Press, 2006.

Clifford, Rebecca. *Survivors: Children's Lives after the Holocaust*. New Haven: Yale University Press, 2020.
Cohen, Dara Kay, and Ragnhild Nordås. "Sexual Violence in Armed Conflict: 1989–2009." *Journal of Peace Research* 51, no. 3 (2014): 418–28.
Cole, Tim. "(Re)Placing the Past: Spatial Strategies of Retelling Difficult Stories." *Oral History Review* 42, no. 1 (2015): 30–49.
Cook, Daniel Thomas, and John Wall, eds. *Children and Armed Conflict*. New York: Palgrave Macmillan, 2011.
Cook, Tim. "Grave Beliefs: Stories of the Supernatural and the Uncanny among Canada's Great War Trench Soldiers." *Journal of Military History* 77, no. 2 (2014): 521–42.
– *No Place to Run: The Canadian Corps and Gas Warfare in the First World War*. Vancouver: UBC Press, 1999.
– "The Blind Leading the Blind: The Battle of the St Eloi Craters." *Canadian Military History* 5, no. 2 (1996): 24–36.
– "The Politics of Surrender: Canadian Soldiers and the Killing of Prisoners in the Great War." *Journal of Military History* 70, no. 2 (2006): 637–65.
Cook, Tim, and Natascha Morrison. "Longing and Loss from Canada's Great War." *Canadian Military History* 16, no. 1 (Winter 2007): 53–60.
Conquergood, Dwight. "Performance Studies: Interventions and Radical Research." In *The Performance Studies Reader*, edited by Henry Bial, 311–22. London: Routledge, 2004.
Corbin, Alain. "Charting the Cultural History of the Senses." In *Empire of the Senses: The Sensual Culture Reader*, edited by David Howes, 128–39. New York: Berg, 2005.
Corbin, Alain. *Village Bells: Sound and Meaning in the Nineteenth-century French Countryside*. New York: Columbia University Press, 1998.
Cruikshank, Julie. *The Social Life of Stories: Narrative and Knowledge in the Yukon Territory*. Lincoln: University of Nebraska Press, 1998.
Daniel, Ute. *The War from Within: German Working-Class Women in the First World War*. New York: Berg, 1997.
Danforth, Loring M., and Riki Van Boeschoten. *Children of the Greek Civil War: Refugees and the Politics of Memory*. Chicago: University of Chicago Press, 2012.
Davidson, Ann C., and David J. Mellor. "The Adjustment of Children of Australian Vietnam Veterans: Is There Evidence for the Transgenerational Transmission of the Effects of War-Related Trauma?" *Australian & New Zealand Journal of Psychiatry* 35, no. 3 (2001): 345–51.

Davidson, Mark. "Preparing for the Bomb: The Development of Civil Defence Policy in Canada, 1948–1963." *Canadian Military History* 16, no. 3 (2007): 29–42.

Davin, Anna. *Growing up Poor: Home, School and Street in London, 1870–1914*. London: Rivers Oram Press, 1996.

Davis, Belinda. *Home Fires Burning: Food, Politics, and Everyday Life in World War I*. Chapel Hill: University of North Carolina Press, 2000.

Davis, Tracy. *Stages of Emergency: Cold War Nuclear Civil Defense*. Durham: Duke University Press, 2007.

Dawson, Graham. *Soldier Heroes: British Adventure, Empire and the Imagining of Masculinities*. London: Routledge, 1994.

De Certeau, Michel. *The Practice of Everyday Life*. Berkeley: University of California Press, 1988.

DeFazio, Kimberly. *The City of the Senses: Urban Culture and Urban Space*. New York: Palgrave Macmillan, 2011.

DeGraffenried, Julie K. *Sacrificing Childhood: Children and the Soviet State in the Great Patriotic War*. Lawrence, Kansas: University of Kansas, 2014.

Demm, Eberhard. "Deutschlands Kinder im Ersten Weltkrieg." *Militärgeschichtliche Zeitschrift* 60, no. 1 (2001): 51–98.

Denov, Myriam. "Children Born of Wartime Rape: The Intergenerational Realities of Sexual Violence and Abuse." *Ethics, Medicine and Public Health* 1, no. 1 (2015): 61–8.

– "Social Navigation and Power in Post-Conflict Sierra Leone: Reflections from a Former Child Soldier Turned Bike Rider." In *Child Soldiers: From Recruitment to Reintegration*, edited by Alpaslan Özerdem and Sukanya Podder, 191–212. New York: Palgrave Macmillan, 2011.

Denov, Myriam, and Atim Angela Lakor. "Post-War Stigma, Violence, and 'Kony Children': The Responsibility to Protect Children Born in Lord's Resistance Army Captivity in Northern Uganda." *Global Responsibility to Protect* 10, nos 1/2 (2018): 217–38.

Denov, Myriam, Leah Woolner, Jules Pacifique Bahati, Paulin Nsuki, and Obed Shyaka. "The Intergenerational Legacy of Genocidal Rape: The Realities and Perspectives of Children Born of the Rwandan Genocide." *Journal of Interpersonal Violence* (2017): 1–22. DOI: 10.1177/0886260517708407

Denov, Myriam, and Atim Angela Lakor. "When War Is Better Than Peace: The Post-Conflict Realities of Children Born of Wartime Rape in Northern Uganda." *Child Abuse and Neglect* 65 (March 2017): 255–65.

Denov, Myriam, Natasha Blancet-Cohen, Alusine Bah, Leontine Uwababyeyi, Jean Kagame, and Andie Saša Buccitelli. "Co-Creating Space for Voice: Reflections on a

Participatory Process with War-Affected Youth Living in Canada." In *Participatory Methodologies to Elevate Children's Voice and Agency*, edited by Ilene R. Berson, Michael J. Berson, and Colette Gray, 423–42. Charlotte, NC: Information Age Publishing, 2019.

Denov, Myriam, Anaïs Cadieux Van Vliet, Atim Angela Lakor, and Arach Janet. "Complex Perpetrators: Forced Marriage, Family, and Fatherhood in the Lord's Resistance Army." In "Masculinidades y feminidades en conflict en el ábito bélico-militar," edited by David Alegre Lorenz and Miguel Alonso Ibarra. Special Issue of Jerónimo Zurita 94 (Primavera 2019): 139–60.

De Pedro, Kris Tunac, Ron Avi Astor, Tamika D. Gilreath, Rami Benbenishty, and Ruth Berkowitz. "School Climate, Deployment, and Mental Health among Students in Military-Connected Schools." *Youth and Society* 50, no. 1 (2015): 1–23.

Dewan, Pauline. *The Art of Place in Literature for Children and Young Adults: How Locale Shapes a Story*. Lewiston: Edwin Mellen Press, 2010.

Dodd, Lindsey, and David Lees. "Introduction." In *Vichy France and Everyday Life: Confronting the Challenges of Wartime, 1939–1945*, edited by Lindsey Dodd and David Lees, 1–14. London: Bloomsbury Academic, 2018.

Dodd, Lindsey. *French Children under the Allied Bombs, 1940–45: An Oral History*. Manchester: Manchester University Press, 2016.

– "'Mon petit papa chéri': Children, Fathers, and Family Separation in Vichy France." *Essays in French Literature and Culture* 54 (November 2017): 97–118.

Dodd, Lindsey, and Wendy Michallat. "Hidden Words, Hidden Worlds: Everyday Life and Narrative Sources (France, 1939–1945)." *Essays in French Literature and Culture* 54 (2017): 7–11.

Dolto, Françoise. *Enfances*. Paris: Le Seuil, 1986.

Donson, Andrew. *Youth in the Fatherless Land: War Pedagogy, Nationalism and Authority in Germany, 1914–1918*. Cambridge: Harvard University Press, 2010.

Doucet, Andrea. *Do Men Mother? Fathering, Care, and Domestic Responsibility*. Toronto: University of Toronto Press, 2006.

Down, Laura Lee. "Au Revoir les Enfants: Wartime Evacuation and the Politics of Childhood in France and Britain, 1939–45." *History Workshop Journal* 82 (Autumn 2016): 121–50.

Dubinsky, Karen, Adele Perry, and Henry Yu, eds. *Within and without the Nation: Canadian History as Transnational History*. Toronto: University of Toronto Press, 2015.

Duder, Cameron. *Awfully Devoted Women: Lesbian Lives in Canada, 1900–65*. Vancouver: UBC Press, 2010.

Dudziak, Mary L. *War-Time: An Idea, Its History, Its Consequences.* Oxford: Oxford University Press, 2012.

Earley, Louise, and Delia J. Cushway. "The Parentified Child." *Clinical Child Psychology and Psychiatry* 7, no. 2 (2002): 163–78.

Edelman, Lee. *No Future: Queer Theory and the Death Drive.* Durham: Duke University Press, 2004.

Eldén, Sara. "Inviting the Messy: Drawing Methods and 'Children's Voices.'" *Childhood* 20, no. 1 (February 2013): 66–81.

Embacher, Helga, Grazia Prontera, Albert Lichtblau, Johannes-Dieter Steinert, Wolfgang Aschauer, Darek Galasinski, and John Buckley, eds. *Children and War: Past and Present.* Solihull, West Midlands: Helion, 2013.

Enloe, Cynthia. *Does Khaki Become You? The Militarization of Women's Lives.* London: Harper Collins, 1988.

– *The Morning After: Sexual Politics at the End of the Cold War.* Berkeley: University of California Press, 1993.

Erjavec, Karmen, and Zala Volčič. "'Target,' 'Cancer,' and 'Warrior': Exploring Painful Metaphors of Self-Presentation Used by Girls Born of War Rape." *Discourse and Society* 21, no. 5 (2010): 524–43.

Ericcson, Kjersti, and Eva Simonsen, eds. *Children of World War II: The Hidden Enemy Legacy.* New York: Berg, 2005.

Evans, Lynette, Tony McHugh, Malcolm Hopwood, and Carol Watt. "Chronic Posttraumatic Stress Disorder and Family Functioning of Vietnam Veterans and Their Partners." *Australian and New Zealand Journal of Psychiatry* 37, no. 6 (2003): 765–72.

Evans-Campbell, Teresa. "Historical Trauma in American Indian/Native Alaska Communities: A Multilevel Framework for Exploring Impacts on Individuals, Families, and Communities." *Journal of Interpersonal Violence* 23, no. 3 (2008): 316–38.

Fahrni, Magda. *Household Politics: Montreal Families and Post War Re-Construction.* Toronto: University of Toronto Press, 2005.

Fahrni, Magda, and Robert Rutherdale, eds. *Creating Postwar Canada: Community, Diversity, and Dissent, 1945–75.* Vancouver: UBC Press, 2008.

Faire, Lucy, and Denise McHugh. "The Everyday Uses of City-Centre Streets: Urban Behaviour in Provincial Britain, 1930–1970." *Urban History Review/Revue d'histoire urbaine* 42, no. 2 (2014): 18–28.

Fass, Paula. "The World Is at Our Door: Why Historians of Children and Childhood Should Open Up." *Journal of the History of Childhood and Youth* 1, no. 1 (2008): 11–31.

Fehrenbach, Heide. *Race after Hitler: Black Occupation Children in Postwar Germany and America.* Princeton: Princeton University Press, 2005.

Fineberg, Jonathan. *The Innocent Eye: Children's Art and the Modern Artist*. Princeton: Princeton University Press, 1999.

Finkelhor, David, Sherry L. Hamby, Richard Ormrod, and Heather Turner. "The Juvenile Victimization Questionnaire: Reliability, Validity, and National Norms." *Child Abuse and Neglect* 29, no. 4 (2005): 383–412.

Fisher, Susan. *Boys and Girls in No Man's Land: English-Canadian Children and the First World War*. Toronto: University of Toronto Press, 2012.

Fraser, Crystal Gail. "T'aih k'iighe' tth'aih zhit diidich'uh (By Strength, We Are Still Here): Indigenous Northerners Confronting Hierarchies of Power at Day and Residential Schools in Nanhkak Thak (the Inuvik Region, Northwest Territories), 1959 to 1982." PhD diss., University of Alberta, 2019.

Fraser, John. "Propaganda on the Picture Postcard." *Oxford Art Journal* 3, no. 2 (1980): 39–47.

Frederikson, Lesley G., Kerry Chamberlain, and Nigel Long. "Unacknowledged Casualties of the Vietnam War: Experiences of Partners of New Zealand Veterans." *Qualitative Health Research* 6, no. 1 (1996): 49–70.

Frühstück, Sabine. *Playing War: Children and the Paradoxes of Modern Militarism*. Oakland: University of California Press, 2017.

– "'And My Heart Screams': Children and the War of Emotions." In *Child's Play: Multi-Sensory Histories of Children and Childhood in Japan*, edited by Sabine Frühstück and Anne Walthall, 181–201. Oakland: University of California Press, 2017.

Fussell, Paul. *The Great War and Modern Memory*. New York: Sterling, 2009.

Gardner, Katy. "Transnational Migration and the Study of Children: An Introduction." *Journal of Ethnic and Migration Studies* 38, no. 6 (2012): 889–912.

Garrioch, David. "Sounds of the City: The Soundscapes of Early Modern European Towns." *Urban History* 30, no. 1 (2003): 5–25.

Gatrell, Peter. *The Making of the Modern Refugee*. Oxford: Oxford University Press, 2013.

Geißler, Gert. *Schulgeschichte in Deutschland: Von den Anfängen bis in die Gegenwart*. Frankfurt am Main: Peter Lang, 2013.

Geist, Anthony L., and Peter N. Carroll. *They Still Draw Pictures: Children's Art in Wartime from the Spanish Civil War to Kosovo*. Chicago: University of Illinois Press, 2002.

Gerber, David A. *Authors of Their Lives: The Personal Correspondence of British Immigrants in North America in the Nineteenth Century*. New York: New York University Press, 2008.

Ghobrial, John-Paul. "Introduction: Seeing the World Like a Microhistorian." *Past and Present* 242, Supplement 14 (November 2019): 1–22.

Giancarlo, Alexandra. "Indigenous Student Labour and Settler Colonialism at Brandon Residential School." *The Canadian Geographer/Le Géographe canadien* 64, no. 3 (fall 2020): 461–74.

Gifford, Shannon, James Hutchinson, and Maggie Gibson. "Lifespan Considerations in the Psychological Treatment of CF Veterans with Post-Traumatic Stress Disorder." In *Shaping the Future: Military and Veteran Health Research*, edited by Alice B. Aiken and Stéphanie A.H. Bélanger, 204–15. Kingston: Canadian Defence Academy Press, 2011.

Glassford, Sarah. "Bearing the Burden of Their Elders: English-Canadian Children's First World War Red Cross Work and Its Legacies." *Études canadiennes/Canadian Studies* 80 (2016): 129–50.

Glassford, Sarah, and Amy Shaw. "Conclusion: Making the Best of It." In *Making the Best of It: Women and Girls of Canada and Newfoundland During the Second World War*, edited by Sarah Glassford and Amy Shaw, 257–63. Vancouver: UBC Press, 2020.

Gleason, Mona. "Avoiding the Agency Trap: Caveats for Historians of Children, Youth, and Education." *History of Education* 45, no. 4 (2016): 446–59.

– "Disciplining Children, Disciplining Parents: The Nature and Meaning of Advice to Canadian Parents, 1945–1955." *Histoire sociale/Social History* 29, no. 57 (1996): 187–209.

– *Normalizing the Ideal: Psychology, Schooling, and the Family in Post War Canada*. Toronto: University of Toronto Press, 1999.

Gleeson, Madeline. "Protection Deficit: The Failure of Australia's Offshore Processing Arrangements to Guarantee 'Protection Elsewhere' in the Pacific." *International Journal of Refugee Law* (October 2019): 1–49. DOI: 10.1093/ijrl/eez030.

Glenn, D. Michael, Jean C. Beckham, Michelle E. Feldman, Angela C. Kirby, Michael A. Hertzberg, and Scott D. Moore. "Violence and Hostility among Families of Vietnam Veterans with Combat-Related Posttraumatic Stress Disorder." *Violence and Victims* 17, no. 4 (2002): 473–89.

Golomb, Claire. *Child Art in Context: A Cultural and Comparative Perspective*. Washington: APA Books, 2002.

Goodnow, Katherine. "Traditional Methods and New Moves: Migrant and Refugee Exhibitions in Australia and New Zealand." In *Museums, the Media and Refugees: Stories of Crisis, Control and Compassion*, edited by Katherine Goodnow, Jack Lohman, and Philip Marfleet, 30–66. New York: Berghahn Books, 2008.

Graff, Garrett. *Raven Rock: The Story of the US Government's Secret Plan to Save Itself – While the Rest of Us Die*. New York: Simon and Schuster, 2017.

Greenspan, Henry. "The Unsaid, the Incommunicable, the Unbearable, and the Irretrievable." *Oral History Review* 41, no. 2 (2014): 229–43.

Grieg, Christopher J. *Ontario Boys: Masculinity and the Idea of Boyhood in Post War Ontario, 1945–1960*. Waterloo: Wilfrid Laurier University Press, 2014.

Grieve, Victoria M. *Little Cold Warriors: American Childhood in the 1950s*. New York: Oxford University Press, 2018.

Gunn, Simon. *Young People and the Shaping of Public Spaces in Melbourne, 1870–1914*. London: Ashgate, 2013.

Günter, Karl-Heinz. *Geschichte der Erziehung*. Berlin: Volk und Wissen, 1987.

Habashi, Janette. "Palestinian Children: Authors of Collective Memory." *Children and Society* 27, no. 6 (2013): 421–33.

Hage, Ghassan. "Migration, Food, Memory, and Home-Building." In *Memory: Histories, Theories, Debates*, edited by Susannah Radstone and Bill Schwarz, 416–27. New York: Fordham University, 2010.

Hagedorn, Ortrud, and Ina Winkler. "Der Wandel des Kunstunterrichts zur Zeit des Ersten Weltkrieges 1914–1918." In *Kind und Kunst: Zur Geschichte des Zeichen- und Kunstunterrichts*, edited by Eckhard Siepmann, 88–93. Berlin: BDK, 1976.

Hamilton, Walter. *Children of the Occupation: Japan's Untold Story*. New Brunswick: Rutgers University Press, 2013.

Halstead, Claire. "Dangers Behind, Pleasures Ahead." *British Journal of Canadian Studies* 27, no. 2 (2014): 163–80.

– "From Lion to Leaf: The Evacuation of British Children to Canada during the Second World War." PhD diss., University of Western Ontario, 2015.

Hamilton, Paula. "The Proust Effect: Oral History and the Senses." In *The Oxford Handbook of Oral History*, edited by Donald A. Ritchie, 219–32. New York: Oxford University Press, 2011.

Hammel, Andrea. "Authenticity, Trauma and the Child's View: Martha Blend's *A Child Alone*, Vera Gissing's *Pearls of Childhood* and Ruth L. David's *Ein Kind Unserer Zeit*." *Forum for Modern Language Studies* 49, no. 2 (2013): 201–12.

Hämmerle, Christa. "'You Let a Weeping Woman Call You Home?': Private Correspondences during the First World War in Germany." In *Epistolary Selves: Letters and the Letter-Writers, 1600–1945*, edited by Rebecca Earle, 152–82. Aldershot: Ashcroft, 1999.

Hanna, Martha. "A Republic of Letters: The Epistolary Tradition in France during World War I." *American Historical Review* 108, no. 5 (2003): 1338–61.

– "The Couple." In *The Cambridge History of the First World War, Volume III: Civil Society*, edited by Jay Winter, 6–28. Cambridge: Cambridge University Press, 2014.

– *"Your Death Would Be Mine": Paul and Marie Pieraud in the Great War*. Cambridge, MA: Harvard University Press, 2006.

– *Anxious Days and Tearful Nights: Canadian War Wives during the Great War*. Montreal and Kingston: McGill-Queen's University Press, 2020.
Haraven, Tamara. "The Search for Generational Memory: Tribal Rites in Industrial Society." *Daedalus* 107, no. 4 (1978): 137–49.
Harlacher, Thomas. "Traditional Ways of Coping with Consequences of Traumatic Stress in Acholiland: Northern Ugandan Ethnography from a Western Psychological Perspective." PhD diss., Université de Fribourg, 2009.
Harrison, Deborah, and Patrizia Albanese. "The 'Parentification' Phenomenon as Applied to Adolescents Living through Parental Military Deployments." *Canadian Journal of Family and Youth* 4, no. 1 (2012): 1–27.
Harrison, Deborah, and Patrizia Albanese. *Growing up in Armyville: Canada's Military Families during the Afghanistan Mission*. Waterloo: Wilfrid Laurier University Press, 2016.
Harrison, Deborah, Patrizia Albanese, and Rachel Berman. "Parent-Adolescent Relationships in Military Families Affected by Post-Traumatic Stress Disorder." *Canadian Social Work Review* 31, no. 1 (2014): 81–103.
Harrison, Deborah, and Lucie Laliberté. "Gender, the Military, and Military Family Support." In *Wives and Warriors: Women in the Military in the United States and Canada*, edited by Laurie Wienstein and Christie C. White, 35–54. Westport: Gergen and Garvey, 1997.
– *No Life Like It: Military Wives in Canada*. Toronto: James Lorimer & Company, 1994.
Harrison, Deborah, with Lucie Laliberté, Marlene Bertrand, Elizabeth Blaney, Jerry Deveau, Penny Ericson, Gaila Friars, and Ann Koller. *The First Casualty: Violence against Women in Canadian Military Communities*. Toronto: James Lorimer & Company, 2002.
Harrison, Deborah, Karen Robson, Patrizia Albanese, Chris Sanders, and Christine Newburn-Cook. "The Impact of Shared Location on the Mental Health of Military and Civilian Adolescents in a Community Affected by Frequent Deployments: A Research Note." *Armed Forces and Society* 37, no. 3 (2011): 550–60.
Hart, Roger. *Children's Experiences of Place*. New York: Irvington Publishers, 1979.
Hartley, Lisa K., Anne Pederson, Caroline Fleay, and Sue Hoffman. "'The Situation Is Hopeless; We Must Take the Next Step': Reflecting on Social Action by Academics in Asylum Seeker Policy Debate." *Australian Community Psychologist* 25, no. 2 (2013): 22–37.
Hartman, Saidiya. *Wayward Lives, Beautiful Experiments: Intimate Histories of Riotous Black Girls, Troublesome Women, and Queer Radicals*. New York: W.W. Norton, 2019.

Hau, Caralee Daigle. "'A Challenge and a Danger': Canada and the Cuban Missile Crisis." PhD diss., Queen's University, 2011.

Hayes, Geoffrey. *Crerar's Lieutenants: Inventing the Canadian Junior Amy Officers, 1939–1945*. Vancouver: UBC Press, 2017.

Henry, Nicola. *War and Rape: Law, Memory, and Justice*. New York: Routledge, 2011.

Heron, Craig, and Myer Siemiatycki. "The Great War, the State, and Working-Class Canada." In *The Workers' Revolt in Canada 1917–1925*, edited by Craig Heron, 11–42. Toronto: University of Toronto Press, 1998.

High, Steven. *Oral History at the Crossroads: Sharing Life Stories of Survival and Displacement*. Vancouver: UBC Press, 2014.

High, Steven, ed. *Beyond Testimony and Trauma: Oral History in the Aftermath of Mass Violence*. Vancouver: UBC Press, 2015.

Hirsch, Marianne, and Valerie Smith. "Feminism and Cultural Memory: An Introduction." *Signs* 28, no. 1 (autumn 2002): 1–19.

Higonnet, Margaret R. "Child Witnesses: The Cases of World War I and Darfur." *Publications of the Modern Language Association of America* 121, no. 5 (October 2006): 1565–76.

Hochschild, Arlie Russell. *The Managed Heart: The Commercialization of Human Feeling*. Berkeley: University of California Press, 2012.

Hoegaerts, Josephine, and Stephanie Olsen. "The History of Experience: Afterword." In *Lived Nation as the History of Experiences and Emotions in Finland, 1800–2000*, edited by Ville Kivimäki, Sami Suodenjoki, and Tanja Vahtikari, 375–84. London: Palgrave Macmillan 2021.

Hogwood, Jemma, Christine Mushashi, Stuart Jones, and Carl Auerbach. "'I Learned Who I Am': Young People Born from Genocide Rape in Rwanda and Their Experiences of Disclosure." *Journal of Adolescent Research* 32, no. 5 (2017): 536–58.

Holland, Maximilian. "Social Bonding and Nurture Kinship: Compatibility between Cultural and Biological Approaches." PhD diss., London School of Economics and Political Science, 2004.

Holt, Marilyn Irvin. *Cold War Kids: Politics and Childhood in Postwar America, 1945–1960*. Kansas: University of Kansas Press, 2014.

Hooper, Lisa. "Expanding the Discussion Regarding Parentification and Its Varied Outcomes: Implications for Mental Health Research and Practice." *Journal of Mental Health Counseling* 29, no. 4 (2007): 322–37.

Hooper, Lisa M., Heather M. Moore, and Annie K. Smith. "Parentification in Military Families: Overlapping Constructs and Theoretical Explorations in Family, Clinical, and Military Psychology." *Children and Youth Services Review* 39 (2014): 123–34.

Honeck, Mischa, and Gabriel Rosenberg. "Transnational Generations: Organizing Youth in the Cold War." *Diplomatic History* 38, no. 2 (2014): 233–9.

Honeck, Mischa, and James Marten, eds. *War and Childhood in the Era of the Two World Wars*. New York: Cambridge University Press, 2019.

Howes, David, and Constance Classen. *Ways of Sensing: Understanding the Senses in Society*. New York: Routledge, 2014.

Huebner, Angela J., Jay A. Mancini, Ryan M. Wilcox, Saralyn R. Grass, and Gabriel A. Grass. "Parental Deployment and Youth in Military Families: Exploring Uncertainty and Ambiguous Loss." *Family Relations* 56, no. 2 (2007): 112–22.

Humphries, Mark. "Willfully and with Intent: Self-Inflicted Wounds and the Negotiations of Power in the Trenches." *Histoire sociale/Social History* 47, no. 94 (2014): 369–97.

Hunter, Kate. "More Than an Archive of War: Intimacy and Manliness in the Letters of a Great War Soldier." *Gender and History* 25, no. 2 (August 2013): 339–54.

Huss, Marie-Monique. "Pronatalism and the Popular Ideology of the Child in Wartime France: The Evidence of the Picture Postcare." In *The Upheaval of War: Family, Work and Welfare in Europe, 1914–1918*, edited by Richard Wall and Jay Winter, 329–34. Cambridge: Cambridge University Press, 2005.

Huxley, Aldous. *They Still Draw Pictures! A Collection of 60 Drawings Made by Spanish Children during the War*. New York: Spanish Child Welfare Association of America for the American Friends Service Committee, 1938.

Iacovetta, Franca, and Wendy Mitchinson, eds. *On the Case: Explorations in Social History*. Toronto: University of Toronto Press, 1998.

Inglis, Ruth. *The Children's War*. London: Collins, 1989.

Innes, Stephanie, and Harry Endrulat. *A Bear in War*. Toronto: Pajama Press, 2012.

– *Bear on the Home Front*. Toronto: Pajama Press, 2014.

Ishiguro, Laura. "'Growing Up and Grown Up … in Our Future City': Discourses of Childhood and Settler Futurity in Colonial British Columbia." *BC Studies* 190 (Summer 2016): 15–37.

– *Nothing to Write Home About: British Family Correspondence and the Settler Colonial Everyday in British Columbia*. Vancouver: UBC Press, 2019.

Ivashkevich, Olga. "Drawing in Children's Lives." In *When We Were Young: New Perspectives on the Art of the Child*, edited by Jonathan Fineberg, 45–59. Berkeley: University of California Press, 2006.

Jackson, Carlton. *Who Will Take Our Children? The Evacuation Program of World War II*. London: Methuen, 1985.

James, Allison. "Giving Voice to Children's Voices: Practices and Problems, Pitfalls, and Potentials." *American Anthropologist* 109, no. 2 (2007): 261–72.

James, Daniel. *Dona Maria's Story: Life History, Memory, and Political Identity*. Durham: Duke University Press, 2000.

Janesick, Valerie J. "Oral History Interviewing: Issues and Possibilities." In *The Oxford Handbook of Qualitative Research*, edited by Patricia Leavy, 300–14. New York: Oxford University Press, 2014.

Jasen, Patricia. *Wild Things: Nature, Culture, and Tourism in Ontario, 1790–1914*. Toronto: University of Toronto Press, 1995.

Jenkins, Jennifer. *Provincial Modernity: Local Culture and Liberal Politics in Fin-de-Siècle Hamburg*. Ithaca: Cornell University Press, 2002.

Jensen, Peter S., David Martin, and Henry Watanabe. "Children's Response to Parental Separation during Operation Desert Storm." *Journal of the American Academy of Child and Adolescent Psychiatry* 35, no. 4 (1996): 433–41.

Johnston, William. *War of Patrols*. Vancouver: UBC Press, 2003.

Jones, John W. *Children of Alcoholics Screening Test*. Chicago: Camelot Unlimited, 1983.

Jug, Steven G. "Sensing Danger: The Red Army during the Second World War." In *Russian History Through the Senses from 1700 to the Present*, edited by Matthew P. Romaniello and Tricia Starks, 219–40. London: Bloombury Academic, 2016.

Kallio, Krisi Paulina. "The Body as a Battlefield: Approaching Children's Politics." *Human Geography* 90, no. 3 (2008): 285–97.

Kallio, Krisi Paulina, and Jouni Häkli. "Are There Politics in Childhood?" *Space and Polity* 15, no. 1 (2011): 21–34.

Kasurak, Peter. *A National Force: The Evolution of Canada's Army, 1950–2000*. Vancouver: UBC Press, 2013.

Kay, Carolyn. *Art and the German Bourgeoisie: Alfred Lichtwark and Modern Painting in Hamburg, 1886–1914*. Toronto: University of Toronto Press, 2002.

– "German Children's Art during World War I." *Global Studies of Childhood* 11, no. 2 (June 2021): 195–212.

Kellogg, Rhoda. *Analyzing Children's Art*. London: National Press Books, 1970.

Kelm, Mary-Ellen. *Colonizing Bodies: Aboriginal Health and Healing in British Columbia, 1900–50*. Vancouver: UBC Press, 1998.

Kennedy, Rosie. *The Children's War: Britain, 1914–1918*. Basingstoke: Palgrave Macmillan, 2014.

Kerbs, Dietrich. "Kunsterziehungsbewegung und Kulturreform." In *Schund und Schönheit: Populäre Kultur um 1900*, edited by Kaspar Maase and Wolfgang Kaschuba, 378–97. Köln: Böhlau Verlag Köln, 2001.

Keren, Célia. "Autobiographies of Spanish Refugee Children at the Quaker Home in La

Rouvière (France 1940): Humanitarian Communication and Children's Writings." *Les Cahiers de Framespa* 5 (2010). https://journals.openedition.org/framespa/268.

Kimber, Stephen. *Sailor, Slacker, and Blind Pigs: Halifax at War.* Toronto: Anchor Canada, 2002.

King, Daniel W., Casey Taft, Lynda A. King, Charity Hammond, and Erika R. Stone. "Directionality of the Association between Social Support and Posttraumatic Stress Disorder: A Longitudinal Investigation." *Journal of Applied Social Psychology* 36, no. 12 (2006): 2980–92.

Kinsman, Gary, and Patricia Gentile. *The Canadian War on Queers: National Security as Sexual Relation.* Vancouver: UBC Press, 2010.

Komulainen, Sirkka. "The Ambiguity of the Child's 'Voice' in Social Research." *Childhood* 14, no. 1 (2007): 11–28.

Korinek, Valerie. *Roughing It in the Suburbs: Reading Chatelaine Magazine in the Fifties and Sixties.* Toronto: University of Toronto Press, 2000.

Kostelny, Kathleen. "A Culture-Based Integrative Approach: Helping War-Affected Children." In *A World Turned Upside Down: Social Ecological Approaches to Children in War Zones*, edited by Neil Boothby, Alison Strang, and Michael Wessells, 19–37. Bloomfield, CT: Kumarian Press, 2006.

Kotchemidova, Christine. "From Good Cheer to 'Drive-by Smiling': A Social History of Cheerfulness." *Journal of Social History* 39, no. 1 (2005): 5–37.

Kozlovsky, Roy. "Architecture, Emotions and the History of Childhood." In *Childhood, Youth and Emotions in Modern History: National, Colonial and Global Perspectives*, edited by Stephanie Olsen, 95–118. London: Palgrave MacMillan, 2015.

Knobloch, Leanne K., Kimberly B. Pusateri, Aaron T. Ebata, and Patricia C. McGlaughlin. "Experiences of Military Youth during a Family Member's Deployment: Changes, Challenges, and Opportunities." *Youth and Society* 47, no. 3 (2015): 319–32.

Krause-Parello, Cheryl A. "Loneliness in the School Setting." *Journal of School Nursing* 24, no. 2 (2008): 66–70.

Kucherenko, Olga. *Little Soldiers: How Soviet Children Went to War, 1941–1945.* New York: Oxford University Press, 2011.

Kuhn, Annette. *Family Secrets: Acts of Memory and Imagination.* London: Verso, 2002. First edition published 1995.

Kwan-Lafond, Dani, Deborah Harrison, and Patrizia Albanese. "Parental Military Deployments and Adolescents' Household Work." *Studies in Political Economy* 88, no. 1 (2011): 161–88.

Lake, Marilyn, and Henry Reynolds. *Drawing the Global Colour Line: White Men's*

Countries and the International Challenge of Racial Equality. Cambridge: Cambridge University Press, 2008.

Layman, Lenore. "Reticence in Oral History Interviews." *Oral History Review* 36, no. 2 (2009): 207–30.

Lease, Suzanne H., and Barbara J. Yanico. "Evidence of Validity for the Children of Alcoholics Screening Test." *Measurement and Evaluation in Counseling and Development* 27, no. 4 (1995): 200–10.

Lee, Sabine. *Children Born of War in the Twentieth Century.* Manchester: Manchester University Press, 2017.

Leeuw, Sarah De. "Intimate Colonialisms: The Material and Experienced Places of British Columbia's Residential Schools." *Canadian Geographer/Le Géographe canadien* 51, no. 3 (fall 2007): 339–59.

Lenette, Caroline, Prasheela Karan, Dearna Chrysostomou, and Anthea Athanasopoulos. "What Is It Like Living in Detention? Insights from Asylum Seeker Children's Drawings." *Australian Journal of Human Rights* 23, no. 1 (2017): 42–60.

Lichtman, Sarah A. "Do-It-Yourself Security: Safety, Gender, and the Home Fallout Shelter in Cold War America." *Journal of Design History* 19, no. 1 (2006): 39–55.

Lorenzkowski, Barbara. "The Children's War." In *Occupied St John's: A Social History of a City at War, 1939–1945,* edited by Steven High, 113–50. Montreal and Kingston: McGill-Queen's University Press, 2010.

– "The Small Spaces of Childhood: Learning How to Feel in Atlantic Canada, 1939–45." In *Making the Best of It: Women and Girls of Canada and Newfoundland During the Second World War,* edited by Sarah Glassford and Amy Shaw, 34–58. Vancouver: UBC Press, 2020.

Lowman, Emma Battell, and Adam J. Barker. *Settler: Identity and Colonialism in Twenty-First Century Canada.* Halifax: Fernwood Publishing, 2015.

Luchs, Michele, and Elizabeth Miller. "On Tour with Mapping Memories: Sharing Refugee Youth Stories in Montreal Classrooms." In *Beyond Testimony and Trauma: Oral History in the Aftermath of Mass Violence,* edited by Steven High, 235–53. Vancouver: UBC Press, 2015.

Lyons, Martyn. *The Writing Culture of Ordinary People in Europe: c. 1860–1920.* Oxford: Oxford University Press, 2013.

– "Love Letters and Writing Practices: On Ecritures Intimes in the Nineteenth Century." *Journal of Family History* 24, no. 2 (April 1999): 232–9.

MacAdam, Murray. *Making Waves: The Grindstone Story.* Toronto: Grindstone Co-operative Ltd, 1984.

Mackie, Vera. "Putting a Face to a Name: Visualizing Human Rights," *Cultural Studies Review* 20, no. 1 (2014): 213–36.

Macleod, R.C., ed. *Swords and Ploughshares: A History of War and Agriculture in Western Canada*. Edmonton: University of Alberta Press, 1993.

Madokoro, Laura. "On Future Research Directions: Temporality and Permanency in the Study of Migration and Settler Colonialism in Canada." *History Compass* 17, no. 1 (2019): 1–6.

Madokoro, Laura, Francine McKenzie, and David Meren, eds. *Dominion of Race: Rethinking Canada's International History*. Vancouver: UBC Press, 2017.

Mahood, Linda. *Thumbing a Ride: Hitchhikers, Hostels, and Counterculture in Canada*. Vancouver: UBC Press, 2018.

Maksudyan, Nazan. *Ottoman Children and Youth during World War I*. Syracuse, New York: Syracuse University Press, 2019.

Malkki, Liisa. "Children, Humanity, and the Infantilization of Peace." In *In the Name of Humanity: The Government of Threat and Care*, edited by Ilana Feldman and Miriam Ticktin, 58–85. Durham: Duke University Press, 2010.

– "Speechless Emissaries: Refugees, Humanitarians, and Dehistoricization." *Cultural Anthropology* 11, no. 3 (1996): 377–404.

Mares, Sarah, and Karen Zwi. "Sadness and Fear: The Experiences of Children and Families in Remote Australian Immigration Detention." *Journal of Paediatrics and Child Health* 51, no. 7 (2015): 663–9.

Marion, Nicole. "Canada's Disarmers: The Complicated Struggle against Nuclear Weapons, 1959–1963." PhD diss., Carleton University, 2016.

Marshall, Dominique. *The Social Origins of the Welfare State. Quebec Families, Compulsory Education, and Family Allowances, 1940–1955*. Waterloo: Wilfrid Laurier University Press, 2006.

Martelly, Stéphane. "'This Thing We Are Doing Here': Listening and Writing in the 'Montréal Life Stories' Project." In *Beyond Women's Words: Feminism and the Practices of Oral History in the Twenty-First Century*, edited by Katrina Srigley, Stacey Zembrzycki, and Franca Iacovetta, 184–91. New York: Routledge, 2018.

Marten, James. "Childhood Studies and History: Catching a Culture in High Relief." In *The Children's Table: Childhood Studies and the Humanities*, edited by Anna Mae Duane, 52–67. Athens: University of Georgia Press, 2013.

Massey, Doreen. "Places and Their Pasts." *History Workshop Journal* 39 (1995): 182–92.

Mathieu, Sarah-Jane. *North of the Color Line: Migration and Black Resistance in Canada, 1870–1955*. Chapel Hill: University of North Carolina Press, 2010.

May, Elaine Tyler. *Homeward Bound: American Families in the Cold War Era*. New York: Basic Books, 1988.

McAllister, Kirsten Emiko. *Terrain of Memory: A Japanese Canadian Memorial Project*. Vancouver: UBC Press, 2010.

McElroy, Gil. *Cold Comfort: Growing up Cold War*. Vancouver: Talon Books, 2012.

McEnany, Laura. *Civil Defence Begins at Home: Militarization Meets Everyday Life in the Fifties*. Princeton: Princeton University Press, 2000.

McIlroy, Andrew. "No Interest, No Time, No Money: Civil Defence in Cleveland and the Cold War." *Ohio History* 106 (1997): 59–86.

McKercher, Asa, and Philip Van Huizen, eds. *Undiplomatic History: The New Study of Canada and the World*. Montreal and Kingston: McGill-Queen's University Press, 2019.

McLaughlin, Carly. "'They Don't Look Like Children': Child Asylum-Seekers, the Dubs Amendment and the Politics of Childhood." *Journal of Ethnic and Migration Studies* 44, no. 11 (2018): 1757–73.

McMahan, Darrin M. "Finding Joy in the History of Emotions." In *Doing Emotions History*, edited by Susan J. Matt and Peter N. Stearns, 103–19. Chicago: University of Illinois, 2014.

Mergen, Bernard. "Children and Nature in History." *Environmental History* 8, no. 4 (2003): 643–69.

Meyer, Jessica. *Men of War: Masculinity and the First World War in Britain*. London: Palgrave Macmillan, 2009.

Mieth, Friederike. "'What Is the Use of Talking-Talking?': Reflections on Talking, Silence, and Resilience in Sierra Leone." *Acta Academica* 47, no. 1 (2015): 38–59.

Millar, Anne, and Jeff Keshen. "Rallying Young Canada to the Cause: Anglophone Schoolchildren in Montreal and Toronto during the Two World Wars." *History of Intellectual Culture* 9, no. 1 (2010–11): 1–16.

Millei, Zsusa. "Temporalizing Childhood: A Conversation with Erica Burman, Stephanie Olsen, Spyros Spyrou, and Hanne Warming." *Journal of Childhood Studies* 46, no. 4 (December 2021): 59–73.

Miller, Elizabeth, Edward Little, and Steven High. *Going Public: The Art of Participatory Practice*. Vancouver: UBC Press, 2017.

Miller, Elizabeth, with Michelle Luchs and Gracia Dyer Jalea. *Mapping Memories: Participatory Media, Place-Based Stories & Refugee Youth*. Quebec: Marquis, 2011. http://mappingmemories.ca.

Miller, Elizabeth. "Going Places: Helping Youth with Refugee Experiences Take Their Stories Public." In *Oral History Off the Record: Toward an Ethnography of Practice*, edited by Anna Sheftel and Stacey Zembrzycki, 113–27. New York: Palgrave Macmillan, 2013.

Miller, J.R. *Shingwauk's Vision: A History of Residential Schools*. Toronto: University of Toronto Press, 1996.

Miller, Susan A. "Assent as Agency in the Early Years of the American Revolution." *Journal of the History of Childhood and Youth* 9, no. 1 (Winter 2016): 48–65.

Bibliography

Milloy, John S. *A National Crime: The Canadian Government and the Residential School System, 1870 to 1986*. Winnipeg: University of Manitoba Press, 1999.

Mmari, Kristin, Kathleen M. Roche, May Sudhinaraset, and Robert Blum. "When a Parent Goes Off to War: Exploring the Issues Faced by Adolescents and Their Families." *Youth and Society* 40, no. 4 (2009): 455–75.

Mochmann, Ingvill Constanze, Sabine Lee, and Barbara Stelzl-Marx. "The Children of the Occupations Born during the Second World War and Beyond – An Overview." *Historical Social Research* 34, no. 3 (2009): 263–82.

Mochman, Ingvill Constanze, and Sabine Lee. "The Human Rights of Children Born of War: Case Analyses of Past and Present Conflicts." *Historical Social Research* 35, no. 3 (2010): 268–98.

Moore, Aaron William. "From Individual Child to War Youth: The Construction of Collective Experience among Evacuated Japanese Children during World War II." *Japanese Studies* 36, no. 3 (2016): 339–60.

– "Reversing the Gaze: The Construction of 'Adulthood' in the Wartime Diaries of Japanese Children and Youth." In *Child's Play: Multi-Sensory Histories of Children and Childhood in Japan*, edited by Sabine Frühstück and Anne Walthall, 181–201. Oakland: University of California Press, 2017.

Moore, Robin. *Childhood's Domain: Play and Place in Child Development*. London: Croom Helm, 1986.

Morin-Pelletier, Mélanie. "'The Anxious Waiting Ones at Home': Deux familles canadiennes plongées dans le tourment de la grande guerre." *Histoire sociale/Social History* 47, no. 97 (June 2014): 353–68.

Moriyama, Raymond. *In Search of a Soul: Designing and Realizing the New Canadian War Museum*. Toronto: Douglas and McIntyre, 2006.

Morris, Amanda Sheffield, and Tolonda Ricard Age. "Adjustment among Youth in Military Families: The Protective Roles of Effortful Control and Maternal Social Support." *Journal of Applied Developmental Psychology* 30, no. 6 (2009): 695–707.

Morton, Desmond. "A Canadian Soldier in the Great War: The Experiences of Frank Maheux." *Canadian Military History* 1, no. 1 (1992): 79–89.

– *Fight or Pay: Soldier's Families and the Great War*. Vancouver: UBC Press, 2004.

Moruzi, Kristine. "'A Very Cruel Thing': Canadian Children, the First World War, and the Grain Grower's Guide." In *Children's Literature and Culture of the First World War*, edited by Lissa Paul, Rosemary Ross Johnston, and Emma Short, 214–25. New York: Routledge, 2016.

Moss, Mark. *Manliness and Militarism: Educating Young Boys in Ontario for War*. Oxford: Oxford University Press, 2001.

Mosse, George L. *Fallen Soldiers: Reshaping the Memory of the World Wars*. New York: Oxford University Press, 1990.

Musgrove, Nell, Carla Pascoe Leahy, and Kristine Moruzi. "Hearing Children's Voices: Conceptual and Methodological Challenges." In *Children's Voices from the Past: New Historical and Interdisciplinary Perspectives*, edited by Kristine Moruzi, Nell Musgrove, and Carla Pascoe Leahy, 1–25. Cham, Switzerland: Palgrave Macmillan, 2019.

Mushynsky, Julie. "Don't Talk about Your Fallout Shelter: Civilian Perceptions of Threat and Structural Responses during the Cold War in Regina, Saskatchewan between 1958 and 1963." *Canadian Military History* 28, no. 1 (2019): 1–35.

Myers, Tamara. *Caught: Montreal's Modern Girls and the Law, 1869–1945*. Toronto: University of Toronto Press, 2006.

Naftel, William D. *Halifax at War: Searchlights, Squadrons and Submarines, 1939–1945*. Halifax: Formac Publishing Company Limited, 2008.

Nasaw, David. *Children of the City at Work and at Play*. New York: Oxford University Press, 1985.

Nethery, Amy. "'A Modern-Day Concentration Camp': Using History to Make Sense of Australian Immigration Detention Centers." In *Does History Matter? Making and Debating Citizenship*, edited by Gwenda Tavan and Klaus Neumann, 65–80. Canberra: Australian National University Press, 2009.

Neumann, Klaus. *Across the Seas: Australia's Response to Refugees – A History*. Melbourne: Black Inc., 2015.

Neumann, Klaus, Sandra M. Gifford, Annika Lems, and Stefanie Scherr. "Refugee Settlement in Australia: Policy Scholarship and the Production of Knowledge, 1952–2013." *Journal of Intercultural Studies* 35, no. 1 (January 2014): 1–17.

Neuner, Frank, Anett Pfeiffer, Elisabeth Schauer-Kaiser, Michael Odenwald, Thomas Elbert, and Verena Ertl. "Haunted by Ghosts: Prevalence, Predictors and Outcomes of Spirit Possession Experiences among Former Child Soldiers and War-Affected Civilians in Northern Uganda." *Social Science and Medicine* 75, no. 3 (2012): 548–54.

Oikawa, Mona. *Cartographies of Violence: Japanese Canadian Women, Memory, and the Subject of Internment*. Toronto: University of Toronto Press, 2012.

Olsen, Stephanie. "Children's Emotional Formations in Britain, Canada, Australia and New Zealand, around the First World War." *Cultural and Social History* 17, no. 5 (2020): 643–58.

Olsen, Theodore, and Gordon Christiansen. *Thirty-One Hours: The Grindstone Experiment*. Toronto: Canadian Friends Service Committee, 1966.

Ong, Walter. "The Shifting Sensorium." In *The Varieties of Sensory Experience: A Sourcebook in the Anthropology of the Senses*, edited by David Howes, 47–60. Toronto: University of Toronto Press, 1991.

Opie, Iona, and Peter Opie. *Children's Games in Street and Playground*. Oxford: Clarendon Press, 1969.
– *The Lore and Language of Schoolchildren*. St Albans: Palatin, 1977.
Parkins, Wendy. "'Feeling for Beauty': Tactile Aesthetics and the Childhood of May Morris." *Senses and Society* 10, no. 1 (2015): 26–38.
Parr, Joy. "Notes for a More Sensuous History of Twentieth-Century Canada: The Timely, the Tacit, and the Material Body." *Canadian Historical Review* 82, no. 4 (2001): 720–45.
Pascoe, Carla. "City as Space, City as Place: Sources and the Urban Historian." *History Australia* 7, no. 2 (2010): 1–13.
Peacock, Margaret. *Innocent Weapons: The Soviet and American Politics of Childhood in the Cold War*. Chapel Hill: University of North Carolina Press, 2014.
Pearson, Geoffrey. "Canadian Institute for International Peace and Security." *McGill Journal of Education* 22, no. 3 (1987): 189–90.
Philo, Chris. "'The Corner-Stone of My World': Editorial Introduction to Special Issue on Spaces of Childhood." *Childhood* 7, no. 3 (2000): 243–56.
Philo, Chris, and Fiona M. Smith. "Political Geographies of Children and Young People." *Space and Polity* 7, no. 2 (2003): 99–115.
Pignot, Manon. *La Guerre des crayons: Quand les petits Parisiens dessinaient la Grande Guerre*. Paris: Parigramme Eds, 2004.
– *Allons enfants de la partie : Génération Grande Guerre*. Paris: Éditions du Seuil, 2012.
– "Children." In *The Cambridge History of the First World War, Volume III: Civil Society*, edited by Jay Winter, 29–45. Cambridge: Cambridge University Press, 2013.
– "French Boys and Girls in the Great War: Gender and the History of Children's Experience, 1904–18." In *Gender and the First World War*, edited by Christa Hämmerle, Oswald Überegger, and Birgitta Bader Zaar, 163–75. New York: Palgrave Macmillan, 2014.
– "Drawing the Great War: Children's Representations of War and Violence in France, Russia, and Germany." In *War and Childhood in the Era of the Two World Wars*, edited by Mischa Honeck and James Marten, 170–88. New York: Cambridge University Press, 2019.
Plum, Colette M. "Lost Childhoods in a New China: Child-Citizen-Workers at War, 1937–1945." *European Journal of East Asian Studies* 11, no. 2 (2012): 237–58.
Portelli, Alessandro. *The Battle of Valle Giulia: Oral History and the Art of Dialogue*. Madison: University of Wisconsin Press, 1997.
– *The Death of Luigi Trastulli and Other Stories*. Ithaca: SUNY Press, 1991.
Putnam, Lara. "Daily Life and Digital Reach: Place-based Research and History's Transnational Turn." In *Theorizing Fieldwork in the Humanities: Methods, Reflections, and Approaches to the Global South*, edited by Debra Castillo and Shalini Puri, 167–81. New York: Palgrave Macmillan, 2016.

Raddall, Thomas H. *Halifax – Warden of the North*. Toronto: Nimbus, 2007.

Ratković, Snežana. "Militarism, Motherhood, and Teaching: A Yugoslav Case." In *Gendered Militarism in Canada: Learning Conformity and Resistance*, edited by Nancy Taber, 147–72. Edmonton: University of Alberta, 2015.

Raynsford, William, and Jeanette Raynsford. *Silent Casualties: Veterans' Families in the Aftermath of the Great War*. Madoc: Merribrae Press, 1986.

Reddy, William. *The Navigation of Feeling: A Framework for the History of Emotions*. New York: Cambridge University Press, 2001.

Reed, Sarah C., Janice F. Bell, and Todd C. Edwards. "Adolescent Well-Being in Washington State Military Families." *American Journal of Public Health* 101, no. 9 (2011): 1676–82.

Reilly, Frances. "Operation Lifesaver: Canadian Atomic War Culture and Cold War Civil Defence." *Past Imperfect* 14 (2008): 46–85.

Richardson, Amy, Anita Chandra, Laurie T. Martin, Claude Messan Setodji, Bryan W. Hallmark, Nancy F. Campbell, Stacy Hawkins, and Patrick Grady. *Effects of Soldiers' Deployment on Children's Academic Performance and Behavioral Health*. Santa Monica, CA: Rand Corporation, 2011.

Robson, Karen, Patrizia Albanese, Deborah Harrison, and Chris Sanders. "School Engagement Among Youth in Canadian Forces Families: A Comparative Analysis." *Alberta Journal of Educational Research* 59, no. 3 (2013): 363–81.

Rodaway, Paul. *Sensuous Geographies: Body, Sense, and Place*. London: Routledge, 1994.

Roith, Christian. *Memory and Critique: Essays on the History of Education and School in Spain and Germany*. Almeria: Editorial Universidad de Almeria, 2015. http://www.ual.es/~chroith/pdf/CDCW.pdf.

Roper, Michael. "Re-membering the Soldier Hero: the Psychic and Social Construction of Memory in Personal Narratives of the Great War." *History Workshop Journal* 50 (autumn 2000): 181–204.

– *The Secret Battle: Emotional Survival in the Great War*. Manchester: Manchester University Press, 2009.

– "Slipping Out of View: Subjectivity and Emotion in Gender History." *History Workshop Journal* 59, no. 1 (2005): 57–72.

Rose, Jacqueline. *The Case of Peter Pan, or The Impossibility of Children's Fiction*. London: Macmillan, 1984.

Ross, Ellen. "'The Country of Fathers' – Review of Julie-Marie Strange's *Fatherhood and the British Working Class, 1865–1914*." *History Workshop Journal* 84 (2017): 265–72.

Rotundo, E. Anthony. "Boy Culture." In *The Children's Culture Reader*, edited by Henry Jenkins, 337–62. New York: New York University Press, 1988.

Rutherdale, Robert. "Just Nostalgic Family Men? Off-the-Job Family Time, Providing, and Oral Histories of Fatherhood in Post-War Canada, 1945–1975." *Oral History Forum* 29 (2009), Special Issue: Remembering Family, Analyzing Home: Oral History and the Family, http://www.oralhistoryforum.ca/index.php/ohf/article/view/248/323.

– "New 'Faces' for Father: Memory, Life-Writing, and Fathers as Providers in the Postwar Consumer Era." In *Creating Postwar Canada: Community, Diversity, and Dissent, 1945–1975*, edited by Magda Fahrni and Robert Rutherdale, 241–67. Vancouver: UBC Press, 2008.

– "Three Faces of Fatherhood as a Masculine Category: Tyrants, Teachers, and Workaholics as 'Responsible Family Men' during Canada's Baby Boom." In *What Is Masculinity? Historical Dynamics from Antiquity to the Contemporary World*, edited by John H. Arnold and Sean Brady, 323–48. New York: Palgrave Macmillan, 2011.

Sarty, Roger. "Admiral Kingsmill and the Early Years of the Royal Canadian Navy." *Canadian Military History* 19, no. 1 (2015): 75–80.

Sangster, Joan. *Transforming Labour: Women and Work in Postwar Canada*. Toronto: University of Toronto Press, 2010.

Schneider, David M. *A Critique of the Study of Kinship*. Ann Arbor: University of Michigan Press, 1984.

Scholz, Joachim, and Kathrin Berdelmann. "The Quotidianisation of the War in Everyday Life at German Schools during the First World War." *Paedagogica Historica* 52, nos 1/2 (2016): 92–103.

Scott, Joan W. "After History?" In *Schools of Thought: Twenty-Five Years of Interpretive Social Science*, edited by Joan W. Scott and Debra Keates, 85–103. Princeton: Princeton University Press, 2001.

– "The Evidence of Experience." *Critical Inquiry* 17, no. 4 (Summer 1991): 773–97.

– "Storytelling." *History and Theory* 50, no. 2 (May 2011): 203–9.

Seiffge-Krenke, Inge. "Adaptive and Maladaptive Coping Styles: Does Intervention Change Anything?" *European Journal of Developmental Psychology* 1, no. 4 (2004): 367–82.

Shalhoub-Kevorkian, Nadera. "Negotiating the Present, Historicizing the Future: Palestinian Children Speak about the Israeli Separation Wall." *American Behavioral Scientist* 49, no. 8 (April 2006): 1101–24.

Shanahan, Fiona, and Angela Veale. "How Mothers Mediate the Social Integration of Their Children Conceived of Forced Marriage within the Lord's Resistance Army." *Child Abuse and Neglect* 51 (2016): 72–86.

Sheftel, Anna, and Stacey Zembrzycki. "'We Started Over Again, We Were Young': Postwar Social Worlds of Child Holocaust Survivors in Montreal." *Urban History Review / Revue d'Histoire Urbaine* 39, no. 1 (Fall 2010): 20–30.

Siepmann, Eckhard, ed. *Kind und Kunst: Zur Geschichte des Zeichen- und Kunstunterrichts*. Berlin: BDK, 1976.

Silverstein, Jordana. "'Because We All Love Our Country': Refugee and Asylum-Seeking Children, Australian Policy-Makers, and the Building of National Sentiment." *Australian Journal of Politics & History* 65, no. 4 (December 2019): 532–48.

Singer, Eric. "Civil Defence in the City: Federal Policy Meets Local Resistance in Baltimore, 1957–1964." *Urban History* 42, no. 4 (2015): 547–63.

Skomorovsky, Alla, and Amanda Bullock. "Children's Positive Experiences Growing Up in Canadian Military Households." *Journal of Military, Veteran, and Family Health* 2, no. 2 (2017): 21–6.

– "The Impact of Deployment on Children from Canadian Military Families." *Armed Forces and Society* 43, no. 4 (2017): 654–73.

Sleight, Simon. *Young People and the Shaping of Public Space in Melbourne, 1870–1914*. Surrey: Ashgate, 2013.

Small, Stephen A. "Action-Oriented Research: Models and Methods." *Journal of Marriage and Family* 57, no. 4 (1995): 941–55.

Smith, Mark M. "Producing Sense, Consuming Sense, Making Sense: Perils and Prospects for Sensory History." *Journal of Social History* 40, no. 1 (2007): 841–58.

– *Sensing the Past: Seeing, Hearing, Smelling, Tasting, and Touching History*. Berkeley: University of California Press, 2001.

– *The Smell of Battle, the Taste of Siege: A Sensory History of the Civil War*. New York: Oxford University Press, 2015.

Spyrou, Spyros. "Troubling Children's Voices in Research." In *Reconceptualising Agency and Childhood: New Perspectives in Childhood Studies*, edited by Florian Esser, Meike S. Baader, Tanja Betz, and Beatrice Hungerland, 105–18. New York: Routledge, 2016.

– *Disclosing Childhoods: Research and Knowledge Production for a Critical Childhood Studies*. Houndsmills, Basingstoke: Palgrave Macmillan, 2018.

Srigley, Katrina, Stacey Zembrzycki, and Franca Iacovetta, eds. *Beyond Women's Words: Feminisms and the Practices of Oral History in the Twenty-First Century*. New York: Routledge, 2018.

Stanger-Ross, Jordan, and Pamela Sugiman, eds. *Witness to Loss: Race, Culpability, and Memory in the Dispossession of Japanese Canadians*. Montreal and Kingston: McGill-Queen's University Press, 2017.

Stargardt, Nicholas. "Children's Art of the Holocaust." *Past and Present* 161, no. 1 (1998): 191–235.

– "Drawing the Holocaust in 1945." *Holocaust Studies* 11, no. 2 (2005): 25–37.

– "Moments of Rupture: The Subjectivity of Children in the Second World War." In

Children and War: Past and Present, edited by Helga Embacher, Grazia Prontera, Albert Lichtblau, Johannes-Dieter Steinert, Wolfgang Aschauer, Darak Galasinski, and John Buckley, 37–56. Solihull, West Midlands: Helion, 2013.

– *Witnesses of War: Children's Lives under the Nazis*. New York: Vintage Books, 2005.

Stearns, Peter. *American Fear: The Causes and Consequences of High Anxiety*. New York: Routledge, 2006.

– "Fear and Contemporary History." *Journal of Social History* 40, no. 2 (2006): 477–84.

Stearns, Peter, and Carol Stearns. "Emotionology: Clarifying the History of Emotions and Emotional Standards." *American Historical Review* 90, no. 4 (October 1985): 813–36.

Stekl, Hannes, Christa Hämmerle, and Ernst Bruckmüller, eds. *Kindheit und Schule im Ersten Weltkrieg*. Vienna: New Academic Press, 2015.

Stevens, Peter. "Cars and Cottages: The Automotive Transformation of Ontario's Summer Home Tradition." *Ontario History* 100, no. 1 (2008): 26–56.

Steward, Jill, and Alexander Cowan. "Introduction." In *The City and the Senses: Urban Culture Since 1500*, edited by Alexander Cowan and Jill Steward, 1–24. London: Ashgate, 2007.

Stivens, Maila. "Gendering Cosmopolitanisms: Hospitality and the Asylum Seeker Other." *Women's Studies International Forum* 67 (2018): 85–93.

Strauss, Anselm, and Juliet Corbin. *Basics of Qualitative Research: Grounded Theory Procedures and Techniques*. Newbury Park: Sage Publications, 1990.

Sugiman, Pamela. "'Life Is Sweet': Vulnerability and Composure in the Wartime Narratives of Japanese Canadians." *Journal of Canadian Studies/Revue d'études canadiennes* 43, no. 1 (winter 2009): 186–218.

– "Memories of Internment: Narrating Japanese Canadian Women's Life Stories." *Canadian Journal of Sociology* 39, no. 3 (2004): 359–88.

– "'These Feelings That Fill My Heart': Japanese Canadian Women's Memories of Internment." *Oral History* 35, no. 2 (2006): 69–84.

Sui, Daniel. "Visuality, Aurality, and Shifting Metaphors of Geographical Thought in the Late Twentieth Century." *Annals of the Association of American Geographers* 90, no. 2 (2000): 322–43.

Suleiman, Susan Rubin. "The 1.5 Generation: Thinking about Child Survivors and the Holocaust." *American Imago* 59, no. 3 (2002): 277–95.

Summerfield, Penny. *Reconstructing Women's Wartime Lives: Discourse and Subjectivity in Oral Histories of the Second World War*. Manchester: Manchester University Press, 1998.

– "Culture and Composure: Creating Narratives of the Gendered Self in Oral History Interviews." *Cultural and Social History* 1, no. 1 (2004): 65–93.

Sutherland, Neil. *Growing Up: Childhood in English Canada from the Great War to the Age of Television*. Toronto: University of Toronto Press, 1997.

Sznajderman, Michael. "A Dangerous Business: Children on the Front Lines." *Alabama Heritage* 70 (Fall 2003): 26–35.

Taber, Nancy. "Introduction: Learning, Gender, and Militarism." In *Gendered Militarism in Canada: Learning Conformity and Resistance*, edited by Nancy Taber, xv–xxviii. Edmonton: University of Alberta Press, 2016.

Tebbutt, Melanie. *Being Boys: Youth, Leisure and Identity in the Inter-War Years*. Manchester: Manchester University Press, 2012.

Thomas, Glyn, and Angèle Silk. *An Introduction to the Psychology of Children's Drawings*. New York: New York University Press, 1990.

Thomson, Alistair. *Anzac Memories: Living with the Legend*. Melbourne: Oxford University Press, 1994.

Thompson, David E., Joyce Baptist, Bryant Miller, and Una Henry. "Children of the US National Guard: Making Meaning and Responding to Parental Deployment." *Youth and Society* 49, no. 8 (2017): 1–17.

Thompson, Matthew. *Lost Freedom: The Landscape of the Child and the British Post-War Settlement*. Oxford: Oxford University Press, 2014.

Thrift, Nigel J. "With Child to See Any Strange Thing: Everyday Life in the City." In *A Companion to the City*, edited by Gary Bridge and Sophie Watson, 398–409. New York: Blackwell, 2000.

Ticktin, Miriam. "A World without Innocence." *American Ethnologist* 44, no. 4 (2017): 577–90.

Titmuss, Richard Morris. *Problems of Social Policy*. London: Kraus Reprint, 1976.

Tomsic, Mary. "Children's Art: Histories and Cultural Meanings of Creative Expression by Displaced Children." In *Children's Voices from the Past: New Historical and Interdisciplinary Perspectives*, edited by Kristine Moruzi, Nell Musgrove, and Carla Pascoe Leahy, 137–58. Cham, Switzerland: Palgrave Macmillan, 2019.

Tonkiss, Fran. "Aural Postcards: Sound, Memory and the City." In *The Auditory Culture Reader*, edited by Michael Bull and Les Back, 303–9. Oxford: Berg, 2003.

Tonkiss, Fran. *Space, the City and Social Theory: Social Relations and Urban Forms*. Cambridge: Polity Press, 2005.

Trepanier, James. "Building Boys, Building Canada: The Boy Scout Movement in Canada, 1908–1970." PhD diss., York University, 2015.

Truth and Reconciliation Commission of Canada. *Honouring the Truth, Reconciling for the Future: Summary of the Final Report of the Truth and Reconciliation Commission of Canada*. Winnipeg: Truth and Reconciliation Commission of Canada, 2015.

Tuan, Yi-Fu. *Topophilia: A Study of Environmental Perception, Attitudes, and Values*. Englewood Cliffs: Prentice-Hall, 1974.

Tuneu, Núria Padrós, Isabel Carrillo Flores, Josep Casanovas Prat, Pilar Prat Viñolas, Antoni Tort Bardolet, and Anna Gómez Mundó. "The Spanish Civil War as Seen through Children's Drawings of the Time." *Paedagogica Historica* 51, no. 4 (2015): 478–95.

Tuttle, William M. *"Daddy's Gone to War": The Second World War in the Lives of America's Children*. New York: Oxford University Press, 1993.

Urry, John. "City Life and the Senses." In *A Companion to the City*, edited by Gary Bridge and Sophie Watson, 388–97. New York: Blackwell, 2000.

Vallgårda, Karen, Kristine Alexander, and Stephanie Olsen. "Emotions and the Global Politics of Childhood." In *Childhood, Youth and Emotions in Modern History: National, Colonial and Global Perspectives*, edited by Stephanie Olsen, 12–34. New York: Palgrave Macmillan, 2015.

Vallgårda, Karen, and Katrine Rønsig Larsen. "Emotional Echoes: Young People, Divorce, and the Public Media, 1960–2000." *Journal of Social History* 55, no. 2 (Fall 2021): 226–53.

Volavkova, Hana, ed. *I Never Saw Another Butterfly: Children's Drawings and Poems from Terezin Concentration Camp 1942–44*. New York: Schocken Books, 1993.

Wall, John. *Children's Rights: Today's Global Challenge*. Lanham: Rowman and Littlefield, 2017.

Wall, Sharon. *The Nurture of Nature: Childhood, Antimodernism, and Ontario Summer Camps, 1920–1955*. Vancouver: UBC Press, 2009.

Ward, Colin. *The Child in the City*. London: Bedford Square Press, 1990.

Way, Niobe. *Deep Secrets: Boys, Friendships, and the Crisis of Connection*. Cambridge: Harvard University Press, 2011.

Weiner, Gaby. "Critical Action Research and Third Wave Feminism: A Meeting of Paradigms." *Educational Action Research* 12, no. 4 (2004): 631–44.

Welshman, John. *Churchill's Children: The Evacuation Experience in Wartime Britain*. Oxford: Oxford University Press, 2010.

Wertsch, Mary Edwards. *Military Brats: Legacies of Childhood Inside the Fortress*. St Louis: Brightwell, 2006.

Westerink, Jan, and Leah Giarratano. "The Impact of Posttraumatic Stress Disorder on Partners and Children of Australian Vietnam Veterans." *Australian and New Zealand Journal of Psychiatry* 33, no. 6 (1999): 841–7.

White, Jay. "Conscripted City: Halifax and the Second World War." PhD diss., McMaster University, 1994.

Wienstein, Laurie, and Christie C. White, eds. *Wives and Warriors: Women in the Military in the United States and Canada*. Westport: Bergen and Garvey, 1997.

Williams, Frances. *The Forgotten Kindertransportees: The Scottish Experience*. London: Bloomsbury, 2014.

Williams, Terry Tempest. *Refuge: An Unnatural History of Family and Place*. New York: Pantheon Books, 1991.

Williamson, Mary, and Tom Sharp, eds. *Just a Larger Family*. Waterloo: Wilfrid Laurier University Press, 2011.

Wittmann, Barbara. *Bedeutungsvolle Kritzeleien*. Zürich: Diaphanes, 2018.

Wittner, Lawrence. *Toward Nuclear Abolition: A History of the World Nuclear Disarmament Movement, 1971 to the Present*. Stanford: Stanford University Press, 2003.

Wolfe, Patrick. "Settler Colonialism and the Elimination of the Native." *Journal of Genocide Research* 8, no. 4 (2006): 387–409.

Woolford, Andrew. *This Benevolent Experiment: Indigenous Boarding Schools, Genocide, and Redress in Canada and the United States*. Lincoln: University of Nebraska Press, 2015.

Zahra, Tara. *The Lost Children: Reconstructing Europe's Families after World War II*. Cambridge, MA: Harvard University Press, 2011.

Zerubavel, Eviatar. *Time Maps: Collective Memory and the Social Shape of the Past*. Chicago: University of Chicago Press, 2003.

Ziino, Bart. *A Distant Grief: Australians, War Graves, and the Great War*. Crawley: University of Western Australia Press, 2006.

– "'They Seem to Understand All about the War': Australian Children and the First World War." *Journal of the History of Childhood and Youth* 11, no. 2 (spring 2018): 227–47.

Zunino, Bérénice. *Die Mobilmachung der Kinder im Ersten Weltkrieg: Kriegskultur und illustrierte Kriegskinderliteratur im Deutschen Kaiserreich, 1911–1918*. Berlin: Peter Lang, 2019.

Contributors

PATRIZIA ALBANESE, PhD, is associate dean, Research and Graduate Studies, and professor of sociology at Toronto Metropolitan University. She is co-editor of *Reading Sociology: Decolonizing Canada* (Oxford University Press) and numerous other titles. Her work focuses on policies affecting children, youth, and families. She is lead researcher on a Women and Gender Equality (WAGE) grant on the post-pandemic economic recovery of women in Toronto.

KRISTINE ALEXANDER, PhD, is Canada Research Chair in Child and Youth Studies, associate professor of history, and co-director of the Institute for Child and Youth Studies at the University of Lethbridge. She is the author of the award-winning book *Guiding Modern Girls: Girlhood, Empire, and Internationalism in the 1920s and 1930s* (UBC Press) and co-editor of *A Cultural History of Youth in the Modern Age* (Bloomsbury). Her current SSHRC-funded research investigates the centrality of age categories to modern race-making and the consolidation of the Canadian settler state.

TARAH BROOKFIELD, PhD, is an associate professor of history and youth and children studies at Wilfrid Laurier University's Brantford campus. She is the author of *Cold War Comforts: Canadian Women, Child Safety, and Global Insecurity* (WLU Press) and the award-winning *Our Voices Must Be Heard: Women and the Vote in Ontario* (UBC Press). Her chapter in this collection arises from her SSHRC-funded research, Experiments in Peace: Activism and Education on Grindstone Island.

ANDREW BURTCH, PhD, has been the historian, post-1945, at the Canadian War Museum since 2006. He obtained his doctorate in history from Carleton University in

2009. His first book, *Give Me Shelter: The Failure of Canada's Cold War Civil Defence*, published by UBC Press, received the C.P. Stacey Prize for the best work of military history in Canada in 2012. At the Canadian War Museum, he has been responsible for temporary, travelling, and long-term exhibitions about the Cold War, United Nations peacekeeping, war and military medicine, war and games, contemporary conflicts, and the Afghanistan War. He is an adjunct research professor with Carleton University's Department of History.

ISABEL CAMPBELL, PhD, is a senior historian at the Directorate of History and Heritage, National Defence Headquarters, in Ottawa, Canada. Author of *Unlikely Diplomats: The Canadian Brigade in Germany, 1951–1964*, she has published on archival standards, declassification, the Cold War, service families, and gender, as well as alliance strategy, oceanographic research, and intelligence history. She is a senior fellow at the Bill Graham Centre in Toronto, Ontario, and an adjunct research professor in Carleton University's Department of History in Ottawa, and she is co-authoring two official operational histories.

MYRIAM DENOV, PhD, is a full professor at McGill University and holds the Canada Research Chair in Children, Families and Armed Conflict. Her research interests lie in the areas of children and families affected by war, migration, and its intergenerational impact. She is the author of *Child Soldiers: Sierra Leone's Revolutionary United Front* (Cambridge University Press) and the co-editor of *Children Affected by Armed Conflict: Theory, Method & Practice* (Columbia University Press). Her current research is exploring the realities of children born of conflict-related sexual violence. She is the recipient of the 2020 SSHRC Impact Award and the Killam Research Fellowship.

CLAIRE HALSTEAD earned her PhD from Western University in 2015 and her master's from the University of Kent in 2011. Her doctoral dissertation focused on British children who were evacuated to Canada in the Second World War. She is also the creator of the British Child Evacuee database and HExD, the Halifax Explosion database.

DEBORAH HARRISON, PhD, is professor (retired) and adjunct professor of sociology at the University of New Brunswick. She is first author of *No Life Like It: Military Wives in Canada* (Toronto: James Lorimer, 1994), *The First Casualty: Violence against Women in Canadian Military Communities* (Toronto: James Lorimer, 2002), and *Growing Up in Armyville: Canada's Military Families during the Afghanistan Mission* (Waterloo: Wilfrid Laurier University Press, 2016). She was a member of the Canadian Forces Advisory

Council to Veterans Affairs Canada and has appeared as an expert witness for the Ontario Superior Court of Justice and the Federal Court of Canada, on matters related to military culture and the Canadian Forces Superannuation Act.

ASHLEY HENRICKSON, MA, is the director of outreach and partnerships at Know History, Canada's largest historical research firm. She previously oversaw educational programing at the Galt Museum and Archives. Her graduate research, with Dr Alexander, focused on the experiences of Canadian children whose fathers or brothers served overseas during the First World War. Ashley was awarded the Medal of Merit for her master of arts at the University of Lethbridge.

CAROLYN KAY, PhD, is a full professor of modern German history at Trent University and the recipient of an OCUFA Teaching Award for outstanding university teaching (2007). Her publications include "German Children's Art during World War I," in *Global Studies of Childhood* (2021); "War Pedagogy in the German Primary School Classroom during World War One," *War and Society* (2014); and the book *Art and the German Bourgeoisie: Alfred Lichtwark and Modern Painting in Hamburg, 1886–1914* (2002). In addition, she has published articles on the history of German childhood in Imperial Germany. She is currently at work on a book on the arts education of German children from 1871 to 1918, focusing upon school drawings of the First World War.

BARBARA LORENZKOWSKI, PhD, is associate professor of history at Concordia University in Montreal and a member of Concordia's Centre for Oral History and Digital Storytelling. She is the author of *Sounds of Ethnicity: Listening to German North America* (University of Manitoba Press, 2010) and has published on the history of migration, transnationalism and national identity, and the history of childhood and gender. Her current research is a large-scale oral history project on children's sensuous and emotional life-worlds in Atlantic Canada during the Second World War.

ELIZABETH (LIZ) MILLER, MFA, is a filmmaker and a full professor in communication studies at Concordia University. Her multiplatform collaborative documentary projects on timely issues such as refugee rights, water privatization, and environmental justice have won awards and influenced decision makers. She is the co-author of "Going Public: The Art of Participatory Practice" (2017) and has written book chapters and articles on co-creation, environmental media, and place-based pedagogies. Her most recent project, Wastescapes, incorporates augmented reality, cycling tours, and educational resources.

MARY TOMSIC, PhD, is research fellow in the Institute for Humanities and Social Sciences at Australian Catholic University. She is a cultural historian whose current research examines visual representations of child refugees, children's voices in literature, and refugee boat journeys. Her work has been published in edited collections including *Visualising Human Rights* (UWA Publishing, 2018) and *Children's Voices in the Past: New Historical Perspectives* (Palgrave Macmillan, 2019) and in journals including *Historical Journal* and *British Educational Research Journal*. She is the author of *Beyond the Silver Screen: A History of Women, Filmmaking and Film Culture in Australia 1920–1990* (Melbourne University Press, 2017).

Index

Page numbers in italics indicate references to illustrative material.

Acholi people, 211, 215–16, 217
activism (antinuclear) by youth, 95, 111, 112–14
adolescents: ambiguous loss theory, 192–3; CAF adolescents and civilian youth defined, 190–1; and Canada's Afghanistan mission, 14, 189–202; chronological age, 15; emotions, 192–3, 196, 198–9; impact of deployment in Afghanistan, 189, 190–1, 193–8, 200, 201–2; isolation problems and support, 193–4, 195, 198–9; peer support groups, 200, 201–2; research findings and recommendations on deployment, 200–2; schools in lives of, 201; self-censorship, 197
adventure playground, 74
Afghanistan mission of Canada: ambiguous loss theory, 192–3; Canadian adolescents during, 14, 189–202; deployments, 189, 190; deployment's impact on adolescents, 189, 190–1, 193–8, 200, 201–2; emergency response team, 190; emotions in adolescents, 192–3, 196, 198–9; impact on families of military, 189, 195–7; mental health issues in CAF members, 198–9, 201–2; and PTSD, 190, 198–200; research findings and recommendations on deployment, 200–2; research methodology and definitions, 190–3; withdrawal of troops, 200
Afghanistan war (2001–14), 14, 189
Allen, Frederick, 73, 74
All I Remember (documentary), 302
All the Way Home (picture book), 308, 309, 310
ambiguous loss theory/paradigm, 128, 192–3, 199

Armyville (Canada, a pseudonym): and deployment to Afghanistan, 190; research findings and recommendations, 200–2
Armyville High School (AHS), 190–1, 199–200
Armyville School District (ASD), 190, 200
art by children. *See* drawings by children
art in German schools: classes in First World War, 37–41; voice of children in, 35–6, 37
art(s) education movement in Germany ("Kunsterziehungsbewegung"), 35–6, 37–8, 40
Ashwin, Clive, 38
asylum seekers (to Australia): children as archetypal figures of innocence, 225–6; debate in Australia, 224; detention facilities and policy, 227–8; drawings collection, 224–5, 226, 231–3, 234–5, 236, 240, 241; drawings, examples, 225, 229, 230, 231, 232, 233, 238; drawings, use and exhibitions, 230–1; identification number, 230–1; journey to Australia, 228–9; number and countries of origin, 228; and refugee policy, 226–7; school for, 229–30, 230. *See also* immigration detention
atomic bomb and attack. *See* nuclear war
"Atomic Generation," 180
Audoin-Rouzeau, Stéphane, 7, 34
Australia: debate on asylum seekers, 224; exhibitions and use of drawings, 230–1; humanness in detention, 236–7; immigration detention camps, 227–8; journey to for asylum seekers, 228–9; politics and emotion in drawings by children in immigration detention, 224–41; storytelling project of refugees, 255–6, 308–11. *See also* asylum seekers
Australian Human Rights Commission (AHRC):

impact of immigration detention, 224; inquiry into children in immigration detention centres, 224, 233–4, 240–1; submissions to inquiry, 234, 240–1
Australian Human Rights Commission (AHRC) and drawings of children: circulation of drawings, 239–41; collection of, 224–5, 226, 231–3, 234–5, 236, 240, 241; confinement representation, 225, 236, 237–9, *238*; examples of, *225*, *229*, *230*, *231*, *232*, *233*, *238*; focus on people in, 236–7; people detained versus others in, 236, 239; political expression in, 236–9, 240, 241
Austria: education during First World War, 34, 58; exhibition of children's work, 37
Austrian National Library, as source of drawings, 36

Baby Tooth Survey, 109–10
Bade, Wilhelm, 48, *49*, 50
Barman, Jean, 251
Becker, Annette, 7
Bedford Basin convoys, 63, *68*, 68–9
Bedford Magazine Explosion (1945), 65, 78–87
Berdelmann, Kathrin, 35
Bernhardt, Minna, *55*
Bernstein, Robin, 16
Bertell, Rosalie, 113
Biess, Frank, 94, 95, 107–8, 109
Bischoff, Frieda, 46, *47*, 48
Boddice, Rob, 9
Boeschoten, Riki Van, 19–20
Bohm-Schuch, Clara, 35
Bolt, Andrew, 240
Bosnia, mines in, 295, 297
Bosnian children, drawings of, 253–4, 294–5, *296–7*, 297–8, *298*
Boss, Pauline, 128, 192–3
Bostelmann, Ella, *54*
Boyden, Jo, 18
Boy Scouts of Canada, and civil defence preparation, 102, 110
Britain, evacuees in Second World War, 170–1, 251–2, 266–7
Brook, Irene, 126, 261
Brook, Isabelle, correspondence, 126, 127–8, 129, 130, 132, 133–4, 135, 261
Brook, Sidney: correspondence, 124, 126, 127–9, 130, 132, 133, 261; correspondence with family in England, 251; description as soldier, 124, 126

Brook children (Gordon, Arnott, Lorne, Glen, and Alice), correspondence, 126, 127–8, 129, 130, 132–4, *260*, 261, *262*, 262–3, *263*, *264*
Brook Family Fonds, 261
Burmeister, Emma, *47*, 48

Cable, Catherine, 72, 79, 82, 84–5
CAF (Canadian Armed Forces) in Afghanistan: description of mission, 189; impact of deployment on students, 190–1; mental health issues, 198–9, 201–2; research findings and recommendations, 200–2; research methodology and definitions, 190–3; research projects on spouses and adolescents, 189–90
Caldicott, Helen, 113
Camp Neekaunis, 179
Canada, as colonial state, 5. *See also* federal government of Canada; *specific topics*
Canadian Friends Service Committee (CFSC): and Grindstone Island, 171–2, 183
Canadian Patriotic Fund, 131, 132
Canadian War Museum, 4, 258–9, *259*
Carpenter, Alison, 113–14
Carwell, David B., 64
Casey, Edward, 67
Cave, Patricia, 269
CBC recording of Halifax sounds, 72
cen, in northern Uganda, 211–12
Certeau, Michel de, 64, 283
Chandra, Anita, and colleagues, 193
Chedabucto (ship), 69, 71
"child-centred reading" of sources generated by adults, 96, 128
children born in captivity (CBC), 208–21, 22. *See also* children born of wartime rape
children born of wartime rape: belonging and stigmatization, 213–15, 216–17, 221; coping and resistance strategies, 217–21; experiences of, 13, 206–7, 208–12; health problems, 209–10; hopes for the future, 216, 220–1; identity of, 212–13, 214–15, 217; knowledge of origins, 212–13; land inheritance or ownership, 215–16; own uncertain futures, 16; participants in research, 208–10; post-war experiences, 206–7, 208; psychological and psycho-social impacts, 208, 210–11, 212; research description and ethics, 208; return to civilian life, 209, 212; sensitization of community, 221; "spirit-related" illnesses, 211–12; stereotypes challenged by, 219–21. *See also* northern Uganda

Index

Children in the World War (Bohm-Schuch), 35
children's art. *See* drawings by children
Children's Overseas Reception Board (CORB), 267, 268
Christiansen parents (Gordon and Mary) and siblings (Steve, Scott, Roger, and Cori), 175, 176, 177, 178–9
chronological age, 15, 287
Chuol, Nyater, 310
City of Benares (ship), 268
Civil Defence Canada: Girl Guides in civil defence planning, 102–3; manual for civil defence, 98; and thermonuclear weapons, 104–5
Civil Defence in Schools (1952), 98
civil defence planning in Canada: Boy Scouts and Girl Guides in, 102–3, 110; "child-centred reading" of letters, 96; as emergency preparedness, 110; emotions and emotional scripts in, 94–5, 96, 114; families' role in, 105–6, 111; film for drills, 99; preparation for and education in, 97–9, 101–2; protection of children, 94; provinces in, 99, 101–2; resistance from children, 103; risks of nuclear war, 94, 95; "self-help" vision of attack, 96–7; as source of information, 95; and thermonuclear weapons, 104–5; voice of children in, 96, 103, 107–9, 111, 114–15
Civil Service Civil Defence corps, 93
Čižek, Franz, 33
Clare Lilley (ammunition ship), 77
Claxton, Brooke, 142
Clifford, Rebecca, 21
Cold War era: bomb race and atomic anxiety, 104–5, 110; decline in tensions, 110; drill of 1953 in Ottawa, 93; and emotions, 94–5, 96; "ideal child" in, 96; lives of families of military, 141, 142–3, 144–6, 147–8; politics of children, 18; risks of nuclear war, 94; social values and norms, 15; view of children in, 95–6. *See also* civil defence planning in Canada; nuclear war
communities of memory: as analytical strand in book, 7, 19–21; children and youth in, 19–21; intergenerational aspects, 20 *See also* oral history
community, in civil defence planning, 97
confinement, representation in drawings, 225, 236, 237–9, 238
conflict-related sexual violence. *See* children born of wartime rape
Conquergood, Dwight, 6

Convention on the Rights of the Child (1989), 10, 234
correspondence: absence and loss of father, 128–30, 134, 135, 260; in archives and collections, 123; case studies description, 124–7; and censorship, 123; conventions and formulas in, 252, 262; dependence on, 251; emotions in, 12, 126, 134–7; empathic inference for, 128; and empire, 251; of evacuees, 266–80; handling by children, 130; health and illnesses of children in, 127–8; importance on home front, 258; as insights on children of soldiers, 123, 124; letter-writing by children, 260–1; as practice and duty of children, 258; as primary sources, 250; production, 123; as social space, 12; of soldiers and children in First World War, 121–37; survival and preservation, 123, 124; use by and usefulness to historians, 123–4; value, 263; wages and money as issue, 131–2, 134; wives and mothers in, 131; writing skills of children, 260. *See also specific individuals*
counterculture of 1960s and 1970s, 180
Crowell, Carolyn, 79
Cruikshank, Julie, 77
Cuban Missile Crisis, 108, 109
"culture de guerre." *See* war culture
Curtis, W.A., 142, 143

Daigle Hau, Caralee, 108
Danforth, Loring M., 19–20
Dartmouth (Nova Scotia), and Bedford Magazine Explosion, 80, 81, 84
Dawson, Graham, 21
Day After, The (film), 111–12
Demm, Eberhard, 37
Dempsey, Gerald, 76, 77
Department of National Defence: preparations for nuclear attack, 97
deployment of parents: and ambiguous loss theory, 192–3; impact on adolescents, 189, 190–1, 193–8, 200, 201–2; impact on families of military, 189, 195–7; with or without family, 142–3; peer support groups, 200, 201–2; research findings and recommendations for adolescents, 200–2
DePoe, David, 181
detention. *See* immigration detention
Dewan, Pauline, 169
Dicker-Brandeis, Friedl, 253
Dickie, Robert, 74

Dieckmann, Martha, 45–6, *46*
disarmament campaign in nuclear era, 95, 110–11, 113–14
Dodd, Lindsey, 11, 66, 85, 254
Dolto, Françoise, 9
Donkeys Can't Fly on Planes (picture book), 255, 308–10, *311*
Donson, Andrew, 33, 58
Douglas, Tommy, 101
drawings by children: and AHRC (*see* Australian Human Rights Commission and drawings of children); analysis and views on, 43–4; by Bosnian children, 253–4, 294–5, 297–8; and children as witnesses, 253–4; collections of, 252–3; desires in, 45; as evacuees, 276, *277*–*9*, *278*; focus on people in, 236–7; gender differences in, 40–1; in Germany in First World War (*see* Germany, drawings by children); and innocence of children, 225–6; interpretation, 253; media representation, 239–40; political expression in, 235–9, 240, 241; politics and emotion in immigration detention, 224–41; tears in, *225*, 237, *238*; voice of children in, 35–6, 226, 235, 241
"duck and cover" drills, 98–9
Dudziak, Mary, 13, 22

Edelman, Lee, 16
education: and civil defence planning in Canada, 97–9, 101–2; in First World War Germany, 11, 33, 34–5, 38–41, 58; on mines in the former Yugoslavia, 295, 297–8; for nuclear attack in Canada, 97–9, *100*, 101–2; on peace at Grindstone Island, 167, 172–3, 174; and war culture, 34. *See also* schools
Elbinsel-Wilhelmsburg Museum (Germany), 36
Emergency Measures Organization, 110
emotions: atomic anxiety, 95–6, 103–10, 112–13; emotional echoes and echoing, 9–10; emotional formations, 9, 95; emotional frontiers, 9, 95; emotional regimes and practices in Cold War Canada, 96, 99, 107–9, 150–3; emotion work/emotional labour, 14, 135–6, 196–8; of families and children in First World War, 12, 121, 122–3, 126, 134–7; of families during Canada's Afghanistan mission, 192–3, 196–9; history of, 9–10, 95; and oral history, 12–13, 159–60; and politics in drawings by children in immigration detention, 18–19, 224–41; and temporality, 109–10

emotion work/labour, 135–6, 196–7
empathic inference, 128
environmental autobiographies, 282–3
Erg (tug), 71
Erjavec, Karmen, 207
evacuees (child evacuees): arrival in Canada, 268–9; Canada as destination, 267; correspondence, 266, 267–9, 270–1, 275–6; dangers of, 268; drawings and visuals in letters, 276, *277*–*9*, *278*; experience as children, 267–8, 274–6; experience of Canada, 268–70; letters from parents, 272; return home, 273–4, 279–80; in Second World War, 17, 251–2, 266–7; as temporary measure, 267

Faille, Maxime, 113–14
Falk, Adalbert, 38
fallout shelters, 105–6, 107–8
Family Herald and Weekly Star, 121
federal government of Canada: and civil defence preparation, 99, 102; families accompanying deployed personnel, 142–3; manual for civil defence, 98; shelter program, 105–6
Ferguson, Marjorie, 67–8, 73
fictive kin, 145
film for drills, 99
First World War (1914–18): correspondence of children and soldiers, 121–37; "culture de guerre" in schools, 7; departures for, 121, *122*, 128–9; emotions of children and families, 121, 122–3, 126, 134–7; health of children, 127–8; and historical memory, 33; images of war from the German home front, 33–59; impact on daily lives, 121–2; suffering of children, 35; writing and children in, 258–64
Forgotten Children, The (report of AHRC inquiry), 233, 234
former Yugoslavia, 16, 294, 295
Foulkes, Charles A., 142
France, 7, 34, 66
Franklin, Ursula, 109, 110
Franklyn Park (Halifax), 286, 290, *291*
Fussell, Paul, 123
future and futurity, for children in wars and conflict, 16–17

Garang, Sunday, 309–10
Gardiner, Lisa, 309
Garrioch, David, 73
Geissler, Gert, 34

Geist, Anthony, 253
George Owen Collection, 271
Gerber, David A., 126
Germany: art classes in schools, 37–41; art in schools, 35–6, 37; art(s) education movement ("Kunsterziehungsbewegung"), 35–6, 37–8, 40; children in schools, 34; children of First World War in Second, 58–9; education during First World War, 11, 33, 34–5, 38–41, 58; fervour for war in schools, 33, 34–5, 37, 58; patriotic ideas in children, 58; sensory experience of war, 66; voice of children in First World War, 35–6, 37; war culture, 34–5; war propaganda in schools, 37, 44
Germany, drawings by children: analysis of children's art, 44–58; classes in schools, 38–9; drawings of war by children, 42–3; drawings of war by children, examples, *36, 39, 46, 47, 48–50, 53–4, 55–7*; exhibitions of children's work, 36–7, 38; German body and enemies in, 44–52; images of war from the home front, 33–59; influences for, 42, 50–2, *51, 52*; nurses in, 54–6; sources of artworks, 36–7, 39, 42–3; subjects explored, 43; weaponry in, 52–3
Gerns, Georg, *57*, 57–8
Gilkie, Ronald, 79, 85
Girl Guides of Canada, and civil defence preparation, 102–3
Gleason, Mona, 20, 128
"Going Places" workshop and bus tour, 301–2, *303*–4
Golomb, Claire, 45
Gordon-Lennox, George, 171
Göth, Ignatz, 41
Götze, Carl, 38
Grantham, Charles, 79, 81, 283, 288
"graphic community" of children, 20
Great War. *See* First World War (1914–18)
Grieg, Peter, 143
Griffin, Laurence, 72
Grindstone Experiment (1965): children and youth in, 175–8, *176*; description and result, 175–6, 178–9; goal, 167, 175
Grindstone Island (Ontario): and CFSC, 171–2, 183; child evacuees from Britain, 170–1; description and access to, 168, 169–70; donation to Quakers, 167, 171; experiences of youth, 167–8; history to 1963, 168–71; peace education, 167, 172–3, 174; politics at, 18; as sanctuary from war, 167, 168, 170, 171, 174, 183;

summer workshops for high school children, 174, 179–83; tensions at, 181–3; wilderness and appeal of, 168–9; workshops and participants, 172–4
Grossman, Bernie, 258, 259

Hage, Ghassan, 310
Häkli, Jouni, 103
Halifax Dockyard, 75
Halifax Harbour Explosion (1917), 79–80, 81, 84, 85, 86
Halifax (Nova Scotia): Bedford Magazine Explosion, 65, 78–87; censorship regulations, 69; civil defence planning, 102; convoys in Bedford Basin, 63, *68*, 68–9; dockyards, *70*, 73; explosion of 1917, 79–80, 81, 84, 85, 86; fire on the *Trongate*, 69, 71; geographies of neighbourhoods, 76–7; ground-level views of children, 64; memories of place, 282–7, *286*; as naval base, 63–4; oral interviews, 64; place- and space-based ways of knowing, 12; sensory experience of war by children, 64–5, 66–9, 71–6, 86–7; sounds in neighbourhoods, 72–4; sounds in Second World War, 65, 66–7, 72–4, 78–9, 80, 82, 86, 87, 289; spatial stories, 76–8, 283; transformation in Second World War, 63–4, 65
Hamlin, Owen, 67, 73–4, 84
Hämmerle, Christa, 34
Hartman, Saidiya, 249
Hayes, Geoffrey, 143
High, Steven, 15, 255
Hill, Jeannie, 69, 284
Hill, Shirley, 73, 81
Hill, Ted, 181
Hochschild, Arlie Russell, 135
Hogwood, Jemma, 207
Holocaust, child survivors, 21, 44, 253
Holt, Marilyn Irvin, 95
Honeck, Mischa, 180
Huebner, Angela, and colleagues, 192, 199
Huss, Marie-Monique, 259–60
hydrogen bomb (or H-bomb), 104

"ideal child" of Cold War era, 95–6
If You Love This Planet (1982), 113
illustrated children's books, for refugee storytelling, 255–6, 308–11, *311, 312*
immigrants in Canada, stories of, 300, 303
immigration detention: camps establishment,

227; description of and life in, 229–30; detention facilities of Australia, 227–8; drawings examples, 224–5, *225*, 229, 230, *231*, *232*, *233*, *238*; feelings of children in, 236; impact on children, 224; inquiry of AHRC, 224, 233–4, 240–1; number of children and adults in, 227–8; policy for asylum seekers in Australia, 227; politics and emotion in drawings by children in Australia, 18–19, 224–41; self-harm in, 230, 232, 233; value of drawings, 224–5; voice of children in, 233–4. *See also* asylum seekers (to Australia); Australian Human Rights Commission (AHRC)
Indigenous peoples in Canada, 5, 17
In My Kingdom (picture book), 308, 309, 310, *312*
Innes, Stephanie, 126
intercontinental ballistic missiles (ICBM), 110
intergenerational memory, 6, 15, 20, 141, 145–6
intergenerational storytelling, 255–6, 308–11
intergenerational trauma, 206–8
Ireland, David, 21
Ishiguro, Laura, 17, 251
islands, meaning for children, 169
Ivashkevich, Olga, 43

Jangaard, Hildegard, 68–9
Japanese Canadians, 3–4, 5
Jasen, Patricia, 169
Jefferson, H. Bruce: sensory experience and observations, 64, 69, 71, 72, 74–6, 78, 81, 82; on transformation of Halifax, 63, 64
Josephy, David, 173, 174, 183
Josephy, Goldie, 173–4
Josephy family, 173–4

Kallio, Kirsi Pauliina, 103, 108
Kaufman, Jack, 107
Kennedy, Rosie, 8
Kids' Own Publishing, 308
Kik, Colestin, 40, 42
Kingsmill, Charles Edmund, 167, 168, 170, 171
Kingsmill family, 170–1
Kingsmill-Flynn, Diana, 170–1
Kingsmill-Wright, Diana, 171, 183
Klein, Barbara, 114
Klein, Bonnie Sherr, 113
Klein, Seth, 113–14
Kolb, Gustav, 41
Komulainen, Sirkka, 11
Kony, Joseph, 207

Korean Conflict (1950–53), 149
Kriegsbilder (Planck), 50–1, *51*
Kronprinsen (merchant vessel), *70*
Kucherenko, Olga, 17–18
Kuhn, Annette, 19
Kuhn, Bernie, 295
Kunzfeld, Otto, 41
Kvas, Peter, 108

landmines. *See* mines
Larsen, Katrine Rønsig, 9–10
Leahy, Carla Pascoe, 8
Lees, David, 11
Lefebvre, Henri, 64
Lenette, Caroline, 234
Leskard, Stephen and Mary, 105–6
Lethbridge, Gerry, 76, 77, 83–4
letters of wartime. *See* correspondence
Library for Research on International Education (Bibliothek für Bildungsgeschichtliche Forschung) (Germany), as source of drawings, 36
Library for the History of Education (BBF, in Berlin), as source of drawings, 39
Lichtwark, Alfred, 37–8
Liebknecht, Karl, 35
Lord's Resistance Army (LRA): abduction, forced marriage, and impregnation of females, 207–8; experiences of children born in captivity, 208–12; importance of children to, 213; life of violence in, 208–9; and participants in research, 208–9. *See also* northern Uganda
Lyons, Martyn, 124, 262

McElroy, Gil, 144
MacFadzean, James, 68
McGraw, Désirée, 113–14
Mackie, Hugh and Austin (uncles), 251, 268
Mackie, Owen: correspondence, 251, 252, 266, 268–70, *270*–2, *271*–3, *274*–5, 276; as evacuee from Britain, 17, 251, 268–9; experience of Canada, 268–70; return to Canada as adult, 274; return to England, 252, 273–4
Mackie, Richard, 17, 251, 268, 276
Mackie, Vera, 236
Mackie parents in England, 251, 252, 271–2
McLaughlin, Carly, 226
McManus, Russell, 81, 85
Madokoro, Laura, 5
Maheux, Angélique, 125, 131, 132, 135

Maheux, François-Xavier (Frank), description as soldier and correspondence, 124–5, 126, 127, 129–30, 131–2, 136
Maheux, Grace, 125
Maheux children (Petuwise, Freddy, Condy, Dolly, and "the baby"), 124–5, 127, 130
Malkki, Liisa, 8
Maluach, Agum, 310
Malual, Abraham, 309
Maluk, Abraham, 309
Manus Island (Papua New Guinea), as immigration detention facility, 227, 232
Mapping Memories project, 300, 302
maps: as knowledge, 6; and memory, 286
Marion, Nicole, 110–11
Marshall, Bob and Jane, 148
Martelly, Stéphane, 255
Marten, James, 7
Massey, Doreen, 283, 285
May, Elaine Tyler, 94, 105
memory, communities of. *See* communities of memory
memory studies, 19
memory work, 19
mental health: of children born in captivity, 210–11; issues in Afghanistan mission, 198–9, 201–2
Mergen, Bernard, 283
Meyhew, Margret, 240–1
Michallat, Wendy, 254
Mile Zero: The Sage Tour, 114
military bases, family-oriented approach, 142
Military Brats (Wertsch), 144
Miller, Bernard, 72–3
mines (landmines): drawings, 295, *296–7*, 297–8, *298*; education about, 295, 297–8; initiatives on, 294–5; use of and as problem, 294, 295
Misheff, Sue, 169
Mishra Tarc, Aparna, 22
Möller, C., 53
Monarch of Bermuda (ship), 266, 268, 269
Mont Blanc (steamship), 79
Montreal, "Going Places" workshop and bus tour, *301*, 301–2, *303*, 303–4
Montreal Life Stories Project (2005–12), 254–5, 300
Moore, Aaron Willian, 11
moral capabilities of children, 17–18
Moriyama, Raymond, 3–4, 17
Moriyama Regeneration Hall (Canadian War Museum), sound in, 3

Morton, Desmond, 123, 125
Moruzi, Kristine, 8
Mosse, George, 8
Müller, J., 55, *56*
Musgrove, Nell, 8
"My Backyard: Point Pleasant Park" (memoir of G. Perks), 285, 286–92

Naftel, William, 69
Nash, Terre, 113
National Defence Demining Action Center (Canada), 294
National Longitudinal Survey of Children and Youth (NLSCY), 190
Nauru, as immigration detention facility, 227, 230–1, 232, 233–4
Newberry, Mary, 180, 181
"New Cold War," 111
Nickerson, Ernie, 76
nightmares, in children born in captivity, 210
non-violence: in Grindstone Experiment, 167, 175, 178–9; and hunger strikes, 178; training and roles in, 175
northern Uganda: casual labour, 220; children born of wartime rape, 207–21; disease conceptualization and "spirit-related" illnesses, 211–12; forced wife system, 207–8; identity of children born in captivity, 212–13, 214–15, 217; intergenerational impact of sexual violence, 206, 207, 208; land inheritance and ownership, 215–16; participants in research, 208–10; research description and ethics, 208; return to civilian life, 209, 212; war description and impact, 207. *See also* children born of wartime rape; Lord's Resistance Army (LRA)
Nova Scotia, civil defence planning, 102
Nowak, Sue, 154
Nowak family, social life with Taylors, 153–4, *155*
nuclear war: and "Atomic Generation," 180; baby teeth and radioactivity, 109–10; bombs development and testing, 103–4, 110, 111; Cuban Missile Crisis, 108, 109; decline in tensions, 110; disarmament campaign, 95, 110–11, 113–14; drill of 1953 in Ottawa, 93; and emotions, 94–5, 96, 114; evacuation and shelter plans, 104–6, 107–8; and growing up, 96–103; manual for civil defence, 98; and politics of children, 18; preparation and education in schools, 97–9, *100*, 101–2; preparation in Canada, 93–4; radioactive contamination (or

"fallout"), 104, 109–10; risks in Canada, 94, 95; role and protection of children, 93, 94, 95; "self-help" vision of attack, 96–7; television simulations, 111–12; voice of children in, 96, 103, 107–9, 111–15

O., Erna, 54
Olsen, Stephanie, 9, 95
Olson family (Theodore, Lydia, Ernst, and Margrit Ann), 175–7
"Operation Turtle" drills, 99
oral history: and collaborative storytelling, 254–5, 300–4; and communities of memory, 7, 14, 19–21, 168, 193, 199–200; and embodied storytelling, 13; emplaced storytelling, 20, 76–8, 252; and intergenerational memory, 6, 15, 20, 141, 145–6; and intergenerational storytelling, 255–6, 308–11; and interior displacement, 12–13; and memoirs, 285–92; and narrative, 6, 21; policy interventions, 221; and sensory memory, 20, 64–5; and silence, 14, 193–6, 214–15; subjectivity of, 15, 19, 21, 146; survival story of, 305–6; and temporality, 14–16, 21, 250
oral testimony, 12, 15, 21, 241. *See also* oral history
O'Rouke, Sue, 308–9

parentification, 196–7, 198
Parkins, Wendy, 88n13
Parr, Albert Eide, 283
Parr, Joy, 67, 74
Partlow, H.R., 99
patriotism, in minds of children, 58
peacetime: civil defence preparation, 102; return to, 14; versus wartime, 13, 14–15
Peacock, Margaret, 95–6, 110
Pearson, Geoffrey, 113
Perks, Gordon: Franklyn Park, 286, 290, *291*; friends of childhood, 284–5, 287; life in Halifax, 252, 282; memoir of stories ("My Backyard: Point Pleasant Park"), 285, 286–92; memories of place, 282–7, *286*
photomontage, 259–60
picture books. *See* illustrated children's books, for refugee storytelling
picture postcards, as evidence, 250, *259*, 259–60
Pignot, Manon, 6, 34, 260
place: and environmental autobiographies, 12; and maps, 286, 291; and spatial stories, 11, 76–8, 252, 282–92; and ways of knowing, 64, 85–6
Planck, Willy, 42, 50–1, *51*
Pocock, Judy, 172, 180

Pocock, Nancy and John, 172, 179
Point Pleasant Park (Halifax), *286*; description, 283; memoir of Perks's stories, 285, 287–92; memories of, 282, 283
political protests, use of children in, 177
politics: as analytical strand in book, 7, 17–19; children as political actors, 17–19; in Cold War, 18; and emotion in drawings by children in immigration detention, 18–19, 224–41; political expression in drawings, 235–9, 240, 241
Portelli, Alessandro, 285, 286–7
Porter, Kenneth, 112
post-apocalyptic films, 111–12
postcards, as evidence, 250, *259*, 259–60
Probe, J.O., 99, 101
"Problem for My Mum, A" (story), 310, *312*
protests, use of children in, 177
provinces, in civil defence planning, 99, 101–2
PTSD (post-traumatic stress disorder): and Afghanistan mission, 190, 198–200; diagnosis, 204n27

Quakers, 172, 179–80
Quarry Pond (Halifax), 283, 288

radioactive contamination (or "fallout"), 104, 109–10
rape in wartime. *See* sexual violence
Raschke, Erich, 50, *50*
Reddy, William, 95
reform movement in arts pedagogy, 35–6, 37–8, 40
refugee children: and politics, 18; storytelling projects, 254–6, 300–4, 308–11; voice of, 308
refugee policy in Australia, 226–7
Regutzki, Wilhelm, *49*, 50, *53*
religious faith, as strategy to forget the past, 218–19
Risser, Beatrice, 81–2
Rogers, Lawrence, 124, 125–6, 130, 134, 135–6
Rogers, May, 125, 134, 135, 136
Rogers children (Aileen and Howard), 125, 127, 130, 134–6
Roper, Michael, 124, 136
Rose, Jacqueline, 8
Rosenberg, Gabriel, 180
Rothe, Richard, 37, 40
Russia, invasion of Ukraine, 22
Rwanda: Leontine Uwababyeyi's story, 301–2, 303, 304–6; youth born of the genocide, 207

St Catharines (Ontario), "Operation Turtle" drills, 99
Samuel, Alexandra, 112–13
Sandy, Sharon, 308
Saskatchewan, civil defence planning, 99, 101–2
Scharweit, A., 55, *56*
Schmidhammer, Arpad, books of, 51–2, *52*
Schmitz-Hertzberg, Eve, 180
Schneider, David M., 162n32
Scholz, Joachim, 35
schools: for asylum seekers in Australia, 229–30, *230*; in civil defence planning, 97–9, *100*, 101–2; and "culture de guerre," 7; drills for emergencies, 98–9, *100*; in evacuation plans, 105; in First World War Germany, 33, 34–41, 44, 58; in lives of adolescents, 201; on military bases, 142; peer support groups, 200, 201–2. *See also* education
Schule und Krieg (School and War) exhibition and catalogue, 36–7, 40
Scott, Joan W., 8, 128, 308
Second World War (1939–45): correspondence of child evacuees, 266–80; evacuees, 17, 251–2, 266–7; impact globally, 266; memories of childhood of wartime Atlantic, 63–87. *See also specific topics*
sensory history: children in, 66–7, 86–7; and embodied knowledge, 64–5, 67, 74, 84–5; sound in, 65–7, 71–4, 78–85
sexuality (of soldiers), and memories, 284, 292
sexual violence: abduction, forced marriage, and impregnation of females, 207–8; in armed conflict, 206; intergenerational impact, 206, 207, 208. *See also* children born of wartime rape
Sharp, Margaret, 276
Sharp brothers (Christopher, Bill, and Tom), correspondence, 276–80, *277–9*
sheet music, 250, 258, *259*, 260
Silverstein, Jordana, 226
Simonds, Guy, 142
Sleswick, Sue, 308
smell of war, 82, 289
Smith, Mark, 66
social ecologies of childhood, 20
social media posts, by war-affected youngsters, 22
sound: of Bedford Magazine Explosion, 65, 78–9, 80, 82, 87; in Halifax in Second World War, 65, 66–7, 72–4, 78–9, 80, 82, 86, 87, 289; as memory of childhood, 3–4, 22; as sense, 65

South Sudanese families, storytelling project, 255–6, 308–11
space: centrality to wartime and postwar worlds, 11–12; description and role, 12. *See also* place
Spanish Civil War (1936–39), drawings of, 253
Speaking Our Peace (1985), 113
Spock, Dr Benjamin, 174
Spyrou, Spyrous, 10–11
Stargardt, Nicholas, 44, 66, 235, 239, 253
"Steven the Donkey" (story), 309–10, *311*
stories, as knowledge, 6
stories of war: and communities of memory, 20–1; of immigrants in Canada, 300, 303; intergenerational stories, 20; as learning tools, 302–3; Perks's memoir, 285, 287–92; and place, 76–8, 283; in print culture, 8; sharing of, 309
storytelling: intergenerational exchanges in, 20, 308–11; mediated forms, 256; as practice, 254, 255; projects of refugees, 254–6, 300–4, 308–11; by survivors, 254, 255
Students against Global Extermination (SAGE), 113–14
Suleiman, Susan Rubin, 21, 127
summer camps, 179
Sylvia (wife of Paul Taylor), 157–8
"symbolic child" construct, 95–6
Sznajderman, Michael, 177

Taube, Elfriede, *39*
Taylor, Annie, 146, 154, *155*
Taylor, Don, 145, 150, *151*, 155
Taylor, Jack, 142, 143, 146, 147–8, 149, 150–1, *151*, 151–2, 154–5, 156
Taylor, Paul, 15, 141, 144–6, 149, 150, *151*, 151–5, *155*, 155–6, 157–60
Taylor, Shelaigh, 15, 141, 144, 145–6, 147, 148–51, 152–3, *155*, 156–7, 159
Taylor family, 144–56, *155*, 158–9
tears, in drawings, 225, 237, *238*
Tebbutt, Melanie, 285
teenagers. *See* adolescents
Terezín ghetto, 44, 253
texts for young people, and war culture, 7–8
thermonuclear bombs, 104–5
Thirty-One Hours: The Grindstone Experiment (Olson and Christiansen), 176, 178
This Is My Home (picture book), 308, 310
Thompson, Matthew, 252
Thompson, Murray, 171
Thorne, Stephen, 107

Threads (film), 111–12
Ticktin, Miriam, 225
Tilch, Elsa, 48, *48*
time and temporalities of war: as analytical strand in book, 7, 13–17; and chronologies of children, 14–15; future and futurity in, 16–17; impact on young people, 13–14; long view of, 15–16; and memories of children, 286–7; as rupture, 13; scholarship on, 13
Tonkiss, Fran, 73
Training Institutes in Non-Violence, 175
Trongate (freighter), fire on, 69, 71
Tuan, Yi-Fu, 65, 88n13
Tuttle, William, 21, 79

Übleis, R., *36*
Uganda. *See* northern Uganda
Ukraine, 22
United Nations Convention on the Rights of the Child (1989), 10, 234
United Nations Mine Action Service (UNMAS), 294–5
Uwababyeyi, Leontine, 16, *301, 303, 304*; collaborative storytelling, 255, 300–2; digital audio portrait of, 301–2; in "Going Places" workshop, 301–2; in Mapping Memories project, 300, 302; survival story, 254, 305–6

Vallgårda, Karen, 9–10, 95
Voice of Women/Voix des Femmes (VOW), 109, 171, 172, 177
Volcic, Zala, 207

Wakefield (ship), 72
Wall, John, 234
Wall, Sharon, 179
war: and children as study area, 7; as "an enduring condition," 22; impact on children and youth, 4, 122

war culture ("culture de guerre"): in education, 34; as experience for children, 7–8; and future of children, 16; in Germany in First World War, 34–5; as idea, 7–8, 34
warship models by boys, 283, 286, 288–9
wartime: vs peacetime, 13, 14–15; resonance through life, 14–15; as way of thinking, 13. *See also* time and temporalities of war
ways of knowing: as analytical strand in book, 7, 10–13; centrality of place and space, 11–12; and children's voices, 10–11; interrelationships in, 10; and oral testimony, 12–13
We Are Here exhibition, 304
Wertsch, Mary Edwards, 144
Wheatley, Thomas, 71, 73, 76–8
white children, race, and protection from war, 16–17
wilderness tourism, 168–9
Wilhelmsburg school and neighbourhood (Germany), war in school drawings, 11–12, 42–3
Williams, Stan, 108
Williamson, Marie, 276
witnessing, and drawings by children, 253–4
Wittner, Lawrence, 111
Women Strike for Peace, 177
Woomera Detention Centre, 231
work of children during war, 132–3
Worthington, F.F., 97–8, 99, 102
writing skills of children, 260

Young, Sarah Hanson, 232
Youth Nuclear Disarmament Tour, 18, 113
Yugoslavia (the former), 16, 294, 295
Yugoslav Wars, 294

Ziino, Bart, 129
Zwi, Karen, 239–40